ELLESMERE ISLAND

und

• Etah
Siorapaluk
Washington Land

Qaanaaq

KNUD RASMUSSEN LAND

TIC OCEAN

The Northwest Coast

G R E E N L A N D

This Cold Heaven

Also by Gretel Ehrlich

The Solace of Open Spaces

Heart Mountain

Islands, the Universe, Home

A Match to the Heart

Questions of Heaven

A Blizzard Year

John Muir, Nature's Visionary

This Cold Heaven

Seven Seasons in Greenland

Gretel Ehrlich

Pantheon Books, New York

All rights reserved under International and Pan-American Copyright
Conventions. Published in the United States by Pantheon Books,
a division of Random House, Inc., New York, and simultaneously
in Canada by Random House of Canada Limited, Toronto.

Pantheon Books and colophon are registered trademarks
of Random House, Inc.

Portions of this book have appeared in *Harper's, Islands,* and
National Geographic Adventure.

Library of Congress Cataloging-in-Publication Data

Ehrlich, Gretel.
This cold heaven: seven seasons in Greenland / Gretel Ehrlich.
p. cm.
Includes bibliographical references and index.
ISBN 0-679-44200-6
1. Ehrlich, Gretel—Journeys—Greenland. 2. Greenland—Description
and travel. 3. Rasmussen, Knud, 1879–1933 — Journeys—Greenland.
4. Greenland—Discovery and exploration—Danish. I. Title.

G743 .E47 2001   998.2'0092'2—dc21   00-069277

www.pantheonbooks.com

Book design by Johanna Roebas

Artwork © by William A. Giese
Endpaper maps and map on pages 118–19 designed by Jeffrey L. Ward

Printed in the United States of America
First Edition
2 4 6 8 9 7 5 3 1

for those who travel the path of ice

I am nothing.
I see all.

—Ralph Waldo Emerson

Contents

Contents

Preface

I first traveled to Greenland in the late summer of 1993, not to write a book but to get above treeline. Still recovering from an accident that affected my heart, I found it difficult to go to an altitude where I felt at home. I learned that treeline can be a factor of latitude, not just altitude—it is a biological boundary created by the cold—and came to think of the treeless polar north as the top of a mountain lying on its side.

The first time I flew north across Arctic Canada toward Greenland I sighed with happiness as the stunted spruce finally stopped; east of Hudson Bay the trees gave way to the polished, undulating rock of the Barren Grounds. Once mountains, the Grounds were overrun by an ice sheet and flattened into a pond-flecked plain. Continuing north, the mountains of Baffin Island came into view, then the ice puzzle of Baffin Bay, and finally, Greenland's rock-walled coast. Treeless expanses, crisp air, and alpine flora at sea level: I had never imagined such a combination existed.

Soon enough I was on hands and knees on a lateral moraine caressing alpine fescue and sniffing dwarf harebells while icebergs, big as warehouses, drifted by. Glistening white, they were the photographic negatives of Greenland's black mountain fringe.

My first summer idyll turned into seven years of Arctic peregrinations. The high Arctic fascinated me because, unlike Antarctica, it had been peopled for thousands of years. Greenland's history is Inuit (Eskimo), and despite all the attention paid to British and European misadventures in the far north, the Inuit people were its first explorers and inhabitants. They are the real heroes.

Descendants of central Asians, Inuit hunters and their families began crossing the 200-mile-wide Bering Land Bridge from Siberia perhaps as early as 30,000 years ago and slowly wandered across the polar north. They reached Greenland 5,000 years ago. Their cold-adapted, boreal culture, a single entity, stretches 6,000 miles across ice caps, pressure ice, barren lands, rivers, mountains, fjords, and frozen oceans. The hunter from Qaanaaq, Greenland, tells his child the same story in the same language as the hunter from Pelly Bay in the Northwest Territories, or from Point Hope, Alaska. The wonder is how these people have lived and thrived in the harshest climate in the world, where the closest village might be a month-and-a-half-long dogsled trip away.

Greenland is the largest island in the world (Australia is considered a continent). Ninety-five percent of its surface is ice. Up there time comes whole, then is divided into four months of dark, four months of light, and two seasons of twilight when the sun hangs at the horizon as though stuck between two thoughts. In Qaanaaq, a town at the far north of the island, the sun goes down on October 24 and doesn't return until late February. With dark and light come two radically different landscapes: the one made of snow and ice and the watery one left after the white floors have melted. These seasons of darkness and light are an alternating current whose opposing pulses represent a union.

Greenland's continental ice sheet is a remnant of the last ice age, as are the people in the northern part of the island who still travel by dogsled, wear skins, and live by the harpoon. We know about the lifeways and culture of the Polar Eskimos because of Knud Rasmussen. Born in 1879 in Ilulissat, Greenland, of Inuit-Danish descent, he became a self-styled ethnographer of the Inuit, a word that means "human being."

In 1910 Rasmussen, with his friend Peter Freuchen, established an Arctic trading station in Thule that became a base for seven major expeditions. During one, Rasmussen mapped the topmost parts of Greenland; four years later he traveled by dogsled all the way across the polar north, ending in Nome, Alaska. His journey took three and a half years.

Stopping at every village along the way and sometimes staying for months, Rasmussen took down verbatim records of Inuit lifeways, beliefs, dreams, songs, and ideas. Shamans, elderly widows, hunters, and orphan children came to live at his camps. There was no one he would not talk to. Without his effort, we would know almost nothing of an ice age subsistence hunting culture unchanged for a thousand years.

Almost a century later I began traveling back and forth to Greenland while poring through more than six thousand pages of Rasmussen's expedition notes. Somewhere in my wanderings the present-day narrative split open to include his notes as well as my own.

My first trip to Greenland was in the summer; the second trip took place in the dark time—January and February—when black days give way to black nights. After that my visits became chronic, as if darkness laid down on ice held secrets I could not yet fathom. Though I visited there in every season and the interstices between, I came to prefer ice and a failing sun to summer's warmth and open water.

It was on the ice that I saw the wild genius and second sight of the Eskimos traveling by dogsled and hunting every day to feed themselves and their families as well as their dogs—twenty or more of them. The complexities of ice had taught the hunters to reconcile the imminence of famine and death with an irreverent joy at being alive. The landscape itself, with its shifting and melting ice, its mirages, glaciers, and drifting icebergs, is less a description of desolation than an ode to the beauty of impermanence.

I saw how skillfully the hunting families refused the impoverishment of materialism to opt for a life of natural communalism, sharing food, love, gossip, feuds, and dogs, as well as weeks of weathered-in, do-nothing days. Fierce individualism is frowned upon. The group matters more. They said: "Everyone wants to be different. We carry our differences inside."

In Greenland I made it a practice to travel alone, never knowing quite how I would get from one place to another in a country of no roads, where solitude is thought to be a form of failure. I made my way slowly, with no common language and the usual Arctic weather-related delays, by dogsled, skiff, fishing boat, helicopter, and fixed-wing plane. The blessing of such awkward movements was that the locals took pity on me: I was passed from friend to friend, village to village, town to town, and slowly climbed the icy ladder up the west coast to Avannaar-sua—the far north.

Once above 76 degrees north latitude, I experienced a euphoria previously felt only above 12,000 feet. Deep, rock-walled fjords, oceans of ice, and changing planes of light strummed the horizon. There I traveled with subsistence hunters—the elite who live at the top of the world, the only boreal society still using dogsleds, wearing skins, and hunting with harpoons. How had their cold-adapted society come into being? How had the ephemeral ice shaped their minds and society?

Though the Polar Eskimos of Greenland have lost many of their old ways, they have also learned to fight for what remains. Stripped of their public ceremonial life in the 1700s, they cling tenaciously to traditional hunting practices and carry forward an old memory of how to endure Arctic hardships and how to thrive in the pleasures it brings. It was not only a life of cold, filth, frostbite, snowblindness, and starvation but also one of intimacy and comradeship, resourcefulness and magic, when shamans in trance made soul-flights under the ice, when parents told children cautionary tales by seal-oil lamplight, when men fashioned harpoons from narwhal tusks and walrus ivory points and traveled on dogsleds made from whale bone with rolled-up frozen peat runners, and ice was cut with knives whose blades were hacked from a meteorite.

The Inuit mind is sharpened by vulnerability. It is a keenness that shows them where to go and how to live. Strong-minded, agile, humorous, cool-headed, and quiet, they have learned from the ice: how its only consistency is movement, how its solidity masks what cannot stay.

The ice cap itself was a siren singing me back to Greenland, its walls of blue sapphire and sheer immensity always beguiling. Part jewel, part eye, part lighthouse, part recumbent monolith, the ice is a bright spot on the upper tier of the globe where the world's purse strings have been pulled tight, nudging the tops of three continents together. Summers, it burns in the sun, and in the dark it hoards moonlight. I liked how the island was almost uninhabitable, how ice had pushed humans all the way to the edge, where they lived in tight villages on a filigree of rock; how on topo maps the white massifs were marked "unexplored."

I wanted to know how the Eskimos made a moral universe of their cold "stone age" empire; how celebration and taboo worked as doorway and wall; how ice worked as a flint on which their imaginations were fired.

One spring at the ice edge I saw narwhal. Their smooth backs rose out of the water and were swallowed again, and their twisted unicorn's tusks needled the air like rapiers. The tusks looked as if they had been unwound from some integral element at the center of the earth. All their swordwork above the water's surface, the corkscrew lances clattering and crossing, seemed a gesture of beings who were lost in battle and who were, like me, trying to cut through to what was real. For seven years I used the island as a looking glass: part window, part mirror.

—Gretel Ehrlich

2001

This Cold Heaven

Darkness Visible:
Uummannaq, Greenland, 1995

Our country has wide borders; there is no man born has travelled round it. And it bears secrets in its bosom of which no white man dreams. Up here we live two different lives; in the Summer, under the torch of the Warm Sun; in the Winter, under the lash of the North Wind. But it is the dark and cold that make us think most. And when the long Darkness spreads itself over the country, many hidden things are revealed, and men's thoughts travel along devious paths.
—Blind Ambrosius

"Do you see that coming?" the old woman Arnaluaq asked.
"What?"
"That—out there over the sea. It is the Dark coming up, the great Dark!"
—Knud Rasmussen

The glaciers are rivers, the sky is struck solid, the water is ink, the mountains are lights that go on and off. Sometimes I lie in my sleeping bag and recite a line from a Robert Lowell poem over and over: "Any clear thing that blinds us with surprise."

I sleep by a cold window which I've opened a crack. Frigid air streams up the rock hill and smells of minerals. In a dream I hear the crackling sound that krill make under water. Earlier in the day the chunk of glacier ice I dropped into a glass of water made the same sound.

The ice came from the top of a long tongue that spills out at the head of this fjord, as if it were the bump of a tastebud that had been sliced off, or a part of speech. Now it has melted and looks floury, like an unnecessary word that adds confusion to insight. But when I drink it down, its flavor is bright, almost peppery, bespeaking a clarity of mind I rarely taste but toward which I aspire.

This January morning a sundog—a rainbowlike ring around the sun—loomed so large it seemed to encircle the visible world. As I moved, it moved. I watched it slide across something stuck: a ship that had frozen into the ice of Frobisher Bay. I was taking off from Iqaluit, a town in Arctic Canada where I'd been stranded for several days. As my plane taxied out onto the runway, the sundog billowed and shuddered, dragging itself across black ice, too heavy to leave the ground. Then the plane did rise and so did the sun's halo—a bright porthole into an Arctic winter's permanent night.

Some Eskimos say such a ring around the sun represents the hand drum used by a shaman to invoke other worlds. They believe there are multiple realms within this one located beneath the sea ice, inside the mountains, at the edge of the ice cap, and up in the sky where other kinds of beings live and interact with us. Some are half human and half animal; some are transparent—pure spirit. Stories are regarded as living things, and the shaman's trance is brought on by the beating of the drum and the slow strobe of seasonal darkness and light.

My plane from Baffin Island to Kangerlussuaq, Greenland, had made an unscheduled, early-morning departure. Every seat but two held strapped-in cargo; the steward and I were the only passengers. It was 20 degrees below zero Fahrenheit, made colder by a hard northwesterly wind. In the cabin we wrapped ourselves in wool blankets and sipped coffee while a mechanic swept snow from the wings. As the plane rose, it passed through the wavering hoop and the sun dog broke.

Below, Baffin Bay was a puzzle that had been shattered. There were disks, plates, slicks, crystals, frazil ice, grease ice, and pancake ice—Arctic lily pads across which seals, polar bears, and hunters leaped. Between tiny islands, broad sheets of ice as big as billboards bumped up into frozen Hiroshige-like waves.

People always ask, Why do you want to go north in the dark time of year? There's nothing up there. But Greenlanders know the opposite is true: "Summer is boring. Nothing for the dogs to do. In winter and spring the fjords and bays are ice. We go for long trips on our sleds—hunting every day, living wherever we want, and visiting friends in villages. That's when we are happy."

Below we flew over an intricate labyrinth of floating plinths. Clouds increased, light waned, yet it was morning. A glow marked the spot where the sun was trying to rise, but we veered north, away from it. Behind us, in the mountains, a river's fast-moving riffles had frozen in place. Everywhere the shifting ice was saffron, then pink, then indigo— the Arctic's austerity both a physical clarity and a voluptuousness.

The hunters I was to travel with said the dogsled trip to Thule would take a month or longer. *Imaqa.* Maybe. Clocks and calendars were still considered irrelevant in the far north, where there were no roads, only frozen fjords and seas traveled by dogsled, where weather metered out time in its own currency, where, in one Eskimo dialect, the word for "winter" also means "a year." Up here, the ephemeral is the only constant; time has not been decimated by the second hand, itself a foreign splinter looking to rejoin the living tree from which it came.

Two years earlier, in 1993, on a similar flight, I had met a young couple, Ann and Olejorgen, who befriended me. Now I was returning to Greenland to spend part of an Arctic winter with them before taking off by dogsled for places north.

Olejorgen is Inuit but born in Nuuk, the capital city below the Arctic Circle, and Ann is a Faroe Islander who had immigrated to Greenland years before. They were on their way home to Uummannaq, a small town on a tiny island halfway up the west coast of Greenland. When they asked what a lone American was doing on the plane, I held up a thick volume by Knud Rasmussen, one of ten compendiums of ethnographic notes from one of his expeditions. Half Inuit, half Danish, Rasmussen had made a three-and-a-half-year epic journey by dogsled in an effort to trace the Eskimos' original migration route from Siberia to Greenland. On the way, he recorded their material and cultural history—including firsthand accounts of how they traveled, lived, and hunted, their shamanic rituals, songs, dreams, drawings, and stories—without which we would know very little about the Greenland, Netsilik, Caribou, Copper, Mackenzie, and Alaskan Eskimos as they lived a hundred years ago.

Olejorgen was surprised that I knew about Rasmussen. Dark-skinned and almond-eyed, he had a slow, soft voice and enough Danish blood mixed into what he called his Eskimo genes to make him tall. Those genes linked him by blood to Rasmussen through one of Greenland's most famous families.

"It's because of Rasmussen that I am going north to live," Olejorgen said. He had never been that far up the coast, never driven a dogsled, never used a harpoon, never killed a seal. "I have quit law school and want to learn to be a hunter. I am an Eskimo. Now I shall learn how to be one."

"Rasmussen . . . ya . . . he is the national hero," Ann said. Buxom and voluable, she spoke in a loud voice, switching effortlessly between Danish, English, Faroese, and Greenlandic—a boon for me since I am a shy traveler. Now she was sorting through a huge bag of presents from Denmark. She was both a collector and a giver, constantly transforming what might have become avarice into unstinting generosity. As a social worker in charge of a regional orphanage and halfway house for children in Uummannaq, giving was a way of life for her. "My family in the Faroe Islands was wealthy. Shipping . . . that's why my professors at university said I wouldn't be good at my job. But I told them that if I'd never known love, how could I give it?"

Ann was returning to Uummannaq with her new companion. She'd met Olejorgen during her sabbatical in Copenhagen and became pregnant with his child. Olejorgen was following her to Uummannaq—a place in Greenland he had never seen, but which for five years had been her adopted home.

When we climbed out of the Twin Otter at Nuuk, I'd found I had no money—no Danish kroner, that is—and there was no place to change currency. The thick volumes by Rasmussen proved to be the only currency I needed: Ann had insisted I come with them to Olejorgen's parents' house.

We sped into Nuuk, Greenland's capital city, in a Toyota pickup-taxi. It was pouring rain. Well below the Arctic Circle, Nuuk has no dogsleds, only apartment buildings, a hotel, a museum of Eskimology, and the House of Parliament. Greenland, a Danish overseas administrative division, gained limited independence in 1979 and is now governed by home rule.

Olejorgen's parents, Motzflot and Maritha Hammekin, were in their late seventies and spoke no English. Greenlandic is an Eskimo language, and is the first language of Greenland. Motzflot was a pale-skinned vicar with a gentle voice and keen eyes. Olejorgen's mother was small and dark, slightly stooped but with thick strong hands. As she took the volumes from my arms, she told me she was related to Rasmussen through a Polish-Jewish-Danish-Greenlandic family named Fleischer. She wanted to show me the treasures she and her husband collected during their travels throughout Greenland. The small rooms were filled with soapstone and walrus ivory carvings and paintings of ice-choked fjords. On the dining room wall behind the vicar's seat hung the long tusk of a narwhal.

West Greenland was colonized by the Danes in 1721 and the entire population was Christianized by zealous Lutherans from Scandinavia. Intermarriage was common, a tool for assimilation, and though the population of Greenland is 85 percent Inuit, there is little pure blood left. What makes the far northern corner of the island unique is that colonization only went as far north as Tasiusaq, leaving the Polar Eskimos who lived along the Melville Peninsula all the way north to Siorapaluk largely unaffected by Europeanization for another two hundred years.

Beneath a chandelier we drank French Bordeaux and ate boiled seal and potatoes. This was the capital city, after all, with a prosperous-looking population of 14,000. Olejorgen's sister, Esther, doe-eyed and high-cheekboned, joined us with her Danish friend, Poul. A midwife, she had already delivered 285 babies that year and was about to set out by skiff to visit outlying villages where she would teach women how to deliver babies. Poul looked on, complacently smoking his pipe. He had left his own Danish family to join this one, and had lost all interest in returning home to Denmark; he had happily settled in with his job as editor of Greenland's bilingual (Danish-Greenlandic) newspaper, and with his Inuit "wife."

The next morning Ann asked where I was going, and I showed her on the map. "Awwkk . . . you can't go there," she said, making a face. "No, no. You must come north with us on the ferry to Uummannaq, the real Greenland, the one that Knud Rasmussen writes about." And I did.

We took the ferry—though it carried no cars, there being no roads between villages—and made a slow passage north. Women smoked and played cards, children ran, and Danish-style food was served in a cafeteria. I spent my time up on deck. Halfway up Viagut Strait, we passed an iceberg with a hole burrowed into its flank like a telescope through which I felt I could see the origins of green and blue, of ice itself.

Ice is what Greenlanders longed for and loved. We careened through pavilions and amphitheaters of ice, past mesas that had been halved and rejoined by summer's heat, exposing a central rift that was all azure rubble. As we proceeded north the ship's wake seemed to close over what was left of time.

A thousand years ago the hunter's world was made of ice and darkness, water and light, meat eaten raw and dried, and skins—dog, seal, polar bear, reindeer, Arctic hare, and eider duck—that were sewn into clothes, tents, and sleeping bags. The seasons rocked back and forth between light and dark and the ice was always moving: the top of Greenland is jostled by 52,000 square miles of Arctic sea, most of it ice. Polynyas—areas of open water—were created when surging tidal currents broke the ice, and stayed open like unhealing sores in midwinter. The land was an ocean that broke against bodies of water, shattering into islands big and small. Tides arm-wrestled pack ice until it accordioned up against itself, finally falling onto the mainland's shore. Glaciers calved great slabs of ice as big as convention centers and as fanciful as the Taj Mahal, and these sailed down the fjords all summer, their arches, towers, and shoulders collapsing in sudden heat as if from a fit of laughter.

Up on deck I met an old woman who had been napping. She asked if I spoke Danish. *Nye*, I said. American. A floe exploded on the starboard side and bits of ice avalanched down into foaming, churning water.

"Now we are going north," the old woman said, standing at the rail, her chin greasy with seal fat because, earlier, she had shared a rack of seal ribs with her grandson. The ice rubble that hit the hull made a thunking sound and the ship veered. "This is not the same world as the one you come from. Even now you are being deceived," she told me. "In early times the people said the land was thin and all kinds of talk between things and animals was possible because all things and all beings were the same; everything was interchangeable." A pod of ringed seals burst out of the water, then dove, leaving in their place a piece of green ice shaped like a harpoon.

Just before dawn, I went out on deck and found Olejorgen standing in the bow. He looked nervous and excited and his cheeks were red. I wondered if he had a fever. He complained of "a polar headache." "Rasmussen used to get them too," he said. A tower of rotten ice collapsed as we glided by. "When I get to Uummannaq I must find an elder who will explain things to me, who will be patient and teach me about using dogs, about the ice, about how to hunt the animals." Neither of us could have imagined then how much he would have to learn just to survive his years of instruction.

Olejorgen had left a wife, a son, and an unfinished law career behind to start a new life with another woman, a child on the way, and a burning desire to claim an Inuit hunting life that, because of geography, he had been denied.

During the night the boat's bow had dipped into deep troughs of open water, then we had glided up the smooth waters of Uummannaq Fjord. The red fin of the island, shaped like a heart, stuck straight up. An almost-full moon rose. "I feel as if I'm going home," Olejorgen had said.

The town is perched on a rock cast off from the main island of Greenland near the head of a fjord. When the ferry docked in the harbor, a crowd of children had cheered as Ann and Olejorgen made their way down the gangplank carrying bags full of gifts. Ann had been gone a year; Olejorgen had never been there, and as he stepped ashore, he shielded his eyes from the sun to look up the hill at the houses bolted to the rock. He had made his pact with the memory of the long-gone Rasmussen, who had also abandoned a European education for the life of an Eskimo. "Give me winter, give me dogs, you can have the rest," Rasmussen had said. Soon Olejorgen would learn the art of driving dogs, reading the ice, surviving storms and cold. At least he would try.

Slightly stoop-shouldered, with fine long fingers and pale skin, Ole-jorgen grimaced as we stepped down the gangplank, rubbed his aching forehead, then smiled. It was easy for the onlookers to see that Ann had snagged a city man.

A year later. We flew toward a black wedge that had been hammered between sea and sky. Behind us the sunken sun laid a belt of light across the water like a path of thought. A moon fell into my arms, a severed head with its brow chipped off, and below us the ice kept breaking. There were blocks of light and blanks of darkness—chronic over- and underexposure. The Arctic's continuously shifting planes of light and dark were like knives thrown in a drawer. They were the layered instruments that could carve life out of death into art and back to life.

The Inuit called this biggest island in the world Kalaallit Nunaat— White Earth. Some 736,000 square miles of it, or 95 percent, is ice, and 1,200 miles of its 1,670 mile-long coast is above the Arctic Circle. On its long back rides the largest continental ice sheet in the world, a remnant of the last ice age, which still lingers here. Snow has been accumulating on this white dome for so long—freezing and refreezing—that the summit has grown to 11,000 feet and its bulk has pushed the land beneath to 1,180 feet below sea level. If the ice cap ever melted, we would have another Hudson Bay.

Since most of the island is a mountain of ice, Greenlanders live on the only habitable land that's left—a rocky fringe along the coast. Of a total population of 60,000 people, 85 percent are Inuit, the rest are Danes. The Inuit are divided into three groups speaking distinct dialects of a polysyllabic Eskimo language they call Greenlandic. The three groups are the West Greenlanders, the East Greenlanders, and the Polar Eskimos. The average wintertime temperature is 25 degrees below zero Fahrenheit.

In early times before Danish colonizers brought diesel generators to villages, the only heat and light during the dark months between October and February came from stone dishes holding ignited seal or whale fat because there was nothing else to burn—no trees at all and almost no vegetation. Villages were moved according to seasons, and families stayed in stone, ice, and sealskin shelters and slept on a single platform covered in caribou or muskox skins. Travel was and still is by kayak and dogsled.

The Inuit were the Arctic's first explorers and had the savvy to live and thrive in this harshest climate in the world. Their travels across the polar north on threads of land and ice were driven as much by their desire to see new places in different seasons as by the need for food, which, weather and ice permitting, was abundant everywhere. Unlike the foreign gold seekers, whalers, and government-sponsored explorers who plied the east coast of Arctic Canada to find a passage to Asia—the very route the Inuit had walked from Siberia without patron, maps, or money—the Eskimos endured hardships with no chest-thumping. Vanity was unknown in the natural communal life of the subsistence hunter. They were an ice age, ice-adapted people who knew how to live in the cold, get plenty to eat, dress warmly, and avoid scurvy—life-saving adaptations that most outsiders who came to the Arctic were too arrogant to learn.

No humans ever lived in the Antarctic. Its coasts and islands are too distant from other continents to make migration possible. Only the Arctic has supported human culture. Twenty thousand years ago or more, people from northern Asia began drifting across the polar north in small extended families including elders, babies, and dogs. They lived by hunting caribou and reindeer with churt spears and marine mammals with harpoons, and they scraped the skins free of fat and flesh to make clothing.

They came from the icy northern regions of Siberia and took the Bering Land Bridge to the frozen flats north of Alaska's Brook Range, continuing through the straits and stepping stones of ice and islands that dot Arctic Canada. Finally, they followed game north to the Eureka Uplands of Ellesmere Island and from there walked across the permanent ice pack of Smith Sound to northern Greenland.

There, the way split. Some followed the tracks of muskoxen north to Peary Land, where they summered before heading down the mountainous, storm-battered east coast of Greenland. Others ventured down the warmer and more placid west coast, hunting seal, walrus, narwhal, and polar bear as far south as Melville Bay, continuing down to the fingering fjordlands of western Greenland, living in ice-bound isolation for thousands of years.

Somewhere over Baffin Bay, my plane droned. It seemed we could not go any slower without falling. Under us thin clouds were white bone rib cages threaded with sinews of pink flesh. As the western edge of Greenland came into view I felt the old euphoria I'd experienced on coming here the first time and asked if there was a creation story, a beginning. "That goes too far back," I was told. "They say it was so dark then, too dark for knowing."

We flew up the sleeve of the 106-mile-long Kangerlussuaq Fjord. The water was black and the mountains were brown, ending in broken snow-covered peaks. Streams threaded through creases in three-billion-year-old rock, the result of roiling magma that cooled into gray, speckled gneiss whose surfaces were later pulverized by incoming meteorites. Now water pooled in smooth catchbasins, and wherever there was enough dirt to support tufts of alpine fescue, muskoxen grazed. Far above, something gleamed: it was Greenland's ice cap—a glittering inflorescence that rode the island like the world's one light.

Greenland had been alive in the European imagination for seventeen hundred years. In the fourth century, a Greek philosopher, mathematician, and sailor named Phyteus sailed north from France and glimpsed a foggy, icebound coast near Scoresby Sound.

The sixth-century Irish monk Saint Brendan used an oxhide-covered willow boat to search for island sanctuaries far to the west, where he might found new monasteries. He described his sighting of an iceberg as "a floating crystal castle the color of a silver veil, yet hard as marble, and the sea around it was smooth as glass and white as milk."

Three hundred years later the Vikings, also known as Norsemen, landed in Iceland only to find that Irish pirates and a few solitary monks had already sought refuge there. When one Norseman, Eric the Red, was exiled from the new Icelandic colony for murder, he and his son Leif sailed to the large island to the northwest. Though it was almost entirely covered with ice, he called it Greenland as a lure to others to join him in his lonely exile. And they did. In the spring of 985, twenty-five ships attempted the crossing. The ice-glutted Atlantic was dangerous: eleven ships were lost or turned back. The rest colonized the grassy alpine meadows at the southern end of the island, unaware that far to the north, Inuit hunters had been living for several thousand years. Four hundred years later, during a cooling trend, the Norse colonists disappeared.

In the meantime, Greenland began appearing in European histories, first in Adam of Bremen's *Historia Hammaburgensis* in 1075, and was put on the map in 1424. In the mid-1500s, the search for the Northwest Passage began. John Davis, a British explorer and navigator, called

Greenland "The Land of Desolation." Unbeknownst to him or the other Euroean explorers, the route they sought had already been traveled by Inuit people for thousands of years.

As more ships plied Greenland's west coast and marginal contact with Inuit hunters was made, disease spread and a grotesque practice began. In 1576 Martin Frobisher ordered his crew members to kidnap an Inuit kayaker who came up alongside the ship. Two others were brought along, and died shortly after arriving in England. By 1660, thirty Eskimos had been captured. As late as 1906, the American explorer Robert Peary brought Minik and his father to New York as "living specimens" for the American Museum of Natural History.

We landed at the old airbase at Kangerlussuaq (formerly Sondre Stromfjord), installed as a line of defense against the Germans during World War II. At the head of the valley muskoxen grazed and a cliff of ice—the edge of the ice cap—glimmered faintly in the near-dark. Once this deep valley was prized for its reindeer. An old woman told me: "Every summer we went to Kangerlussuaq to live. We rowed umiaks from Illorsuit and Uummannaq. It was good hunting. The place was always full of flowers. We were happy there. So many reindeer. Some we ate, some meat we dried. There were many, and when we rowed back to the villages, the boats were full of meat and the blood ran under our kamiks [boots] like fjord water."

I transferred to a smaller plane and flew north to Ilulissat. There, in the afternoon, the sun was like a fire burning on the horizon, but after a few hours it dropped out of sight. The weather turned bad and the helicopter to Uummannaq was grounded. I walked into town, where I was to stay next to the hospital in a yellow house belonging to a doctor, Elisabeth Jul, a friend of Ann's I had met the previous year.

Ilulissat, just above the Arctic Circle, is a bustling town alive with the noise of 8,000 sled dogs howling. Elisabeth had just been made chief of staff at the town's regional hospital. She visited her outlying patients all winter by dogsled. "Doctors in Denmark and Greenland don't make much money, not like America. We do this work because it's interesting," she said. Her face reddened when she talked about herself, yet she had a physician's confidence and speedy abruptness. She was tomboyish and stocky and wore her blond hair in two thin braids. Her slight New York accent came as a surprise, since she had been raised in Denmark. She explained: "My parents were World Health Organization workers who met on the job. My father was a Dane and my mother a New Yorker."

She gave me a tour of the hospital. "The first thing I noticed when I came here was that the Greenlandic patients refuse to be alone in a room or have the door closed. They grew up communally and they don't want to die alone. A room with the door closed—that's a Dane."

We drank coffee at a window overlooking the fjord where the world's most productive glacier, the Sermeq Kujalleg, calves 10 percent of all icebergs in the water between Greenland and Canada. "The iceberg that sank the *Titanic* probably came from here," Elisabeth said.

Elisabeth relished the variety that geographical isolation brought to her work, describing herself as a jack-of-all-trades doctor: internist, surgeon, obstetrician, psychiatrist, and public health worker. "I give out pills, condoms, do autopsies, vaccinate, deliver babies, and operate. I try to pull the patient through with the equipment we have and our combined experience."

Once she had to do a surgery she had never performed before. They rigged her with a headset connected to the Royal Hospital in Copenhagen, where a surgeon talked her through the procedure. "The patient had internal bleeding and was going to die if I didn't do something. . . . Well, the thing is," she said blushing, "he lived. These Greenlanders are tough, that's why they survive." She continued as we walked to her house: "I had one guy with a perforated ulcer. It had gotten bad when he was out on the fjord and it was a two-hour trip by dogsled to town. Before anything else, he sorted his fish and fed his dogs. Only then did he come into the hospital. A friend brought him; the day after surgery, he walked home."

Elisabeth's house smelled sour from the kitchen scraps she begged from the town's hotel to feed her dogs. She hated housework. "I keep the clean part of my life in the hospital," she remarked. When there was ice, she harnessed her dogs and traveled alone to isolated villages along the coast to treat her patients and give vaccinations. "When I was first learning how to drive dogs the people in town stopped their transactions at the bank and the grocery to watch me. They had a great many laughs: there were a lot of wrecks. It helped them accept me."

From the window she could watch her dogs, who were chained up nearby. She had trained guidedogs for the blind in Denmark. "I like having them close. That way I can see what they are discussing among themselves."

Ice had not yet formed over the rough waters of Baffin Bay. A glut of icebergs stood like shining towers where the fjord let into the bay. It was hard to believe that once Greenland was lush with ancient poplars, chestnuts, oaks, laurels, walnuts, and magnolias, all of which froze in the Pleistocene and stayed frozen. "We are still in an ice age up here," Elisabeth reminded me.

Knud Rasmussen was born in Ilulissat. As soon as I stashed my duffle with Elisabeth, I walked across the road to Rasmussen's childhood home, now a museum. Climbing the narrow stairs, I stood at the window in the library that looks down on a floating city of icebergs. Rasmussen must have stood there many times, waiting for the ocean to freeze so he could go out with his dogs.

Everywhere I went, there were stories about Rasmussen as if he were still alive and off somewhere on his dogsled. A woman from Ikerasak said her mother had sewn his kamiks; someone else was his grandson; yet another was the granddaughter of Qavigarssuaq, the man with whom Rasmussen traveled for three years.

Earlier the sun had been a small fire burning on the horizon, but now the bay was dark. My head felt strange, not aching or dizzy, but leaden. I wondered if Rasmussen's "polar headaches" felt that way, if they had been brought on by magnetic storms; if Olejorgen was still having them.

Rasmussen's headaches were legendary. Perhaps they were born of the rift between the primal, restless, meat-hungry Arctic nomad that he was, and the cultured, educated European husband, father, and hero that he became. It was said that Rasmussen was really two people, one a Danish gentleman, the other an Eskimo truant—but that his laughter, energy, and charm mortared the rift; his heart's home was always Greenland.

Born June 7, 1879, Rasmussen was the son of a Danish pastor and a mother of mixed Danish-Inuit blood. He had a whip in his hand as soon as he could walk; by the time he was ten, he was driving his own dogsled. He grew up bilingual, speaking Danish with his father and Greenlandic with his mother and all his schoolhood chums. His maternal grandfather was from the Fleischer family. The first Greenland Fleischer was a Norwegian Jew of Polish descent who had come to Greenland to start a trading post and a new life. This he did by marrying a young Inuit villager from Qasigiannguit (just south of Ilulissat) who was orphaned, illiterate, and close to starvation. Young Knud grew up hearing his grandmother's stories of seal hunting, drum dances, and communal living, as well as the legends that came down in the dark times from five thousand years of living on the ice—stories of giants, dwarfs, and spirits who dwelled there.

As a boy Rasmussen was enthralled by what he saw around him: the drifting icebergs and the sealskin tents of summer camps on barren islands that dotted the coast, then the icing over of the fjords, and the dogteams going out to hunt for weeks and months at a time.

His mother understood Knud's passion for the Eskimo life. When his sister May was born, a Greenlandic orphan girl was also brought into the family: Knud's mother shared her milk with both babies.

School and all the intricacies of European living eluded him. He had to be dragged into the classroom. Playing hooky, he sought out the elderly women in Ilulissat and listened to their strange stories of the pure-blooded Eskimos who lived farther north, dressed in bearskins, and killed walrus, polar bears, and whales with harpoons.

At age twelve Knud went with his father to visit his uncle Carl Fleischer, who lived in a subsistence village north of Ilulissat. There he heard more strange stories: of a *kivitog*—a person who abandoned his family to live alone at the edge of the ice cap, and could never go back to normal life. If he tried, the villagers would shoot him. Another story told of a woman who was lost when an iceberg toppled over on her kayak. The husband went mad with grief and wandered into the mountains. Ten days later he was found dead, with brown hair sprouting from his legs and arms; at the end of one withered leg was a hoof.

Knud eagerly awaited the return of the hunters at the end of spring, their sleds loaded with seal, whale, and walrus. The meat was shared and there were great feasts which he joined, listening to tales about hunting. In the winter the young Rasmussen went out with his boy's sled. He had a way with his dogs, an understanding of their minds that in later years enabled him to travel with them for thousands of miles.

When his father was transferred back to Denmark, Knud's icy paradise was taken from him. They moved to Copenhagen, where it was flat, rainy, and leafy—the opposite of Greenland. Knud struggled with homework, especially math, and graduated with the lowest score in the whole school. At the university he studied acting and worked as a journalist on the side, but everything was pulling him back to Greenland.

In 1902, when he was twenty-three, he found a way home. He was asked by Ludvig Mylius-Erichsen to join "the Literary Expedition" to west Greenland. Knud eagerly agreed and asked a Greenlandic friend, Jorgen Brönlund, to join them. Their first adventure in Greenland was in his own old backyard: they attempted to get to the top of Disko Island's ice cap, but failed.

Later, they took the trail from Ilulissat over the mountains of Nuussuaq Peninsula to Uummannaq. Stopping at the island of Ikerasak, Rasmussen spent a few weeks with his other uncle, Jens Fleischer, who was a renowned dog trainer—the perfect mentor for the young explorer.

When the ice was good they traveled north to the town of Upernavik, far north of Uummannaq. On the way, they spent a few nights at Illorsuit, where the American painter Rockwell Kent would later spend a year. Upernavik became their headquarters. The town was never the same again after Rasmussen was there. "Laughter preceded him everywhere," it was said. He dreamed up every excuse for a celebration—Eskimo-style costume parties, singing, dancing, and feasting.

Finally the expedition went north up the long and sparsely populated coast to Cape York. Rasmussen's dream was coming true: for the first time he would meet the Polar Eskimos. The going was tough. Ice conditions and the ferocity of the weather far exceeded anything they had known in Ilulissat. They almost froze in their canvas tents and the dogs ate their sealskin harnesses. One of the members of the group, Harold Moltke, fell gravely ill and the dogs came down with distemper. It was Rasmussen who saved them all, forging on ahead to a village where he could get food and warmer clothes for himself and the others. When Moltke recovered, they built a headquarters on Saunders Island just off the coast from Thule, in the northernmost inhabited corner of Greenland.

On Rasmussen's return to Denmark from this first expedition, he met and fell in love with Dagmar Andersen, the quiet and thoughtful daughter of a wealthy Danish businessman. But already he was divided: no earthly love could mitigate his appetite for the far north. Knud and Dagmar were married in 1908, and afterwards she waited patiently at home for a husband who was almost always away.

In 1910, Rasmussen invited his friend Peter Freuchen to join him at Thule in northern Greenland, where they would build an Arctic station—a trading post, bank, clinic, and headquarters from which to launch journeys into the heart of Eskimo culture.

Peter was young, big-boned, gregarious, steadfast, and daring. By his own description, his childhood had made him a perfect candidate for

Arctic living. "Hardly anything was forbidden in our place," he wrote, "and our garden was the meeting ground for all the children of the neighborhood. The result was a group complex which has followed me all through my life. I like best to be one of a crowd."

Like Rasmussen, Freuchen had not found university to his liking. He had enrolled in medical school but felt restless and bored. His resolve to live as he pleased was toughened by a bout of tuberculosis. He worked as a coal stoker on a ship to Greenland; he was ready for Thule.

There was great excitement in the air about the Arctic since Robert Peary's trip to the North Pole in 1909, and with funding from Denmark, Rasmussen and Freuchen headed for Thule as planned. In Dundas Village on North Star Bay, they built a trading post and bank. From there they launched six expeditions around Greenland. Between 1921 and 1924, the Fifth Thule Expedition took Freuchen to Arctic Canada and Rasmussen all the way to Alaska by dogsled.

Rasmussen took to heart what a Caribou Eskimo once told him: "All true wisdom is only to be found far from the dwellings of man, in the great solitudes; and it can only be attained through suffering. Suffering and privation are the only things that can open the mind of man to that which is hidden from his fellows."

Between trips, Rasmussen went home to Denmark to see Dagmar. He managed to father two children—daughters—and buy a farm not far from the western edge of Copenhagen. His returns were festive events, but soon society wore thin and he'd go north again. He still had an abiding interest in theater: during his Seventh Thule Expedition, he made a theatrical film on the east coast of Greenland called *Palo's Wedding*, using local Greenlanders as actors.

Pleased with the results, he had plans to make more movies, but he was struck down suddenly by salmonella after eating a big bowl of *kivioq*—an Arctic-style delicacy made from dead auks sewn inside a seal gut and left to rot for two months. Antibiotics were still unknown. He rallied for a few weeks, was shipped home to the Royal Hospital in Copenhagen, but died in 1933. He was fifty-four years old.

Rasmussen once described midday in winter as "white darkness." Now, sixty-two years after his death, Ilulissat's sky was dark blue, but the snow gave off its own diffused light, as if the sun had been buried beneath the ground and was trying to get out. After three days of waiting I boarded an aging Sikorsky helicopter. It lifted up through lingering snow showers that turned Ilulissat's few hours of daylight gray. Up above, over the waters of Disko Bay, the sun burned a hole on the horizon, its long wake of light a torch striking north at the darkness into which we had begun to fly.

I began to think of Greenland's light as being multiple—a ladder of suns which, like candles, had been blown out one by one, and just as slowly were being lit again. The island of Greenland itself was a ladder reaching for the North Pole, each step bringing progressively colder weather and darker skies.

I had climbed a rung and now I was headed for Uummannaq, where Olejorgen and Ann were waiting for me. Far to the south I could still see the last of the twilight, a metallic glow wavering, trying to spear the enveloping darkness, but to no avail. Icebergs sailed under us, each one a miniature continent with its own turquoise inlets and long-fingered fjords, sharp peaks and sloping plains. One had collapsed into itself; its broken parts had curdled and were floating in black water. In other places the ice floor had shattered into elongated rectangles like blocks of basaltic rock.

Instead of flying over the mountains, we went out and around the Nuussuaq Peninsula, the idea being that, in case of an emergency, it would be safer to autorotate down onto ice than into a snowy mountain. We rounded the tip of the peninsula, then followed the fjord, passing the village of Niaqornat out on the western end. The father of my Greenlandic friend Aleqa Hammond drowned in this fjord when she was seven years old. He had been hunting when he fell through the ice with all his dogs. "I asked my grandmother why people have to die, and she told me it was something arranged by the spirits. Some people have thick candles that last a long time. His wasn't so big. And so he went down to where the goddess of the sea lives." Once the storm overtook us, violent winds buffeted the helicopter. Its one blade of hope held us above the ice, ocean, sea goddess, and the certain death that Arctic waters can bring.

In early times there was no light and people did not die. Then there were too many of them, and two old women began one day to talk to each other. "Let us do without the daylight if at the same time we can be without death." "Nay," said the other. "We will have both Light and

Death." As the old woman said those words, it was so. Light came and with it, death.

If light brought death, then I was safe. We were flying in darkness, in a lost sky, across a black blank. Then I saw stars. The Inuit once thought that stars were holes through which snow, rain, and the souls of dead people spilled. I wanted to break open the helicopter's windows to keep the skulls from tumbling, to let in more light.

Everything in the helicopter shook. We continued on. How could we have slid so far from the sun? What kept the ice-heavy North Pole from tipping even further? This was not just an oncoming winter storm that would soon pass, but the shadow of the earth falling across the whole top of the world.

We flew up the black sleeve of the Uummannaq Fjord. Snow-covered cliffs rose up wounded and scarred by the glacial traffic that had passed over their rocky flanks. For a moment a half-moon rose up above the storm as if greeting us. Then we augered down into a chaos of falling snow toward dark pitching water where there should have been a smooth floor of ice.

I was in Uummannaq again, a town of 1,400 people and 6,000 dogs at 72 degrees north latitude. It is perched on a rock island, cast off from Greenland near the head of a fjord. Long ago the sun stopped rising here and I could only wonder if it would ever come again. It was three p.m. and the lights were on all over the settlement. What was called day here was something else entirely; here, the sky had not yet become a lamp for human beings. I only wanted to sleep.

Ann and Olejorgen greeted me at the heliport. A tiny face peeked out of a sealskin anorak: it was Pipaluk, their daughter, now two. Ludwig, Olejorgen's ten-year-old son from Denmark who had come to live with his father, shook my hand. The snow was deep as we made our way into town. Everywhere around the island there was open water except in the harbor, which had turned to ice.

Ann had arranged a house for me. It was reached by a long series of rickety stairs. At the top sat a two-room house, bolted to rock. It was uninsulated, with no running water, and looked down on the harbor below. From my window I could see the grocery store, the post office, the warehouse, the administration building, and the bakery; from another window, the Uummannaq Hotel, the Grill Baren (a hot dog stand), and a clinic. On the far side was the Royal Greenland fish factory. Fishing boats were frozen in place and the seal hunters' skiffs were scattered helter-skelter on top of the ice.

Four p.m. looked like midnight and the dog noise was cacophonous. Bundled up in wool pants, down parka, and sealskin mittens with doghair ruffs at the wrist, I trudged through the village lined with prim Danish-style houses painted yellow, blue, red, or green. Only forty years ago the Greenlanders lived in peat-and-stone houses trussed with whale ribs. In winter the rooms were lined with rime ice; when the sun returned, they removed the roofs to let the rooms thaw.

There was Arctic clutter everywhere: sleds stacked up, sled dogs tethered by long chains, dog shit, drying racks hung with halibut, and seal and polar bear skins pulled taut on stretchers laid against houses to dry. Greenlandic dogs are descended from the first canine migrants who came to Greenland from Ellesmere Island. No other dogs are allowed into Greenland. In this way, the bloodlines are kept pure. Slightly smaller than the Alaskan husky and more fine-boned, they have the same shaped head, ears, and upturned tail. Some are dark brown with white chests, others white-blond, the color of polar bears. They live in groups and seem to have their own society. When I walked near, there was no response, not even a glance. They pay attention only to the one who feeds them; otherwise they are unconcerned with human affairs.

Kids shot by, four to a sled, narrowly missed by a dogsled climbing up the other way. Men and women pushed prams with babies whose tiny hands reached up to touch dangling mobiles of soft-sided whales and seals. Female dogs in heat ran loose through town, as did all puppies, and as each passed through a new neighborhood of chained dogs, howls and moans erupted—the sounds of excitement and longing. I felt rather unnecessary in that world of dogs. Local taxis zoomed up and down the hills taking grocery shoppers home. Through the window of a tiny woodworking shop whose lights were on, it was impossible not to see two graphic posters on the wall—beaver shots of naked white women.

In the morning the temperature dipped to 12 below zero. The sky was still black. Everyone went down to the water to see if the ice was coming in. "You'll be able to tell when you look way out and the water is completely still. That's how you know the ice is coming." The crisis was that the fjords had not iced over. Stormy weather kept breaking it up. Without ice, there was no way to get to other villages. We were prisoners on our Eskimo Alcatraz, and I wondered if my dogsled trip to the far north might not be doomed.

Far out near the head of the fjord I saw a piece of ice shaped like a heart within a heart-shaped opening of black water. My own heart—which had stopped once and started again unaided—was now almost too cold to beat. Down there in the water the sea goddess Nerrivik lived. Her long hair was tangled and full of lice and no one would comb it clean. She was unhappy, the old people said, and there were no angakoks anymore—no shamans—to pacify her. That's why there was no ice.

In early times the nomadic life of the Eskimos was contained by a moral universe kept under the thumb of various powers. The "powers" were an array of busy, pestering spirits. And Sila. In Greenlandic, *sila* means both weather and consciousness. Weather itself was thought to be an organism, a power with a personality and an ever-changing shape that could ambush, kill, or resurrect. Some shamans said that in early times Sila was a baby giant who had fallen out of his mother's amaut (the hood in which a baby is carried) and was lying on the ground. Women gathered around and played with the baby's penis. It was so big that four of them sat on it at one time. Suddenly the baby giant was lifted up and away from those women and landed in the sky. There he became Sila, the weather. When he loosened his caribou-skin diapers, wind and snow were let loose. For an angakok to appease Sila, he had to fly into the sky and tighten the diaper.

For Inuit hunters, weather ruled. Humans were puny figures who lived in a voracious and everlasting country of winters. Mental prowess was as important as physical agility. Psychological perseverance had to match physical speed. Fear of Sila drove the Eskimo to unbending self-discipline. Though often disguised as nonchalance and a disdain for order, it was the glue that bound internal and external weather events together.

Adherence to local rituals was critical: "It is how we hold our world and each other up, so that we do not offend the powers," one old hunter said. Taboos were lifelines: water had to be poured into the corner of a newly killed seal's mouth, a woman's left nostril had to be plugged after childbirth. If these acts were ignored, things would go badly.

Arctic weather had a mind of its own and the mind had an intemperate climate. Against the power of Sila, humans learned to act as a group. Individual expression had no place in communal strategies for survival. Wind could blast at 150 miles per hour, blowing people and dogs away, never to be seen again; cold devoured limbs and all thinking. Sudden warmth and ocean currents broke up ice; dogsleds disappeared in the holes. Spring snows obscured crevasses on glaciers, summer fog engulfed coastlines and could disorient the hunter like a drug.

Seasons of darkness and light passed like a blinking light, first bright, then black, and the bicameral mind blinked with it. Sila was a single multitude: Arctic weather was a know-it-all, a major divinity, and mind was a tangle of strict etiquette and wild imagination that grew in direct proportion to the extravagance of polar beauty, cold, and storms.

Nerrivik (sometimes spelled Neqivik) was the goddess of the waters. She was beautiful, haughty, disdainful of humans, and easily angered. She had been an orphan who lived in a settlement where she was badly treated, as orphans often were. She had to fend for herself, eat the scraps left over by the dogs, and mend her ragged clothes. The day the hunters decided to move on, they tied their kayaks together to make a raft, loaded their belongings on it, and sailed away. Nerrivik came running after them but they left her behind to starve. Desperate, she jumped in the water and swam after the raft. She finally caught up and grabbed hold of the side, trying to pull herself into a kayak, but one of the people chopped her fingers off and she sank back into the water. So great was the evil committed against her that she became the most powerful of the spirits. Her amputated fingers became seals and walrus and whales. That is how the marine mammals were created, and she guarded them jealously and with revenge in her heart, so that if a human broke any rule or insulted the souls of the animals, she snatched the animals up and hid them under her house at the bottom of the sea. People starved and the shaman had to be sent down to appease her.

Nerrivik's house was like a human dwelling but without a roof. A wall was built in front of the entrance which the shaman had to break into. Her long hair always got tangled when she was angry, and since she had no fingers, it was the shaman's duty to stroke her locks to smooth them, saying, "Those above can no longer help the seal out of the sea." And she would say, "It is your ill-doing that bars the way." Sometimes her hair was full of lice. He had to remove the vermin and promise that the human offenders were sorry for their actions and would no longer misbehave. When her anger had been appeased, she released the animals one by one. After a violent commotion, they swam up into their breathing holes. In this way, they offered themselves to hunters as food.

Late in the day Uummannaq's rock walls ran black with meltwater and the inky fjord jostled against the island's cliffs. It was too warm for ice. I set aside a few hours to study Greenlandic, the polysyllabic Eskimo language common to Inuit people across the polar north to Alaska. The add-on words could grow so long they became a whole sentence or two, impossible to mouth. At first, to look at one of those giants was defeating. I only later began to identify the individual words within. The dialects differed, but they could all be understood. I learned lists of words in West Greenlandic but could not grasp where to fit in the verbs and so add wings to a sentence—if I could have formulated one at all. After, I went walking.

That day I met a man who knew all about trees but had never seen one growing. He was the local dogsled maker. Each district has a distinct sled-making style: in Ilulissat and Uummannaq the sleds are short with curved handles for maneuvering in the mountains; in Thule, far to the north, they are long with shorter straight uprights in the back and upturned runners.

The carpentry shop was high-ceilinged and lined with handsome Danish-modern workbenches where the sleds were being constructed. As we walked between them he explained that for the runners, which must be strong but flexible for traveling over rough ice and rock, he bought whole trees from Denmark that had been split in half and air-dried. When cutting and shaping them he was careful to match the left or outer convex side of the log to the left side of the sled, and the right to the right side. Otherwise the runners would break.

Sleds varied in size according to function and time of year. The long sleds used in the spring to hunt narwhal when the sea ice was breaking up were eighteen feet long, while sleds for local travel and seal hunting in Uummannaq District were only six to eight feet long. On sleds to be used for long trips, like the one being made for Olejorgen, he reinforced the handles and joints with sheet metal, and the crossbars that made up the floor of the sled had to be fastened at alternating lengths into the runner. If not, the runner would break through the grain of the wood.

It was Friday afternoon and the carpenters were drinking warm Tuborg beer. I laid a topo map of Uummannaq District and the Nuussuaq Peninsula on the floor. They gathered around to show which route they take to cross the top of the mountains, the place where they sleep at night, and where last year hunters were rescued by helicopter after a piece of ice they were standing on broke away during a storm. They also showed me places where friends of theirs had disappeared through the ice—dogs, dogsled, and all.

When I asked the sled maker if the fjord would freeze, he looked out the window and shrugged. "The time between the full moon and the new moon—that is when ice always comes. The weather grows calm and very cold. If there are no more snowstorms, there will be ice." As I left I asked if he had ever wanted to see a tree grow. He looked at me and grinned. "I'm happy where I am."

Qilaq taatuq. The sky is dark. *Segineq.* The sun. *Siku.* Ice. *Tarraq.* Shadow. *Aput.* Fallen snow. *Tartoq.* Darkness. *Kisimiippunga.* I am alone. That was my vocabulary lesson for the day. In reading the expedition notes of Knud Rasmussen, I learned that words used in seances were different from secular words, so that the shamanic word for sea is *aquitsoq* (the soft one), rather than the usual *imaq.* Mental and spiritual prowess was inextricably linked to weather: *silanigtalerarput* means "working to obtain great wisdom."

On my way home from the sled maker's shop, I noted that the skim of ice that had formed was gone and the pathway out to the piece of annual ice used for drinking water had gone liquid. Near the harbor in the center of town I stopped to look at the one traditional peat-and-stone house left in Uummannaq from the old days. The old man who was staying there invited me in. The air inside was dank and the peat smelled like burnt heather. One window, once made of seal gut, now of glass, was lined with candles. The man sat on his sleeping platform and watched me in silence. A rifle was slung over the back of the chair and an old harpoon rested in the corner. I asked if he had known Rasmussen and he nodded yes, that Knud had been here when he was a little boy. How little? I asked. He held his hand a few feet above the floor and laughed toothlessly.

There was a dogsled outside but no dogs—they had all died of old age. But the old man seemed ready to go hunting. Later someone told me that he had been born on a moving dogsled far from home, and people born that way only want to travel, never staying in one place very long.

The paleo-Eskimos—known as the Independence I people—who walked to Bronlund Fjord in Peary Land five thousand years ago from neighboring Ellesmere Island, were muskox hunters who wandered across the top of Greenland and down the east side. Their tool kit included notched lance blades, knife blades, scrapers, arrow points, and burin spalls made of churt, as well as bone needles for sewing using thread made of the long sinews of whales.

This group gave way to the Saqqaq, a group of perhaps four or five hundred hunters who lived between 2000 and 1500 B.C. Also users of stone and bone tools, they lived in egg-shaped houses made of peat and stone with ceilings of stretched animal skins, situated on low promontories overlooking the water.

A 600-to-800-year silence in Greenland was followed by the coming of the Dorset people from Foxe Basin and Hudson Strait. They traveled far down the western coast of Greenland and lived on caribou, seal, whale, and the now-extinct great auk. The Dorset people were known for their elegant walrus ivory carvings of human and bear spirits, sealmen, and bear-men, and believed that humans and animals were incomplete without each other. They disappeared by the middle of the ninth century A.D.

The last group, the Thule, still living a stone age existence, arrived in Greenland in A.D. 1050, just as the Normans were preparing to invade Britain. Ice and weather kept them isolated. They didn't even know there were any other people in the world. By 1450 they had made their way to the east coast of Greenland and settled at Ammassalik, hunting muskox and making skin clothing from Arctic fox, seal, polar bear, and caribou—just as Greenlandic hunters are doing now. From the Canadian Arctic they brought new technology: sinew-backed bows, kayaks, umiaks, and dogsleds. A cooling climate later pushed them south down Greenland's west coast.

The last migration of Thule people from Baffin Island came in 1865, the year Tolstoy wrote *War and Peace*. They brought back tools that had been lost and forgotten—the kayak and bows and arrows. This last group of Eskimos walked to Greenland via Pond Inlet and Ellesmere Island in 1862 led by Qidlaq, a local shaman who had dreamed about

Greenland. It took them seven years to make the trip. They made their first camp at Etah, north of present-day Qaanaaq. Some stayed, but those who returned to Pond Inlet were hounded by misfortune. The shaman died and many starved to death on their way home. Those families who stayed on the north coast of Greenland fared better. The hunting was good and the weather was better than in eastern Canada. Many of the people now living in Siorapaluk and Qaanaaq are descended from these ice age pilgrims.

Ann and Olejorgen invited me for dinner. Before we ate I helped Olejorgen feed his dogs. He had inherited the team of Ann's deceased boyfriend, and they were chained up behind his house. Sled dogs in Greenland are fed only every second or third day because it's thought that if they eat regularly they will lose their ability to survive days when the hunting is bad and there is no food. They are kept half-wild and hungry.

When Olejorgen appeared holding buckets of halibut, an explosion of barking and yelping erupted as morsels of fish flew through the air. The dogs lunged, straining at the ends of their chains and pawing the air for more. When the ice came in, the dogs would be staked out on the frozen fjord.

In the house we drank sparkling water popping with glacier ice. In summer, a bank of windows on two sides of the living room let in a surfeit of light. Now the windows were black and blank, but the windowsills danced with votive candles. Olejorgen had started driving his own dogsled and had shot a few seals, but he still had the graceful figure of a scholar, slightly stooped, with long fingers turned up at the ends—nothing like the short, broad-handed hunters.

Townspeople sometimes referred cruelly to Olejorgen as Ann's *kifak*—her housekeeper. She had the job and he cooked and cared for the children, which is fine in Denmark but unheard of here. Out on the ice he was still very much a beginner, and who wouldn't be? His dream of finding an elder who would become his mentor hadn't materialized. But he had found a hunter—the husband of a woman who worked for Ann at the Children's House—who took him along.

During dinner Pipaluk, named for Peter Freuchen's daughter (who, like her, was born prematurely), sang and danced for us. Then she pulled me outside to see the dogs sleeping in snow, noses tucked under tails.

Feeling cabin-feverish, we all went for a midnight spin in Ann's small Russian car—an orange box on four tiny wheels. She'd taught one of the local hunters to drive because she didn't know how. She'd grown up with a chauffeur. "Everyone would be asking me to take them around," she said. Instead, that's what she asked others to do for her.

The town's loop road was a steep, snow-packed rock path. After five of us jammed into the tiny vehicle, we could barely make it up to the top. The car lurched, spun its wheels, then slid backward. Finally we made it. Dogs were chained up everywhere—thousands of them, as anxious for the ice to come in as we were. We passed the mayor's house, the banker's house, the comptroller's house, and at the far end of town on a cliff overlooking the mouth of the fjord, we stopped at a blue house under construction—one that Olejorgen longed to buy. But not Ann. "It's a dreamer's house," she said. Olejorgen smiled.

We descended, skidding past the church, skirting the edge of the harbor, then started up the hill for home. On the way we passed a small cemetery and stopped. "People come to Greenland for one of two reasons," Ann said. "Love or tax problems. Mine was the first." She had followed her boyfriend, a young doctor, to Uummannaq. Soon after, the helicopter he was riding fell into the fjord and everyone drowned. "All they found was a boot. So I buried it in his grave. Everything in the Arctic is provisional," she said. "The ice and our lives."

Later that night a little girl was brought to the Children's House and Ann was called. The girl had just seen her mother kill her father with a skinning knife. The policeman who went to the scene was a friend of the family's, and as in all Greenland towns, there was no jail to house offenders—the censorious looks of the neighbors were prison enough; it was merely suggested that the child spend the night elsewhere.

Ann left her own child, who had come down with the flu, to attend to the newcomer. Badly shaken, the girl was given hot chocolate and cookies, a fresh nightgown and toothbrush, and a clean bed in a brightly painted room with a window that looked at the mountain. Ann stayed there almost all night in case the girl woke and was afraid.

Greenlanders have always known that the psyche is a difficult place to navigate—as difficult as ice—and had to be undertaken with great care. They practice tolerance toward those in distress. *Perleroneq*—Arctic hysteria—could break out as darkness came on and dogs as well as people might foam at the mouth and try to kill innocent bystanders or themselves. In one of Rasmussen's texts, an explorer reported that simply petting the dogs relieved them of their anxiety; he didn't comment on how to treat afflicted people.

Polar days are the same as polar nights: the streetlights in town are always on. Behind the houses of this village, the wall of Uummannaq Mountain rises straight up, a pale, lobed heart in a body too big to see. I tried to keep to a schedule: coffee in the morning, dinner at night, then sleep. But the schedule yielded to the body's own understanding of constant dark. I slept when I should have eaten and ate in the middle of the night.

A recent study suggests that the eye may have its own biological clock, separate from the one in the brain. Now it's possible to think of eyes as circadian timepieces with resettable daily rhythms in the retina that orchestrate the ebb and flow of the hormone melatonin. In the dark and near-dark, I wondered what dances my eye rhythms were performing and if, upon reentering the world of all-day sun, I would be blind.

Morning and afternoon the sky was black. I read Rasmussen, practiced Greenlandic, and visited the Children's House. The young girl who had been brought in the night before said she had dreamed about people who weren't really people, but spirits who lived in the ground and left no hole when they emerged, who disliked men and would jump through them, leaving no mark, then kill them.

I strolled one day along the rocky edge of town, past the inlet where a wave, generated by a calving glacier, washed fifteen anchored boats onto the road. The Danes were so busy trying to save their pleasure boats that they forgot about the dogs tied up at the shore and the dogs drowned. "That's how it is nowadays," an old woman said. "In early times, they dared not behave that way."

My daily walks were the one constant. I checked my watch and tried to make my body understand that it was day. Past the heliport, I came to the dump. The view from there looked inward toward the wet black cliffs at the head of the fjord.

Traversing the rockfall at the foot of Uummannaq Mountain's red spire, I found that its thickness barricaded my way around the island. I could go only so far up its slope before it rose vertically, then I scrambled back down into town. Town was dark and light, studded with streetlights, the government offices buzzing with people who, a hundred years ago, would have been dressed in polar bear pants, riding sleds. Now they governed themselves with a thirteen-member council—six from the town and one from each outlying village; time formerly spent hunting for seals was now spent in meetings. The weekly helicopter from Upernavik landed and took off. Weeks earlier, when nosing up above the clouds while flying north from Ilulissat, it was easy to see how all storms and all loves are merely local weather, how, with patience, one can always find a hole through which to fly. . . . Looking down from the steep side of Uummannaq Mountain, I saw that the island was a circle drawn in deep water, and the water was a circle whose one hole had been plugged by an island of rock.

My rooms were frosty. The snow I tracked in on the floor never melted. I kept candles lit on the bare table where I read and wrote as the electricity stopped and started according to the whims of the town's diesel generator. I'd bought food at the store: seal ribs, potatoes, tea. Every few days an older man I didn't know hauled buckets of water up the long stairs and refilled the tiny oil heater by the couch that had become my bed. He spoke to me in Danish, then Greenlandic; thinking I must be mute, he shrugged and walked out of the house, climbing the steep hill to a house that looked just like mine.

Evening. My window framed bits of town life like a proscenium: a hunter traipsed through carrying a rifle. He walked across the harbor ice to his skiff, which he shoved over to the one lead—a crack in the ice—started the engine, and headed out into the fjord's ink-black water. I walked to Ann and Olejorgen's house for dinner. Theirs was an Inuit-style marriage, no ceremony, no rings, just an unspoken vow to live "so as not to injure each other's minds."

The three of us quickly finished off a pot of reindeer stew and afterwards lay on the couch, lazily sipping coffee and eating chocolates. Wind rattled the windows and the temperature plunged. When the door creaked open I saw my old friend Aleqa Hammond standing there. We had met the year before. Born in Uummannaq, she had only just returned from university studies in linguistics and Eskimology. Tall and big-boned, with long hair pulled straight back in a knot, she had a glinting, white-toothed smile. "I heard you were coming," she said.

The history of the Arctic was written in Aleqa's surname and her countenance: the name Hammond had been passed down from her great-grandfather, an Englishman who had come north on a British whaling ship in the 1880s. At one of the ports he'd had a dalliance with an Inuit woman and was put off the ship as punishment. His exile proved to be a reward: he quickly settled down in the village with his lover, learned to hunt with a harpoon, and fathered many children. "I think he was happy at what happened to him," Aleqa said smiling.

Two generations later, the trend reversed. Village life was not enough for Aleqa; she was always on the move. She'd guided hunters in Quebec, studied linguistics at Arctic College in Iqaluit, lived with a German lover in Europe and a Danish one in Copenhagen. Then she'd come home again. "It's important for people to know that we are not just specks of ice. Our culture is very valuable. Here in Greenland we are no longer pure Eskimos and we are not Danes. We are a race between. We make a new boundary. We look different, and we are finding our balance as we live in two worlds. The Danish government, once our colonizers, have been tolerant. Not in the beginning: that's why we lost so much of our spiritual life. But now we are surviving. No one is hungry. Everyone has a good place to live. Help isn't difficult to get. And we still have our dogs and traditional hunting. In Canada, they have lost all that: they now use snowmobiles."

More coffee was passed, and cookies were brought from the kitchen. I asked if it was possible that twenty thousand years of shamanism could have disappeared in less than a hundred years. Olejorgen and Aleqa looked at each other, shrugged, then said no.

The last shaman was baptized in 1900. The first one to be Christianized was converted when Hans Egede came to Greenland on July 3, 1721. Born in 1686, Egede was a Norwegian priest and the son of a sailor. When the king of Denmark approved a recolonization plan for Greenland and started a trading company in Bergen to sponsor a mission, Egede immediately sailed with his family and set up house in a village. Wisely, the local angakok would not let him stay. He had to move on to the larger colony of Nuuk.

In Egede's effort to annihilate the ceremonial life of the Greenlanders, he forbade extended families to live together under one roof (the old divide-and-conquer strategy). This destroyed the mutual support needed to row an umiak, hunt from a kayak, haul in a bearded seal. His crowning achievement was to make the word *Toorianaarsuk*, which means "spirit," into a swearword, "goddamn." But this made no sense to the Greenlanders, who have no swearwords. "Only white people speak badly about each other in front of others," Olejorgen told me. "Greenlanders show their disapproval by saying nothing."

Aleqa and I cracked a window wide and stuck our heads out: street-lamps were on, dogs slept in tight circles, two teenagers strolled up the hill arm-in-arm, and icebergs drifted by in the fjord. "I'm glad it's not warm here," Aleqa said. "I love the icebergs. They have a wonderful smell, and every day they make themselves into different shapes." When our cheeks froze we pulled our heads back in. The village of Uumman-naq was once a hill of lumpy peat-and-stone houses with blubber lamps in the windows, waving their pale lights at passersby. Umiaks and kayaks lined the edge of the harbor, not skiffs with outboard motors. Sleds were stacked out on the ice foot—the belt of ice at the shoreline that forms between high- and low-water marks—and the dogs ran loose and wild. In the dark months, stories were told about how earth, humans, dogs, and death came to be, how, when starvation edged in or violence erupted in the village, certain people—mostly women—prac-ticed *ilisineq*, the black arts. Animal and human natures overlapped, intertwined, and were considered to be one and the same, as were ani-mate and inanimate objects. A man could become an iceberg; a shaman could live as a bear, suckle two cubs, then return to being a shaman again. The outward forms differed, but not the essential nature. People and animals talked to each other, shared a common language, and changed skins on a whim. Interspecies erotics thrived. There were odd couplings and strange progeny: girls married dogs, men slept with foxes, bears abducted women, women suckled caterpillars and gave birth to dogs. "The way to do it is still here, but not many know it anymore," Aleqa told me.

Another night Ann, Olejorgen, and I were invited to dinner at a local painter's house. An ashtray flew toward us as we opened the door: our host and his wife were having a fight. They insisted we come in. The painter had recently suffered a stroke and couldn't walk, so he held court on a low daybed, surrounded by household debris like a doomed, deposed king. But his conversation was bright.

Dinner was a traditional soup made of seal meat and potatoes. The wine was vinegary. In the middle of the meal, the painter's wife vomited in the kitchen sink; she'd had too much of the bad wine already. He showed me some of his pen-and-ink drawings of icebergs and glaciers and gave them to me. He was talented, and when the evening ended, I thanked him for the gift. A fire truck zoomed up the hill. We rushed out, thinking Ann's house might be on fire, but it wasn't. After coffee drunk in a sullen silence, we went home. Later, alone in my green house, I bundled myself up in my made-to-order Feathered Friends sleeping bag, sat by the window, and breathed in the tranquillity of perpetual night.

Mid-January and still no ice. A hundred years ago, the failure of the ice would have meant certain starvation: if there was no ice on which to travel, there was no way to hunt, no way to obtain food. Rasmussen often came upon hungry people as he traveled. Hunters didn't have outboard motors and skiffs in which to hunt seal in open water, only kayaks, and when the water was rough and ice-studded and the sky was dark, finding a seal was like finding a needle in a haystack.

It was thought that Sila and Nerrivik worked together against human beings: it wasn't only bad weather that killed them, but misconduct. When the rules of society were broken, things went wrong. People got sick, died, and the animals on which they depended for food failed to appear. That's when they had to ask the shaman for help. Some tried the black arts, what Rasmussen alluded to as "the machinations of Darkness."

Looking over the watery fjord, I wondered if anyone here still knew magic formulas—*serratit*—that could bring the ice back. *Serratit* are "old words, the inheritance of an ancient time when the sap of man was strong and the tongues were powerful," a woman told Rasmussen, "and were to be used only in dire necessity or when direct danger threatened."

Sometimes the formulas were meaningless words strung together from people's dreams; others were actual words handed down from generation to generation. *Serratit* could be said only in the early morning. The hood of one's anorak had to be up. Just before saying them, the fourth finger was placed so far back in the mouth as to cause gagging, and only then the magic words came out and were sometimes repeated twice. *Serratit* could also be used to chase away a *tupilait*.

If magic words had power, nothing in Inuit society was as potent as a *tupilait*. Some thought them to be living creatures, though they were human-made and used to do harm or bring misfortune. They were tiny sculptures made of various substances—a combination of animal parts—seal and dog bones, pieces of skin from seals, bears, and dogs, bits of moss, and long pieces of sinew. The shaman or an apprentice would gather the materials, stash them in some secret place—a cave, or up along a stream, or on the beach at night—then go to that place before dawn and prepare to create something evil.

"The ways in which ilisineq could be practiced were as varied and grotesque as the Eskimo fantasy is luxuriant," Rasmussen wrote. One woman who had been spurned by her husband for another sought an old sorceress, who told her that she must first go inland and kill a fox and a ptarmigan. Then she had to find the husband and the new wife when they were sleeping face to face, and only then put a fox breast under one pillow and the ptarmigan belly under the other without waking them. After, the scent of the fox and the ptarmigan would go into their thoughts in the form of disagreement and they would part. In case she was unable to accomplish this feat, another suggestion was made. To prevent there being any children, she would have to catch, but not kill, a sparrow in the summertime. Then she must say things to the captive bird: "May he never have children; carry away the woman's offspring every time one is born, until there are no more."

Making a *tupilait* could entail another kind of procedure. The sorcerer would sit, take his anorak off and put it on backwards with the hood over his face, then proceed. He would sing a magic song, then have intercourse with the bones, rubbing against them and inserting his penis between the parts. Little by little the *tupilait* came together, almost assembling itself over a period of days. Finally the maker gave the object life. He sat astride the bones once again and sang until a shiver passed through the object and it began to breathe—what was reported (by Rasmussen) to be a "gasping, groaning respiration." Then the *tupilait* moved, disappearing right through a rock and reappearing in an inland lake or river. It changed forms: it was a seal, then a dog that kept diving into deep water and emerging again, asking, "Where is it I must go?" Finally the sorcerer would give the *tupilait* its instructions.

A person who cast such spells had to be sure about his abilities, because if he failed, the misfortune intended for the victim would turn against the sorcerer and kill him.

I walked the cliff edge looking for strange objects on the rocks or a man fornicating with a pile of bones, but found nothing. The dark seemed darker in the hours without a moon. Sometimes clouds rolled in and the sky and ground were one gray ball. The distant thunder I heard meant an iceberg was rolling all the way over like a roving eye trying to see something that wasn't clear. Waves radiated out from the disturbed floe and undulated toward shore. I walked to the far edge of the island and looked toward the head of the fjord. Something bright caught my eye: a full moon began to rise, a moon too enormous for the towers of rock that flanked it. I watched, mesmerized. Any clear thing that blinds us with surprise . . .

The moon lifted so slowly I was afraid it would drop back down— but moons are not betrayed by gravity. Finally, it topped the cliffs at the head of the fjord and brightened, suddenly reddening, as if it had just been cut from ice and thrown up in the air—the absent sun's pale twin.

Morning. I'm not living on earth or ice but rock and the sharp tooth of Uummannaq Mountain jutting up behind the town like a harpoon. At eleven the peak caught light like the poisoned tip of an arrow and the cliffs that gave birth to the moon last night were pink, crimson, and gold. By noon there was a bit of light in the sky, but not enough to read by.

At two a.m., against the dogs' constant conversation about urgent matters of food, sex, and rank and their general angst at being chained on dirty patches of rock and snow and not being fed enough, I lay alone. The moon was down. Unable to sleep, I drank a cheap bottle of blanc de noirs—the white of the black, the foam of the night, the light hidden within dark grapes and made to sparkle. But how did they get white from black, how did they separate the two?

It no longer mattered whether I closed my eyes. The operations of the mind were the same: darkness made being awake seem dreamlike. I wondered how it would be to live in a house made of ice, and thought of the way light filtered through shoji screens. Japanese culture, like that of the Eskimos, evolved in relative darkness without electric light. Racially linked, both cultures might have produced the same theater: in No plays, the whitefaced actor was meant to be the only light on the stage, teeth blackened as if to simplify human physiology to a ghost acquainted with death or to toothless infancy. Up here, an Eskimo's moon face grew darker and darker the more months he lived out on the ice; in the all-light spring months, his face was a negative image of the sun.

When all the blanc was gone there was only noir, *obscurum per obscuris*, a path leading nowhere, or maybe to the town dump. The Inuit never made much of beginnings or endings and now I knew why. No matter what you did in winter, how deep you dove, there was still no daylight and no comprehension that came with light. Endings were everywhere, visible within the invisible, and the timeless days and nights ticked by.

Greenlanders say that only the *qanuallit*—the white people—are afraid of the dark, while Eskimos like nothing better than long winter days of storytelling and talking to spirits. Rasmussen told the story of two Danes—Gustav and Olaf—who overwintered together every year on the east coast of Greenland, where they hunted foxes and sold the skins in the spring. Olaf made dinner one night. Later, Gustav said he had a bad stomachache. Shortly after, he died sitting in his chair. In Olaf's grief and the shock of utter solitude, he found he could not part with his friend. He set Gustav's corpse, still in the chair, outside to freeze and in the evenings brought him back inside, seating him at the dinner table so he would not have to eat alone. In the spring, when Gustav began to thaw, Olaf took him home to Denmark to be buried.

In my frigid room I read about dark nebulae—immense clouds composed of the detritus of dying stars. The nebulae are made of molecular hydrogen, high concentrations of gas and dust whose effect in the universe is to produce "visual extinction." Yet the nebulae are detectable because of the obscuration they cause. I looked up at the sky: the dark patches between constellations are not blanks but dense interstellar clouds through which light from distant stars cannot pass. They are known variously as the Snake, the Horsehead, the Coalsack. Darkness is not a blank, a negation, but a rich and dense obstruction, a kind of cosmic chocolate, a forest of stellar events whose presences are only known by their invisibility.

A skin of ice formed, smoothing watery wrinkles to glass. Somewhere out in the darkness I heard the rhythmic drone of a ship's diesel engine, then a sound like sheet metal collapsing: it was the ship breaking a path through the ice. Inside the harbor, the captain turned the ship around and backed to the dock. He would have to break ice with the bow to leave again.

When the harbor was quiet again and the crew had walked home, ice began to congeal around the ship's bow. One decklight was left on.

In its hard, downward beam I saw that snow had begun to fall. When I looked again, the ship's decks had turned white.

In winter, light sources are reversed. Snow-covered earth is a torch and the sky is a blotter that soaks up everything visible. There is no sun, but the moon lives on borrowed time and borrowed light. Home late from hunting, two men pulled a sledge up a hill laden with freshly killed seals, dripping a trail of blood in the snow. As I dozed off, I dreamed the paths were all red and the sky was ice and the water was coal. I took a handful of water and drew with it: in a frozen sky, I drew a black sun.

Later I couldn't sleep. The half-moon's slow rising seemed like a form of exhaustion, with night trying to hold the moon's head under water. It bobbed up anyway, and I, its captive audience, caught the illuminated glacial cliffs on the surface of my eyes. The moon's light was reflected light, but from what source? The sun was a flood that blinded us, a sun we couldn't see. When I lay back in the dark, the pupils of my eyes opened.

At birth, one group of Eskimos held the newly expelled placenta in front of a chosen infant's face as if it were a piece of glass. From it came light and the ability to see inward. I looked out my window: it returned my reflection. Beyond, I saw nothing.

Once Rasmussen asked a shaman, "What do you think of the way men live?" The shaman answered, "They live brokenly, mingling all things together; weakly, because they cannot do one thing at a time."

I tried to do less and less every day, tried weeding out the mind. To obtain awareness was once thought by the Inuit to be an essential aspect of personhood. The confines of village life in early times meant that behavior had to be moderate. Even-temperedness, humor, and modesty were highly valued; cautionary tales warned people about the harm anger and self-pity could cause. Once, a woman who had been wronged by her husband became so distraught that she flew on a bearskin to find him, and when she did, she mutilated him until he was dead. After, the bearskin sewed itself to the front of her body and she was never able to get it off again.

Seeing was the ultimate act of the angakoks. Whether it was seeing into the source of a famine or the source of an illness, they had to pierce all obstacles. In eastern Greenland and in Alaska, some shamans and their apprentices wore masks. Others hid their faces behind sealskins. In both cases, the idea was to banish the obstructions of ego, greed, contempt, or self-importance that might get in the way. The neutrality of the face-cover provided a passageway to another world.

To believe that the single soul was made up of many strands of beings was normal. What else could be expected from a people who lived in total darkness for three months of the year and spent their lives driving dogsleds over ice that concealed the very thing they needed to see in order to survive?

The Inuit scratched their imaginations against their frozen world as if it were a flint: light came into their bodies, enabling them to see, to pierce ice, to fly under water, or go to the moon. Once when a European explorer arrived at a camp and set up a telescope, the hunters laughed at him; their shamans could already go to the moon or the stars without help.

Olejorgen and I have started a countdown until the day the sun appears. Days pass. I try to distinguish the shadowed path from the shadowed world but fail. Then it is February.

The real is fragile and inconstant. The unreal is ice that won't melt in the sun. I walk partway up Uummannaq Mountain and look south. The sun's first appearance of the year will occur in three days, but for now, the light is fish-colored—a pale, silvery gray, like the pallor between night and day. The cold seems to deepen as the sun comes near as if driven by some mathematical equation in which relativity has been relegated to the attraction of opposites. I try to remember the feel of sun on my face, but the dark mass, the rock body of Nuussuaq Peninsula, drives the sensation away.

In the night there is none of the old terror of the sun going down and never coming up again—the terror that heart patients feel—because the sun is already gone, and I am alive, and the darkness is a cloak that shelters me. As I walk down the mountain to the town dump, patches of frostbite, like tiny suns, glow on my cheeks. They burn like lamps and I wonder if, later, they will cast enough light to read by, if they can help me to see.

Tonight the darkness jolts me. I walk around the room trying to lift the dark cover of night with a flashlight in my hand, as if its fading beam were a shovel. I am trying to understand how one proceeds from blindness to seeing, from seeing to vision. A trance befalls me, a waist-deep lull of boredom. But boredom can be a friend. The mind empties out and refills, oh so slowly, with another order of things.

The Eskimo world was once full of invisible spirits. Some were people or animals who did not die peacefully. Some were evildoers, others were helpers, others were simply mischievous beings who inhabited specific territories. All were odd beings who came and went as quickly as the ice.

The *innerssuit* were shamans' helpers, beach spirits who looked like humans but had no nose and grew out of clumps of sand. Some were giants and some dwarfs. The *innerajuaitsiat* could transform themselves into giants and cover immense distances in a few strides. The *isserqat* lived in the ground and tickled people to death. Another spirit was a living stone that loved to frighten people. The *erqigdlit* had human bodies and dogs' heads; they lived on the ice cap and liked to kill people in their villages. They were used to scare children into sticking close to home.

A hundred years ago a young shaman went to the old angakok and said: "*Takujumagama.* I come to you because I desire to see." After purifying himself by fasting and suffering cold and solitude, he sat on a pair of polar bear pants beside the old man, hidden from the villagers by a curtain of skin as if to make himself invisible. At that moment, the seeker received *qaameneq*—a light suddenly felt in his body, an inexplicable searchlight that enabled him to see in the dark.

One young shaman told Rasmussen that his first experience of enlightenment was a feeling of rising up—literally, up into the air so that he could see through mountains, could see things far away, even blades of grass, and on the great plain of earth could locate all lost souls.

I don't know where I am. Wind comes through the walls. Maybe the walls have fallen away and merged with the walls of the galaxy. In this place it seems there are only undefined distances that grow wider. I pick up a two-week-old *New York Times* science page brought from America, and it confirms this notion. "Deep Images Favor Expanding Universe," the headline reads. Following the repair of the Hubble Space Telescope, which gives detailed images of galaxies far out in space and far back in time, astronomers learned that the universe is at least five times as vast as they had thought and is still expanding. Because of the telescope's power, many fainter galaxies are now being counted for the first time.

From the window I look into indigo space, and indigo space, like an eyeless eye, looks back at me. The thirteenth-century Zen teacher Dogen wrote: "To say that the world is resting on the wheel of space or on the wheel of wind is not the truth of the self or the truth of others. Such a statement is based on a small view. People speak this way because they think that it must be impossible to exist without having a place on which to rest."

In the harbor, we walk on crystal. The ice has come in at least that far. Night is a transparency and ice the cataract over the eye that won't see. Only the finlike keels of fishing boats touch water under ice and the fish look up through their cold lenses at our awkward boots.

Twilight gone to dark. I lie naked, careless, not quite destitute under a waning moon on a polar night. Greenlanders thought the moon and sun were brother and sister and had unknowingly slept together. After the discovery of their incest, they sailed up to the sky holding torches, and lived in separate houses from then on. In summer, only sun, the sister, came out of her house; in winter, the brother moon came out, though sometimes he had to go away to get animals for the people to eat. Which is why, when the new moon came, they were thankful for the good hunting and for the return of its light.

Out the window thin clouds cover the sky, then break into gauze and strew their opulent shadows about like discarded clothes. I light two candles and open a bottle of Fitou, a red table wine from a French village I once visited—strange that I can get it here. Sitting by the window I must look like a character from a Hopper painting—almost unmoving, but not unmoved. Stuck here on this Arctic Alcatraz, I don't know what I am moved to, except too much drink and a low-fever rage against geographical restraint. But as soon as I say the word "rage," my claustrophobia melts.

I write and drink by candlelight. No leaf, no shadow, no used-up senses finally coming to rest, nor the lover's postorgasmic sleep. Only this: a cold room where snow fallen from my boots does not melt and the toilet in the unheated entry of the house stinks because it has not been emptied for days. It occurs to me that the only shadow seen since last autumn was the wavering one a candle made, casting its uncertainty on the wall.

Later in the evening the wind stops and a skin of ice hardens over the water. Groups of villagers come down to the harbor to look and wait. The old people shake their heads. It is said that they know in October how the ice is going to be. If there is a layer of ice on the shore where it goes into the water, and it holds, then the ice will be good. This year there is that kind of ice, but for two days only, then it goes. They already know it won't come this year, or if it does, it will be dangerous.

An old woman standing next to me says, "If people go out, they will die. They will fall through the ice and go down to where the sea goddess lives. No one knows about ice anymore."

February 2. Tacitus said that the sun made a noise when it rose in the east and cried out at the end of the day as it drowned in the ocean. But here, the sun rises in the south when it rises at all. Learning to see in the dark seems more important now. Jorge Luis Borges reprimanded his readers for thinking that blind people live in a dark world. Behind his blind eyes he said there were always colors. Milton, also blind, wrote of burning lakes and inward conflagrations.

So much about the Arctic has to do with blindness and seeing, lucency and eclipse. Milton went to visit Galileo, who had been put under house arrest by the Inquisition in Arcetri, near Florence. The scientist had gone blind, his starry world taken from him; Milton would lose his sight later, but the calamity that disabled the astronomer gave inspiration to the poet. The two men sat outside at night, heads tilted back, and tried to remember the stars. After, Milton began his epic poem *Paradise Lost*:

> *Hail Holy light!. . . . Thee I revisit now with bolder wing,*
> *Escape the Stygian pool, though long detained*
> *In that obscure sojourn, while in my flight*
> *Through utter and through middle darkness borne. . . .*

Later, in *Samson Agonistes*, he wrote:

> *O dark, dark, dark, amid the blaze of noon,*
> *Irrecoverably dark, total eclipse*
> *Without all hope of day!*

Noon. The supply boat slides through a lead in the ice like pencil lead on white paper. Its running lights are two eyes growing ever fainter. Now only the engine sound remains, a muffled drumming. The eye is an island, a domed piece of drift ice floating in bone and flesh. It is an acquisitive organ, metering in brilliance and shadow, conjuring shapes. When it has only darkness to sift through, what shapes does the imagination make? Early Greek theories held that vision resulted from particles continually streaming off the surface of bodies, or that the eye was made of water, or that streams of light issued from the observer's eye and coalesced with sunlight.

The sun is an eye. Its coming means that the boulder rolls away from the front of the cave and we are set free. Yet I am still night-foundered, blind so much of the time.

Later. I'm done with daylight. It reeks of carbonized toast crumbs left behind after breakfast, of the kind of bright decor that hides a congenital blindness to what is real. Today in my house, with no lights, no water, only a view of the darkness outside from the darkness within, from the unlighted room of the mind and the unheated room of the heart, I know that what is real only comes together in darkness, under the proscenium of night's gaunt hood.

It also occurs to me that the real and the imagined have long since fused here. Truths are relative to the imagination that invents them. It's not the content of experience that we end up with, but the structure of how we know something.

In the next days there is more daylight, three or four hours at least. Not bright, but enough to read by—that has become my measuring stick. Tomorrow the sun will peep over the ridge, then disappear. Now I don't want it to come. I've grown accustomed to the privacy and waywardness of night. In daylight all recognitions turn out to be misconceptions. During one of my naps I dream that I can hear the sun beating behind the rocky peninsula like an expectant heart.

February 3. "Day breaks in the body's night." But the body is frozen and heavy. I've been reading about dark matter and dark energy. Astronomers know that the dark matter permeating the universe has a weight sixty times that of the stars and seven times that of the baryons, the material that makes up stars, planets, asteroids, comets, and people. Dark energy, also called quintessence, or the cosmological constant, has a weight almost twice that of all matter, dark or visible, and is pushing so hard against gravity that everything could fly apart and disappear into the universe from which it came.

February 4. The cosmological constant breaks. It is Sun Day, Sontag, Sunday, Solfest. At ten in the morning light heaves up. It is 17 degrees below zero and the sky over the Nuussuaq Peninsula is a pink lip trembling. The wind is sharp. Ann and Olejorgen spread a yellow cloth on the dining room table for our post-sun feast. Elsewhere in the higher latitudes of Greenland, at 78 and 82 degrees north latitude, it is still dark. Solfest will not reach Thule for another three weeks.

Here in Uummannaq, panic sets in. Do the children have on their mittens, caps, and boots? Gitte, the neighbor who works at the Kommune, comes in her pickup to take us to the topmost viewpoint on the island—her house. Up there, we run to the edge of the cliff, which looks south across roiling fjord waters toward the mountains. There is a moment of utter breathlessness, then a pale light begins to move into the sky and smears itself from the sharp point of the heart-shaped mountain down into the village. Every object of Arctic clutter momentarily goes from shade to gloss—sleds, harnesses, dogs, drying racks, clotheslines, skins, cars, baby carriages, empty bottles, gravestones. House by house, the dead windows come alive. The sled dogs stand up and stretch in the sun, shaking all the secrets of winter from their coats.

11:47 a.m. Olejorgen counts down: five, four, three, two . . . A spray of cloud lifts, an arching eyebrow lights up from below and fires to the color of salmon. From behind the upside-down proscenium of rock, incandescent daggers spike the sky. In the square notch between two peaks, a tiny crescent of sun appears, throwing flames into the forehead of morning.

"Look, I can see my shadow!" Olejorgen says.

Do shadows prove existence? "*Sono io,*" Gitte yells out across the mountain as if yodeling. "I am."

For six minutes the cuticle of sun burns inside the notch like a flame. When it scuttles behind the ridge again, our shadows dwindle to nothingness. I am not I.

Everyone goes inside to eat and drink: *kaffe,* tea, *mattak* (whale skin with a quarter-inch of fat), rye bread, cheese, smoked salmon, and a dark Danish liqueur that tastes like night. Outside, the sky is still bright and the sun pushes west behind the mountain as if behind the back of a giant, almost appearing again in a crack, then goes blank again.

We toast Knud Rasmussen and Peter Freuchen; we toast the return of the sun. After all, we are still alive despite our various bouts of cancer, tooth loss, divorce, marriage, childbearing, and barrenness, and, in my case, lightning. As I drink down my liqueur, it occurs to me that there are all kinds of blindnesses and all kinds of seeing, that a dark world is not emblematic of death but of a feral clarity. In this sudden flood of sun, have I seen anything?

Afternoon. The pink light is going, not down but up, a rising curtain lifting light across the face of the village, up the long tooth of Heart Mountain, leaving in its wake the old darkness. The diesel-powered lights of town come on as we stumble home. Dogs are fed. An old man chips away at an iceberg, carrying off a chunk in his pail to melt for drinking water. The world has returned to its dark normality and our shadows will not reappear until morning.

Walking back to my perched house, I see that out on the bay one collapsed iceberg holds a tiny lake in its center, a turquoise eye glancing upward. The moon comes up in the east as if it were a sun rising, and for the second time in one day the mountains go bright.

Today winter was a burning lake and I watched it catch fire.

Elisabeth, 1995

Near the end of February I find myself in Ilulissat again on Elisabeth Jul's doorstep. The key to her back door is still on the hook in the shed and I let myself in. She's surprised to hear from me when I call the hospital. While I've been in Uummannaq, she has delivered a set of twins, performed an appendectomy, treated two cases of pneumonia, and vaccinated twenty-two children in a nearby village, which she travels to by dogsled.

She has been planning to hook up the dogs this evening to check on a patient and wonders if I care to come along. Though there is no sea ice yet, it is possible, in Ilulissat, to go up the long valleys into the mountains by dogsled.

"You must come," she insists, and I agree to go. I sleep much of the day. The dogs' howling—thousands of them—echoes against a wall of basalt on the far side of town. Elisabeth comes home so late I ask if we should still be going. "Why not?" she says. "Who cares what time it is?"

Ilulissat sleds are small. Their shortness makes them more maneuverable in the mountains. We put on layers of clothes—fur over Polartec—and start catching and harnessing dogs. At the thought of being freed from their chains, they are frantic with delight. My job is to keep them from running off. "*Nye, nye,*" is all I can think to say. I shake the long whip over the dogs but their cowering is unconvincing, a mockery of fear. As soon as Elisabeth ties in the last dog, they erupt in a snarling fight, jerk forward, and fly.

Cars come toward us and veer off quickly: sled dogs have the right of way in Greenland. Hooked up in the traditional fanlike array, the dogs don't alter their course for anyone or anything. We drive through the middle of town, turning left at the red house where Knud Rasmussen was born, zinging past the *brottlet* (an open-air market), the bank, the Italian ex-pat's tourist shop, and the harbor, then pick up speed on the snow-packed northbound road. "This is called the Round the World Loop," Elisabeth yells as we bump up and over a lip of plowed snow and follow a trail into the mountains.

In Rasmussen's days sleds were sometimes made of walrus bone with frozen peat runners and rolled hides or frozen fish for handles. Now the runners are hard plastic with metal edges that emit sparks as we scrape over rock. This night they sing deliverance from Uummannaq's prison of icelessness. The sky clears. In 1921 Rasmussen wrote: "An hour after midday the light was gone and we drove on through the white darkness of the Polar night. The details of the landscape melted strangely one into the other like frozen fog, and little ice-covered hills looked like mountains."

Away from the all-night lights of Ilulissat, we bump through foothills, guiding ourselves by the stars. The North Pole, a few hundred miles away, is a mathematical, moving point in a sea of sloshing ice, but the polestar is a constant. "I wish you had a cabin out here and we never had to go back," I tell Elisabeth.

The ground is uneven—rock, snow, ice, and more rock. When the dogs come to the top of a ridge they know to stop so that Elisabeth can find a safe route down. They begin to tire and are more manageable—that is, they listen to Elisabeth's voice. When we take off downslope, dragging our feet to brake the sled, the dogs settle into a steady trot.

At the bottom I try to jump off the moving sled and stand all in one movement, but just then we hit a bump and I find myself rolling and laughing. I run in deep snow to catch up, pumping my legs on uneven ground in heavy oversized boots, grabbing for the sled handle, then get dragged until the dogs slow. Elisabeth rests on the sled while I drive.

We stop once to let the dogs rest. Elisabeth's face and hair are frosted white and her round cheeks are bright red. It is 20 below zero but we are almost hot. Elisabeth wears no gloves or hat. "I only do that when it's really cold," she says. The dogs sleep curled in tight knots—white and pale yellow on snow. Over us, the Big Dipper puts its bowl down on our heads as though blessing us.

After several hours we come to a tiny village. We stop at a house lit up with candles. They are having a *kaffemik*—a birthday party where cake and coffee are served. Elisabeth knows the women in the room because she has delivered their babies. One woman sits alone in the corner. Elisabeth whispers, "She's here in lockup. She killed her first and second husbands. The first one came home late one night and she shot him. The second husband failed to get the things she wanted at the store, so she shot him too." The lone woman fiddles with the dial of a radio, which emits nothing but static. Elisabeth kneels down by her, takes her blood pressure, and asks how she is feeling. "Fine," she says. "Fine." A week earlier, a local man had asked the woman in lockup out on a date. He didn't know about her bad temper. The older women shooed him away. As he backed out of the room uneasily, not understanding what he had done wrong, the women laughed.

After cake and coffee, we set off for home. The dogs trot in an easy gait. Elisabeth crouches behind me on the sled, her arm around my shoulder to keep from falling off. At that moment I experience an extraordinary sense of well-being. Bundled into polar rotundity, linked and crouching, we fly from abyss to abyss. We look up: the northern lights flare—hard spotlights focused on dark nebulae, new planets, and nothingness. The aurora expands and contracts as if its white purse strings were being loosened and pulled tight. It extends so far up into the sky, it appears to be holding the universe together.

Darkness reconciles all time and disparity. It is a kind of rapture in which life is no longer lived brokenly. In it we are seers with no eyes. The polar night is one-flavored, without past or future. It is the smooth medium of present time, of time beyond time, a river that flows between dreaming and waking. Behind the dogs, in their streaming wake, we move over white ground fast. The ground is alive like a torrent, a wild cataract. Which one is moving?

We take a different route home. "I'm not sure where we are," Elisabeth says, "but we're not lost. It's impossible to be lost. That would mean we were nowhere." We cross ridges, slide down icy slopes, zing over snowless patches striking rock into sparks as if our sled runners were matches trying to light our way. But the moon does that, and seeing in the dark is no longer a difficulty.

To our disappointment, the lights of Ilulissat soon flare ahead of the team. "Let's not go back," I plead. But we have to. Elisabeth will have new patients by morning. Finally we bump over the plowed cornice of snow and hit the road that leads back to town. On ice the sled fishtails, wagging with a kind of unspoken happiness, and as the dogs go faster and faster, I am swept forward over the glass eye of the earth.

The Arctic Station, 1910–1917

At the very top of Greenland is an oasis of unglaciated land that in the briefest of summers—roughly, the month of July—bears alpine vegetation and supports populations of muskoxen, birds, insects, polar wolves, and Arctic hares. It was across this land, fretted with fjords—St. George, Sherard Osborn, Victoria, and De Long—that the early Eskimos walked all the way over to the east side of Greenland.

Since childhood, Knud Rasmussen dreamed of founding an Arctic station at Dundas Village on a horseshoe-shaped bay from which he could launch expeditions to study the plants, animals, and lifeways of the people of the entire polar north. At the University in Copenhagen, while studying acting, Rasmussen had developed empathy and learned to listen, which he combined with practical knowledge to put wheels under the central dream that fueled his life: to live like an Eskimo.

He carefully nursed his dream to fruition. From 1910 to 1933 he would launch seven expeditions to study the origins, history, migration routes, and cultures of the Inuit people. He traveled the whole of Greenland, then ventured west across Arctic America on an epic journey from Greenland all the way to Siberia on what was called the Fifth Thule Expedition, the likes of which had not been seen since Lewis and Clark walked from St. Louis to the Pacific Ocean.

While still living in Copenhagen, Knud had invited his friend Peter

Freuchen to join him in the experiment; Peter, who had already given up on becoming a doctor, quickly agreed. The Arctic station would function as a bank, a home, and a trading post, a spot to plant the Danish flag, claiming the land for Denmark, as well as the headquarters from which to launch their expeditions.

Lacking finances, the two young men rented lecture halls all over Denmark and gave a series of talks about Greenland and Arctic lifeways. Charming, bright, and affable, both Freuchen and Rasmussen became increasingly popular. Yet at the end of the tour, they had no more money than they had started with because, in their exuberance, they had allowed their travel expenses to eat up their profits. Just when they'd run out of fund-raising ideas, two wealthy friends came forward and supplied them with the money needed to start what would be an extraordinary adventure that lasted more than twenty years.

In the summer of 1910 Rasmussen and Freuchen sailed for Greenland. On seeing its southernmost tip, Freuchen wrote: "We saw the huge mountains on shore, ominous foreboding of the sternness of the land. The sea ran high and the rocks offered no solace. They are black and towering, and there is no pity in them. As I stood at the wheel, I realized for the first time that I had burned my bridges and was up against something which would demand the utmost from me."

When the two men arrived at Dundas Village, at the bottom of the fist that is northwest Greenland, at 77 degrees north latitude where a long spit of sand marked by a flat-topped hill curves into a peaceful inlet called North Star Bay, they established a small store and immediately set to work building a small house with imported Danish wood. The Thule

District had been visited by outsiders before. In 1818, the English explorer John Ross called in at Cape York and Saunders Island and was greeted by Inuit hunters, who called Ross's two ships gods.

When Rasmussen unpacked a globe given to them by a well-wisher, they set it outside on a box and a group of curious hunters gathered around. One old man pointed and began talking. Seeing him, Peter, who could not yet understand Greenlandic, stepped into the circle and tried to explain the globe. Rasmussen intervened: "The old man is telling them about conditions at the South Pole. You don't have to teach them anything."

If their Arctic station, which they called "Thule," seemed remote, solitude was not one of their problems. A constant stream of visitors came by on dogsleds, and four old women moved into the house with the two bachelors, not only to help with household chores but also to tell stories. Over the years they served as informants for Rasmussen, who sought to record the Inuit culture of the entire polar north from Greenland to Alaska. "He [Rasmussen] was the Arctic Elsa Maxwell," Freuchen reported, "never happier than when he could celebrate something or other, and I never knew a man who could find so many occasions for celebration."

When winter came and the sea froze solid, Rasmussen hooked up his dogs to go muskox hunting across Smith Sound on Ellesmere Island. Freuchen and a Greenlandic couple accompanied him part of the way. The woman was pregnant. Near the camp of Neqe, a storm overtook them. Atiak's water broke and she went into labor. The men tried to build an igloo—an ice hut—but nothing held. Instead, they stood around the sled blocking the wind. Atiak's husband split her pants open—it was too cold to take them all the way off. Supported by her husband and another man, she got on her knees and pushed the baby out. She lifted up the infant, wrapped him in skins, and put him to her breast. Soon after, the storm abated. Rasmussen gave his sled to the couple, and with the new baby tucked into her amaut, they took off across the frozen sea to her home village on Ellesmere Island.

After a whole winter of hunting, Rasmussen and Peter returned to Thule. On the way, Rasmussen stopped in a village to see the local angakok, an old woman named Sermiaq. But she had been lost in a snowstorm, and they joined the others in a search for her. The snow lay in deep drifts and eventually they could go no farther. Rasmussen drove the dogs over the ice foot, looking for shelter, and came to the opening of a cave. When his eyes adjusted to the darkness inside, he saw the old shaman sitting there.

Cold and hungry, she had no sleeping bag and had eaten only the foxes she had trapped to make an anorak for her grandson. Knud and Peter took her back to her village and hired some women to make her new clothes. That was her payment for telling Rasmussen stories.

One day Rasmussen's dogs became sick. Sermiaq was summoned. She looked at the poor animals and said they were ill because they were wearing other dogs' harnesses, that something harmful from the outside had been brought in. Overnight she made a new set of harnesses, and immediately the dogs revived.

The day Rasmussen and Freuchen set out to leave, Sermiaq jumped on Rasmussen's sled and would not get off. "You need an experienced woman's protection," she exclaimed. They tried to persuade her to stay where she was, but she wouldn't budge, and they had no choice but to take her. Uninvited, yet useful as an informant to Rasmussen, she lived with them for many years, traveling when they traveled, staying at the station when they stayed.

During the dark time, from October through February, Sermiaq busied herself with collecting boxes and bags. "I collect shadows and darkness," she said, "so that the world will get light again, and I keep it all locked up here in these boxes." Every spring the light returned.

Rasmussen was living two lives. After the Literary Expedition to Greenland of 1902–1904, and before coming to northwest Greenland, he had met a young woman, Dagmar Andersen. She was quiet, well educated, and aristocratic, and she admired Knud. Men who spend years in the Arctic don't take long to get things accomplished at home. He and Dagmar were married in the fall of 1908 with the understanding that he might not be home very often. And he wasn't. When a letter from Dagmar arrived in Thule—who knows how many months after it was written?—Rasmussen discovered that he was the father of a baby girl. Peter reported: "Both of us were so excited we scarcely knew what we were doing." A big celebration ensued.

Soon after, Rasmussen had an almost fatal accident. It was summer and they were hunting narwhal from kayaks. Knud harpooned the animal when it was on the left side of the kayak (harpoons are always thrown from the right). The sealskin thong attached to the bladder shagged on his chest and tipped the kayak over.

Knud became entangled in the line. His head went under. The other hunters quickly paddled over, cut the line, and pulled him from the frigid water. When asked if he wanted to change into dry clothes, Rasmussen looked surprised. Why would he do that when he had a chance to catch a much-needed narwhal? The hunt continued and the narwhal was successfully speared.

By early September the annual supply ship from Denmark had still not arrived. Provisions were becoming scare and soon there would be no open water. By the time the schooner came, the ice was closing in: they could stay only twenty-four hours before turning around.

Peter had been expecting his girlfriend from Denmark to be on the ship. She had written the previous year and said that she would join him in Thule. He searched the ship and did not find her. The idea of spending another winter alone was almost too much for him to bear. He was shattered—but not for long.

South of Thule they had met up with Minik, famous because he and his father had been kidnapped in 1897 by Robert Peary and taken by ship to New York. Soon after arriving the father died, leaving Minik an orphan in a strange land. The boy was put in the care of someone at the American Museum of Natural History. It was there that Minik found his father's skeleton on display. The shock was almost more than he could bear. Minik survived twelve more years in New England. He asked to be taken home in 1909, but Peary refused. By the time the young man returned home, he was destitute and cultureless, struggling to relearn his language and hunting skills.

Minik asked Rasmussen and Freuchen if he and his wife could move in with them at the trading post. They agreed, and a small house was built beside the station. When Rasmussen went north to hunt polar bears that spring, Peter moved in with the young couple. Then Minik left too, and a young woman, Navarana, was sent to keep Minik's wife company.

Weeks went by. One night, finding himself alone with Navarana, Peter asked her to stay with him. "I only asked her to move from the opposite side of the room to mine—that was all the wedding necessary." When Knud returned home and learned the good news, he hosted a three-day celebration.

The station at Thule was to function as a jumping-off point for research into Eskimo culture, its origin and migration to Greenland, as well as for scientific expeditions that would focus on the geology, botany, and biology of the polar north.

With that in mind, Rasmussen and Freuchen embarked on what they called their First Thule Expedition in the spring of 1912, and set out with thirty-four sleds and 375 dogs to cross the ice cap between Clements Markham Glacier at Pitoravik and the Danmark Fjord on the east coast.

The going was tough: incessant wind, drifting snow, barely enough to eat, and on top of it all Freuchen was going snowblind. Coming off the ice cap on the other side was even worse: they had to belay down a perpendicular, fifty-foot wall of ice using sealskin thongs; on the way, a harpoon point tore through Freuchen's thigh.

Peter's leg healed, but his snowblindness grew worse. At the bottom they ran into the now-deserted summer camp of their old friend Jorgen Brönlund, who, shortly after their arrival, lost his life. On the way home Rasmussen came down with a severe bout of sciatica, but eventually, hardened to pain, cold, and hunger, they were able to return safely to Thule.

Rasmussen left for Denmark to see his wife and children and to raise money for the next trip. He now had two daughters and the time he needed to work on his book. But Freuchen, who had been co-opted into going to Copenhagen, only wanted to return to Greenland. After five weeks he shipped out for his adopted home.

Desperate to see Navarana, Freuchen grew frantic when an engine on the ship, the *Cape York,* broke down. They were racing the ice, and it didn't look as if they would win. In the middle of the night some girls ran into his stateroom shouting, "Knud, Knud!"

Peter couldn't understand what had happened. Then Rasmussen appeared. He had heard in Denmark that the ship was delayed and worried that Peter wouldn't make it home before the ice closed in, so he made his way by commercial vessel to southern Greenland, then bought a small motorboat and came to Peter's rescue. Typical Rasmussen. No one else could have understood Freuchen's dilemma, no one else would have leaped effortlessly over so many obstacles to help out. Or perhaps it was just that home life in Denmark bored him.

By the time the sailing schooner had started its route north to deliver the year's supplies, the ice in Melville Bay had already closed in. Undaunted, Rasmussen organized the hauling of goods by dogsled. "Melville Bay became a highway that winter," Freuchen noted in his journal.

> *The anxiety of driving tired dogs through darkness, snowstorms, and the everlasting cold was disheartening. But Rasmussen blossomed under the grueling routine. I can still see him standing in the middle of Melville Bay, the going bad through deep snow or rough ice, the dogs balking, the Eskimos disgruntled, no dog food, no fuel or provisions, and home far, far away. Then he was at his gayest and most at ease. (Freuchen,* I Sailed with Rasmussen, *p. 152)*

Rasmussen returned to Denmark just as World War I erupted. No supply ships embarked for Greenland for another year and Rasmussen was stuck at home. He was horrified by the atrocities. More than ever, he longed for the hunter's life in northern Greenland. Eventually he managed to get aboard the very first vessel allowed to cross the North Atlantic and joined Peter and Navarana in Thule. By then it was June 1916.

Peter recalled the night when Navarana went to eat *mattak*—the fat and skin of a whale, which provides all the vitamins and minerals needed. Peter had stayed home to write. In the middle of the night Navarana came home complaining of a stomachache. A few hours later she went into labor. "I was frightened half out of my wits," Peter said. He went to get Knud, who could only think of boiling water, which in Greenland is a lengthy process.

By the time the ice had melted and was boiling, Peter's son was born. By eight in the morning, Navarana was up and went visiting with the infant tucked into the amaut on her back. Knud organized a celebration and Peter recalled that Navarana "danced with abandon all night."

The Second Thule Expedition, initially planned for 1914, then canceled, was set to begin in the summer of 1916. Rasmussen wanted to map the north coast and the top of Greenland and to botanize, but the ship that was to bring their yearly supplies had been sunk by a German U-boat. Just as they had given up hope for a vessel to come for the second year in a row, a ship appeared.

One of the passengers was a Swedish botanist, Thorbild Wulff. He had come to Thule to collect plants and asked if he could move in. Since Rasmussen and his cartographer Lauge Koch were planning to winter in Tasiusaq, there was room. Anyway, Rasmussen never said no.

Wulff had traveled widely in Asia but treated "the natives," as he called them, with disdain, which did not sit well with Peter or Knud. When Thorbild and Peter, plus several villagers, made the trip south to Tasiusaq in February to join Rasmussen, there was trouble. On February 22, while were crossing the inland ice going south, they stopped to watch the sun rise for the first time that year. Observing tradition, the Greenlanders removed their hoods and mittens and faced the rising sun, palms out, faces up. They asked Thorbild to do likewise. He refused, scoffing at them. Ulugatok, from Cape York, admonished him: "You should not laugh at us. We think that if we do this we shall not die at least until the sun returns the next year. Even if it does no good, we enjoy life so much that we do anything to keep it."

Still, Wulff refused. All during the journey he continued to be difficult, insisting on sleeping late when the others were ready to go, and complaining of cold. Once, the hunters took off without him and descended the ice cap at Parker Snow Bay. Peter and his unwelcome friend continued on, traversing "the big glacier," as the ice cap was called. There were days of delay, bivouacking between snow-covered crevasses, because Wulff claimed he was too tired to move. But a storm was moving in and they had to get off the ice. Once more, Wulff refused and started unloading the sled despite Peter's vehement protests. "In desperation I took my whip and cracked it in the air. He looked at me in bewilderment, and cried out that I dared not whip him. I said: 'I not only dare, but it is my pleasure to do so, and I intend to do it immediately unless you get a move on.' " Again Wulff refused. Peter cracked the whip closer and closer until he jumped. "Never once did he try to defend himself, and a wave of sickness swept over me," Peter wrote.

The Second Thule Expedition Begins, 1917

After three years of false starts and delays and a decision by the accident-prone Peter Freuchen to stay behind, the Second Thule Expedition began on April 7, 1917. As usual, Rasmussen was in a state of intoxication: "The weather is glorious with a high sun above the white snow. The ice-mountains of the fjord gleam in the light and the basalt of the mountains out toward Cape Parry flash in merry colors," he wrote.

The first night was spent in Netsilivik (now the town of Qaanaaq), a camp of three houses that looked across the bay at Kiatak and Herbert islands. While there, Rasmussen visited Iterfiluk, "a gossiping widow of fifty years" who had often come to Thule to make his kamiks (sealskin boots).

As Rasmussen squeezed through the narrow passageway and up onto her greasy stone floor, she squealed with delight. "Her house is also filled with travelers and while her visitors are asleep she herself sits stark naked by her lamp, like one of the holy virgins guarding the lamp so that the precious light shall not be extinguished during the night."

As per custom, Rasmussen removed his clothes and pressed in between Iterfiluk and one of her friends, "the fat Kiajuk who wears the same paradisical costume as the hostess." They talked for hours, until finally Rasmussen lay back and fell asleep wedged between the others.

At Ulugssat, another camp on the south side of Herbert Island, they bought meat for the men and dogs and paid for the kamiks that the women there had made for them. Ilanguaq's house was filled all night long with the sound of drum songs. Rasmussen went to bed but was awakened by the sound of footsteps squeaking in the snow. It was Simiaq (the Corked-Up One), the oldest women of the settlement, who had come to repay a debt: Rasmussen had once saved her from a desolate mountain where her son-in-law had left her to die.

Once she had been the most desirable woman in northern Greenland: tall, buxom, with a happy carefree temperament, and "thick hair which, like a waterfall, hung down about her naked body." Rasmussen used his charm to get her to tell stories.

She told him about her early life before white men had come to stay, before Peary brought guns, before kayaks had come back into use. There were often famines then, she explained. One time, her husband, whose name meant "Little Throat," disappeared from their summer camp with a sack full of puppies. When she found him, he had eaten all the puppies and had not shared them with her. She left him for another man.

Simiaq told Rasmussen that she had come that night to get him on good terms with the spirits "who rule over mountains and abysses; the loneliness also has its powers, of which puny man must be aware," she told him. While he lay on his caribou skins, she sat close and mumbled these songs:

> Day arises
> From its sleep,
> Day wakes up
> With the dawning light.
> Also you must arise,
> Also you must awake
> Together with the day which comes.

She sang other songs to disperse fog, bring game, lure polar bears, subdue mountains, and drive away death. By the time Rasmussen woke up the old woman was gone.

In the next days, the sleds continued on with stops at Neqe and Etah to pick up more meat and additional hunters. Fifteen sleds would continue on to Humboldt Glacier, thirteen to Cape Constitution, eight to

Thank God Harbor on Polaris Promontory. Six sleds would remain to make the trip to explore the country mainly between Sherard Osborn Fjord and De Long Fjord in the north of Greenland.

The expedition had started out in high spirits and continued that way. At Etah, they were welcomed and entertained by the American Crockerland Expedition, which had overwintered there. From there they continued up the coast to Anoritoq, then on to Renssalaer Harbor, where a hunters' camp called Aunartoq was located on a bend of the coast. Of it Rasmussen wrote:

> *The inner bend of this bay gives an exceedingly friendly impression. The country hereabout consists of beautiful rounded hills of light granite, with moss and grass peeping out wherever the snow is blown away. Along the coast, tall, elegant and proud sandstone mountains stand on both sides of the bay like a majestic porch leading to the little cove where the Eskimos have built their camp. (Rasmussen,* Greenland by the Polar Sea, *p. 48)*

Happily ensconced in one of three houses at this, his favorite place on the coast, Rasmussen told the story about Miteq (Eider Duck), Aunartoq's last inhabitant. No one else had lived there for fifty years. He had gone north up the coast with his wife to escape her admirers. Bad luck had befallen them and they were beginning to starve. When famine came it was customary to do away with the children first. These were Darwinian rules: the fittest meant whoever was able to contribute to survival, not take from it. They sealed all but one child in a hut and rolled a stone across the front, harnessed the team, and with great sadness drove away. But things did not improve and the favored child was left behind as well. After, the couple made camp in Anoritoq, but they found they could not live with themselves or other people and so moved north to a camp whose name means "Where Spring Comes Early." There they lived alone and eventually killed themselves.

Among the remains of Miteq's house Rasmussen found part of an ancient sled made of whale ribs. One purpose of his expedition was to study the remnants of a vanished boreal civilization: ancient house sites, clothing, food, and tools to help prove that ancient Eskimos had indeed migrated across the top of the world from Siberia and landed here.

Rasmussen's men replenished the stores of food needed to feed 185 dogs and thirty-eight men. Still in a celebratory mood, Wulff loaded the movie camera and filmed the hunters performing various antics; then, for the rest of the evening, they all feasted on *kivioq*, rotten auks or seal.

Traveling up the coast, Rasmussen took the smooth ice foot along Kane Basin and made camp far out in the frozen bay, building snow houses with a view of the seventy-five-mile-wide face of Humboldt Glacier. Rasmussen reread Elisha Kent Kane's notes on the place:

> *The mountain-line raised itself like a massive, glass-like wall, 300 feet above the sea with unknown, unfathomable deeps at its foot; and its arched surface, sixty miles long from Cape Agassiz to Cape Forbes, lost itself in unknown spaces, no more than a single day's train ride to the North Pole. (Rasmussen,* Greenland by the Polar Sea, *p. 59)*

They continued on to Washington Land and Akia, "the country on the other side of the great glacier," which the Inuit had told him was all white—chalk cliffs. At Cape Benton he found the ruins of six winter houses built by paleo-Eskimos, one square and the others in the shape of beehives, plus a dance house—two houses built together with a passageway between and whale ribs used as roof supports.

Near Cape Independence they made their last large camp before sending the other sleds back, but not before Rasmussen, Wulff, and Koch wrote their last letters home. These would be taken by their hunters to the hunters at Aunartoq, who would take them to the whalers off Cape Seldon, who would transport them to Upernavik, where they would be sent on to Denmark by ship during the summer.

It was April 26 when Rasmussen and the others started off again, dependent on luck, weather, and hunting skill for their survival. They struggled with towering slabs of pressure ice and *sikussaq* in Kennedy Channel. When a snowstorm halted them they rested for the first time since leaving Etah.

The storm raged for two days. When it cleared they made their way to Cape Morton, where they came upon an old depot from the Nares Expedition of 1875–1876, which had been sent out by Queen Victoria to traverse the frozen sea to the North Pole. "It consisted of six boxes, each containing four 9-pound tins of Australian mutton, fresh and delicious as if it had been left only the previous day." The food they were eating belonged to men who had died before Rasmussen was even born.

"North! North!" Rasmussen wrote in memory of Captain Hall,

who had died there in 1871 aboard the *Polaris* while trying to reach the North Pole. Rasmussen camped on the ice foot and walked to Hall's grave. A bear had recently scratched the wooden monument erected in the captain's honor.

Some days they traveled, other days they had to hunt. The weather was so fine they gave up their sealskin tents and slept outside under the stars. The going in Hall Basin was smooth and fast. Undulations of gravel and sand were fringed by the wild mountains that buttressed the hump of inland ice from which storms rolled down.

North of Hall's grave the coast steepened, as did the pressure ridges of ice between Greenland and Ellesmere Island. "May 2nd. We started at ten o'clock. We expected bad driving, and we got it." Past Cape Lupton the slabs of ice were sometimes ten to fifteen meters high: "It was quite impossible to drive across these huge blocks, which lay piled together as if thrown here by a giant's hand. For hours we had to stop in order to make a road for the sleds with our ice picks." They pitched their tents in what Rasmussen called "an awkward neighborhood," between pressure ridges, in an attempt to find shelter from the storm.

It was sobering to walk in the footsteps of explorers who had come to those places and failed, and it appealed to the European side of Rasmussen. As they made camp at Cape Sumner a southeast wind gusted so strongly it was impossible to stand up. A reconnoitering trip up the ice foot was made on hands and knees. They sought shelter behind hummocks of ice. There, for the first time, Rasmussen could look out across the Arctic Ocean toward the North Pole. He wrote: "I had no words to express the feeling with which this living though ice-bound sea overwhelmed me."

During one such rest Rasmussen recalled the fate of the Nares Expedition. The second of Sir George Nares's two ships, the *Alert,* had overwintered at Floeberg Beach in Grant Land within sight of where Rasmussen was now sitting. Rasmussen recalled the fateful journey:

It was April, 1876 when Clarence Markham set out with 19 men. Each man pulled a sled with 230 pounds and dragged two wooden boats too heavy and unwieldly for the trip. Within a week the crew began suffering frostbite—after all, they wore only leather boots—and soon enough they began suffering from scurvy since they ate only salted meat instead of fresh seal. By April 19th they crossed Lat. 83 degrees N. By May 10th, five of the men were unable to walk and had to ride on the sleds pulled by the healthy men. Markham went on ahead, leaving the others behind to rest. He reached Lat. 83° 26′ N, farther north than anyone else. By the time they returned to their ship on June 5th, several of the men died just as they reached the harbor. (Rasmussen, Greenland by the Polar Sea, *p. 94)*

Rasmussen's "awkward neighborhood" was "a wilderness of pressure ice" from which there was no escape. Near Repulse Harbor, they found a note in an empty brandy bottle written by Robert Peary on June 1, 1900: "Am passing here on my way to Ft. Conger. I left Etah on March 4th and Conger April 15th. . . . reached a point on the sea ice at N. Lat. 83° 50′ May 16th; and a point down the east coast about N. Lat. 83° May 21st. There followed over a week of fog, wind, and snow, this made travelling very heavy and the return slow."

The rough ice smoothed into a long, monotonous coast of sand, snow, and gravel. Between Blackhorn Cliffs, Cape Stanton, Hands Bay, Frankfield Bay, and Cape Bryant, they saw polar wolves and ptarmigan but nothing else. Just around Cape Bryant the view opened up into big country split apart by the gaping Sherard Osborn Fjord. "The sky was dazzling clear, the air deep blue and fresh, and it was as if the wind itself had other songs here than on the dead coasts from which we had come. On the uttermost horizon of the ice-ocean one sees occasional mirages lifting the sun-bathed pack-ice up towards heaven, giving relief to the monotony which rests over the frost-bound ocean."

On the smooth ice of St. George's Fjord, Rasmussen and his team drove their dogs to Dragon Point, where, "for the first time for a long period we stand where the rays of the sun are allowed to warm us right through. Not a wind stirs, and a tiny, curious bunting circling above our heads gives us a welcome to our first spring camp."

Rasmussen cached half their provisions for the return trip and continued on with six sleds and seventy dogs to hunt muskoxen. Traveling to Victoria Fjord, they had shot six muskoxen and two hares by May 12. The dogs filled up and rested, as did the men, feasting on the fattest parts—the fat around the heart and kidneys and in the hollows behind the eyes. Twenty-two shoulders of muskox were cached back at Dragon Point amid a storm that dumped so much new snow that the hunters had to break trail for the dogs. On May 19, returning to Sherard

Osborn Fjord from Victoria Fjord, they saw a seal, missed it, ate a hare, and saw wolves.

For the rest of May they encountered typical Arctic spring weather: heavy snow followed by fog and bad hunting. Because they had stock-piled their meat for the return journey, which had to be made quickly to beat the melting ice, they soon ran low on food. The young cartographer Lauge Koch came down sick with diarrhea and Ajako, one of the hunters, went snowblind.

When Koch was better, he and Rasmussen skied fourteen hours to survey Sherard Osborn Fjord. Rasmussen was seemingly tireless, which made it difficult for him to understand how other people fared in adversity. Koch was so tired he had to lie down on the ice to keep from fainting. Food was scarce. Then Rasmussen had his comeuppance: they quickly found themselves on the brink of starvation.

On Sunday the sun came out. Sun was like food for Rasmussen. He wrote: "We sit here in an ocean of light which blinds our eyes, in the midst of the winter-like Arctic spring, with pure new snow round our feet, the sun-gilded horizon of the glaciers behind the russet mountains."

The teams were split in half: Rasmussen, Ajako, and Koch were to go to Peary Land, Cape Glacier, and Cape Morris Jesup in the very top of Greenland, while Wulff and the others were to hunt on the De Long Fjord. They would meet again at the Nordensfjord and start home.

Rasmussen kept a journal:

June 4th. . . . it was at once evident that we were in Peary Land for such fertile oases we had not seen before. In some places we found thick, lush grass, not merely the miserable meagre tufts to which we were accustomed. Everywhere polar willow grew abundantly, and poppies, saxifrage, and cassiope, but everything is yet withered with winter. Here is at any rate plenty of fuel, if only we can find something to cook. (Rasmussen, Greenland by the Polar Sea, p. 125)

Ajako went off to hunt, Koch to chart the inner reaches of the fjord, and Rasmussen stayed with the dogs. After waiting fifteen hours with no sign of either man, Rasmussen wrote: "The dogs are raging with hunger; nearly all of them have bitten themselves loose from harness and traces, and are repeatedly attacking the tent where a small piece of boiled meat is still kept."

Koch returned twenty-five hours later with nothing. A sense of doom befell them; then Ajako came with two seals and three hares. "Our joy . . . is so intense that we feel as if warm waves beat through our bodies and we cannot prevent ourselves from shouting meaningless words."

In the next few weeks more difficulties arose. Ajako went completely snowblind and Koch suffered the old nausea. Even the dogs became ill and when seals were shot and blubber offered to them, they couldn't eat. Such is the effect of starvation. Food had to be administered in tiny portions.

In mid-June they moved on to Cape Salor. Sudden heat was followed by dire snowstorms. At one point they had only a single piece of seal and some *mattak* (the skin and a quarter-inch of fat from the whale) to feed themselves and their dogs. But once again Ajako, whom Rasmussen described as "light, with tense muscles, hardy, and used to starvation," saved the day: barely able to see, he managed to shoot a large seal.

At no other time in his life did Rasmussen suffer from the rigors of the subsistence hunter's life as he did then. It was this experience that gave him the breadth of mind to understand the life of all polar people. Though he straddled two cultures and was himself a halfbreed, he was now, in spirit and experience, one of them.

Rasmussen and his team continued their survey of what is now called Nansen Land and De Long Fjord, a long thumb of mountains and water just to the west of Cape Morris Jesup, which marks the tip of Greenland. It was the time of year when temperatures dipped and rose whimsically and banks of fog shifted from mountaintops down to ice. The constant sun, when it shone, threw heat so intense upon the backs of the explorers that they felt almost as miserable as they had during the cold spells. As soon as they shed their polar bear pants, anoraks, and winter kamiks, another snowstorm would whizz through, and they had to put them on again. Muskoxen came and went, but hares and ptarmigan were ever-present; the shooting of a seal was only occasional.

At Cape Mohn, a low promontory on De Long Fjord, Rasmussen found a small beacon containing a report from the American explorer James Lockwood of the 1881 Greely Expedition. The paper had been stashed in a tin and untouched for thirty-five years.

Greely's winter quarters were in Lady Franklin Bay. A house was built at Fort Conger, where they stayed during the first winter. Supply boats failed to reach them there and they overwintered a second year.

On April 3, 1881, Lockwood left the fort with twelve men and two hunters on dogsleds. He reached Cape Britannia by May 1. Instead of staying put, he continued north. On May 13 he planted the American flag on an island (now named for him) in De Long Fjord at 83° 24′ north. He returned safely to Fort Conger by June 1.

Things there weren't any better than when Lockwood left. Since no relief ship had come for two winters, Greely and his men started south before another winter came on, hoping to meet the ship somewhere on the coast of Ellesmere Island. That southward journey proved to be their undoing.

Four hundred miles south at Cape Sabine, the men found a note left for them reporting that, of two ships sent to rescue them, one had wrecked and the other had turned around, unable to penetrate the ice. A third winter approached. The shelter they built on Pim Island consisted of the hull of the wrecked boat. There were insufficient supplies to last them a year. As winter began, one of the Inuit hunters died of starvation while looking for seals; another drowned in his kayak. A man who shared his sleeping bag with another team member to help stave off frostbite found his mate dead in the morning. By the time a ship reached them in June 1884, all but Greely and six other men out of twenty-four had perished.

The Homeward Journey, 1917

Everywhere Rasmussen went at the top of Greenland he found remnants of European and American misadventures. He knew how easy it was to run out of food. A single change in weather—fog that would not dissolve, bad ice, a blizzard's whiteout—could bring hunting to a halt and hide the animals, if there were any around at all. The island was immense and the frozen sea that separated Greenland and Canada was a country between. The population of land animals was relatively small. Marine mammals were plentiful, but seldom visible to the eye.

Rasmussen understood that the only hope for survival was to live Eskimo-style. Those explorers and whalers who failed to do so faced almost certain death unless they were very lucky. And in the Arctic, luck was meted out in doses almost too small to do any good.

On June 22, Midsummer Night, Rasmussen, Koch, and the others decided to return home. Despite illness, snowblindness, and hunger, they had successfully explored the top of Greenland, disproved Peary's claim of an inland waterway, and charted every inch of the De Long Fjord. Now they had to face the hardships that summer weather can bring. The sun that warms and heals the body also eats the ice away, making travel with dogs difficult if not impossible.

Rasmussen wrote: "This is a stage rightly feared by all Arctic travelers; for at any moment the sledge may be sucked down by the wet snow." But nothing was going to interrupt their solstice celebration. At Rasmussen's insistence they feasted on a fat barnacle goose they shot when it happened to fly by.

By late June the snow was melting on the coast and great pools of water lay below the ice foot and ran down through fissures. Every few days rain and fog stopped travel altogether. When they could see enough to move, they covered their skis and sled runners with sealskins, which slip easily over snow, and kept hunting despite the deep slush through which the dogs could barely drag the sleds.

At the beginning of July, Wulff and his party rejoined the others. Alpine flowers began to blossom and all seemed well. But soon food became scarce. Rasmussen wrote that northern Greenland was "a land without heart where everything living must fight a hard battle for life and food."

More than anything else, it was the wet conditions that drove the men crazy.

> *The journey goes through ice-water, and it is only occasionally that we have an opportunity of a moment's rest on "dry ice." The warmth has converted the rough Polar-ice into a hopeless system of channels and pools, where from occasional blocks push up as islands in a huge swamp of ice. In the beginning we sought obstinately for the best places where a zigzag advance was possible; but this method has been given up long ago, for everything is wet through in spite of all our efforts. All through the day we wade up to our waists under the work with the sledges, which constantly get stuck in the holes, the same fate overtakes our reserve clothes. First the water pours over the sledges in front, then behind, according to different positions it occupies in the melted hollows. (Rasmussen, Greenland by the Polar Sea, p. 166)*

A week later, near McMillan Valley, muskoxen were sighted. But on inspection it was found that they were on the other side of a river of melt ice that the travelers were too weary to cross. The hunt was put off for another day. The meat, if they got it, meant not only food for themselves and the dogs, but also a few days of rest in a beautiful valley where they could dry their clothes.

To gain strength for the muskox hunt they had to shoot and eat a few hares first. Within an hour's walk they found themselves in range of five bulls, lying down and chewing their cud. The hunt itself had carnival overtones. Dogs were let loose in an attempt to drive the animals closer to camp. One dog was charged, tossed over the bull's head, and killed. Another disappeared over a cliff in a cloud of dust. Eventually two bulls were shot. Men and dogs ate, rested, and ate again.

Only Ajako had the strength to go out and hunt down the other three muskoxen. "He seized his gun, loosened the dog which usually followed him on all his hunting excursions, and disappeared behind the nearest ridge, light and supple, as if he had just got up from a long and refreshing rest. Over his walk and all his being rested a beauty that only youth and strength gives."

He returned twelve hours later, having shot six more muskoxen plus two barnacle geese. Afterward, he slept twenty-four hours without moving. In the next days the explorers gave their dogs a proper and well-deserved holiday, turning them loose along a stream, bringing freshly cut-up muskox meat to them, letting them sleep and laze and drink water as they wished. Of the seventy dogs they started with, only eighteen had survived, and they were badly needed to get home.

When they left their idyllic camp, some of the hard-won meat had to be left behind because the sleds were too heavy to push through the wet snow. Ten days later they were hungry again. "Hunger and death stalked us from all sides," Rasmussen wrote. They divided up into two parties: Wulff, Koch, the Greenlanders, Hendrick, and Bosun were to be in one group that would go inland; Harrigan, Ajako, and Rasmussen would be in the other to take a route across the sea ice. At the last minute, Hendrick asked Rasmussen if he could be excused from going inland. Rasmussen considered the request and denied it. Hendrick was needed in the mountains for hunting.

When the two parties met again, Hendrick was missing. Days went by and still he failed to appear. They hunted for him, taking valuable days from their southward movement as the ice became more rotten and the pools of water and rivers grew wider. Finally they gave up. Hendrick was gone. A mood of destitution came over the men. They were hungry, the ice was bad, and the going intolerably slow.

One evening Rasmussen met up with three wolves. They had come from the direction where Hendrick was last seen. One wolf had blood on his muzzle. Rasmussen observed, said nothing, and continued on.

Forced to travel out on the ice, the men had to walk in front of the sleds to assure the dogs that the going was safe, which of course it wasn't. One bad piece of ice and the whole sled could disappear, and because the edges of the holes were so soft, getting out would be impossible. A seal was shot but lost behind an ice floe. They went on, passing the last possible place where Hendrick could have appeared to meet them.

Drizzle alternated with snow and fog. It took twelve to fourteen hours to go ten kilometers. Their clothes never dried. On the last day of July, lacking food, they killed a dog. Rasmussen wrote: "Contrary to our usual custom we take our meal without joy."

Wind and rain lashed the tent. Rasmussen, who had the capacity to be ruthlessly cheerful, was now unconsolable. His diary entry for that day was titled "Stormy Thoughts": "Heavy in heart, we observe how every day which goes makes our dogs thinner and thinner; we ourselves are not much better off, but we understand the purpose, so we shall soon be accomplished in the art of starvation."

After another meal of dog he wrote:

When a little handful of men like us live by ourselves by degrees into a unity on the harsh and desolate coasts, we form, as it were, a small society of our own. The great living world which we left soon becomes so distant as to exist for us merely in our thoughts and in our longings. . . . We live life as it must be lived in these surroundings, simply and primitively; we execute our task as conscientiously as each man knows how, and in the solving of the problems which the expedition has set us to learn to know each other more intimately than do people as a rule. The best qualities of each man here meet with the weaker ones, but we help each other according to our ability." (Rasmussen, Greenland by the Polar Sea, *p. 208)*

A page later his mood had shifted: he was finding it difficult to come to terms with the loss of the once-orphaned Hendrick, whom he loved, and the bad weather underscored his grief. At six in the morning they could stand their hunger no more and broke into the provisions to stir up a bowl of oatmeal. When the oatmeal was gone they ate rabbit droppings and lichen.

"The new month started unusually hopelessly," Rasmussen began. It was August. Then the sun came out and Ajako saw a seal. He lay on his belly in deep, frigid meltwater and fired. Luck was with him: he got the seal. Dogs and humans ate and slept. In the morning they woke up under "a flaming sky." Sailors take warning: the temperature soared, mare's tails flew, and a ring formed around the sun—changing weather was on its way.

By afternoon rain had begun. During a letup, while their clothes dried, they built a beacon by a river in memory of Hendrick Olsen. Rasmussen spoke: "The Polar Eskimo has a proverb which says that no man will settle down and take up new land for good until death overtakes him and the stone mound ties his body to that place. Only then is it possible to attach a man to his country. I therefore propose that we hold to this idea, born of the enormous spirit of the hunting man, and to this island, where Hendrick found his grave, give his name."

All through August the men and dogs struggled. Up over the inland ice, down again on rotten ice, up and over several more times. Some days they ate, others they did not; they lived in a state of semistarvation. Rasmussen doctored their various ailments—boils, sprains, lacerations—and rationed out the food strictly but fairly, striving to keep up their spirits.

Sometimes in the middle of the day or night when the men were sleeping, Rasmussen would light his pipe and reflect on things. After months of Eskimo-style group living, he knew how to find moments of solitude.

Their home was the tent and the tent was always moving. They had camped on the endless expanse of the *mer de glace*, sheltered from wind between towering slabs of pressure ice, on the low stony deserts of the northernmost coast, in the inviting oases of alpine valleys carved out by glaciers. They had watched rivers come into being after winter's long dormancy, and seen snow rot into great expanses of gray. Most of the time they were hungry, but whenever game presented itself and they had food to eat, they were always grateful and remembered how to have fun and to feast. "The best qualities of each man here meet with the weaker ones, but we help each other according to our ability."

Despite everything, Rasmussen still felt the old camaraderie. Despite great differences in character and strength, they were sharing a common fate and a great intimacy that, with the impetus of comradeship and cooperative living, turned into love.

Near Daniel Braun Glacier they struggled down 1,000 meters into what Rasmussen called "a cauldron" and up again. The mountains were bare, brown, and vertiginous, with no sign of life, no birds, no plants.

But in the midst of that Arctic desert, he found beauty: "We find great, beautiful branches of coral, bearing witness that even here in this heart of winter was once a tropical climate, where the waves of a living ocean, driven by mild breaths of wind, merrily lapped across the stubborn remains of a bygone period."

The next day they found the ten-million-year-old fossil of an octopus next to a hundred-year-old skull of a muskox.

By August 10 they were on the inland ice, where cooler weather made the going easier. They could ski, and with lightened loads the dogs made good time. Soon, Washington Land was in sight, blotted out eventually by a storm that held them in their tents for two days. On August 25 they came off the ice cap and reached land, where they hoped the hunting would be better. It was still 200 kilometers to Etah and all they had left for food was a teaspoon of tea.

Rasmussen decided that he and Ajako would walk to Etah and bring back a relief party, but not without eating a feast of newly shot hares. After, they set off with only their guns, extra kamiks, and Rasmussen's diaries—no sleeping bags or change of clothes.

Red willow leaves, coolness that comes before winter's cold, glacial rivers that have swept away coastal ice, an ocean full of seals, reindeer tracks, small lakes and ground covered with alpine fescue, stony moraines, wet clothes, days without food, meadows of willow and heather, three hares shot and consumed, gray days, worn-out kamiks, fog . . .

On the fourth day of walking, Ajako yelled, "*Inussuaq! Inussuaq!*" A human being! They jumped up and saw a figure walking toward them. Their first thought, after five months of total isolation, was that the man must be a ghost. But it was Miteq, whom they knew well and whose fall hunting camp was at Kukat on the Inglefield Gulf.

Another long stint of walking and they were at Miteq's camp, where he gave them food and clothes and, best of all, news from home. A ship had come for the Americans on the MacMillan Expedition and all was well in Thule.

But of World War I Miteq reported:

A terrible blood-thirst has seized the white man. Nobody goes hunting or traveling now. . . . the white man uses all his cunning and great wisdom for the purpose of destroying each other. Nowhere in their land was shelter and safety to be found; they attack each other from the surface of the soil, from the sky, from the sea, and from the deeps of the great waters.

Usually they shoot blindly from a great distance, killing people whom they have never seen and with whom they have no quarrel. (Rasmussen, Greenland by the Polar Sea, p. 249)

The next day Rasmussen and Ajako borrowed some dogs, hooked them up, and continued on to Etah as it began to snow. The point was to get a relief party back to the others without delay. The news about the war had shocked Rasmussen. The contrast of their "primitive" nomadic life, full of congeniality and shared hardship, with the horrors of an impersonal war raging within the "ordered world" was an irony not lost on him.

They arrived in Etah in a raging storm at nine in the morning on the last day of August. The villagers had all moved into the vacant house left by the Crockerland Expedition. As the two men walked through the door they found themselves in a crush of people and noise. "Questions rained over us. . . . it was as if big waves beat together above our heads and swallowed us," Rasmussen wrote of their welcome.

Later they sat down to a feast—food left behind by the American explorers: potatoes, pemmican, biscuits, tinned tomatoes, beans and bacon, porridge with treacle, brown bread, fried hare, boiled seal, gulls in rice soup with dried turnips and spinach, tea, coffee, and American cut-plug tobacco. All set out to the accompaniment of music played on MacMillan's Victrola: Wagner plus tangos from Argentina.

"The whole thing was a hallucination," Rasmussen reported. "Like one of those which used to mock us during our periods of starvation. . . . We struggled for breath in the face of this abundance."

The next day the relief sledges started out for Cape Agassiz, where Wulff, Koch, Bosun, and Harrigan were waiting. They arrived on the evening of September 10. When Rasmussen appeared on the rocky coast to greet them, his young friend Koch sat down on a rock and started crying. The prophecy given seven months earlier had come to pass: Wulff was dead.

Koch described his last days with the botanist. They had cooked the hares left by Ajako, but Wulff had refused to eat hare meat. The hunting thereafter was so poor that they decided to look for game together. After a twenty-minute hike, Wulff refused to go farther. He and Koch sat down and drank the soup of a dog they had killed, then slept for thirteen hours while the others hunted.

Even so, Wulff could barely walk the next day, taking three hours to go four kilometers. He hallucinated about food and complained of his heart. When two hares were shot and cooked, he again refused to eat their flesh. They continued on the next day, walking, eating, resting, but Wulff got weaker and weaker. Even so, he continued to make botanical observations, dictating his thoughts when he became too weak to write:

August 25th—Harrigan got another two hares, all three young with grey heads—one was eaten raw, two others were boiled. Potentilla nivea, rubicaulis, emarginata, Dryas, broad-leaved, smooth, octopetala-like typical integrifolia and var. canescens. Very commonly Myrtillus uliginosa, scattered extensive mats, Salix arctica, with broadly oval and narrow lance-shaped leaves, highly variable, Pedicularis hirsuita. . . .

Knud and Ajako started out on foot this evening at 6 o'clock for Etah, the straight road across land to send us relief sledges and provisions. . . . Drank warm water for supper.

August 26th. Thrown away theodite, two cameras, bandages, clothes, everything we can yet do without. Remains now the most serious fight for life. To think of collecting plants now impossible. If we manage to get off with our lives it is great. We four men have absolutely nothing edible and obviously bad prospects of hunting. All weak but in good spirits. This helplessness, when strength leaves is hideous. I am only a skeleton now and shiver with cold. . . .

5:30 p.m. We make clear to continue westward. Everything is left behind. I have only my reindeer skin and an extra pair of kamiks. . . . This will be a march toward death unless a miracle happens. Gun and cartridges are brought.

Harrigan shot a small hare, 7 cm. long. Lesquerella, Hesperis, Cerast. alp. Kobresia, C. nard, Erioph polyst. Poa cenisia. Triestum, Hierochloa, Luzula nivalis, Sax. opposit. Flower. Alsine verna, Silene acaulis. . . .

Rather good sleep in spite of boil. Start noon. Grey cold fog. Along the edge of the inland ice. . . . Think mostly of a visit to some health resort for my poor worn-out gaunt body and suffering soul.

Drag along for two hours in cold fog, heavy, stony, cliff-terrain until 9 p.m. Minus 1.4 degrees. Camp for the night on the moss. . . . Were I only at a Sanatorium. This is worse than death.

August 27th. As we brought nothing but 2 guns, 3 rugs, my coat, 5 boxes of matches and a pan, our rig-out for 2–3 weeks' autumn campaign is very simple and "Eskimo." To sleep at 11 p.m. on mossy slope. Fog sets in. minus 0.5 degrees and a little snow. The Eskimos—those energetic savages—again after hare—return.

4 p.m. Entrails eaten as usual raw, the blood goes into the soup, then a fresh cooking of hare. . . . A loon, geese, terns, buntings in flocks. Midnight gloom, gneiss knolls, tracks of reindeer.

August 28th. Bosun a hare during the night. Cold. Fog. Falling snow. Diarrhoea. Misery. Start 1 p.m. through snow. Colpodium, Cystopteris (com.) Lycopod. Selago, Rhododendron, red-polls in flocks, terns, falcons, plenty of animal life and rich plankton in several little lakes. . . .

*August 29th. I am half-dead, but found Woodsia ilv. Lay down at 7 p.m. for I will not hamper the movements of my comrades on which hangs their salvation. (Rasmussen, *Greenland by the Polar Sea*, pp. 280–83)*

After a long rest, Rasmussen started home for Thule. He already knew he would never attempt a trip like this one again. The deaths and hardships had tempered his celebrity. He hadn't gone to prove himself, but in fact that's what had happened. He had been deeply humbled by the experience, and his empathy for the Eskimo greatly widened. He wanted now to turn his full attention to studying the lives of these people; he wanted to dive deeply into the boreal culture of which he was now, more than ever, a part.

Arriving home—the Arctic station—in the middle of the night, Rasmussen threw open the door of Peter Freuchen's house. Peter woke up startled. Later, Peter said of his friend: "The look of the icecap was upon him, months of starvation and hardship was written on his face."

N by E: Illorsuit, July 1996

Twenty-four-hour-a-day sun and I'm living in a skin turned inside out.
All privacies externalized.
Light spills onto the top of the world and keeps spilling.
Not burnished light, but a searing turned up to incandescence.
Sometimes blue rinses the white walls of floating islands.
Only the water is black—a burnt-out flame.
I dream I can snap my fingers and make water boil, just like that.
To take bearings at the horizon—I get lost in splinters.
A breeze quickens the water into hammered silver, ribbed light.
The straight-up sun sends shadows straight down like stakes.
Can shadows "impale" ice?
Even timelessness can be wasted.
Again I take bearings at the horizon—no reference point.
Not knowing is the other name for a Greenland summer day.
Night gives itself completely to day like unearned affection.
No escape from overexposure. Only this pale lambency called air.
A Dane sent to eastern Greenland was so bored he wrote six months
    ahead in his log book but died before his daily entries ended.
I shiver. The sun's cool passion.
In the "hadal regions of the sea," 1,000 fathoms deep, are beings who
    live in darkness and have no eyes.

Even shut, my eyes are lightstruck.
The clock is divided into bodies of water: we leave a fjord, enter a bay,
    leave it for a strait, come to a half-moon bay with a village.
Where a corner of thought breaks off—no blood, only a trapped blaze.

Summer. There's an island fifty miles northwest of Uummannaq called
Ubekendt Ejland—Unknown Island. Mostly uninhabited, it lies like a
brown sliver in a narrow strait. Its only village, Illorsuit, is at the north-
eastern end. Remote and protected, it faces inward, not on the open
water of Baffin Bay.

Sixty-five Julys ago Illorsuit served as a temporary sanctuary for the
American painter Rockwell Kent (1882–1971). He came to Illorsuit at
the suggestion of Knud Rasmussen and Peter Freuchen, who happened
to be on the same ship with him going from Nuuk to Copenhagen. Kent
had been trying to get home to New York after his thirty-three-foot sail-
boat had wrecked on the southwest coast of Greenland—an escapade he
wrote about and illustrated in his book *N by E*. Though it had survived
the rough waters off Nova Scotia and Labrador and the icefields of
Davis Strait, the boat dragged anchor in a sudden June storm and broke
up on the rocks in a fjord.

From the wreckage Kent salvaged his paints, brushes, and bits of
canvas to which he added pieces of burlap and bedsheets, though his
illustrated journals of the voyage were lost. He stayed in Greenland
for two months, painting and enjoying the embraces of young Inuit
women as they walked the valleys, glaciers, and mountains around
Nuuk. He became so infatuated with Greenland—and its women—that

he pledged to return. And return he did, on a placid sun-bright night in July 1931, staying through the winter, and coming back for another year in 1934–1935.

Kent's meeting with Rasmussen had been pure chance. Everything in Kent's life worked that way. He traveled impulsively, recklessly, pushed by the feverish unease he felt in society, pulled by a lust for remote places, his appetite so voracious that it could be satisfied only by geographical extremes. His travels took him not only to Greenland but to other cold places too: he sailed the Magellan Straits, wintered on Fox Island in Alaska, painted in Newfoundland and Ireland, and built a house on Monhegan Island off Maine, as if only treeless open spaces suited his all-day, all-night binges of painting.

In his book *Salamina,* written as a tribute to his Inuit companion, Kent describes that July evening:

> *It is a tranquil cloudless evening in July. The shadow of the hills of Umanak lies on the settlement; brown rocks, brown soil, brown native houses built of turf, and Danish houses bright with paint. And all around, seawards and landwards, on the blue bay islanded with ice, on mountainous islands, on the snow-tipped ranges of the mainland, on the near hill crests and on the towering flanks of Umanak's peak, the golden light of the Greenland summer's never setting sun.* (Kent, Salamina, p. 3)

As with Kent, it was July, and I was trying to make my way from Uummannaq to Unknown Island fifty miles north. I spied the green house where I had spent part of one winter but its windows were shuttered closed, and Ann and Olejorgen's house was locked. They were away on holiday.

I wandered the town looking for help with no luck. Late in the day I was given the name of an Illorsuit fisherman who was due in and would probably be going back that night. Perhaps he would give me a ride on his boat, they said. His name was Kristian Möller. When exactly he was coming, no one could be sure. All I knew was that his boat was blue, and we did not share a common language.

If you sit anywhere long enough, the drunks will gather around. I waited on a bench at the harbor all day with two boozy-breathed young men. Boat after boat came into the small, U-shaped harbor. I'd ask, "Kristian Möller?" "*Nye . . . nye,*" they said.

At six in the evening a good-sized blue fishing boat rounded the breakwater. They were Inuit, but they spoke Danish. "*Navn?*" I asked, inquiring about the name of the boat. Their glazed eyes registered nothing. Could they even see? The boat swung close and glided by. "Kristian Moller," one of them said softly, nodding his head.

I ran to the end of the pier where the boat was being tied. An Inuit man looked up from the aft deck. In his early forties, his hair was black and his body was carved rock, but his dark eyes were gentle. "Kristian Moller?" I asked. He stared at me—was it my pronunciation he didn't understand? I said his name again, timidly. He smiled. "Illorsuit . . . Hans Holm . . ."—before I finished, he held out his hand to help me aboard. Pointing at his watch, he indicated that we would get under way at 19:00, *imaqa*—maybe—which meant we could leave anytime. Who cared when we left?

At ten in the evening we glided out of the harbor. The boat was thirty-five feet long with a high, ice-nicked bow made of heavy timbers and a narrow wheelhouse and a two-cylinder diesel engine that drummed rhythmically. Strips of seal jerky swung on the stays between mast and deck. At the breakwater, a discarded plastic glove filled with water bobbed up and down as if waving good-bye. I couldn't be sure if Kristian had understood me and wondered if we were actually headed for Illorsuit. I didn't care; it felt good to be under way.

I'd already been on the ferry that plied the west coast in the summers with a voluptuous green-eyed Swedish opera singer for a roommate and a jaunty Danish captain who took his twelve-hour shifts at the helm smoking cigars and listening to Mozart. Now I found myself at the seabirds' and seals' level and my perspective changed. Greenland's immensities loomed even larger: massive, water-blackened rock walls rose up from a mirror made of water as big as the sea.

I stood on the foredeck shivering. I was bare-armed and bareheaded and could see my breath. The airline had lost all my luggage: parka, hiking boots, sleeping bag. I had no way to keep warm and wondered how I would fare during a cold Greenland summer. But I did have books. As the boat inched out toward the wide mouth of Uummannaq Fjord, I held Kent's illustrated memoirs about Greenland against my chest—*N by E, Greenland Journal,* and *Salamina*—using them to shield myself from the frigid wind. Once more I asked Kristian if we were going to Illorsuit. He grinned as the boat putt-putted oh so slowly . . . Yes.

I had hitched a ride on a fishing boat going to Unknown Island in cold, bright sun that shone all night.

"Nikolai," Kristian bellowed. The hatchcover lifted and a man appeared who looked like no one I had ever seen before—a wild Eskimo with a heavy brow, raven hair, a bony face, and, most startling, deep-set turquoise eyes. He didn't talk. His look was fierce; he seemed to part the air as he strode into the wheelhouse. He took the helm while Kristian lowered himself down into a skiff tied aft, and, clutching a rifle, sped off so fast I barely had time to see him vanish behind an iceberg. He had gone to kill a seal.

With Nikolai steering we droned through corridors of water between tall islands, the boat's wake opening behind us like a flower. Thousands of resting fulmars flew up—curtain after curtain of birds. Once, a boat with two hunters sped past just as we slowed: a pod of seals lifted out of the water in a single capriole. Then the lip of the other boat's wake curled over the seals' vanishing heads.

We entered a forest of icebergs. The path between was chrome and slate, a mirror that did not reflect. It was ripple-battered, then smoothed. Icebergs creaked. Bits of rubble skidded down sleek walls. Arctic gulls shrieked, rising up, looking for food. The glazed wing of an iceberg caught light. From one translucent arch, a row of blue tears fell.

By the time the steamer carrying Rockwell Kent, Knud Rasmussen, and Peter Freuchen docked in Copenhagen in 1933, a friendship was launched. Frances, Kent's new wife, met him there. Rasmussen invited the couple to visit his farm, Hundstead, on the outskirts of Copenhagen, and they accepted. Rasmussen had already completed his three-year journey across Arctic America and had begun visiting the little-known east coast of Greenland, taking down the intellectual and cultural history of the Inuit hunters there. At Hundstead, Kent worked on a commission to illustrate *Moby-Dick*. By November he had completed 157 drawings. In exchange, Rasmussen later sent Hanne, one of his daughters, to stay with Kent at his Adirondack farm in upper New York State.

Kent kept journals of all his voyages, later assembling them into illustrated books. While plying these same fjords he wrote: "Man is less entity than consequence and his being is but a derivation of a less subjective world, a synthesis of what he calls the elements."

The wind died and freshened. A single cloud took the sun and a blue wash poured forth. Nikolai stepped from the wheelhouse and cut off a hunk of dried seal. His big hands shone with grease as he ate. Sweet-eyed, barbaric, he saw I was shivering from cold and beckoned me inside. I squeezed onto a narrow bench beside him. At the end of Uummannaq Fjord we crossed a slice of Baffin Bay and turned north. There was a chop on the water and the wheel kept hitting my knees as it turned. Nikolai wore red overalls with a white wool sweater buttoned over the top. His fingernails were long. He opened a small window and stuck his head out into the breeze. Pale light flooded in and its sheen lay like something viscous on his cheekbones.

A long brown coast rose before us—Ubekendt Ejland—all tumbled peaks and scarps that in the geologic past had been turned upside down: the peaks were in the basement and the basement had been hurled to the top. The glacier-carved seabed was 1,000 kilometers deep and the bottom was a repeat of what we were seeing topside: a world of underwater mountains.

Had I been sleeping? My head was resting against Nikolai's hip. It must have been the sudden warmth that made me drift off. He looked down at me, smiling. The boat putted north into Illorsuit Strait.

Kristian reappeared from behind an iceberg with a dead seal draped over the bow of his skiff. I held the wheel while Nikolai helped haul the animal aboard, then Kristian took the helm.

Glass is what the boat cut through as we continued north. The sea was indigo—it stood for night, which had fallen from the sky. A line of silver demarcated blue water from blue cliff, and there, a thin band of haze rose. I wondered why anyone came to Unknown Island, anyone at all.

Something broke the surface of the water: another pod of seals. Kristian grabbed his rifle, the whites of his eyes flashing as he leaped to the foredeck. The hatchcover lifted again: Nikolai appeared on deck from below—not Ahab, but Caliban. His blue eyes were feral. He was detached, sullen, calm; he watched Kristian shoot. The seal got away. Unfazed by failure, the two men squeezed into the warm wheelhouse beside me.

For two more hours the boat's slow thrumming was the only voice heard. In silence we were pressed so tightly together that the turning wheel made a groove in my side. As we chugged into Illorsuit Strait rock walls rose up on the starboard side, and on the port the brown island slid—a dry sliver.

Seen from above on a map, Ubekendt Ejland looks like a flounder with a flattened head and a long tail. From water's edge, it was a fifty-mile-long palisade with shadows clenching tight canyons, bold scarps, and razorbacked ridges curved like chair backs. Once, a village called Ingia sat at the island's northern tip. Rockwell Kent had gone there to hunt whales one October during the belugas' southward migration. Now the village was gone. I wanted to ask, but didn't have the Greenlandic words for it: Why was this island "Unknown" when all the others in the vicinity had names?

On arriving in Illorsuit, Kent wrote:

> Both by the suggestion of its name and by its position and character—its seagirt isolation, the simple grandeur of its stark, snow-covered tableland and higher peaks, the dark cliff barrier that forms its western shore—there is the glamour of imponderable mystery about the island which dignifies it even at the gateway of a region of stupendous grandeur. Its cliffs, proclaiming inaccessibility, preclude the thought of human settlements. *(Kent, Salamina, p. 6)*

As we made our way north, I wondered where in the village Kent's house would be; where he went to paint; what he traveled to see; what the Arctic taught him about light. Two months earlier I had written a letter to my contact on the island—the only English speaker—about renting Kent's house. The response was vague. He said only, "Please come. You are welcome here." In Illorsuit there were ninety-nine Greenlanders and one Dane, Hans Holm, with whom I was to stay.

At two a.m. we rounded a headland topped by a graveyard and glided into a half-moon bay. The village of Illorsuit (pronounced *Is-slor-sluit*) lay before us. At the bottom of a brown-walled amphitheater lay a string of houses on a half-moon bay. The black sand beach glittered with ice; the narrow fjord was black and the rock wall on the other side rising from it—another island, unexplored, uninhabited—was topped by the ice cap's wavering edge of white.

I climbed the metal ladder from the boat to the dock. Kristian handed up my daypack and pointed vaguely to the far corner of the settlement, indicating that I would find Hans's house there. How would I know which one was his? Was I to knock on doors at two in the morning until I found him? I began walking . . .

I walked past small houses and the usual Arctic clutter. Clothes flapped on lines frozen stiff in the all-night sun, and sled dogs tethered by long chains slept in dirt, their noses tucked under their tails. Fish and seal meat dried on racks poled far enough off the ground so loose dogs couldn't get at it. Children's toys lay in the sand and sleds were stacked three high, the boiling pots for water from the previous winter's hunts still hanging from the handlebars.

All Arctic settlements have the same acrid smell: of dog shit, seal guts, unwashed bodies. But the sun in the northern sky casts a light so lucid, all impurities are erased. Fjord water slapped the black sand. Soon the village proper gave onto a half-mile-long wooden boardwalk that led to a few houses at the end of the spit. Where the boardwalk ended, sand began, sand mixed with dog shit, ice, and seal bones. How I would know which house was Hans's wasn't clear.

A lone Greenlandic woman approached. Stupefied, I could say only "Hans Holm?" She nodded and I followed her. Mistakenly I had searched the bay for the biggest and most brightly painted house, but Hans was no colonial master. His was one of the smallest and most humble abodes.

Six puppies greeted me, jumping up and searching my pockets for food. Then the children—Hendrik, age two, and Marie Louisa, age six—ran to me, grabbed my hands, and pulled me indoors. The room was mustard yellow, almost bare. Two windows with lace curtains looked out at the ice-glutted fjord and the rock-walled island beyond.

Hans came into the room. In his early fifties, he was tall and fine-featured, with a nervous, string-bean gauntness and a furrowed brow. Fair-skinned, his face had begun to show the ravages of the Arctic climate and age. But when we shook hands his worried look dissolved into a smile. The house had about it the air of hippiedom: a handmade skylight over the kitchen table, an unfinished addition, single-paned casement windows, no bathroom in which to bathe. One wall was hung with a gallery of family photographs—snapshots of dogsleds, children, relatives. When I apologized for arriving so late, Hans laughed and said, "It doesn't matter. The last thing anyone worries about in the summer is sleep."

The children rattled off questions in Greenlandic as I opened my two dictionaries—one was English to Danish, the other Danish to Greenlandic—and for a few minutes we struggled with words. The woman who had greeted me on the path was Arnnannguaq. Not Hans's wife, he said, but the mother of his children. Something caught my eye out the window: it was Kristian's boat coming toward shore. Nikolai was on deck, leaning down to tie up at the long line next to Hans's house.

"Who is he?" I asked Hans, pointing to Nikolai.

"That's Kristian's brother," he said. "They are the best fishermen and hunters in the village. Their mother was very strong, very clever. I even have her picture on my wall. When I moved here I knew nothing, and she taught me what I know about Greenlanders."

Nikolai and Kristian came ashore. Their house was only a few yards away and much grander than Hans's.

Forget that it was 2:30 in the morning—the children cavorted. They were small, black-haired, dark-eyed, good-natured, and dexterous. We sat in the tiny kitchen. "Would you like some toast?" Hans asked. "I remember when I worked at the American airbase at Sondre Stromfjord the American men all liked to eat toast." I gladly accepted.

Marie Louisa climbed onto the table, her tiny legs like poles in front of my face, and lifted the skylight. She peppered the glass with muesli. "For the birds," Hans told me. "She likes to watch the snow buntings eat the cereal." In the corner cordoned off by a curtain was the bed where Hans, Arnnannguaq, Marie Louisa, and Hendrik slept all together, Greenlandic style. Was I to sleep there too? I could see no other bed.

The middle of the night was bright, sunny, cheerful, windless, and everyone was wide awake. I looked at the clock on the kitchen wall. It read 12:24. Day or night? Regardless, it couldn't be right. By then it must have been 3:00 a.m. Hans chuckled. "That clock has been broken for ten years."

Rockwell Kent was an emotional and political cannonball, shooting off in several directions at once for the sake of a cause or for love. He was by turns truculent and passive, vengeful and generous. His family life was messy: he kept a wife and young children at home while bragging about the other women in his life and expecting them all to get along. As his marriages crumbled, he made hasty retreats to remote and often tree-less domains to write and paint and get away from it all. When at home, he fought one cause after another, becoming so disgruntled with both art and politics that he allied himself with Germany during World War I, then with Russia just as Stalin was coming to power. He bequeathed much of his work to the Pushkin Museum in Leningrad, an act that rendered him almost unsellable in the United States.

In a Greenland village, an outsider with money and enough gusto to drive a dogsled and eat raw seal could live like a king in the 1930s. To Illorsuit Kent brought music, carpentry tools, booze, and food—cans of fois gras with truffles, bottled fruit juice, cigarettes, coffee, and hundreds of records—in response to the hospitality he knew would be forthcoming.

He was not only a painter but wrote about the remote places to which he traveled. The books are rambling, homey, and gossipy. He was a man at war with his own loneliness: he thrived on remote landscapes but couldn't stand to be alone. In *Salamina*—which recounts a year in a Greenland village—he gives a feel for the mad swings between placid do-nothing days, seething small-town intrigues, and the robust activity of hunting. One treasures his books as much for the slice-of-life view as for the rock-ribbed woodcuts, spare drawings, and luminous paintings.

A dog ran by. Someone yelled. Hans looked: "That dog's been on the loose for months. Once they get a taste of freedom, they can't be caught. I don't try to catch that dog . . . he's too much like me."

Hans came to Greenland after dropping out of architecture school in Copenhagen in 1968, while his brother went on to become a doctor. He took a summer job at Sondre Stromfjord—now called by its Greenlandic name, Kangerlussuaq—which had been a U.S. Air Force base during World War II and maintained an American presence through the Cold War. A French friend there who was in trouble and needed money to go home asked Hans for help. Hans gave him his airplane ticket and a small amount of cash—whatever was in his pocket—in exchange for the Frenchman's five dogs, sled, and shack in the village of Illorsuit—a place Hans said he had trouble locating on the map or in his mind.

When the job ended, Hans and a cousin, who was related to Rasmussen, traveled to Illorsuit. "I came to see about the dogs I had inherited. I had to make sure they were being cared for and fed . . . I guess you could say that I came here and never left." He looked out the window at the black beach where his puppies roamed and the iceberg tilted precariously in the midnight sun.

"I wasn't prepared for winter. I had no clothes, no equipment for hunting. The supply ship hadn't been here for a long time and there was almost nothing in the store—just a few canned goods. I had to learn to hunt, not just for myself, but for the dogs too. We all eat the same thing. The neighbor who had been feeding them taught me how."

Before coming to Illorsuit, Rockwell Kent arranged for lumber and building supplies to be sent from Denmark. The lumber and all the makings of a house arrived by ship—cement, stove, chimney, stovepipe, paper, doors, and windows—but there were no nails.

The villagers helped him build a small house high on the hill overlooking the bay that fronts the fjord. Construction only took a few days. They called him Kinte, for Kent, and like Paul Gauguin in Tahiti, he settled into village life quickly. Instead of Gauguin's hot tropics, Kent sought out his own icebox paradise. Though he had an American wife and children at home, Salamina, whose husband had died of tuberculosis, became his Eskimo wife while he was there.

Hans had come to Unknown Island less well prepared, but with the same results. When he decided to add on to the shack he'd bought with his return ticket home to Denmark, he had to wait a long time for supplies. The first winter he used shark oil as a fire starter and burned broken pallets left by the supply ship in his tiny Danish woodstove for cooking and heat. There was no money for insulation or double-pane windows. Like Kent he ordered only bare essentials, but had the opposite problem: "The nails arrived in the spring, but not the lumber," he recalled. "Then one morning a piece of driftwood came to the shore. It is now the main beam of the house."

Another fishing boat anchored out front—friends of Arnnannguaq's from Saattut, a village near the head of Uummannaq Fjord. The woman was short-haired and mannish and her husband slim, almost feminine. They jumped into their skiff, came ashore, knocked on the door, and burst in. Their toothless grins indicated they'd caught a seal and wanted to share it with us. Not later, but now. "It is the Inuit custom," Hans told me.

We drank coffee crowded around the tiny kitchen table. It occurred to me that I should ask about renting Rockwell Kent's house, but in my exhaustion that seemed unimportant. I had traveled five days to get there and all I could think of was sleep.

Hans searched my face: "You must lie down. It won't bother any-one." He laid an old foam pad and a dirty comforter on the floor.

My clothes were already sour from three days' travel from hot to cold climates, on planes, helicopters, benches, and boats, and there was nowhere to bathe, nothing to change into. One of Kent's books fell open to a page where I read: "See me liberated by the blessedness of the disas-ter from the confinement of the boat, shorn of property, stripped of clothes, wandering, an unknown alien-beachcomber in a generous land." I slept.

Sometime later the visitors retreated to their boat to sleep and the house went quiet. From my mat on the floor I watched cool sun flood the windows. For a moment, the light seemed deathly, not life-giving, as if affording me the last glimpse at the end of the tunnel or maybe the beginning of something. Nothing that august occurred to me now. I was only weary. In all this light, it was easy to reduce time to a mathematical calculation. Light did not separate out the moments but amassed them into a single cell—maybe we were being taken all the way back to the beginning, I couldn't tell. I felt dizzy. My body was time and it had been hurtled through space a long way.

Kent had hired Salamina to be his *kifak* (housekeeper) in Illorsuit. She had been born on the island of Ikerasak, near Uummannaq. Her family was prominent. She was taught to read and write at an early age, could shoot a gun, prepare skins, sew, cook, flense a seal, and drive dogs. After her parents and sister died of tuberculosis, she married a first cousin, but he too succumbed to the disease after their third child was born. When Kent met her and asked her to work for him, she said she couldn't because she had three children. Kent said simply, "Bring them along."

Soon enough Salamina and Kinte (as she called him) were cozy in their one-room Greenland house. She lorded over the household and his bed, fiercely protective and jealous. Life was sweet despite Sala-mina's wild rages. Kent's only work was to go where he wanted with his dogsled to paint and write, sleep in his dogskin sleeping bag, sometimes with Salamina, sometimes with a woman from a nearby island. He joined in village life and celebrations when he wanted or tramped the fjords and mountains to paint when it suited him.

In Illorsuit Kent saw to it that there were parties with Eskimo-style dancing and singing and celebrations during holidays. He made a

Christmas tree from a narwhal tusk. Seal-hunting expeditions went out in the spring, whale hunting in the fall, and there was fishing, egg gathering, and berry picking in summer, plus continual customary visiting year round. During the dark months, Kent put together an intimate compendium, *Greenland Journal,* whose chapter headings are woodcuts—small windows into the village and its surroundings, mountains and glaciers, sled dogs and sleds, the night sky, and villagers playing under the midnight sun.

About *Greenland Journal* Kent wrote: "Of life without the luxuries that we enjoy in America, without most of the gadgets that we have come to call necessities, of life in a barren country where even bare existence is precarious and the means of getting it a hazard, this book is a record."

Laughter woke me. Dazed, I looked out the window. Arnnannguaq and the woman from Saattut had dragged the dead seal up on the beach. Rubber-booted, with cigarettes hanging from their lips, they sharpened their knives. The woman from Saattut held her blade up to the sun: its honed edge glistened. One long cut from chin to back flippers and the skin broke open, glutted with curds of fat. Another deeper cut and something was pulled up from the gaping cavity on the tip of her knife: it was the liver, steaming in the frigid air. When I looked again, they were laughing and chewing, and their mouths and chins were dripping with blood.

They motioned for me to join them and offered me a piece. I took the rubbery slab from their red hands, chewed, and spit; a puppy ran over and ate the masticated bit voraciously. They laughed, helping themselves to more.

Another nap delivered me into the middle of the day. I drew a calendar at the back of my notebook, determined to keep track of time. But I kept napping. When I woke again, the house was quiet because the children were gone. The visitors from Saattut had taken them fishing. The sun had circled around to the eastern part of the sky. When I asked again about the possibility of renting Kent's house, Hans said, "Oh, that house was taken down a year ago. Now a school has been built there." It suddenly became clear that the mat and blankets in the empty living room were to be my summer home.

I had ridden a fishing boat into a world of light, light with no darkness, no moon lunacy, no giving over to ordinary night after the exhaustions of day. Here, light gave off more light and sun was a rolling torch on ball bearings, igniting what it had already oxidized.

When Hendrik and Marie Louisa returned we walked to the schoolhouse. Marie Louisa took my hand and led me around to the back, where we crouched down and looked: I could see the stone foundations of what had been Kent's house. The site was as far up on the hill as we could go; the view down was of the entire village, the harbor, the strait, and the desolate cliffs of the uninhabited island opposite. Far off there was a speck on the water: a fisherman returning home from hunting, a seal draped over the bow of the skiff. All else in the bay was unmoving—a gilded, silvered silence.

Kent was first and foremost an illustrator; his woodcuts were bold, dramatic, and physical, almost Blakean in their striving for a metaphysicality, but one that was cut from dark and light, muscle and sinew, not gold and illumination. In the Arctic landscape he found what was already in his mind's eye: the stark, bare, glinting surfaces. He knew that stripping everything down to bone caused more emanations. He lived through all the seasons, witnessed the coming of dark in October, then the sudden brightening as the sun returned in February; he had found an Arctic home.

From his house he wrote:

> Standing on the sloping foreland of Illorsuit, one looks out as though upon the stage of a great theatre. Of that stage, the level plain of the sea is the floor, the great circle of the heavens is the proscenium arch, the two headlands are the wings. . . . Despite man's littleness out there, let him just be there, enter on that scene, and as far as the eye can reach all eyes have found him. The speck is the event. (Kent, Salamina, p. 107)

On Sunday we loaded the skiff with food and motored to a group of tiny uninhabited islands to collect tern eggs. We were the speck and the event. The islands were so small they appeared only as dots on the topo map, but they were the summer home to thousands of seabirds—Arctic terns—that had come all the way from the Antarctic to lay their eggs. It has long been the practice in Greenland to vacate the village and camp out—a cleansing rite to rid oneself of cabin fever. From their summer campgrounds, the villagers hunted seals, fished, gathered eggs, and cooked over smoky heather fires, enjoying the warm July sun.

We piled into Hans's skiff and headed north. Rasmussen mentions in his Fourth Thule Expedition notes that the tern eggs he and Freuchen found on a deserted island had kept them alive one summer when hunting had been bad. But we were not starving; we had thermoses of coffee and sandwiches.

Arnnannguaq was angry with Hans. I couldn't figure out why. They bickered and I held on to Hendrik, who lay on the seat of the boat sleeping. Marie Louisa, bright-eyed and wiggling, wedged her small body into the boat's bow as we flew across the fjord, the spray lapping her face. Every few minutes she turned and smiled at me. I moved forward and sat behind her, getting sprayed too.

A. couldn't decide which island she wanted to go to. We stopped at one, got out, looked around, then went to another. The islands were hollowed out in the center like nest cups lined with soft green grass and feathers. Finally A. settled on the big island. As we entered the cove I saw the blue fishing boat that had brought me to Illorsuit. Nikolai, Kristian, and his family were gathered around a smoking turf fire by a hut. They had come to hunt eggs too. As we pulled in and tied up the boat to rocks, Nikolai looked up and smiled.

The sky was thick with circling, diving, shrieking terns. We had invaded their sanctuary. Terns annually migrate approximately 22,000 miles from the Antarctic to the Arctic and back, following the sun. They spend more time in daylight than any other bird. Their pair bonds are long-term and they are faithful to their established territory.

Now I was robbing their nests and I didn't want to. But what choice did I have with A. pushing from behind to make me put eggs in my basket?

The children fanned out, scanning the grass. The eggs were small and olive-colored with brown speckles, and we found them lying on rocky outcrops and grass. The birds dived at us as we filled our sacks with what would have been their progeny. I tried to calculate the impact our petty thievery had on their population. Finally I could steal no more and deliberately walked by eggs hoping no one else saw them.

Back at the boat we ate lunch and moved on. Passing between two islands, we ran into the visitors from Saattut, who invited us on board. Since they had shared their seal with us, we shared our eggs, boiling them in the boat's tiny galley. We cracked the olive shells on the boat's rail and popped them into our mouths like marbles. Strongly flavored, they tasted like duck eggs. This was the only time of year villagers ate eggs, which were considered a delicacy. In the distance I could still hear the terns' cries.

When the sun left the southern sky and circled to the north, passing behind mountains, riding in the open skiff was cold. Hans loaned me a pair of insulated coveralls to keep warm for the ride home. We zoomed past islands and grassy inlets where Kinte had painted.

Kent used his images as a narrative tool. His woodcuts—finely carved, bold, and handsome—changed the way we thought about going somewhere. We didn't have to see the actual place, he gave us its essence. His Greenland images were full of shadows and brightness—the black, blue, and white world of the Arctic. The slices of village life veered from the dramatic. No blood and gore, no blizzards, no ghosts—just the head-on stillness of a summer night, or the brittle blaze of a winter day.

Once it was all night here; now it was perpetual morning. I slept again and woke in the same dirty clothes (it was too cold not to sleep in them), surrounded by people. Arnnannguaq's friends from Saattut had followed us back and were talking, smoking, laughing, and eating the last of the boiled seal. Out front the skiffs and fishing boats were lined up around the bay tied by long lines to the beach. When icebergs were collapsing, the lines were lengthened so that the waves made by falling ice would't carry the boats to shore. In the afternoon an iceberg drifted perilously close in; Kristian and Nikolai re-anchored their fishing boat until the ice went by.

On Sunday evening the villagers strolled on the shore. As Hans, A., the children, and I started out, I thought of the great parks and avenues made for such walks: the Champs Élysées, the Paseo de la Reforma, and the cobblestone piazzas of Italy. Here, we walked a dirt path strewn with seal guts and dog shit. Dogs howled and busied themselves with canine activities—nuzzling, growling, playing. Kristian promenaded arm in arm with his wife Marie, and Nikolai, freshly bathed and dressed in khaki pants and white shirt, walked a few paces behind.

In Hans's house harmony returned, or at least a tense peace. The big iceberg in front heaved and tilted, but didn't fall. And so it was with us humans. A. and Hans stopped bickering; when Hendrik had a tantrum, Hans picked up the thrashing child and carried him around the room until he stopped crying.

Hans had lived in Illorsuit for fifteen years and had recently taken a job with the fish factory fixing machines and unloading supplies when they came. When I asked him why he stayed, he shrugged. "I just couldn't leave. I didn't exactly know that I didn't want to go back, I just couldn't make myself go." For years he lived alone. The quiet life suited him. And like Kent, he took on a *kifak*. Arnnannaguaq came from a small village up the coast. She was nineteen when they met and Hans was thirty. The children came later.

"Now I have been here so long, I can't stand any settlement that is bigger than Illorsuit," Hans said. His coming to Greenland in the first place wasn't mere whimsy. His father, Mogen Holm, was the first doctor to diagnose and treat tuberculosis in the villages of the northernmost settlements.

Hans had never been that far north, nor did he seem to have plans to go there. He had become so fragile in his isolation that just traveling the fifty miles to Uummannaq was a trial for him; he went there only once or twice a year. Education for the children beyond the six-grade village school was going to pose a problem. When I asked if he was planning to move when his children were ready to enter a middle school, he said he didn't know if he would be able to leave, yet he knew something would have to be done.

Arnnannguaq baked bread and I cut up the cucumbers brought from Uummannaq, but only Hans and I ate them. A. didn't care much for vegetables. She preferred raw seal liver to lettuce, avocados, and asparagus, and had never tasted corn on the cob.

Once the Inuit women washed their long hair with urine. Even now, the houses in villages like Illorsuit had no running water. What was meant to be used as a bathtub in Hans's house was filled with boxes of winter clothes. No real bathing went on there. Buckets of water were hauled from the spring in back of the house near where the dogs were tied and were used for washing dishes. Ice hacked from first-year icebergs was melted on the stove for drinking water.

After a very late dinner and a story, the children sprawled on the communal bed. In *Salamina,* Rockwell Kent describes a typical Greenlander's bedroom:

> *From the kitchen you looked onto the bedroom; you looked in because the door stood open. Opened so that the fetid warmth of the kitchen could pass in, and the family fumes pass out. That room was crowded too. There was one big double bed for all the family. Some were in it, some were*

on it, some were sitting around on chamber pots. Ane, the buxom wife, was seated in the midst of it all lending her Holstein breast to an orphan child that they had taken pity on. (Kent, Salamina*)*

In the morning we emptied the slop bucket used by the children for middle-of-the-night peeing. There was an indoor compost toilet located in the corner adjacent to the entryway. No door separated them, so that a visitor's first sight on entering the house might be someone using the bathroom. Life in all aspects was lived communally and without privacy.

Every morning for breakfast, at Hans's urging, I made toast. After breakfast Marie Louisa climbed on the roof to refill a bird feeder and jumped down in one flying leap. I saw her legs pass by the window, then her black hair. Who needs a ladder? she seemed to be saying. On walks she was a natural gymnast, scrambling over boulders and scaling cliffs with complete ease, so at home was she in her skin. She used her eyes to get my attention, to point out curiosities, to question me, to express pleasure at what we discovered as we went along. The fact that she and I could communicate with only a limited mixture of Danish, English, and Greenlandic gave our outings a unique feel. Hilarity combined with an unexpected intensity reigned.

The sun is a star, I told her. It looks like it's moving, rising and setting, but it isn't. We are moving around it as if it were a god. She looked at me quizzically, unable to understand anything except the word for sun. We inspected the low-lying flowers that had just come into bloom. I took out my guidebook. *Gronlands Blomster.* When she pointed to a delicate yellow flower on the ground, I opened to the page with a photograph of the polar pontentil, Arctic cinquefoil. There were red flowers strewn through the rocks and a broad-leafed willow herb. Astonishment! How could flowers on her island be in a book belonging to me? Were there flowers in other places? she wondered.

About trees she knew nothing. Like most Greenlanders she had never seen one, or smelled the vanilla bark of a yellow pine; never sat under the shade of a cottonwood, never climbed a sequoia, never tasted maple syrup freshly tapped, never broken open an acorn from an oak. She grew wide-eyed as I drew pictures of trees in the dirt, then I stood and showed her how tall a tree could be.

Rocks were examined as we ambled, her curiosity unflagging. Volcanic or sedimentary, hard or soft, pushed up from what depths, laid over on which side, compressed at what temperature, lifted to what heights, and how long ago . . .

I pointed to stars, though we couldn't see them. Orion's belt, the Big Dipper, the Pleiades. They were there: could she understand? If only they were visible . . . But we would have to wait for winter. The sky's pale face was moonless, starless, and unchanging.

Village life was quiet. Women with small children visited one another; others worked in the fish factories. Those married to subsistence hunters waited for their men to come home, then the work of flensing the seals and tanning the skins began. There were always skins to be mended, skin garments to be made, dog harnesses to repair, food to be cooked.

As I walked around I noticed that Illorsuit was devoid of teenagers. To go to high school required moving to a larger town, like Uummannaq. There were two vocational schools in southern Greenland towns, but enrolling in a university meant living in Denmark. The only option in a village such as this was to be a hunter or a hunter's wife, or to move away.

Arnnannguaq came from Sondre Upernavik, a village up the coast. She hadn't been to school much and couldn't really read. Sometimes at night when the one television channel came on with a subtitled foreign film, she simply turned off the sound and watched the images. To make money she cleaned two bachelors' houses and when payday came, she spent it on beer. While I was there she stayed away from the booze. Instead, she cleaned a bit and played solitaire. Our hikes didn't interest her. While Marie Louisa and I went out, she stayed home with the young boy, Hendrik.

Hans had taken a full-time job with the Royal Greenland fishery driving the one and only front-end loader. They were rebuilding the dock and Hans delivered pilings from the warehouse to the site. Anyone without a village job was out hunting. At any time of the night or day you could hear a skiff taking off across the fjord. The women waited at home, visiting and watching the children, awaiting the sound and sight of a boat returning.

"Up north," Hans told me, "it is more traditional. The women often go out for long periods of time with the men and in the summer they still hunt in kayaks with harpoons. But down here, we have been colonized by the Danes too long. The old ways get mixed up with the new much faster in west Greenland."

The children and I wandered the length of the island, and the other village children, sensing an adventure, began to follow, sometimes seven or ten of them. We made loops from the easternmost house, where a whale rib was stuck upright in the sand, through the village, to the *butik* (the tiny general store) for candy, along the boardwalk, onto the beach, past Hans's house, all the way to the western tip of the island. There, dark cliffs rose straight up. We climbed them, pressing our faces against the rock, and tilted our heads back: from summer's great blank, the glitter-drizzle of meltwater drained down into our mouths.

It's said that Rockwell Kent's paintings and illustrations stand for the inviolability of the self, the radiance of the natural world, the dignity of creation. I looked out at the vista he had painted so often: the rooftops of village houses sloping down to water's edge, the six-mile-wide fjord filled with white mountains of ice that drifted beneath the immobile black walls of islands on the other side, and the ice cap bulging like a bulb.

In the paintings *Greenland Winter* and *New Fallen Snow,* light from some enormous, unseen source slants in, throwing cartwheeling, triangular shadows on the white ground. The scene looks otherwordly—not the nineteenth-century view of the sublime, but a realist's heaven: bold and bare, with a hard sun and sharp shadows—a bit like Rockwell Kent's face.

Greenland could not provide a colonialist vision of the pastoral. There were no plowed fields, dairy cows, or sheep. This was a lunar plain, skinless, as if one were peering directly at the bare flesh of light.

"Igdlorssuit, July," Kent wrote, "—and not a soul was doing anything. The women were not at their housework—they had none. The men were not hunting—there was nothing to hunt. The children were not at school—it was vacation time. And everyone was out of doors. It was a breathless sunlit afternoon."

After all the American can-do busyness, Kent thrived in this make-do subsistence village. He wrote: "Out of nothing at all, are the good times had in Greenland life; that may be typical of happy living everywhere. . . . Despite the hazards of the hunter's work, the rule is uneventfulness; and people thrive on it. They live in peace, and peace, I think, means happiness. A bitter thought to us Americans!"

The strait had a pulse as did the village, but one that was barely perceptible. Metronomic time—the lawful ticking marked by a swinging pendulum—had no place there. It dictated a puritanical efficiency rather than one driven by weather and pure need. I tried to visualize time's shape but couldn't. Like the ice cap, it was too gargantuan to see.

From my driftwood perch in front of Hans's house, the July sun's hoop dance lengthened into an elliptical arc. Its persistence represented a fanatical loyalty to the season. What lay before me was six miles of glass stopped at the other side by black mountains. The drifting icebergs were like photographic negatives—smaller white mountains passing in front of the black ones as if they had been cut loose, become ghosts, and were floating away.

Kent's palette was made of blended mist and ice, aquamarine and gray. It was milk with the cream skimmed off and all that was left was the watery, blue-veined whiteness of a world without night. Mountains and rocks looked like sea monsters, and hard shadows paved the ice with oblique black sails. There was never any breathing in these paintings, no winds, no storms, as if the brushstroke itself were velocity enough. All the rhythms of village life were contained—the furtive lovemaking in a communal bed, the glide of sled runners over imperfect ice, the incessant dogtrot and huffing. If the still point is movement, then what does movement refer to? Every time Kent made a swipe with his brush, Greenland's bowl of ice was smoothed crevasse-free.

Dead calm and refulgence. Only the fjord vacillated, shaking out ink, pale blue, then shattering into colorless glass. On the water's surface reflections of other mountain islands shimmered and went still, coming into being and shaking into nothingness again. Then the false fronts lay upside down in water and were cut clear through by a floating iceberg.

In the back of my blue notebook, I drew squares on a lined page, wrote in numbers, and X'd off days: days and nights of light. July 3: Hans Egede Day passed. July 10: Rasmussen stopped here today at the beginning of his Fifth Thule Expedition. Now it was Bastille Day. Would my lost luggage arrive? Clean clothes had ceased to be a concern. I no longer cared if everything was lost. Like Kent, I was "shorn of property, stripped of clothes, wandering." I tore out the calendar page and threw it away.

Kent described Greenland time this way: "March days crept up as though in fear of me, each moment trembling as it neared, then halting in its tracks. And having passed, they'd leapt away to lose themselves in the abyss of yesterdays. That first of February was a lifetime ago, a date before my lifetime; tomorrow was a lifetime off."

My head had begun turning with the sun, tropistically. I saw boats, ice, dogs, Hans's lone Danish flag, burn barrels, socks and sealskins drying on the same clothesline. The 3,773-foot-high brown mountain behind the village was a dull shield. Light moved through light and ice opened upon itself into chamber after chamber of blue. Later in the year the sky would draw a different blank: darkness would wash over darkness. Then, in early March, a match would strike: light would be rekindled.

Scientists say that the sun's outer rim is illusory, not a boundary but an ephemeral place where solar gas becomes transparent and solar winds flow ceaselessly. Just beneath, the corona is an engine of million-degree heat that propels the solar wind and its pulsing, dancing, polar plumes outward.

No one danced here, though in Kinte's time there were dances on every occasion. But general activity was constant. We went days with almost no sleep until one morning, when the sun went behind a cloud, everyone was suddenly sleepy and lay down, not getting up again until the sky went bright.

I wondered how deeply our circadian rhythms were affected by continual sunlight. There is no one central clock in organisms—but often many. The eye of the mollusk aplysia and our own eyes have their own circadian cadence. Even single-celled algae waltz to their own beat. Different rhythms can drum within a single organism simultaneously, the leaves and flower petals of one plant adhering to different timetables.

Human biological clocks run on a twenty-five-hour day, not twenty-four, which is why we have an innate tendency to let schedules drift. The arrow of time bolts and drops like a missile gone wild, its contrail visible—spectral, shining, and twisted. In the brightness I slid into new habits, eating four or five meals a day, with dinner at one or two in the morning, then resting between five and nine.

Unbeknown to me, my biological clock is constantly undergoing minor adjustments to the inevitable slide. The twenty-four-hour cycle is the middle C of our biological ensemble, ruling our sense of timekeeping. The cues that make us tick come from light. A specialized group of nerve cells called suprachiasmatic nuclei (SCN), located above the two optic nerves, are linked to the retina of the eye and organize cycles of rest and activity, skin temperature, and secretion of hormones. Sunlight triggers all this. It plies a route from eye to midbrain and winds our clocks.

On the flip side is melatonin, the "darkness hormone," secreted only in the night hours by the pineal gland, part of a light-darkness cycle that causes rhythmic increases in a nocturnally activated enzyme. Melatonin provides vital information about time—day-and-night cycles as well as seasons. Below the Arctic Circle, sugar rises in trees, leaves turn, weasels change fur color from brown to white, and in some fish the dorsal skin becomes lighter at night. States of inactivity and hibernation are controlled by the pineal gland: the more melatonin, the more hours, days, and months of sleep.

I lay on the floor with my eyes wide open. Undoubtedly I was short on melatonin. There was no night in me. I felt lit up, translucent, as utilitarian as a lightbulb. Perhaps the best way to sleep in this season was to stay wide-eyed and stand like a horse. To shut my eyes against light was to go against the rhythm. I imagined my body as tympanic, a composite of clocks, hundreds of ticking mechanisms buried inside my eyes, in cardiac cells, and under my skin, all pointing toward the sun, all beating and oscillating synchronously and keeping me wakeful.

I cupped my ear and listened. All I could hear was the occasional grunt and groan of ice, the slapping of little waves on the black beach, and my own skewed body clock thirsting for night, pulling away from time's obedience like a skiff that had come loose from its long line and drifted to shore. In the fjord, sun-contorted icebergs went soft. Glazed by heat, they rained down turquoise tears.

On one of our walks, Marie Louisa and I stopped to touch the whale rib's curved length. The bone was four inches thick. Whale ribs served as structural beams for Inuit houses at the same time that flying buttresses were being erected in Europe. In 1931, Rockwell Kent had used a narwhal's tusk for a Christmas tree.

I searched the coasts of the surrounding islands and wondered where other villages might have been during the 5,000-year history of habitation here. "Anywhere you see a settlement now, there was probably a village on that site before," said John Pind, a young archeologist I met in the National Museum in Copenhagen. He was in Greenland for the summer mapping archeological sites because most of the northern part of the country was still uncharted. "I study the Thule culture," he told me, "because it was the first time the Inuit met outsiders. Whalers from Scotland and Norway had come, as well as missionaries and explorers. I'm interested especially in cultures in transition."

The Inuit traditionally lived as small groups in long rectangular houses, but were later forced by Danish missionaries to live apart in nuclear families. For the Inuit, to be set apart couple by couple was immoral—a sin against the good of the whole. Several family groups had once lived together in the common house, hunted together, and jointly owned an umiak which the women rowed. The meat was cooked and eaten communally. There were no territorial disputes about who got what and how much. The residents of the house formed the crew of the boats, and the house, the umiak, and the meat were all communal property. But when the families were separated, it became unclear who owned what. There was no longer a crew for the umiak—and no one knew who owned the meat after a hunt. The whole society changed.

By the time Rasmussen and Freuchen passed by Illorsuit at the beginning of the twentieth century, the slope was dotted with small peat-and-stone houses that gave shelter to several generations of single families, though orphaned or excess children were sometimes passed freely between families as they are now. It was easy to see how the socialist ideals of the Danes accorded with Inuit communalism. There is no private land ownership in Greenland. Citizens own their houses but not the land. When they apply for permission to build at the Kommune office, their application is considered: will it block another's view of the harbor, will it cause ecological problems? If so, changes are made. Litigation is almost unknown. There are no fences, no gates, and few locked doors.

Kinte, as they called him, loved children. Salamina's daughters lived with them. Even though families lived as separate units, the doors were always open, visiting was a compulsive activity, and children ranged freely. They'd go anywhere they could get a nibble of *mattak* or have some fun. Kent thrived on village life. As a child he had been willful and rebellious, and later he dodged most social conventions. His claustrophobia drove him to treeless isolation; the view had to be enormous. But once there, he luxuriated in human company, always able to relax in his pleasure with things.

Hans, Arnnannguaq, Hendrik, Marie Louisa, and I walked to the graveyard on the headlands at the entrance to the village. From there the dead could see who came to this place, A. told me. I wandered through gravestones looking for Kinte's friends and found them: Rudolph and Margreta Quist, Abraham Zeeb, Louisa Zeeb, Severin Nielsen, and Henorich, Sophia, and Elisabeth Lange. All except for Salamina, who was buried on the island of Ikerasak near Uummannaq. Kent delighted in his Greenland neighbors, describing one couple as "incorrigibly genuine, a good-natured, old-fashioned, free-and-easy Greenland couple, distinguished in their elevation by their heedlessness."

A trail meandered up the hill from the graves. When I asked where it went, Hans said, "Nowhere." We followed it to the top.

"I've always wanted to go nowhere," I told him.

"You're already there," Hans quipped. With that, he hiked back to the village to his job.

From the top Marie Louisa and I could see down the spine of the island. It was all Arctic desert—unwatered, precipitous peaks that were gray, bare, and dry. Below, the strait's westward current seemed unbidden, infusions of salt slowly mixing with thousand-year-old glacial flour, the tides rolling it all together into a calm geological soup. Beyond the end of the trail, a knife-edged ridge spilled dirt and rock down sharp couloirs. The end was where we started from. But where could we go from there? When I looked at my feet I noticed that our shadows had disappeared.

At night the July sun poured in the window. It was hard to sleep. Hunters took off in their skiffs at odd hours to hunt seals, children played, and the melting icebergs made sounds like someone beating on sheet metal. Turrets of ice collapsed. Sleep came in fits and starts because the body in daylight wanted no rest. Full of energy, there was no place to go. The hours were languorous, sun-drenched, air-chilled. My clothes were foul. Even if I washed them by hand, how would they dry? There was sun, but the air temperature was too cold.

Night, unattainable now, seemed like an opulence, a dusky diamond. In a book I came on the image of a sun buried in the palm of a hand: it was an eye that saw clairvoyantly. We didn't have to be blind to see. Sitting, I felt as though I was rising up; walking the beach was the same as standing still.

Some days Hans and I went by skiff to places where Rockwell Kent had painted. The distances were deceiving, since the air was so clear and there were no visual clues as to how close or far away the mountains were. Sometimes he cut the engine in the middle of the fjord and we drifted between city-states of icebergs that were pocked, striped, stretched, glassed, fringed, split, steepled, bent, gull-splattered, till-frosted, toothed, triangulated. Some had broken off from glaciers whose edge had deformed and split open into crevasses; fluttering walls of lace.

Big icebergs can weigh as much as ten million tons—but these had already been water-drenched and molested by sun; we were seeing only crumbled fibulas and broken clavicles. I felt small, lost and happy. If we followed the tide and kept going, we would be caught by a current that moved us south toward what Leif Eriksson called Vinland—Labrador.

Instead, we went ashore on Karrat Island, Kent's favorite camping place. It was a small island with a ragged, grassy edge—plenty of places to get off the ice or out of the water and set up an easel. His painting *The Artist in Greenland* gives a view downslope over Karrat's beach to the other side of the fjord. At shoreline the sides of a white tent are secured by rocks and the artist himself is walking by, carrying an unfinished canvas. In this picture Kent translated silence into a flat plain. No tidal rising and falling registered: the fjord is only mirror, a narcissist's looking glass, a ground for double images of mountains where summer fog pillows between peaks, and the painter, in self-portrait, is a small figure standing on copper-colored tundra that has oxidized to verdigris.

While painting there he wrote: "Sunlight to see by, ice to travel on, and work to do. The work was painting. It was for that that I had come to Greenland; by that and maybe for that, that I lived and found it almost good most anywhere, alone."

Greenland Winter, painted from his house in Illorsuit, is a view over the top of the village toward the mountains on the other side of the strait rising in spring light. The brushwork is fine and flawless, giving a sense of illumined, unending space. Ice paves the fjord and the icebergs are stuck, unmoving, like shark's teeth casting long shadows. In the foreground are two Inuit houses, a drying rack hung with fish, and villagers walking home. The forms are massive, undulating, graceful. Of the Arctic hues, Kent wrote: "Blue sky, white world, and the golden light of the sun to tune the whiteness to sun-illumined blue."

Another day Marie Louisa and I followed the ravens' tracks around the side of the mountain, dammed up a stream, and took a cold bath. I had come from a great plain of money—America—where greed supplants regeneration, litigation supplants intimacy, and envy supplants aspiration. We hide the beautiful desolation of our landscapes with ostentatious façades and exotic species of plants that require more water than we have. The actual contours of our topography—inward and outward—are hidden. But here, from my niche in the amphitheater wall, I looked out on a barren coast that was all richness, where everything was revealed, everything was measured in immensities and scintillas.

Walking, I imagined that cells roamed freely here, if they could do such a thing. That's how much space there was. The uninhabited islands across the fjord were not coveted by anyone. They were mine to explore, camp on, hunt from—or anyone's. And whatever happened there, it would, at some later date, be taken away by the advance of a glacier.

The life is simple; the language, on the other hand, is complex. Greenlandic can be understood all the way across the polar north and is polysynthetic. That is, words are created from a stem with one or many—often many more—modifying syllables and an ending. Verbs have thirty-four to sixty-eight endings, and stem words can have any of 420 affixes used freely. The words are aggregates and are impossibly long.

A shoulder of ice collapsed into the bay. I fooled with the spelling of "isolation," changing it to "iceolation." The latitude here—72 degrees north—began to represent a measurement of solitude. *Imaqa*. Or maybe not, because I was not lonely at all. The strait was liquid night and icebergs were continents drifting, pieces of light that stirred me. Sun's intoxicant made my mind unfurl.

Marie Louisa and I continued to take walks, timidly at first, then more and more enthusiastically. She was small for her age but physically fearless. With her fishing pole—a stick and a string and a hook—she caught a fish that resembled a horny toad, held it lovingly in her hand for me to see, then threw it back—catch-and-release in Illorsuit Fjord. Other times she wandered around on the beach prodding rocks in the black sand. The sun at midnight was a halo on her head.

Even at the time of day most people called dawn, when a mist gathered and passed behind the icebergs like an Arctic fox's thick tail, there was nothing in the air out of which to make rain; at the time people called night, when it was so cold we could see our breath, there was nothing in the bright air to make snow. Sun reigned, hot and cold. Water burned. Sun scorched ice, carving it into beads; sun blasted rock, scarring it deep with its uninvited brilliancies.

Rockwell Kent wrote:

Painting; painting incessantly. Pursuing beauty in bewilderment at its profusion, greedy to get in one short year the whole of what might thrill a man a lifetime. As well might one by spinning a kaleidoscope hope to exhaust its permutations in one day. I mention art to tell how time was filled, not to enlarge on it. Art talk; that's the true perversion of our faculties. We travelled the fjords, camped where it pleased us most, and worked. (Kent, Salamina, p. 315)

My breathing changed. It came in long slow pants, cougarlike. The sun's pulsing orbit, a dilapidated halo, had been made elastic by its own fatigue. Twenty-four hours a day it torched around and around as if to say, all of life is one slow-burning day. In the late evening an iceberg tipped over, sending shock waves toward the house. The villagers emerged from their houses and children ran down to watch. Skiffs bobbed and spun sideways as waves tumbled in. "Surf's up!" I yelled, but no one understood. When the disturbance subsided, Kristian ventured out alone in his skiff. The light at that time of night, as the sun turned the corner from the west to the northern part of the sky, cast a gold dash down the length of the fjord—a path that Kristian followed.

"In Greenland one discovers, 'as though for the first time,' what beauty is," Rockwell Kent wrote. "God must forgive me that I tried to paint it. I did incessantly. I would attach a large canvas to the stanchions of my sledge as upon an easel; I'd hang my bag of paints and brushes from the crossbar, lay my palette on the sledge. I'd catch my dogs, and harness them. And then, after the mad stampede downhill and over the shore ice which was inescapable prelude to the trip, I'd recline upon my reindeer skin with the indolence of a sultan and drive off to my rendezvous."

All afternoon Marie Louisa bounded over boulders, up scree slopes, jumping thin streams of water. Her natural grace and curiosity astonished me. I made curried seal and rice for dinner and she ate heartily, never complaining. When I showed her photographs of African animals and demonstrated (comically) how they traveled across the savannah, she leaped like a gazelle around the living room.

She drew pictures. When thinking about the limited way our eyes work, the foveal aperture that lets so little in compared to our Neanderthal ancestors, I wondered how big our mind's eyes were, where our "blindsight" led us, the way the mind still sees when there is nothing before its eyes. Marie Louisa drew a whale, a house, an iceberg, and the sun.

The next day Hans, Marie Louisa, and I buzzed across the fjord in the skiff headed again for Karrat Island. We'd borrowed a tent, some sleeping bags, and an old Primus stove, plus dehydrated food that I'd brought from America. We would find camp at one of Kent's old haunts, a place where a stream oozed by and the view took in the entire end of the fjord. Near Karrat, a wind pushed brash ice against the northern beaches and jostled us sideways. Then the outgoing tide broke the ice loose and cleared the way.

From Illorsuit Strait we glided up a long tributary—Kangerlussuaq Strait. A glacier calved thunderously and the grassy meadow at the bottom, where Kent's tent might have been pitched, was a foot deep in meltwater. We climbed to a place farther up the slope. The tent was staked and sleeping bags were thrown inside while we went hiking. Karrat Island is an eyelash of rock at the mouth of a fjord with alternating fingers of land and ice streams on either side. The mountains all around each bore its own set of high lakes and glaciers. Above everything the inland ice gleamed.

"I am a colossal egoist. . . . I am not going to do any fool, little thing. . . . I am . . . reaching to the stars. . . . I don't want petty self-expression, I want the elemental, infinite thing. I want to paint the rhythm of eternity," Kent wrote.

Up and up we climbed. The fringes were green, the walls of rock were black, and knuckling glaciers poured meltwater down. Light touched the plank-backed mountains iced with last winter's snow, which covered glaciers from some other millennium. A wind-spun cloud was a winding stair that climbed to the top of Karrat's sharp peak. We came to wide meadows and stepladders of tiny lakes. There was enough soil in there for wildflowers—Arctic cinquefoil, saxifrage, beach pea, broadleafed willow, harebells, and, unbelievably, clumps of alpine fescue, the most beautiful grass in the world. Alpine vegetation at sea level, for God's sake! And the sun-glazed sheen of water dribbling over broad hips of granite.

Careening down the island's mountain, we splashed through pools of water and slid on overhanging gardens of moss, lifting our boot heels so as not to hurt the plants. As in all alpine plant communities, where there are mosses, there are also lichens, I told Marie Louisa. Mosses have chlorophyll in their cells, but their spores are contained in small oval capsules teetering on top of wiry stalks. Lichens are two plants that look like one: a fungus and a green alga. The fungus provides the minerals needed and the alga synthesizes food for the fungus. As one Arctic botanist put it: "A lichen is a fungus that grows its vegetables inside itself."

Unlike in most ways, both plants lack roots. They simply absorb water when it falls on them as rain, snow, or dew, and when the water dries up, they go into a state of dormancy. This is, after all, a polar desert. I stopped to look at disks of black lichen lift in the breeze. They looked like paper medallions—some kind of ancient money gone to ash: I walked across the only millions I had.

We climbed high onto a lip of ice and saw where, like a flap, it was joined to the ice cap that rose even higher, then turned and glissaded downhill. Water leaked from the edge of the white-knuckled glacier and runneled in glistening streams under our feet. We ran against a wind so hard it almost pushed us backward. Marie Louisa laughed as she fought her way down. At the bottom there was no tent. It had all blown away.

One day an old man, Karl Ottosen, sat on the steps of the dance house Rockwell Kent had built and smoked a cigar. A plaque with Kent's distinctive design was still nailed above the door. Ottosen said he didn't remember an American by the name of Kent. Then I asked if he had known "Kinte" and his eyes brightened.

"Yes, I remember him well. I was ten years old and I went with him on some of his trips. He'd pack up his brushes and canvases and take the dogs and go painting. He used the village of Nuugaatsiaq for a base; he loved the little island of Karrat, just up there." Karl nodded to the northwest. When I asked what had become of Salamina, he couldn't remember.

Karl had grown up to become the village kayak and umiak maker. By the 1930s kayaks were made from wood brought in from Denmark. He carved narrow ribs, bent them into place, then covered the shell with four overlapping sealskins sewn twice. The string was made from narwhal ligaments—several strands twisted together—and the seams were made from skin with some fat left on so the water wouldn't seep through. Umiaks used twenty-four skins, he said, and were made the same way. The paddles were carved from wood—often driftwood—with a bone tip smoothed so finely that a seal couldn't hear it dip into the water; the sandpaper was made of shark skin. Karl also made the harpoons with which he killed the seals, proving the Inuit adage that the hunter, the tools, and the animals must be one.

Karl and his wife made their own clothing for hunting. "I wore a caribou anorak with a skirt sewn with the sealskin string we used for the boats. Also, dogskin trousers and kamiks—boots—worn with sealskin socks. When the colder weather came, I changed to a reindeer anorak—it's warmer—and my cap was made from a reindeer's ear. I made a hole in the ear as a vent so I wouldn't sweat. My gloves were sealskin and in the coldest weather, I wore polar bear pants which I had made in Upernavik. In this way I could travel in any weather and not feel cold. The same for my wife. Often she followed me on her dogsled and I'd go back and ask if she was cold and she'd always say, 'I'm just as warm as when I started.'

"I had ten or fourteen dogs, but ten would do. I always raised my own dogs and they were thought to be some of the best in the village. That's because they are the same as humans. They had to be clever, smart, and strong. I looked for the same qualities in a dog as I did in a woman or man. When I weaned the puppies I gave them the best food so they would grow big, but not too much to make them fat. They were never mean. I didn't need that. They didn't bite. They worked for me because they wanted to."

Karl told us about the winter trip he made by dogsled from Illorsuit to Thule. "I left in February and came back in May. In Melville Bay we slept on our sleds. The farther north we went, the flatter it became. Up by Thule there were no mountains at all. I felt scared. There was something wrong with the land there."

He paused as he looked up the long fjord. "Now I have no sleds and my wife is dead," he said, puffing on his cheap cigar. And that was that. He had no more stories.

On the way back to the house, Hans and I visited Ann Hansen. Born in 1909 in Illorsuit, she was one of eight women who rowed an umiak during reindeer-hunting season. She was short and wide with thick arms—

what used to be her rowing muscles, she told me. Long hairs grew from her chin and she had sparkling blue eyes.

"We went all the way down to Kangerlussuaq to get the reindeer. It took several days to row there and we stayed in camps all along the way. There were always six or eight of us, always women. The men were in their kayaks but the big boats were used for carrying the meat back. Sometimes we rowed to these islands just north of Illorsuit to collect eggs and hunt birds. The rowing was hard, day after day. We were very strong. But it was the best time of the year to live in the camps and get ready for winter.

"In the winter, the men went out on their sleds to the west side of the island, where it was better for getting whales. We waited at home. I didn't like that as much. There was a man here who played the fiddle and we had dances with his music in the dance house that Rockwell Kent built. That was Karl Ottosen. I can still hear his music now."

As she spoke a thick fog came in and lay across the fjord, clasping even the pointed and tumbling tops of icebergs. Twelve ravens browsed on the little plain at the bottom of the mountain. I parted ways with Hans and walked up the mountain behind the village, where I found a tiny waterfall. The water came from an unseen source and squirted out from the middle of a barren, chocolate-brown cliff. I quickly undressed, splashed myself, brushed my teeth, and, shivering, put on the same filthy clothes.

Halfway down I lay in the sun. It had begun to shine through the threads of fog. The water was placid. I dreamed the sky was a palm frond made of suns waving over our heads. Sun was a flood, but, as in all floods, we were swept this way and that, lost. It was all brightness, all blindness, all chaos, reminding me of how deaf and dumb we were to the clear nature of things. The fjord water was black;. I looked into its ebonied darkness. The sun was the world's lamp; earth moved its giant forehead toward and away from it, awaking in light, sleeping in shadow. In the *Denko-roku* (Transmissions of the Lamp), a fourteenth-century teacher wrote:

> *The water is clear all the way down.*
> *Nothing ever polished it.*
> *That is the way it is.*

> Merwin, Sun at Midnight, *p. xxvi*

Back at the house everybody seemed on edge: Hans aloof, Arnnannguaq bored, Nikolai sober but melancholy, smoking a pipe. Then I realized it was probably because nobody had slept enough. When the fog came in we all went to bed; the lowered light level made our bodies think it was dusk. Later, Hans and I had midnight tea and cookies. "We have only had electricity [generated by a huge diesel generating plant] since 1984, and a phone for one year. I have the only international phone and fax machine in the village." He smiled. "I'm the liaison to the outside world." He laughed. "If only they could see me."

Culture is always refashioning itself. In this village at the end of the twentieth century, the hunters fixed new things in old ways, taking what they needed from modern technology and using it to maintain the old ways with better methods. "One old man in the village inherited an outboard motor for his skiff," Hans told me. "It was very old and didn't work and when he asked me to order new parts, the company said they didn't make them anymore. So the old man made the part he needed from a reindeer antler. And the engine still works!

"Another hunter, coming home alone one winter from a long hunting trip, found that his sled runner had cracked and he could go no farther. So he shot a seal, rolled the skin, and tied it to the side of the sled as a runner. It took him a little longer to get home, but he made it. Otherwise he would have frozen to death or starved. That's how we do it here."

Another week went by and I bathed in what was left of the stream. In summer, everything is a permutation of light, and light is electromagnetic radiation, only a small part of which is perceptible to the human eye. Marie Louisa and I sat on the rocky slope and tried to exercise our eyes: we wanted to see what we couldn't see: the moon and stars in daylight.

Later we went down to the house to find five Danish geologists in the living room. They had arrived by boat and stopped in to say hello. The mood in the house lifted. They were scouring the northwest coast for geological clues, up and down every fjord. We gave them coffee and cookies and they explained the local geology to us: the rock wall behind the village is basalt resting on a foot of sandstone. The beds of rock are laid horizontally, sometimes as thick as one hundred feet, sometimes dwindling to a thin stripe. These are divided by sheets of slate, or mudstone, reddish in color, and in some places hardened and massive and rising straight up, then sinking into curving slopes at the bottom.

After they left, Marie Louisa and I climbed a three-layered rock to the top of the waterfall where it drove straight into the slope and disappeared, only to spew out a few hundred feet below. It was earth's needlework: a stream of water looping in and out of a chocolate-brown cliff. Was that the way a mountain strung together its stories?

Later Arnnannguaq joined us and we made our daily pass at the *butik,* open only a few hours a day. We bought a sack of onions and a bouquet of red silk tulips. A shipment of tired-looking Danish vegetables had arrived and the prices reflected the effort it took to get them there. The choices were a three-dollar zucchini or a five-dollar head of lettuce, the leaves limp and translucent because it had frozen and thawed.

Clouds lowered. Now only the foot of the mountain across the fjord showed and brash ice rammed its soles. Above, the glaciers were moving in patterns of ablation and accumulation, though neither advance nor retreat could be immediately perceived. Calf ice at the base of a distant glacier was sunlit, and closer to shore an iceberg had come apart, the internal organs and inner lakes all turquoise bodies that belonged to another order of things.

In the late afternoon I went to take my daily bath, only to find that the stream had frozen. From midslope I noticed that Nikolai's and Kristian's blue fishing boat was gone. How had I missed hearing them leave? The halibut catch had been so robust that the processing plant in Uummannaq couldn't accommodate all the fish, and now fishermen like Kristian and Nikolai had to take their catch north to Upernavik.

The bay looked empty. Where the boat had been anchored, icebergs had moved in—white continents, new worlds revolving by. I imagined I was the geographer forced to redraw the map. Just as I finished one chart, the ice rearranged itself and I had to start again.

Ice floated north out of Illorsuit Strait with the outgoing tide, finally dumping into Baffin Bay. Then it sluiced down between Greenland and Baffin Island. It was captured by the Labrador Current and swept south along the coasts of Labrador and Newfoundland to the Grand Banks, and was finally cast out into the shipping lanes of the western North Atlantic.

An iceberg is an unstable mass, big, angular, bulky, sometimes as big as a football field, and capable of generating its own foggy weather. Its tongues of subsurface ice are sharp feet that work like levers, upending anything that gets in their way. With eight-ninths of its immensity

hidden beneath water, it drags through polar shelves of pack ice, often moved by deeper, unseen currents, the pack ice pushing one way and towering ice mountains pushing in the opposite direction, warped and wrapped in veils of mist.

Ice shelves break from the coast of Ellesmere Island and drift away. These ice islands stay intact for years and have been used as moving platforms by scientific research stations, marooned polar bears, and Inuit hunters. On the berg's thin topside are patches of soil and gravel where a few blades of grass sometimes grow.

During the Hall Expedition in 1871–1872, meant to find Sir John Franklin and his crew, it was thought that the expedition ship, the *Polaris,* was about to be crushed by ice, so the crew began unloading important supplies and a lifeboat. During the process, twelve men, two of them Inuit with their wives and children, found themselves drifting on a loose floe. It was October. From 79° 35′ north, they drifted south in the Greenland Current, catching seals on the way and living quite comfortably. Seals provide vitamin C as well as protein, so no one eating the Eskimo diet suffered scurvy. The fat was used for light and fire.

By April they found themselves off the shore of Labrador, but the coming of spring made their journey more dangerous: the pack ice began to break up in stormy seas and the floe grew smaller and smaller. A child had been born and thrived. On April 30 the travelers were picked up in perfect condition. The party had been drifting for 193 days and had covered 1,300 miles.

The strait was a piece of blue cord with a bite taken out. It was so cold, even in full sun, that my hands and feet grew numb. I paced up and down the curved beach as Rockwell Kent once did waiting for a letter from his wife. I longed for word from home, anything to reconnect me, though I was expecting no mail. One fax arrived, but it bore no news. The children used the paper to draw on. Over the radio we heard that an American jetliner had exploded in midair on the way to Paris from New York. But Hans couldn't make out which airline or why.

Sun's intoxicant filled me like helium. It had no odor, nor could I touch the exact place where it leaked in. Its glaze was limpid, translucent, pure porcelain. If I shoved my hands into sunlight—not a landscape I could relish, but an eye-aching gascape—gold leaf with no velocity covered my hands.

Recent images sent from *Soho*'s sun-orbiting observatory showed the sun's gascape to be both violent and musical. Oscillations from the depths of the sun strike the surface gases, causing them to lift and fall like curtains and sound out ten million separate notes, none of which we can hear because they are trapped inside the sun, unable to push through the vacuum of space. Meanwhile, the sun's magnetism pirouettes, pushed by a rotational shear that moves faster at the equator than at its poles, as well as by convectional flow velocities, each one independent of the other and moving at one kilometer per second.

The night was windless, the fjord was glass. Mountains floated, were water-made. The sun's wide halo in July made an elliptical orbit that widened every day. Clouds blew in from the south and hovered over a glacier's crammed nursery of calf ice, turning icebergs into black shields that rose from a darkening mirror.

A front pushed through. I longed to be set adrift.

When Rockwell Kent got restless he took off on his dogsled or skiff, or else changed wives, girlfriends, or houses. He'd build a shack in Maine, then take off sailing to Greenland; or fix up a southern Vermont farmhouse and move to New York City; or go on sabbatical to Alaska or Tierra del Fuego. Restlessness was the excuse he used for being a ladies' man and a vagabond, but it also freshened his eye, opening it to more light.

Standing by the window in the middle of the night I felt someone touch my shoulder and turned: no one. Ghost or mouse? But there were no mice here. I kept still and waited. Nothing. An iceberg groaned, its innards collapsing. Later in the night, in full sun, Kristian came home with a seal.

Near the end of his life Kent settled down with his third wife on an Adirondack farm in New York. On a spring night in 1969 they were sitting in the living room reading when a thunderstorm erupted. Lightning struck a transformer; a blue ball of fire rolled into the house, setting it on fire. All Kent's canvases and woodcuts, books and notes, and collections from the Arctic and South America were burned to cinders.

Later, while he was away on a trip, his friends and neighbors rebuilt his house. But he was eighty-seven, and a few years later he announced to Sally one evening that he was very tired. He leaned over to pick up what he thought were flowers on the rug, and collapsed. He died shortly after.

In the middle of the night I sat up with a jolt, then scrambled over to the window and kneeled there as if at an altar. I wanted to talk to this ghost, whoever it was. I waited, but nothing stirred. Before my time and Hans's, and Kent's, people on this island lived in parallel worlds and knew that reality is at least as permeable as ice, pierced through as it is with emptiness. I looked out: the Arctic sun was a note held; under it, walls gave way to unobstructed vision.

That night I asked Stephen Hawking's unanswerable question: Is it possible to remember the future? Light penetrated my eyelids and landscape slipped from sight in the curvature of space-time; over the falls in a barrel it went. To talk about a future seemed wrongheaded, calling up the old insistence on linear time, and so did the Christian fantasy that we are living out some sacred tragedy of sinful lives from which we must seek redemption.

Time proceeds without measurement; there is no original sin, only a confluence of waters mixing, separating, and mixing again. $I = E$. Instant equals Eternity. Perhaps it is possible to remember where we have not yet been.

Across the fjord the white ends of glaciers tongued the flattened rubble they had uprooted. Sun disappeared behind more clouds. Was there a storm brewing? Sandwiched between high cliffs, I couldn't see the horizon's horizon, only what the mountains wanted me to see.

I read "Talk of the Town" in an old *New Yorker* magazine found curled in my rucksack. The urbane conversation brought me back to some temporarily lost world—a world I was usually content to live without. But in Illorsuit, there was not much talk and no town at all, so I was happy for what seemed like "local gossip." How many weeks of no conversation did it take for verbal agility to slip? In place of verbiage, I laid ice and rock on my tongue and swallowed vistas more beautiful than I could bear.

Near midnight I heard a diesel engine put-putting into the bay. From the window I saw Nikolai at the helm, weaving through house-sized chunks of ice. His red coveralls were an ember from an old fire, still glowing.

In the store I bought a new shipment of Danish cheese and rye flatbread and a five-dollar box of California raisins to eat on our walks. Nikolai was drunk and had been drunk for three days. He was sitting on a stack of pallets by the warehouse, smoking his pipe. I felt him watching me as I passed. The collar and cuffs of his white sweater were black with grime; his pooling turquoise eyes were red. I heard him say something to Arnnannguaq, who looked at me and laughed. When Hans came home that evening he translated: Nikolai had asked to marry me.

For the rest of the week I lived in what must have sounded like silence, but wasn't. My sign language with Marie Louisa had become extravagantly efficient. I felt ardently attached to her, too much so, and she to me. I hardly did anything and she knew what I meant; I barely remembered that we didn't share a common language. We weren't patient enough to fuss with dictionaries. We had things to do, like walk, look under rocks for bugs, pick flowers, look for ravens, and let the feathery waterfall douse our skin.

We were being carried by the vital force of Sila. Of that I was sure, and Nuna—earth—registered our soft tracks. The old angakok's secret words might have been spoken if we had known them, the way hunters used to speak to the animals they pursued or sing to the ones they killed. In the old days a woman walking the barren slopes of Ubekendt Ejland might have been snatched up by a bear to be his wife, abducted by a dwarf, or impregnated by a dog.

A culture can be anything it wants to be; it is always and only an aspect of memory and imagination. But as we approached the end of this millennium, we found our minds had narrowed. As the shaman said to Rasmussen, we lived brokenly and didn't know how to be.

How could I say these things to Marie Louisa? I asked Hans to tell her that she should listen when she was walking or going by dogsled in the winter, she should try to learn those secret words and songs. Then she could teach them to me.

The wind picked up and I heard something slapping the side of the house. Marie Louisa and I went out to look. The sound was made by thongs cut from seal guts used to lash sleds together and repair dog harnesses. They hung alongside the nylon straps bought in the store. Soon it would be winter. By November 14 in Illorsuit, the fjord would be ice and the sky completely lightless.

I looked at the clock. Still 12:20. On Ubekendt Ejland time was told by ice and light, not seconds and hours. Time was not some fenced pasture we could mow or second hands we could watch. To be moving was to be still and to be still was to dance for the man who played a fiddle sixty years ago. That was in the era before time had begun, when people spoke to animals and animals to people, and angakoks flew under the ice. It was the time before darkness ended, before daylight had come and decided to stay. Now that light wouldn't go.

Marie Louisa burst into the house. She had been playing alone on the beach, had stripped and gone swimming in the 42-degree Arctic water. Now she shivered on the bench in the kitchen. Her mother did nothing but throw a comforter over her, but it wasn't enough—she began crying. I touched her feet, arms, and cheeks: she was ice-cold and turning blue, and slurring her words. She was hypothermic. I found dry clothes, socks, a wool cap, and dressed her, then wrapped two blankets around her, tucking them in like a sleeping bag. I held a mug of hot water with sugar to her lips, then soup, a candy bar, and herb tea. The tears stopped and laughter began. She looked up: two snow buntings came to the skylight to eat the muesli she had left there.

It was time to leave the island. I waited for the Royal Greenland fishing boat whose crew said they would pick me up at the end of the summer on their way home to Uummannaq. The boat would be coming from the northwest, the direction of Karrat—Kinte's favorite island—and so it became a day of waiting. Marie Louisa and I sat on the beach. We drew figures in black sand. She ran back to the house for her fishing pole and net. While I watched, she caught two tiny, ugly fish—aquatic horned toads.

We collected rocks. I picked one up and gave it to her; in turn, she gave one to me. Rock for rock we made our way down the long half-moon arc of the beach toward the dock, then back again. At seven in the evening the boat finally appeared.

Still in the same clothes in which I had arrived at the beginning of July, I hitched my book-filled rucksack on my back, walked the narrow strip of beach I now knew so well, and headed for the dock. Marie Louisa started screaming. I turned and hugged her, telling her that I would be back, but she couldn't understand, nor did she want to. Hans came from the village and, on seeing her state, carried her to the skiff. I followed. Instead of walking, we sped to the waiting boat.

It was a thirty-five-foot cabin cruiser with six bunks, a kitchen, and a head. Four young Greenlanders helped me aboard. Hans and Marie Louisa handed up my rucksack from the skiff. Behind them, near the village storehouse, sitting on pallets, I saw Nikolai, wearing his newly washed white sweater under bright red overalls. He had been watching us.

The young captain revved the engine as I took one last look at the village, trying to memorize every house, every dog, every person. Had I looked hard enough in all that light? Had I been sun-blind? Had I seen anything of what had been revealed?

The day Rockwell Kent left the island he wrote:

It was raining the next morning. Many and sad were the leavetakings. People hung about the house to help us move our goods on board. At last, at one, we were at the shore to sail. We shook the hand of every man, woman, and child. Rudolph and Abraham came aboard with us. We were all crying. On the wharf the people began to sing a hymn; it was the last touch of beauty to make our sadness complete. A crowd followed along the shore as the Naja sailed away, along the shore and up onto the headland, waving their hands and handkerchiefs, and firing guns. Farewell Idglorssuit—as though to life. (Kent, Greenland Journal, p. 300)

That was 1932. Kent went home to New England and returned in June 1934 with his son Gordon. Salamina had waited for him; on his arrival she moved in and resumed her domestic place in his life. Later, it's said that she had his child. (Salamina's daughter lives on Ikerasak and a grandson, Jacob, lives in Uummannaq.)

The boat moved away from the dock. I waved to Hans. I waved to Nikolai, who laughed, then looked away—uninterestedly, cynically, or sad, I couldn't tell which. Marie Louisa was crouched in the prow of the skiff crying. "I'll be back soon," I kept saying, then remembered the unmoving clock in their kitchen. For a child, there is no past or future. I was either here or gone. There was no hope in between.

As the boat pulled slowly away, Hans and Marie Louisa followed us out into the fjord. It was a cool evening. No wind. It had not rained once since I'd been there—just the ever-present sun blasting the water white. Up on the headland I saw the graves of those who had gone before. All of Rockwell Kent's friends were buried there, and in the future perhaps Hans, Kristian, and Nikolai would be too. From their high perch they could see who came, who went, who was allowed to return. Would I be one of them?

Hans's skiff drew close and Marie Louisa stood up like a bowsprit, raven hair flying, laughing and waving, and wiping away tears. As we gained speed, so did they, then we began to pull away, out into jet-black water. For a long time I stood in the stern looking back at her, waving as if there really was an end to time and to ice and to light. One last glimpse of the dock before we went around the bend: Marie Louisa growing smaller; Nikolai lifting his head, looking in my direction, walking away; Hans waving. Then they were out of sight.

All objects are created in the service of light. They are the obstructions on which light bumps itself into a shaped existence: black-headed seals pop up, then disappear; a duck dives; an iceberg topples. Does ice exist because there is light, or is it the other way around? I'd been there so long I couldn't remember. Now I was leaving. It was more like dying, having to go back to a place where there is night.

The trip to Uummannaq from Illorsuit is fifty miles. Out in the middle of the fjord, the captain backed off on the power and we inched along. Barely moving on unmoving water, they hunted seals and seabirds for seven hours. Three of the men stood on the foredeck holding rifles, scanning the water. Straight ahead five seals broke the surface. The men fired and in the next second everything moved fast. Guns were dropped, long-handled hooks were picked up, the boat lurched forward toward the dead animals. It was the time of year when seals are thin and unbuoyant; if shot, retrieval is almost impossible. We came alongside one dead seal just as it sank. The men's hooks went down, but too late: the seal was gone.

All speed stopped. We resumed our slow-motion drifting. Below, in the galley, the young men snacked on raw seal liver. A duck—a *lomvie*—was shot, netted, its neck twisted, and dropped into the hold, then another and another. To starboard was the long flank of Unknown Island, like the flank of a fifty-mile-long whale. On the port side cliffs and rocky peninsulas towered. I looked up the long arms of Inukaqsiak and Kangerlussuaq fjords. Narrow and winding, they ended in a cecum—a blind gut of ice.

Above, the late summer sun's circular orbit had grown almost too wide for the sky, but still it shone. The foot of the mountain was incarnadine, and the pocked, split, derelict face of the ice cap was gold. Another seal was shot and lost, another burst of speed surged and dwindled. We looked like soldiers or pirates scanning the banks for the enemy on a river, but those men were only hunting for food.

In Uummannaq I bathed for the first time in a month. The next morning, still dressed in filthy jeans, I heard a knock on the door. A man who worked at the harbor threw my lost dufflebag inside. He couldn't say when it got here or where it had been. I didn't care. I put on clean clothes.

The helicopter took me south. In Ilulissat Elisabeth and I went dancing. The disco was crowded and smoky and all her friends were there. A handsome man named H. sat with us. Part Danish, part Inuit, he had the build of an athlete, short-cropped hair, and a starched cotton shirt unbuttoned halfway down his chest. His dancing was exuberant, with the vertical elevation of a Mikhail Baryshnikov. "He's one of my psychiatric patients. Don't worry, he's well medicated—just don't say anything that will upset him. If he wants to dance with you, dance," Elisabeth said matter-of-factly. And so we danced.

Home at two, all sweaty. My plane left at six. On the way to the airport I stopped by the bakery where H., my dancing partner, worked and bought a loaf of his muesli bread. It was the best I had ever tasted.

Black summer nights lay before me like millstones and I wanted none of it. Marie Louisa's tears rained down in me, as did the dead seals left to sink, the wringing of the ducks' necks like the winding of a clock. Why did time have to begin again? In Illorsuit, Hans's kitchen clock was still unmoving. Now I returned to a shuttered world of black and white, a land of paradox. Soon the dark-faced cliffs here would go white with snow and the icebergs would no longer be silhouettes sailing by, but white mountains sprouting in ice, and the summer sun would dissolve to black.

By the end of the first day of traveling I had encountered trees, heat, and night. A boat had come for me, then a helicopter, then a twin-engine plane, then a small jet, then a larger one. I flew into the universe remembering the future which is nothing but light, remembering the past which is all light, breathing in the present which seems to run on linear time but doesn't. Six months earlier, after spending part of a winter in Greenland, I'd crouched on the floor of the bathroom with a migraine on my first exposure to daylight; now, I reeled into despair as night came on. The smell of grass growing and the humidity of human bodies made me nauseous.

Where I'd been, there were no roads, there was no path, and narrative was a meandering cloud that gathered suddenly over the fjord and lay like hair in the sky swishing this way and that, becoming one thing, then another. So that the traditional story of Arnattartqoq's wandering spirit becoming a seal, then a fox, then a bear, then a seal again could also be about a man or a woman, you or me. Above all that, the ice cap, a seventeen-hundred-mile-long diamond, gave simultaneous, bloodless birth down every glacial canal, its nurseries crammed with calf ice that glistened all summer. "Is the world flat?" Marie Louisa had asked. They say it is, but I'm not always so sure, I told her. From the island's rocky fringe we watched the world melt under a sun whose halo had stretched into an ellipse and would soon fall over the edge of what we know.

We go; beauty stays. That's what Joseph Brodsky wrote about his beloved city Venice. Arctic beauty resides in its gestures of transience. Up here, planes of light and darkness are swords that cut away illusions of permanence, they are the *feuilles mortes* on which we pen our desperate message-in-a-bottle: words of rapture and longing for what we know will disappear.

One more Greenlandic word: *qarrtsiluni.* It refers to acts of creation, to the creative mind at work, but translates literally as "waiting for something to burst." A final look as the plane lifted away from Greenland: pancake ice all shattered and islands giving way to more islands—stepping stones to the central mountain of ice as if it were a new sun. My pens and paper are arrows all bent and time is the fuel buried deep inside that propels us toward our much-anticipated extinction.

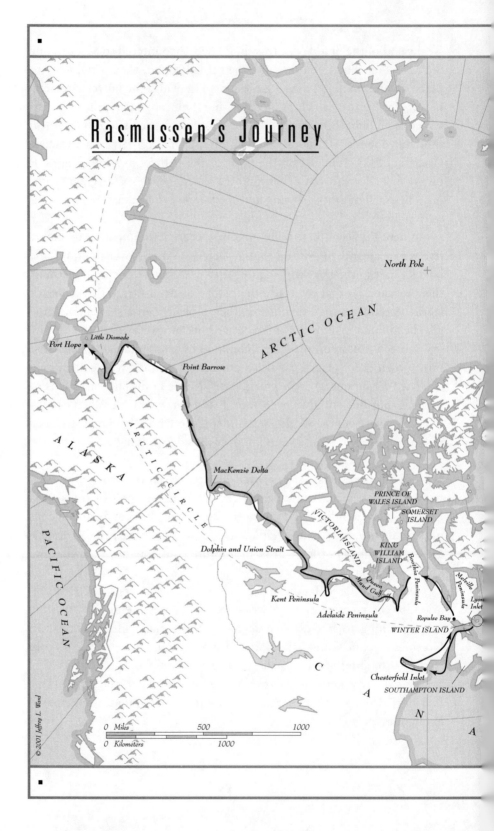

Rasmussen's Journey

North Pole

ARCTIC OCEAN

Little Diomede
Port Hope
Point Barrow

ALASKA

ARCTIC CIRCLE

MacKenzie Delta

PRINCE OF
WALES ISLAND

SOMERSET
ISLAND

VICTORIA ISLAND

KING
WILLIAM
ISLAND

Boothia Peninsula

Melville
Peninsula

PACIFIC OCEAN

Dolphin and Union Strait

Queen
Maud Gulf

Lyon
Inlet

Kent Peninsula

Adelaide Peninsula

Repulse Bay

WINTER ISLAND

C

Chesterfield Inlet

SOUTHAMPTON ISLAND

N

A

A

© 2001 Jeffrey L. Ward

0 Miles   500   1000
0 Kilometers   1000

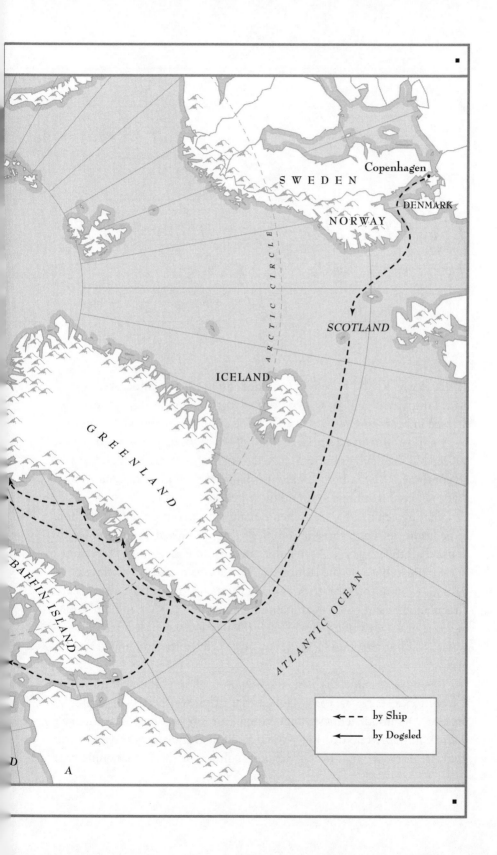

SWEDEN

Copenhagen

NORWAY

DENMARK

SCOTLAND

ARCTIC CIRCLE

ICELAND

GREENLAND

ATLANTIC OCEAN

BAFFIN ISLAND

D

A

- - - by Ship
——— by Dogsled

The Fifth Thule Expedition Begins,
1921

"When I was a child I used often to hear an old Greenlandic woman tell how, far away North, at the end of the world, there lived a people who dressed in bearskins and ate raw flesh," Knud Rasmussen wrote after his 1917 trip to northwestern Greenland. "Their country was always shut by ice, and the daylight never reached over the tops of their high fjords," he continued. "Even before I knew what traveling meant, I determined that one day I would go and find these people."

That day came in 1921, when Rasmussen set out on the Fifth Thule Expedition, an epic, three-and-a-half-year journey of 20,000 miles by dogsled all the way across the polar north from Greenland to Siberia.

After establishing the station at Thule as his home, his trading post, bank, and jump-off point for investigations of life and ice in northern Greenland, Rasmussen began planning a journey so vast and ambitious in scope, it took twelve years to raise the money, assemble a team of scientists and hunters, build a ship, buy dogs and equipment, and get under way.

Rasmussen made his first *isumaluit*—a plan—for the Fifth Thule Expedition as early as 1909. Unlike that of most other polar explorers (except Diamond Jenness and Vilhjalmur Stefansson), Rasmussen's interest in the Arctic was not part of a self-aggrandizing strategy to win gold or glory. It was the history and culture of the Inuit people that

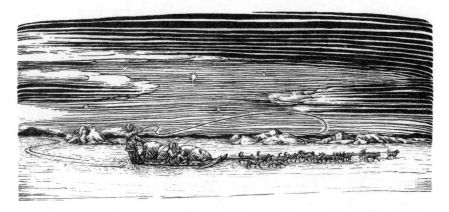

obsessed him. "The ethology of Greenland comprises a material so colossal that it is impossible to probe it to the bottom on a single journey—it requires a lifetime, preferably even longer," he wrote.

Rasmussen is said to be the founder of Eskimology. His aim was to portray Inuit people all the way across the polar north through their own voices, stories, dreams, songs, and drawings. "The Eskimo is the hero," he said. His methodology was simple and unobtrusive. He was savvy enough not to ask too much too soon. "I determined to begin by doing nothing, but simply to live amongst them, be as communicative as possible myself, and wait for an opportunity when the desire to narrate should overmaster their reserve."

He usually traveled simply and matched Inuit reserve with his own modesty. On entering a village he befriended shamans, old women, young hunters, children—anyone who would tell stories; he lived with them, hunted and ate with them, and as the stories unraveled, he took them down, sometimes on notepaper, sometimes memorizing them verbatim, Inuit-style, until he too could tell them correctly. He was admired and trusted because he had arrived by dogsled and left by dogsled and they knew he was going a long way, knew he was planning to tell their history from their point of view, and that like theirs, his movement was determined by Sila. Rasmussen was ambitious, but ambitious for them. He would collect 20,000 artifacts and compile more than 6,000 (published) pages about natural history and Eskimo folklore, culture, and customs from the eastern Canadian Arctic to western Alaska.

All Arctic travel is fraught with difficulty. It takes patience and money to wait out the bad weather, ship and sled wrecks, illnesses, and missed connections. With his team of seven Greenlanders, three scientists, and their two assistants, Rasmussen's expedition made a slow start. On June 18, 1921, Rasmussen, Peter Freuchen, Therkel Mathiassen (a botanist who couldn't drive a dog team so he walked everywhere, maintaining an invariable speed of exactly three miles per hour), and Kaj Birket-Smith sailed from Copenhagen on the Swedish ship *Bele*, which was carrying most of the expedition's equipment. They called at Nuuk to join in the festivities of Hans Egede Day, docking alongside the ship of the king of Denmark, one of the patrons of the expedition.

The king invited Rasmussen and Freuchen to board his ship. After the celebration Freuchen's wife Navarana came down with what they thought was a cold. She worsened and soon they knew that she had the Spanish influenza. Peter sat at her bedside for days. One evening when she was delirious with fever, he went to the kitchen to make tea. When he came back, she was dead.

Grieving over the loss of Navarana, Freuchen gave his daughter Pipaluk to his parents to raise. Then he rejoined Rasmussen and the others aboard the schooner *Sokongen* and headed north up the coast with the *Bele*. On July 13, on the way to Upernavik, the *Bele* ran aground in the fog near Svartenhuk at the southern end of Unknown Island. The ship began breaking up and the equipment had to be saved. Rasmussen, Freuchen, and the others proceeded in the *Sokongen* on to Thule.

In Thule they picked up the dogs, sleds, and the Greenlandic members of the expedition. These included Iggianguaq and his wife Arnarulunguaq (Arn), Arqioq and his wife Arnanguaq, "Bosun" and his wife Aqatsaq, and the unmarried Qavigarssuaq (Qav), who was Arn's cousin. Farther south they picked up Jacob Olsen. Before they even started across Davis Strait, there were several deaths. On September 6, Iggianguaq, Arn's husband, died. When asked if she wanted to stay or go, Arn chose to continue. She would sew skin clothing, cook, help drive the dogs, and ultimately be Rasmussen's companion. On the 7th the ship sailed for Arctic Canada.

Their destination was Winter Island, where Sir William Edward Parry had wintered during one of his unsuccessful attempts to find the Northwest Passage one hundred years before. Near Southampton Island they ran into heavy ice upon entering Foxe Channel and changed course, then headed northwest toward Melville Peninsula. When they saw land, they assumed it was Winter Island, but it turned out to be a much smaller spot on the map just below Vansittart Island. They anchored and went ashore. This would be their headquarters for the first third of a three-year-long journey. When they realized they had landed in the wrong place, they dubbed the speck of land Danish Island.

On landing, Freuchen and his helpers immediately began building a house while Rasmussen and the Greenlanders went out hunting. They returned after a few days with twelve caribou and five seals. Freuchen had already spotted walrus in the waters nearby. This time they were determined not to starve.

Rasmussen was eager to begin meeting the Iglulik (Hudson Bay) Eskimos of the east central Arctic. It had been two months since they arrived on their tiny island and they had not seen another human being outside their own party.

On December 4, Rasmussen and Freuchen, each with his own sled, began looking for villages. People who have been hungry and hunt for their own food develop the keenest of senses: Rasmussen had stopped to rest the dogs and have a smoke when he heard the sound of a sled a few miles away.

With binoculars he spotted hunters in the distance. They had halted to see who this stranger was. Then one of their party started running across the ice toward him. Knud gave his dogs the signal to go. "In a few minutes I had come right up with him, and the dogs, themselves ex- cited by the strange smell of him and his unfamiliar dress, would have attacked him had I not shouted to him to stand still. I stopped the team at the same moment, cracked my whip over their heads, and leaped clear of the sledge in front of the dogs so as to place myself between them and the stranger." He jumped so hard that he inadvertently fell into the man's arms. They both began laughing. That was the beginning of three years of such meetings with Inuit people across the polar north.

At Repulse Bay on the Arctic Circle just below Rae Isthmus, Ivaluart- juk, an old man with red, snow-burned eyes and a white beard, drew with uncanny accuracy a map of the coastline between his village and Pond Inlet, five hundred miles away on the north side of Baffin Island. The oldest man of his group, he hated living alone, so when his wife died, he married one of his own adopted daughters and bought her a child, paid for with a frying pan and a dog. He recalled his early days: "When I was young, every day was the beginning of some new thing." Now he was getting ready to die. He sang:

Cold and mosquitoes
These two pests
Come never together.
I lie down on the ice,
Lay me down on the snow and ice,
Till my teeth start chattering.
It is I. . . .

As always, the camp at Danish Island attracted neighboring Eskimos, and during the winter people began to appear. Akrat, an old man with a young wife and daughter, decided to settle in. He was prized for his ability to build igloos, some large enough to serve as dance houses.

They met Kutlok, who, when asked to take a letter to someone near Hudson Bay, was gone two years to make the delivery. He had returned just in time to see his wife having a baby—obviously fathered by another man.

When the shaman Padloq and his wife Takornaq visited Danish Island, they decided to stay on, though according to his wife Padloq was not good at working, thinking, or hunting. When a snowstorm buried the house, Padloq didn't bother digging out. Though the others were out hunting, he knew the bad weather would bring them back to do the digging for him.

Unaleq, also a shaman, and his wife Tuglik showed up on a frigid night scantily clad, with poor dogs and nothing to eat. Rasmussen allowed them to stay in exchange for stories.

Unaleq told about the first human beings who lived in a world before this one, when the earth rested on pillars. When the pillars collapsed, "the world disappeared into nothing and the world was emptiness." Then two men came up out of the ground. When they wanted to have children, a magic song changed one of them into a woman and children were born, people who now inhabit all the lands.

Unaleq had ten helping spirits. The most important of them was a giant in the shape of a bear with fangs; there were also two women and two men, two mountain spirits, and Tuneq (Tunit)—a mythological paleo-Eskimo woman. Unaleq promised Rasmussen that he would hold a seance in exchange for a snow knife. He insisted on holding it in Rasmussen's tiny study in the dark. He crawled under the desk while his wife Tuglik hung sealskins all around. The audience waited. Then there was the scraping of claws and a deep growl, frightened groans, and a shriek. Tuglik ran to the edge of the desk and began talking to the spirits in the special language known only to shamans.

Sometimes his voice was falsetto, sometimes a low baritone. Between the magic words were the sounds of nature: water running, winds, oceans, a walrus, and a bear. Then all was quiet. Tuglik told Rasmussen and the others that her husband had become a bear and had been walking along the route Rasmussen would be taking across Canada, that the bear spirit had swept the path clean and they would have a safe trip with no misfortune.

Another Arctic nomad who came around the winter house at Danish Island was Anarqaq. He came from an island near the Magnetic North Pole. Up there, where women were scarce, polyandry was the custom, but when the other husband rented out the shared wife to a stranger while Anarqaq was away, Anarqaq left in a rage and started wandering.

Anarqaq's specialty was curing indigestion. Other than that he had few practical skills. He speared salmon in the rivers for food, but had little to wear. High-strung and temperamental, whenever he went out on the ice to hunt caribou he was besieged by visions of spirits who, he said, "took his eyes through to the center of things." Rasmussen asked him to draw pictures of these spirits and he did.

Igtuk

Nartoq

As described by Anarqaq to Rasmussen, "Igtuk, or the boomer . . . [has] legs and arms on the back of his body, whilst his nose is hidden in his mouth; when his jaws move, one can hear booming out in the country . . . . Nartoq (the pregnant, or the one with the big stomach) . . . rushed threateningly at [Anarqaq] but disappeared when he prepared to defend himself . . . . The cause of its hot-headedness was that Anarqaq himself was too easily angered. In future he need never be afraid of it, if only he changed his disposition." (Rasmussen, *Fifth Thule Expedition,* vol. 7)

In midwinter, when the light started to come back, Rasmussen and the others split up. Birket-Smith went south to study contact between Eskimos and Indians (they have always been enemies), Peter Freuchen and Mathiassen traveled north to map Baffin Land, and Rasmussen went inland to the Barren Grounds.

The sleds of Hudson Bay were longer, narrower, and heavier than Thule sleds and the runners were wider for going across snow rather than ice. North of Lyons Inlet near Cape Elisabeth, where Rasmussen had been hunting walrus, a sled pulled by fifteen white dogs and carrying six men came alongside. A small man with a long beard plastered with rime ice jumped off and shook Rasmussen's hand, then showed him where they lived.

The man was a shaman named Aua, and he whisked Rasmussen to his village—five domed snow houses all connected by passageways so that no one needed to go outside to visit their neighbors. Sixteen people lived in these gleaming Arctic ice apartments. Orulo, Aua's wife, took Rasmussen on a tour:

> *They have been here for some time now and the heat from the blubber lamps has melted the inner layer of snow to a hard crust of ice. Icicles hang down by the entrances, gleaming in the soft light from the lamps. All the sitting places look comfortable and inviting, well furnished as they are with handsome soft caribou skins from the last autumn's hunting. We pass through winding labyrinths, all lit by small, faintly burning lamps, going from one apartment to another and greeting those within. (Rasmussen, Fifth Thule Expedition, vol. 7, no. 1, p. 46)*

At the beginning of March Aua's people left for spring camp to hunt walrus on Cape Elisabeth. Moving day was busy: they packed the sledges with their belongings—skinning tools, cooking things, soapstone lamps, vessels, guns, bows and arrows, harpoons, knives, as well as spring, winter, and summer clothes—passing the caribou skins on which they slept through a hole cut in the side of the igloo because it was taboo to remove them through the front passageway.

Aua said a prayer over a baby making her first journey on a sledge: "I arise from rest with movements swift as the beat of the raven's wings. . . ." According to custom she was taken out a hole cut in the wall at the back of the igloo and was laid on top of a sled piled five feet high with household goods. As soon as they arrived at the new hunting area, new houses were built within a few hours and they moved in.

The days were short. Rasmussen, Aua, and the other villagers drove in the dark to the ice edge. While they were gone, Orulo repaired kamiks, anoraks, caribou trousers, and mittens, collected snow to melt for drinking water (there was no glacier ice here), and thawed and cut up meat to feed the dogs when they returned. Then she collected, froze, and rendered blubber for use in the lamps, which required constant care to keep them from smoking. The heat from the lamps, which remained lit day and night, melted the roof of the igloo and Orulo had to replaster it with snow. The skins had to be scraped, stretched, dried, and chewed to make them soft enough to sew. She was always making new mittens and kamiks because they wore out quickly when the men were hunting walrus and seal at the ice edge or running overland after caribou.

Orulo remembered seeing *ierqat*—mountain spirits—when she was a young girl. They had come as messengers to warn of her father's impending death. *Ierqat* means "those who have something about the eyes"; the mouth and eyes of the spirits are set vertically on the face. They live in stone houses inside cracks in the hills and can run faster than caribou. Their special power resides in something they carry that is like a mirror. It glitters like mica and when looked into reflects back everything about human beings and where they live. That is how the *ierqat* know when someone is going to die.

When Orulo's father died, she helped her mother sew a caribou-skin bodybag and dragged him out on the snow between villages, where they said good-bye to his body and waited for his spirit to announce itself in some new form. Her brother died shortly after. He had seen the *ierqat* too, but had kept it a secret, which was a fatal mistake. If you don't tell others about the spirits, they kill you. They want to be known.

In the evenings at Aua's hunting camp outside Lyons Inlet, where it was dark in the afternoon and stayed dark until midmorning, Rasmussen and Aua would return from hunting walrus at the ice edge and seals at their allus (breathing holes). They fed their dogs, ate boiled seal ribs and walrus, and talked about rules and taboos by the light of soapstone blubber lamps flickering on icy walls. But Rasmussen wanted to know more.

Aua answered Rasmussen's question with another question: Why is life so hard? Then he took Rasmussen on a tour of the igloos. In one, belonging to a hunter who had failed to get a seal, the lamp barely flickered and the children were shivering and hungry. "Why should it be cold and comfortless in here?" Aua asked. In another hut a woman lay on her *illeq* (sleeping platform) coughing. "Why must people be ill and suffer pain?" he asked. "All our customs come from life and turn towards life; we explain nothing."

The Iglulik don't believe, Aua said, they fear—because they know there are no answers, no cures. Like all Arctic people they fear the weather, hunger, illness, cold, evil spirits, the souls of dead humans and of the animals they have killed for food; they fear the unknown, the invisible spirits that lurk everywhere. Everything is alive and every being knows about every other being. It's important to "keep a right balance between humankind and the rest of the world."

The Iglulik weren't theists—they called the powers that held sway over their lives *ersigifavut,* meaning "those we fear." They were Sila, the spirit of the weather, consciousness, and the universe; Arnaluk Takanaluk or Takanapsaluk, the Old Woman of the Sea, from whose fingers fish and marine mammals came into being, a vengeful dictator who punished anyone who broke taboos by impounding all the animals; and Aningat or Tarqeq, the moon-being who lived with his sister in a double house up in the land of the dead, and who protected against the punishments of Takanapsaluk and regulated fertility. Aningat also presided over the tides and currents of the sea and brought boys good luck.

Sentient beings had two souls, the *inusia,* which was the spirit of life, and the *tarnina,* which gave life and health but at the same time was the site where sickness could come in. People live on after death and the dead become fully alive again in dreams. Sleep and death are allies. When someone sleeps their soul is turned upside down and they hang on to the body by the big toe. That is how tenuous life is. It can slip away any time, Aua told Rasmussen.

One of the villagers, Inugpasugjuk, told two stories about death and rebirth. One was about Sereraut, a man who returned from the Land of the Dead and went hunting with a friend. Sereraut wanted his friend's wife so badly, he pushed him down the breathing hole of the bearded seal he had caught, harpoon, bladder, and all. Later in the year, during a song festival, the man whom Sereraut had killed shot up through the floor of the dance house and stood there with the bearded seal and cried out, "Sereraut killed me, tied me to a bearded seal I had caught, and sent me to the bottom of the sea." After saying these words, he disappeared.

Again he shot up, closer to Sereraut now, and repeated the same words, and again disappeared. The third time he rose up, he was standing right in front of his killer, and as he sank back down, the line attached to the seal wrapped around Sereraut and pulled him into the hole. A moment later, the dead man shot up, fully alive. His parents were called to the dance house; Sereraut was never seen again.

Inugpasugjuk told another story, about a ghost that came out of its grave as a fire and tickled a mother and child to death. The woman had lost her husband and gone out with her two boys to visit his grave. While building a snow hut where they would sleep that night, the smaller boy, lying on a skin on the snow, began laughing and could not stop. The woman realized it was the child's father. They jumped on the sled and hurried away, but the ghost of the father succeeded in killing the smaller boy with its tickling hand and the mother as well. As the older boy fled on the dogsled, the father appeared on the sled as a flaming torch. But the boy struck at the fire with his whip, extinguishing it every time it came back. He returned home safely. There was a shaman in the feast house and he charmed the fire away and saved the young man's life.

Orulo told Rasmussen more about death. In early times, before there was death, before there was light and darkness, when there was no difference between humans and animals, the perceiver and the perceived, the spirits that rule human life were plain human beings, but Orulo couldn't say how they rose to power. Trying to go beyond or behind these spirits was not possible, she warned. "Too much thought only leads to trouble. All this that we are talking about happened in time so far back there was no time at all."

The Time Between Two Winters,
1922

In what Rasmussen called "the time between two winters," in 1922, Rasmussen and Freuchen went separate ways. Freuchen transported the archeological, botanical, and geological specimens collected by Mathiassen and Birket-Smith from Repulse Bay to Danish Island, and Rasmussen went in search of the inland Eskimos who had not yet had contact with outsiders.

From the western shore of Repulse Bay, Rasmussen traveled south down the coast of Hudson Bay. At Chesterfield Inlet, he sifted through the ruins of paleo-Eskimo houses, then began following the Kazan River inland. His first stop was to visit the people who lived on the Barren Grounds near Hudson Bay. The Barren Grounds were once big mountains that had been "run over"—worn down to undulating plains of rock by an ice cap called the Keewatin Glacier, much like the one that still covers Greenland. In its wake the ice indentations were small ponds that glinted in sun and, when not frozen, watered the caribou.

Rasmussen had never met Eskimos who knew nothing of the sea or the hunting of marine mammals. These people subsisted entirely on caribou; only caribou could live on the lichen-and-water diet provided by the Barren Grounds. From there, they migrated toward the coast at the end of May, then back again in late September. If weather interfered, postponing or altering the caribou's course, and the hunters had not cached enough food, there was no recourse. With only one main source of food, starvation was common.

From Baker Lake Rasmussen skied in front of the sled to lighten the load as they moved across the hard spring snowpack, stopping here and there to feed starving people, take on guides, or rest and have tea. Stories followed Rasmussen like seagulls behind a fishing boat. They met a blind man from the Qaernermiut tribe on the southwest side of Baker Lake who begged Rasmussen to stay, then a starving Harvaqtormiut on the lower Kazan River whose name meant "Fat Man." It was there that Rasmussen heard the story of the time when houses could move on their own, and how they lost the power when someone complained that the rushing noise made his ears hurt.

Farther on, Rasmussen came to a village where a jilted suitor turned all the people and even the dogs to stone. Upriver were the two sisters who stole a caribou skin and a firestone (a piece of pyrite) and had to escape by becoming thunder and lightning.

He heard about the mother-in-law who killed her own daughter, skinned her, and wore the skin to fool the girl's husband, Kivioq, into thinking she was his wife. When he discovered the deception, he tried to escape, but each time an obstruction barred the way. Somehow he clambered out the other side of a mountain with a mouth that opened and closed. He passed through a wall of sealskin thongs below which human bones lay piled up, slid over the lip of a boiling cooking pot, and shot through the jaws of two fighting bears until he came on a *tarpana,* a dwarf woman who was cooking food in her house.

Seeing her through a hole in her roof, Kivioq spit on her. She looked up and said, "What is that standing in my light? Is it here the shadow comes from?" He spit again and she cut her cheek off and put it in the pot, then her nose. Then she ran out of the house clutching her *ulo* (knife) and cut large boulders in half. Kivioq killed her.

Traveling on, Kivioq came to a house where a woman with an iron tail lived. He spent the night there, carefully covering himself with a flat rock; sure enough, in the middle of the night she tried to pierce him, but her tail broke on the stone and she fell over dead. Now in a kayak, Kivioq paddled straight through a giant mussel and continued on until he reached home. His parents had been sitting on two rocks, waiting for him so long that the stones were worn down. When they saw him, they were so happy, they fell over backward and died from joy at seeing him again.

Amid these tales of love, Rasmussen and his female companion, Arn, were drawn close by the intimacy, arduousness, and wonder of dogsled travel. It was common for men and women to become lovers on a long sled trip, regardless of their marital status. Whatever happened while out hunting was their business and no infatuation lingered into their lives at home.

They continued up the Kazan River until they reached the most remote group of Eskimos, the Padlermiut. A spring rainstorm had nearly drowned them. "The camp was in a state of complete confusion: morass, melted mud, whipped up by the rain, a mire of soft, bottomless snow and uncountable little streams that shot up out of the ground and ran away in all directions," Rasmussen wrote.

The Eskimos in the village nearby fared worse. The walls of their snowhouses were "a yellowish mass that looked like brown sugar and as the rain constantly tore holes in them, they tried to plug the worst places with old footwear, trousers, and frocks." The caribou-skin roofs had been swept away by rain and wind. But when Rasmussen peered in he saw them gathered around, wet through, singing, laughing, and gambling with cards imported from Winnipeg.

Up the Kazan River Rasmussen traveled in what he described as "furious weather"—rain and sleet that undermined the river ice and softened snow to slush. The caribou were migrating in small groups, keeping the dogs in constant excitement.

On June 30 he came to a large lake called Hikoligjuaq. There he saw a man on top of a rise who held up his arms in a gesture of friendship. Wasting no time, Rasmussen drove to the man's village.

He was Igjugarjuk, "Little Testicle," about whom Rasmussen had already heard. He was famous for having killed his wife's relatives because they opposed his marriage to her. She had gone willingly with him when the opposition was disposed of.

Igjugarjuk invited the Greenlanders into the tent of his second, younger wife, who had been obtained by more peaceful means. They feasted on caribou. A month before, he told the visitors, they had been starving, and it was his older wife, Kibgarjuk, who had gone off with her tiny son in a snowstorm to find food. They walked through a blizzard for two days with no sleeping skins and no provisions to a small lake she had dreamed contained *iqaluit*—trout. Her dream was accurate. She caught enough fish to carry the village through until the migration began.

Rasmussen observed that they laid into the cooked caribou "like ferocious dogs," tearing meat off the bone with their teeth. He had never seen anyone eat so ravenously. But their population had been decimated by starvation and, ironically, by the introduction of the gun, whose noise scared the caribou away.

Once the village had boasted 600 inhabitants. That number had been reduced to 100. It wasn't a lack of game animals, merely that they kept changing their migration route. The Barren Grounds were so difficult to traverse, the caribou often passed by undetected, and the hunters had to wait until they returned in the fall.

The entire life of the Padlermiut was centered on the caribou. They provided food and skins for clothing, summer tents, and sleeping bags. The hunters drove the animals down avenues of stone cairns, behind which archers hid and killed them with bows and arrows as they passed. Or they hunted them in the lakes from a kayak with an *ipo*—a caribou lance—or trapped them in pits covered with a thin crust of snow and moss scented with the urine of a dog or wolf.

Until late May the Padlermiut lived in unheated snow houses, since they had neither wood nor blubber. Colder than Greenland, the Barren Grounds' winter temperature averaged 30 below zero. In June they moved into caribou skin tents with no smokehole. They traveled mostly by foot. It was not uncommon to see a sled pulled by a man plus one or two dogs and a woman walking alongside.

After the feast to welcome Rasmussen and his companions, there was singing and drumming. A female shaman, Kinalik, was asked by Rasmussen to "examine the road that had to be traveled." She was in her thirties and wore a shaman's belt hung with a piece of a gun butt because her initiation had come about through a ritual shooting.

During her initiation, she was hung from tentpoles above the ground during a blizzard and left there for five days. Then she was laid down on a skin and Igjugarjuk shot her in the heart with a stone. She died and lay there the whole night. In the morning she woke. The stone was removed from her heart and was kept by her mother. She had become a shaman.

Kinalik stood alone in the middle of the floor, eyes closed, her body trembling. "This was her manner of 'seeing inward,' into the secrets of the days to come," Rasmussen wrote. She made strange noises and contorted her face as if in pain. Rasmussen was taken outside and told to stand where there were no footprints in the snow. Later, Kinalik said she had spoken to Hila (the Padlermiut name for Sila). The powerful weather spirit assured a safe journey for the traveler.

Igjugarjuk told Rasmussen that the caribou came out of a hole in the ground and populated the world as they wished. No one guided them. They were of the earth and belonged to the earth and no shaman or spirit could influence their wanderings. That is why when starvation came, there was no spiritual recourse for Igjugarjuk's people, because he could not to dive down though ice to pacify Nerrivik and comb the lice from her hair.

Divested of these powers, all a Padlermiut shaman like Kinalik or Igjugarjuk could do was to heal the sick and rescue people from evil charms that had been cast, usually by women. A shaman's training entailed exposure to cold, hunger, drowning, and "death" by shooting.

Igjugarjuk's training was especially severe. He went five days with nothing to eat or drink; after a mouthful of warm water, he went hungry for another fifteen days; after more water, he suffered a further ten-day stint of starvation. Then his instructor (also his father-in-law) dragged him behind a sledge in the middle of winter to the other side of the big lake.

The old man built a snow hut for Igjugarjuk, then carried him inside and left him there for thirty days, during which time the novice was to give himself over completely to Hila.

"Only towards the end of the thirty days did a helping spirit come to me, a lovely and beautiful helping spirit, whom I had never thought of: it was a white woman; she came to me while I collapsed, exhausted, and was sleeping," Igjugarjuk said. At month's end, the father-in-law came. Igjugarjuk was so weak and emaciated he had to be carried. In the village he was declared a full-fledged shaman. Nevertheless, he remained humble: "I do not think I know much, but I do not think that wisdom or knowledge about things that are hidden can be sought in that manner [by trickery, low lights, and magic]. True wisdom is only to be found far away from people, in the great solitude, and it is not found in play but only through suffering. Solitude and suffering open the human mind, and therefore a shaman must seek his wisdom there."

That spring of 1922 Peter Freuchen started transporting the collections to Repulse Bay, where they would be picked up by a schooner in the summer as soon as the ice broke. Peter set out during a cold spell. The temperature, he reported, "hovered at about sixty below zero." A week into the trip they reached soft snow and the sleds were too heavy for the dogs. They offloaded some of the cargo.

Later, Freuchen went back for the goods he had left behind. Just as he finished packing the sled, a ground blizzard whipped up. "The drifts were alive under my feet and it was impossible for me to follow the tracks. The wind turned into a storm, the storm into a gale," he wrote.

With no shelter, he decided to try for camp anyway by dumping the load and traveling lightly. He carried only a pair of extra kamiks, a bearskin, and a sleeping bag. He walked in front of the dogs to show them the way.

It became impossible to head into the wind: he couldn't breathe and was frequently blown over. He stopped at a large rock for shelter. There was no chance of building a snow hut—the wind drifts were packed so solidly he couldn't cut through the ice. Trying to stay warm, he walked back and forth, then dug a hole in the snow, got in, and pulled the sled over his head. Soon, he was asleep.

When he woke, he had no feeling in his feet. He tried to dig out but failed. When his hands started to freeze, he took a piece of sealskin, wound it tight, spit on it, and when the spit froze he used it as a digging tool. In the process, his beard froze to the side of the sled. When he finally had the strength to pull it away, much of the skin on his chin went with it.

Lying back to rest, he saw that snow had begun filling his hole. He needed another digging tool. He had once seen an Eskimo use a frozen dog turd as a snow knife. Lacking the excrement of his dogs (they were lying under the snow away from him), he used his own, fashioned it into a blade, and let it freeze.

A day and a night passed before he dug himself out of his grave. He discovered that he couldn't walk—his feet were frozen solid. He tried to get the dogs hooked up but couldn't, nor would they pull him. They ran away. Freuchen crawled for three hours to camp.

Padloq and Apa nursed him. One foot swelled, then turned gangrenous. They cut a hole in the igloo so he could rest with his smelly foot outside. Skin and flesh started to come off, leaving the bones of his feet exposed. He wrote: "At night when I could not sleep I stared with horrible fascination at the bare bones of my toes. The sight gave me nightmares and turned my nerves raw. I felt the old man with the scythe coming closer, and sometimes we seemed to have switched roles and my bare bones to have become part of him."

Observing his pain, one of the Eskimo women offered to bite off the ends of his feet, but he politely refused. Instead, he asked for a pair of pliers and a hammer. Sitting up, Peter knocked off the gangrenous stumps by himself.

In early autumn Freuchen reached the ship anchored at Chesterfield Inlet on the west side of Hudson Bay and asked the ship's doctor to cut off the rest of the foot. It had been torturing him. He spent the rest of the fall recuperating on Danish Island.

The other members of the Fifth Thule Expedition had ended their work together and would now say good-bye. Rasmussen had returned from visiting the Caribou Eskimos, and Therkel Mathiassen and Jacob Olsen had returned from Southampton Island after an eight months' absence. Now Mathiassen would go to Pond Inlet; Birket-Smith and Jacob Olsen would continue their study of the Caribou Eskimos, then move south to Churchill to study the Chippewa Indians.

By the end of December Freuchen felt well enough to travel again and set out from Danish Island for Baffin Island with three hunters, their wives, and a newborn baby. They had to stop and resew Peter's stitches when they came open during the exertion of driving a dogsled. Along the way they met a childless couple who had bought a baby in exchange for a frying pan. It turned out that the baby was sick. On the other hand, the frying pan had been cracked, so it was determined to be a fair deal. The Greenlandic woman who'd just given birth suckled the sick infant to help him get well.

In Pingerqaling, they met a cannibal named Atakutaluk. She was famous all over Baffin Land for having eaten her husband and three children. When she met Freuchen, she told him of the ordeal that had taken place many years before.

Thirteen people had set out for Baffin Land to trade for driftwood for making dogsleds. Halfway there, the weather changed suddenly. Oddly, it wasn't the cold that nearly killed them, but heat. During the night their snow huts caved in and the frozen bits of skin, rolled meat, and bones used to construct their sleds thawed and were eaten by the dogs. They had no food and no way to travel. After eating their dogs, they began to starve. Atakutaluk then ate the bodies of her husband and children.

When Peter met Atakutaluk she had since married the village leader. She was, in Peter's words, "well dressed, merry, and full of jokes." Atakutaluk saw the uneasy look on Peter's face and consoled him: "Look here, Pita," she said. "Don't let your face be narrow for this. I got a new husband, and I got with him three new children. They are all named for the dead ones that only served to keep me alive so they could be reborn."

In Eclipse Sound just south of Bylot Island, a gale hit and the ice where the Greenlanders had made an igloo broke off. For thirty hours they drifted and fought breaking ice, trying to stay together, trying to keep from falling into open water. "We ran up and down the ice searching for a spot to cross to each other. Finally Boatsman [Bosun] shouted that he had found a place. I took off my coat, turned it inside out, and poured the child into it. Then I shouted to the father to come and help catch her, and I tossed her like a sack."

But the edges of the floe Arqioq and his wife were on kept breaking off until there was hardly room to stand. Half the contents of the sled fell overboard—all their food and warm clothing—but eventually they clambered onto a bigger piece of ice. Together again, Freuchen, the two couples, Bosun, and the baby drifted around Lancaster Sound between Devon Island and Baffin Island. For the next two days they could not dry their clothes or cook. The baby cried and his mother was in a bad temper. Arqioq pulled Freuchen aside and apologized for his wife: "She belongs to those who are angry when adrift on an ice pan if they have small babies."

Pushing and pulling at the ice and leaping across gaping holes, they finally reached land after five days with little food and almost no sleep. Soon they came upon people who were worse off than they were. Freuchen wrote: "Their faces were hollow and their eyes sunk deep in their skulls. They had no real clothes but were covered with scabrous-looking rags and filth. They were starving. Their voices were eerie. I had seen many shocking things in my life but nothing like this."

They too had been caught in a storm, but one that lasted a whole month. It was the old story of starvation and the eating of dogs. But these dogs were diseased and caused a plague among the hunters. Thirteen villagers died. There were twelve left. Freuchen immediately gave them raw seal to eat, but they could eat only a little. Then a broth was made, which they drank. One of the young men, Mala, who had lost his entire family, joined Freuchen and the two of them went on foot to Pond Inlet for help with only a gun and a harpoon.

Hunting was bad along the way. They ate rabbit dung and lichen. When Freuchen saw a seal out on the ice, he lay down and acted like a seal for three hours, gradually crawling within range. When he managed to shoot the seal, both men lapped the fresh blood, then roasted the meat on a flat stone heated in a fire fueled by turf and blubber. Three days later they reached the village of Toqujin and help was sent to their starving friends.

Peter Freuchen's participation in the Fifth Thule Expedition was coming to a close, as planned. He walked to Pond Inlet and met the ship that was to take him first to Thule to pick up his son, Mequsaq, then home to Denmark. Because of bad weather they did not make a call at Thule and Peter had to go on to Copenhagen without the boy.

In 1927 Peter had his entire leg amputated. He had spent fifteen years in Greenland and the Canadian Arctic. Mequsaq, his son, finally came to live with his father, but could not adapt to European living and was returned to Greenland to be raised by his adopted parents. Peter was twenty-three when he and Rasmussen had first gone to Greenland. Now, at thirty-seven, his Eskimo life had come to an end.

Qaanaaq, 1997

*Sun at midnight. Ice is a clear mirror
and beneath it, the broken sea. Which
is which? No clarity can flatten
torment; no fragment can undo clarity.
That's how it is. They are the same.*

—*Muso Soseki*

There's a place on the map of Greenland where the coastline bulges out into knotted, ice-capped headlands and tight-fisted islands. The fjords lie back in wide, lakelike hideaways where narwhal mate and glaciers calve ice mountains that in winter stand in frozen cordilleras and in summer drift slowly into Smith Sound and are taken south by the Labrador Current into Baffin Bay.

Sometimes it takes five or seven or ten days to get to Qaanaaq from California, then to Siorapaluk, the northernmost continuously inhabited village in the world. Because at 76 degrees north latitude, which is 600 miles north of the Arctic Circle and 600 miles south of the North Pole (or the Puili, as the Greenlandic people call it), the only constant, the only god, the only common denominator is weather and the movements of ice, and once there, the only mode of transportation is dogsled.

On a Tuesday in May I waited all day to board the once-a-week plane from Kangerlussuaq to Thule. My Greenlandic friend Aleqa Hammond, whom I had first met in Uummannaq four years earlier, was to accompany me as my translator. But she failed to show up, even though we'd been planning the trip for a year. When I asked around at the airport if they'd seen her, they said no. The plane she was supposed to be on landed at eight in the morning and it was now four in the afternoon. She wasn't in her office or house in Nuuk; she had disappeared.

When the plane to Thule was announced, I decided, right or wrong, to go anyway, even though I had no pass to transit through Thule Air Base, no helicopter ticket to Qaanaaq, and no way to communicate with the hunters with whom I was to travel for a month. After all, I had already come a long way.

We flew north, following the west coast of Greenland. A milky fog poured over the fingered network of fjords, mounding up until even the island tops were lost and a haze lay in front of the all-night sun in a single transparent veil. Farther inland, something rose: not *nuna*, earth, but the ice cap whose unseen tides broke rock and carved canyons.

We flew along the spine of Unknown Island, the speck of Illorsuit where Marie Louisa lives, its half-moon harbor of ice lined with sled tracks. We flew over the high black rump of Svartenhuk, and the grave of Peter Freuchen's wife Navarana at Upernavik. From there, a long stretch of coast pulled us north into Melville Bay.

There, the land widened, still rebounding from the retreating ice cap—a remnant of the ice age that ended 10,000 years ago. The wildly irregular fringe exposed by the meltoff was mostly naked rock. Between Tasiusaq—once the northernmost outpost of colonized Greenland—and

Cape York—where Polar Eskimos first saw a European—the habitable brown fringe disappeared altogether under the snouts of glaciers that had sealed themselves at right angles to the fjord ice. Their false fronts were blasted with sunlight, their pinnacled colonnades half-toppled as if they had once supported an entablature, now razed.

On my lap I spread out a topographical map of Avannaarsua—the Far North—a district so isolated that, besides Qaanaaq, there are only a few inhabited villages, and the next-nearest town can't be measured in miles—it is a month-and-a-half trip south by dogsled. The peninsula where Qaanaaq is located is shaped like a four-cornered hat, flanked by two bowlegged fjords, and is called Piulip Nuna, Peary Land, named after the American explorer Robert Peary.

By chance I was sitting next to Robert Peary's Inuit granddaughters, the progeny of one of the sons Peary fathered with his Greenlandic companion, Aleqasina, who traveled with him on his seven failed expeditions leading up to his final "conquest" of the North Pole on April 6, 1909. (He also had an American wife, Josephine, and a child.) The sisters, both in their mid-fifties, were ogling pictures of the Danish queen they called "Daisy" in a movie magazine. I slid the topo map over Daisy's face and asked them to show me where they lived. They pointed to Herbert Island, ten miles across the water from Qaanaaq. This island's sole village had only four inhabitants—so small, they said, that they would soon have to move to town.

The older sister looked out the plane window, then marked the spot on the map over which we were flying. Her wrinkled hand cut precise arcs in the air to indicate the shape of a lake that she knew, and the hundreds of grounded tidewater glaciers along Melville Bay that kept loosening their belts and calving out pinnacled blocks of ice. Maps were an unnecessary luxury to her. She and her family had never used them. She could outline the ragged edge of the coast in perfect detail, the polynyas, hidden rocks, and fog-shrouded islands. Greenlanders have lived for 5,000 years without maps (even now, the last quadrangle on the west coast available is Qaanaaq and there are only two maps of the entire east coast). Ninety-four years after Robert Peary finished his explorations of the North Pole, Piulip Nuna's ice-capped summit is still marked "elevation unknown," and Prudhoe Land to the northeast, which is mostly ice, is marked "unexplored."

In the Inuktun dictionary of the northern dialect, I had looked up words for ice. They are *kaniq, qirihuq, qirititat, nilak, nilaktaqtuq, hiku, hikuaq, hikuaqtuaq, ilu, hikuiqihuq, hikurhuit, hikuqihuq, hikuliaq, manirak, hikup hinaa, qainnguq, manillat, kassut, iluliaq, ilulissirhuq, auktuq, quihaq, hirmiijaut*—rime frost, freshwater ice, sea ice, thin ice, ice on the inside of the tent, pack ice, new ice, a smooth expanse of ice, the ice edge, solid ice attached to the shore, hummocky ice, pressure ridges, pieces of floating ice, icebergs in the water, melting ice . . .

The Peary sisters pointed excitedly down at leads (cracks) in ice, stranded icebergs, polynyas, long-legged fjords, mountaintop lakes where they had camped in summer and gathered bird eggs. I couldn't stop looking at the frozen ocean's cracked root and brain maps, its dendritic grid; how the whole island resembled an overturned hull, a ghost ship made of ice no human had sailed.

Earlier in the month, shadows owned the sun. They moved it around the sky like a lost chess piece. Now, sun shoveled shadows out from under things in a cubist, angled reality, an oblique suggestion that changed into actual dogs, sleds, humans, mountains, and pressure ice. At the top of it all was the North Pole, which wasn't land at all, but a moving buttonhole, a floating world whose only constancy is its fleshless shine.

The plane veered sharply. We flew over a fist of inland ice and started our descent. Around the mountainous bend was North Star Bay, a deep U-shaped body of water edged by a long strand of beach, with a flat-topped sentinel mountain guarding the harbor entrance. This was Dundas Village, where Knud Rasmussen founded his Arctic station and launched his expeditions. Hardly anything is left of the settlement where Rasmussen and Freuchen lived. Known by many names—Qaanaaq, Thule, Dundas—it is no more. In a covert arrangement between the American and Danish governments during the Cold War, the historic area became the site of an American air force base, built to protect the world from attack by the Russians.

As soon as the plane touched down at the base, I was arrested. In the small lobby I was asked to show my helicopter ticket to Qaanaaq. My no-show translator had my ticket and the Danish consulate in Los Angeles had told me crisply that I didn't need a special permit to transit through the air base. She was wrong, and the helicopter scheduled to take me to Qaanaaq that evening, a short trip of sixty kilometers, had been canceled, even though the sky was clear.

Someone was whistling a tune from *The Big Valley* as I was being interrogated. The Peary sisters laughed at the officiousness of the American and Danish military. "Who are you? Why are you here? Where are you going? What do you do? Why are you in Greenland?" the liaison officer asked in halting English. When I told him I was going out with some hunters in Qaanaaq, he said, "But you may be a Russian spy." I laughed. They didn't think it was funny. "Oh, come on," I said. "The iron curtain dropped some time ago, or hasn't that news gotten to you yet?"

I couldn't see who was whistling, whether it was Guy, the French Gronlandsfly representative, or the Danish representative from SAS, both Europeans who could have cared less who I was. Finally, I was released and sent with the others to Barracks 136, reserved for Greenlanders on their way home. "But we'll be back for you in the morning," the officer said. "And you'll have to take the plane back to Kangerlussuaq."

A van took us to the barracks, one of hundreds lined up on grim dirt streets. When I stepped out there were none of the welcoming sounds of a Greenlandic village—no dogs howling and children playing—only the constant shuddering of gigantic, aboveground pipes shunting steam, water, and heating oil.

My assigned room was narrow with a small window at one end. Out past the last hangar, the valley known as Pituffik stretched nine miles toward the glistening ice cap. The valley was once prized for its fox hunting, and North Star Bay was a majestic inlet of water rich in seals, whales, and walrus, with turf-and-stone houses clustered at the edge. Now the old Qaanaaq was a ghost town used occasionally by hunters passing through. In 1952, the villagers from Dundas were removed against their will to the shore of Inglefield Sound, sixty kilometers north, now known as the "new" Qaanaaq—my destination, though it seemed now that I would never get there.

Under arrest or not, I walked around, not to spy but to stretch my legs and glimpse the historic valley and Saunders Island, where the Greenlanders camped in late spring to catch birds.

Thule Air Base—the Twelfth Air Command Squadron—is an $800,000,000 state-of-the-art Star Wars–style base with mostly civilian personnel—engineers, computer specialists, and a horde of Danish and Greenlandic workers to keep the facility going. When the base was built in the 1950s, there were 25,000 men stationed here. Now it's a third that size and shrinking.

On the fringe of the tin-can barracks and the archways of grunting steam pipes, I passed a four-story hotel, underground missile sites, the Knud Rasmussen Library, a gym, a bar, a massive dining hall, and a PX. On a height overlooking a river made unbeautiful because it flows through the base is an immense radar installation that can look over the edge of the earth, just in case anyone needs to see what's there.

The military association between the United States and Denmark began during World War II, when two air bases were established at Sondre Stromfjord and Naarssarsuaq to provide important defense positions against Germany. During the Korean War, a large hospital in Naarssarsuaq received soldiers so badly hurt that the Americans sequestered them in Greenland, so the extent of American injuries would not be seen. But why was the base plunked down in one of the most beautiful, productive, and historic valleys in all of Greenland?

I went to bed late. The sun shone hard at 2:00 a.m. and Arctic foxes begged at our windows. The Peary sisters left their door wide open. I said good night and lay on my narrow bed in my red union suit awaiting the MP's who would roust me later in the morning.

The sound of a jet woke me. It was First Air—the once-a-week plane that had brought us, taking off. The Peary sisters peeked into my room grinning: I had been spared. There was no way for the police to send me back now.

We walked to the dining hall for breakfast. Imina, a tax collector from Qaanaaq, spoke English and translated for me. One of the sisters wore a T-shirt with the words, "Thoughts of Summer Sun with Happy Memories." It was snowing. The array of fresh American food in the cafeteria was staggering: cantaloupe, apples, grapes, and bananas— things unseen here in northern Greenland, and as much as you wanted. We ate crowded together at the far end of the dining hall, segregated from the American military personnel. A young couple at our table worried aloud that their whole one-week vacation to see her parents in Qaanaaq would be swallowed up here at Thule if the weather didn't improve.

Back at the barracks, a young Inuit woman and her tall, handsome Danish boyfriend pawed sweetly at each other while watching *Back to the Future III*. "I'm from the future and tomorrow I have to go back to the future," one of the characters said. Greenlandic pop music played in the kitchen where Safak Peary chewed on a piece of sealskin, softening it to make a pair of mittens. We were not on our way to the future, but to a place where men and women live by the harpoon.

So far no one had sent me away and I felt free to roam. Imina and I visited Jack, an American weather forecaster who also works as a coordinator for the Peregrine Fund and fills his rooms with classical music. A Brahms piano sonata was playing when we arrived. Fussy and pedantic, he was a Vietnam vet who found it too hard to go home: "I needed to find a refuge. I read about a job up here so I came. It's the beauty of the nature all around that holds me. I've been here twenty-seven years now."

We were peering at a photograph of baby peregrine falcons in the nest when the liaison officer and his sidekick burst into the room. "We were supposed to arrest you this morning but we didn't," he announced sternly, as if his error was my fault. Then he admitted that he had overslept. "Anyway, Aleqa Hammond called and said you are a guest of Nuuk Tourism. Is that so?"

"Yes," I replied.

The officer loosened up. "Well, I guess you can keep staying here."

When they left and I asked Jack how they knew where to find me, he shrugged.

That afternoon, Jack took a group of us for a drive, passing around a box of fresh strawberries as we sped by the two-mile-long runway where the C-150 that had brought the fresh fruit was being refueled. "Sinful, isn't it?" Jack said, gloating.

We were stopped on the road to P Mountain by drifts of snow. Foxes and Arctic hares ran everywhere. We got out and looked at rocks. A caterpillar lay curled on a clump of dead grass. Imina exclaimed, "You came to no-man's land and found a butterfly."

Time slid by. The sun was always shining on this wild valley transformed into a hell. Nowhere else had I seen so clearly how industry trivializes the subtle workings of landscape: the base's steam pipes grunted and gurgled and the noise of massive generating plants worked as a baffle against the strumming Arctic silence. Out on the slope of P Mountain, the Arctic woolly bear caterpillar I had seen was a time traveler. Its body, frozen through for nine or ten months of the year, thaws out for only two or three, so its development from egg to butterfly can take twenty years.

Into the time warp we leaped. Days, we watched movies on TV during sun-tinged nights; nights, we hung out at Jack's. One night he treated us to a DVD of Monteverdi's *Orfeo*. The blue blinds were drawn and we sat on a sheepskin rug eating pizza. The libretto translation read: "I make my way through the blind air, but not through hell, for where there is so much beauty, there is paradise. . . ." The Peary sisters dozed quietly.

Bad weather continued. The women in Barracks 136 kept busy knitting, sewing skins, and playing cards with the radio on over the sound of the television. The phone rang incessantly. "Teléphonée!" whoever answered sang out.

A storm warning came over a loudspeaker positioned in the corner of the barracks. "Big Brother Weather," Imina called it, but no blizzard materialized. I walked to the weather station to look at the "Progs"—the forecast. Thyge Anderson, the Danish weather observer, greeted me, bounding around the room with the grace of Baryshnikov in socks and sandals. Throwing the window open, he stuck his head out and said, "The most dangerous thing about this job is getting stabbed in the neck by an icicle."

Storm-alert instructions were posted, along with the time it takes for flesh to freeze and the wind speed at which you were required to stay inside. When I made fun of the dramatic storm alert, Jack said, "Last year we had one of the worst winters on record. There were fifty to sixty big storms. Thule sticks out in a bad place. There's lots of wind. It gusted to 152 miles per hour just recently. In one storm a guy went hand over hand on a rope strung between two buildings. Suddenly the rope went slack. He blew away and was never seen again. Another guy was blown down flat in the snow and died of asphyxiation."

Jack shuffled through computer printouts. "We put together the prognoses with the surface systems we can see, plus a WAG—a wild-assed guess. Of course we're wrong a lot of the time, but since there's no one above us, the pilots have to keep coming back. And when the storms are really bad, everyone gets off work. So we're popular."

Thyge grinned sardonically: "I guess you could say the shaman function has now been taken over by weathermen. Our wisdom and dependability are no better, probably worse."

By the time I got back to the barracks, the Peary sisters had made four pairs of sealskin mittens with doghair ruffs and two pairs of kamiks.

The next morning the helicopter was canceled again. I walked my usual loop around the base: down to the shore ice, past the "tank farm," then up to the hill that divided the base from the village site. Up there the drifts were chest high and the river that ran down the middle of the wide valley was still frozen. Later I cornered the helicopter mechanic, a tall, gangly Swede who said, "It's cloudy out, but the windows are also dirty. Maybe it's really sunny. Anyhow, we don't fly yet today." Morning announcements came and went: more information by noon. But we knew what it would say.

On Friday night snow fell heavy and fast and the requisite storm warnings were announced all over again. Guy, the Frenchman who ran Greenland Air in Thule, stroked the side of the helicopter as if it were a cat. "She is a good one. Of course, she is French. We've only lost three. We have a very good flying record." Two years earlier the hangar roof had blown off in a blizzard and the helicopter filled with snow. "Almost anything can go wrong here and it always does."

An Arctic storm was blowing our way. Another day and night went by. The morning movie was *Black Rain* with Michael Douglas. The Peary sisters turned the sound off but kept the image, then told stories with Imina translating: "The strait between Greenland and Canada is not very big. But the ice is dangerous. Men from one side used to come over and steal women from the other side. That was a thousand years ago. When the Norwegian-Danish priest came to Greenland in 1721 there were sixteen thousand Greenlanders. He told them they had to stop listening to their shamans, that they were frauds and couldn't cure anyone or anything. Shortly after, the smallpox hit and the population dropped to one hundred ten people in all of Greenland."

Sunday. Snow fell and the sun came out. An icefield on Saunders Island shone like the side of a silver bowl. In a few weeks millions of murres would land there to nest and fledge their young. Behind us, the monumental radar installation looked like a large plate that had been painted black. Arctic foxes wandered between barracks—bedraggled because they were shedding. Patches of white fur hung from their delicate bodies like dreadlocks.

Foxes don't give you the kind of ingratiating looks we're used to getting from dogs, and they make a sharp *kak-kak-kak-kak* sound, more like a bird than a member of the canine family. They are absolutely monogamous. If a third fox happens by during spring mating, the pair chase the intruder away.

I walked to the ridge that overlooks Dundas Village, passing four American servicemen barbecuing steaks and corn in what had become a blizzard. Under the mountain stream's crumpled lid of ice we heard rushing water. I wanted to walk through what remained of Dundas Village to see where Peter Freuchen and Knud Rasmussen had lived and to look out on that once-fecund bay. Now the flat top of the solitary mountain that stood sentinel at the entrance to the bay is used as a golf course by American officers on the Fourth of July.

Ten thirty p.m. The sky cleared. Gaiety in Barracks 136. The first helicopter was to leave for Qaanaaq. The second would take me, the Peary sisters, and one other. If the weather held, there would be five trips that night. The van came for our luggage. I felt a moment of panic. Thule had begun to feel comfortable. Now I was being foisted into the unknown.

At the edge of the runway we huddled together like sheep. The sky had darkened and a wind dropped the temperature to zero. We heard the thumping beat of the returning helicopter. It was a toy in the sky slowly descending at our feet. Gitte Mortensen climbed out first. I had known her the winter I spent in Uummannaq—it was at her house that we glimpsed the February sun when it showed itself for the first time that year. She had moved to Qaanaaq to work in the Kommune, but a love affair gone bad was sending her away.

My nose slid from her fur hat to her sealskin anorak as she embraced me. There were tears in her eyes. "I wanted so much to see you and talk to you. We have both been stranded. Too bad it wasn't in the same place. Now we must say everything we have to say on this runway. I have been sick, so sick. Not in my body, but in my mind. The north has not been easy for me. So much darkness. And also a man, a hunter . . . Now I must go home to Denmark and get well."

Over her shoulder I saw the Swedish mechanic running. The passenger door of the helicopter had fallen off. Hurriedly, he began screwing it back on. Wind hammered us. In the blur, Gitte pulled away from me.

I was crammed between the Peary sisters on the helicopter's bench seat. Behind our heads the humped-up cargo loomed, held in place by a rope net. The pale Danish pilot climbed in. He was new on the job and he looked it. The Arctic had not yet carved its hard lines into his face, or set his mouth with the usual insolent contempt for death. Now I understood why we had been delayed so long at Thule: he was afraid. An Arctic hand would have flown in iffier weather.

I was relieved to see the Swedish mechanic slide into the copilot's seat. The engine thrummed and the door held. As the helicopter surged forward, I felt an immense relief to be getting away from Thule. I had been in the Arctic all right, but not the real Greenland. The Peary sisters smiled as we lifted up. I wondered about metal fatigue—how long would those door screws last? It was past one in the morning as we rose through a diminishing snow squall into all-night sunshine and the huge, menacing air base vanished from sight.

No one spoke. The helicopter's vibrations shook us up and up. We saw where glaciers had unpooled their ice into Smith Sound and flew through streams of mist that lay feathery on mountains. The Peary sisters called the rock faces that pushed up "walrus heads." The ice was a skin, all cross-hatched, blasted, and scratched, its lobed fissures bending. A frozen river appeared to flow backward up a white mountain. The ice cap was a *dzong*—a fortress—whose interior had never been hollowed out.

It was impossible to tell if we were flying into a wall or sliding over the edge of the earth. Depositions of ice were serrated by silver light and aquamarine pools. I remembered what Jack had said about the location of Thule Air Base: that it was located on the earth's geomagnetic center. Now I wondered what kind of forces were working on us, if they would pull us down or lift us. The farther north we went, the more I felt as if my body was imploding.

Under the thumping blade my eye followed the sinuous coast. Mountains alternated with fjords, ice with land, land with ice—all were strobing currents. Here was the birthplace of this world's horizon, its single universal line frazzled into a million slender threads. How they were combed straight and laid out told us where we lived, the one reference point keeping us from oblivion.

We arrived in Qaanaaq at two in the morning. The sun shone bright. As I stepped off the helicopter I could hear village sounds—dogs barking, the slow rhythms of Greenlandic being spoken, the squeak of snow under feet. A kind-faced Greenlander came forward and took my bags. In my excitement I'd forgotten that I didn't have a place to stay, but the problem seemed to have solved itself. The man was Hans Jensen from the Qaanaaq Hotel. "Aleqa called and told me you were coming. You will stay with us until you go traveling with Jens Danielsen. I have found a translator for you. He and Jens will come to the hotel tomorrow to meet you."

The "hotel" was five spartan rooms, a shared bathroom, and a dining room and kitchen with a bank of windows overlooking the fjord. Children's cutouts of the sun hung everywhere. Beyond was the frozen ocean, then Ellesmere Island.

Jens put my dufflebag in one of the rooms. "If you are hungry help yourself. I'm sorry, but we weren't sure if you were coming tonight, so there is no dinner. In the morning we will eat."

I made a cup of tea and some toast and stood at the windows. In front of the small Danish-style houses, sleds were parked willy-nilly and everyone's dogs were tethered to long chains on the ice. Their howling and shrieking drowned out other sounds. The air was still. A calm had fallen over the village. The dogs lay down. With their noses tucked under their tails, they looked like rocks.

Everything in the world was frozen in place except the sun, which moved its gold leaf here and there, torching the tops of stranded icebergs and filigreeing the sharp-bladed ends of the Greenland coast. Beyond was ice—or was it only light laid flat, a whole prairie?

In the morning Birthe, Hans's wife, laid out a Danish-style breakfast of rye bread, cheese, and ham. Buxom and wild-eyed, her laughter was infectious. Her long black hair floated over her shoulders when she walked. We sat drinking coffee, stumbling through a mishmash of Greenlandic and English. I practiced the Inuktun dialect and she corrected my pronunciation. In this tiny hotel I was the only guest.

Later, Jens Danielsen and Niels Kristiansen came by. They were huge men at six foot four and six foot one with brown faces and black hair. Jens blinked shyly as we discussed the trip, never looking me in the eye. Niels translated slowly and laconically. Jens had the loose, nonchalant air of a man who had circled the globe more than once, but had finally come home. "Just for the adventure. You know, to get out and see some things," he told me. He had shipped out of Nuuk when he was eighteen and had only recently returned to his hometown of Qaanaaq to live as a hunter. "Wherever I traveled people asked what nationality I was. They thought maybe I was Japanese or Mexican or Tibetan. When I said I'm Eskimo they never believed me. So I had to say something in Greenlandic. It didn't matter. They called me 'Sumo' because I was so fat. I weighed one hundred twenty kilos then, mostly from beer."

Jens was married to Ilaitsuk, a woman eight years his senior whose grandfather had traveled with Rasmussen to Alaska on the Fifth Thule

Expedition. In 1991 Jens and his partner, Ono Fleischer—a great-nephew of Rasmussen—followed Rasmussen's tracks. From Greenland they flew to Resolute, Northwest Territories, then traveled by dogsled across Arctic Canada to the Seward Peninsula in Alaska. Their journey took one hundred days—not three years. I asked if they might do it again and take me along. Jens looked at me and shook his head.

We sat in silence. I wondered aloud if the weather would be good. Jens stared blankly. I didn't know if his reticence was contempt or shyness, and hoped it was the latter. On the other hand, he had every right to feel disdain. I was out of my element in the Arctic and couldn't begin to understand the complexities of ice. That would take a lifetime and I had already used up most of the one life I had.

Struggling to get up, Jens said that we would leave the next day and go north to the village of Siorapaluk and beyond to Etah, then out to the ice edge to hunt narwhal and walrus. I had questions but didn't ask them: where would we sleep, how would we eat, did I need to buy groceries? Jens asked if my clothing was warm enough. I went to my room and brought out what I had. He fingered the four-inch-thick parka and pants, tattered hand-me-downs from a Himalayan climber. "Maybe too warm," he said, laughing. "Come tomorrow, about eleven, down to the sled."

"*Sumiippa?*" I asked finally—Where is it? He looked exasperated, then turned and went out the door.

Snow began. Then sun burst out, accompanied by the snow buntings' song. I had mild chest pains and slight nausea. Nothing more serious than abject fear. It was impossible to sleep. I stood at the windows of the dining room looking west toward Canada. A thick mist separated the top and bottom of the islands. I could see only the flanks of the mountains. Then the clouds merged, taking whole islands with them. I looked toward what had been the horizon—that invisible wall at the end of the world—and hoped that on a dogsled we would be able to travel beyond.

After midnight there was the usual calm. The future had been abandoned and the past had been annihilated by tranquillity. Ice mesmerized time. The horizon shifted from silver to blue. I knew it was only an illusion: the human mind groping for boundaries, but in no way did it hold me that night.

A loose female dog in the village wandered among suitors. The males, tethered by thick chains, howled with longing. The sky was moonless. Was gravitational attraction still at work here? Under the ice unseen tides came and went. I drank more tea. The midnight sun cast shadows that leaned sideways from dogs' legs, rooflines, and the gracefully upcurving sled runners. Then clouds covered the sun until sky and ice were one thing. I worried about the journey ahead of me, traveling alone with two strange men. There was no turning back. It had been agreed that we would leave the next day.

Morning brought light snow. I carried my duffle down a path between houses to the shore ice where the sleds were parked helter-skelter between hummocks and hundreds of dogs lay waiting—all cream-colored with brown spots or dark with light chests and paws. Which ones were Jens's I couldn't tell. Dogs, people, harnesses, children, parkas, plastic bags with food, and sleds stretched in both directions.

A pear-shaped man in bright blue overalls approached. It was Niels. "How can you be lost?" he asked. A smile crossed his wide face. We ambled down onto the ice. No self-respecting Greenlander would ever behave as if he were in a hurry. It didn't matter if we left at ten in the morning or four in the afternoon. As long as the ice was good, there was always light.

"You can just follow me," Niels said softly. A cigarette hung from his lips as he led me far out from the others to where Jens was harnessing dogs. The sled was long—thirteen feet—its bed made of wood imported from Denmark and covered with a blood-stained blue tarp. Onto this we loaded our duffles, boots, anoraks, a small satchel of food, and two kitchen boxes with boiling pots, fuel, and two Primus stoves. A few pads were thrown on top and reindeer hides were lashed over the cargo making a smooth soft seat. Extra thongs (made of sealskin), nylon ropes, and a burlap sack with a Made in Mexico label were hung from the two curved sled handles at the back. Inside was a sewing kit, a hand planer, extra sealskin mittens, ammunition, and more nylon rope.

Jens's twenty dogs were already harnessed. He stood bent at the waist in a tangle of ice-clotted trace lines, sorting and pulling the uneven lengths apart. These were the lines that connected dog to sled, not in pairs as in Alaska (where there are narrow trails between trees), but in a broad array, fanned out in front of the sled. In this way, the dogs had more freedom to move among themselves, to pull hard, hang back to rest, or sidle up next to a friend.

Niels held the older dogs while Jens turned his attention to four young ones, who squealed with delight at the prospect of going. He patiently tied them in with the others. As their excitement mounted, Niels snapped the whip to keep them from taking off. They ducked, retreated, and lay in a huddle.

Just before Jens tied the traces into the *pituutaq*—the ivory half-moon hook that connected the main line to the sled—he looked back to see what I was doing. Niels whispered, "You can just sit down!" The sled jerked forward. I didn't know what was happening, but I sat. The dogs lunged. Running now, both Jens and Niels made flying leaps and landed heavily on the sled, Jens sitting sideways at the front and Niels at the back, with me sandwiched between.

We careened through broken ice at the shoreline, now sitting sideways three abreast with one leg tucked up under the other. The sled jounced, tilted, and came down hard as we slid over the rough ice. I was the *aluupaq*, the passenger, a novice on a sled. I shoved my fingers hard under the lash lines to keep from falling off.

"*Haruuu, haruuu*," Jens cooed in a soft, gravelly voice. Go left, he was saying. "*Attuk, attuk*"—go right. There are no reins to control the dogs, just voice commands. The ice was a constant obstacle course and the dogs scrambled over whatever came their way. Knife-edged bits of rough ice grazed my legs and broke off. As we headed north up the coast, the ice smoothed out and the dogs trotted euphorically. This was a Greenland highway—a frozen sea, all white. We were on our way to Siorapaluk, the northernmost village in the world.

A dogsled is a moving platform from which to see. The ice looks like a place where Ockham's razor has made a swipe, taking unnecessary loved ones, animals, homes. Once I had everything. Now it's lost. Then the losing of it was lost. The sled does not move toward one point and away from the other. It just glides.

A sharp breeze hit my face like the back of a hand. "Pay attention," it seemed to be saying. We passed the deconstructed cathedral of a half-melted iceberg and the sharp ends of two large islands, Kiatak Island and Herbert Island (Qeqertarsuaq). On my right was the frozen coast of Greenland, on my left a plain of ice that led to Ellesmere Island. We were the only beings moving.

The summer before I watched icebergs move down Illorsuit's narrow fjord. I was stationary and they were the travelers, floating legless like ghosts, white against the wet faces of rock. Now the icebergs were grounded and we moved. Even though our course was north, we never crossed the sun's halo; it seemed to enlarge as if to accommodate our journey. Such is the generosity of the place. Later, snow clouds crowded in; our sled runners sliced through straightedged shadows and the light went flat.

"There's no better way in the world to travel than by dogsled," Niels said, and he had tried everything—motorcycles, ships, helicopters, bicycles, horses, and airplanes. We slalomed through a line of towering floes—"an Eskimo picket fence," he called it. The week before, a polar bear had gone all the way up the fjord, hiding behind the "ice mountains," and escaped its hunters.

I looked at the sky through dark glasses. The spacecraft *Soho* sent back images of gas pouring around the sun in rivers 64,000 kilometers wide. Between these bands sunspots appeared, intensifying the sun's heat and magnetic fields and adding to global warming. Up here, at the top of the world, we were indeed the sun's prisoners, never out of its sight. Ahead of us, horizon gave way to horizon like doors swinging open, and portholes kept appearing in the upper walls of ice floes through which to view the all-day, all-night peep show of continuous light.

A bone lay on the ice. One of the young dogs snatched it up as he trotted by. That meant trouble: if the other dogs saw it, there would be a fight. In one quick motion Jens flicked the whip—the handle was made from the legbone of a reindeer and attached to it was a twenty-foot-long sealskin thong. Perfectly aimed, the tip wrapped around the end of the bone, pulling it from the dog's mouth without ever touching the animal.

"*Ai, ai, ai, ai, ai,*" Jens cried out, urging them on, his deep-bellied voice rising to a near-falsetto. A bright sun's ray knifed the snow squall and burnished his face. Despite his size and gruffness, I saw and heard only gentleness: when he talked to the dogs, his voice had the same tenderness that I'd heard him use with his grandchild before we left.

Snow deepened and the dogtrot slowed. Our load weighed nearly a thousand pounds. The dogs constantly repositioned themselves, the ginger-colored lead dog staying at the front, and two small black-and-brown females with fluffy tails hanging back on each side. Sometimes Jens cut the youngsters loose and they ran free alongside the team. When the pulling got tough, the smaller dogs and some of the females pressed their bodies together and strained against the lines—three dogs pulling as one. They had already traveled 1,500 kilometers this season, Jens told me. The ice wouldn't melt until July, so they could expect to travel that far again before summer.

Avannaarsua. North Land. The scale was grand and distances were hard to calculate. Instead of the cloistering revetments of rock rising straight out of narrow waterways that I had seen in west Greenland, here the coast was a wider hand whose fingers were roundtop mountains cut through with wide fjords. Glaciers presented their ice walls at the ends of these white floors, white giving onto white. Land that looked ten miles distant might be fifty miles away. And much of it had never felt the weight of a human foot or even an animal's.

A long, melodic whistle brought the dogs to a stop. "*Arittet,*" Niels whispered, jumping off the sled. The dogs sat huddled together as it began to snow. I looked up: the edge of the ice cap blurred—it looked as if it was made of mist that had dissolved—and the dove-gray sky drove down to our feet. Jens unhooked and untangled the traces, giving the dogs a rest. As they rolled in the snow to cool themselves, we pulled on sealskin mittens. All around was white: sea surface, mountainside, the ice cap mounded up in whipped clouds. The only sound was made by the dogs. When Jens asked them to stop panting, they did; he turned to me and smiled. All we could hear then was the dry hiss of snow blowing off the ice cap.

After a short rest Jens tied the other two young dogs in. "You can just sit down," Niels said to me again. We glided around the tip of Piulip Nuna and peered in at the head of of MacCormick Fjord. "Up there is a beautiful lake where I like to go fishing in summertime," Niels said. He was a man of leisure now and his bulging belly showed it. He'd sold his motorcycle and his seaman's house in Denmark and was living on the proceeds.

On the other side of the frozen sound, the land curved out like a wing. In midsummer—the mid-weeks of July—its green point would be dappled with alpine flowers—saxifrage hyperborea, salix herbacea, salix articus, alpine chickweed, and common koenigia, among others. At the guest house, Hans Jensen had described northern Greenland's summer glories to me: "Summer happens for two weeks in July. The sun is very bright and the flowers bloom all over the hillsides. The little river rushes through the middle of the town, sometimes taking out the footbridge. The children love it when that happens. They jump back and forth across the torrent of water, never falling in. Last year the wind blew so hard, all the icebergs went away. But this year we were lucky. The sun was hot and the fjord was like a parade ground full of drifting ice."

The way was smooth but the snow had deepened, so the going was slower. Jens busied himself repairing dog harnesses on the moving sled. He sewed the thick yellow nylon straps together, pushing his needle through the tough material and binding the cut edges with the wavering flame of a butane lighter. "In the old days, the harnesses were made of sealskin thongs, but the dogs ate them. Nylon is better. They can't chew their way out of these." Laid out on his lap, his sewing kit had bone needles and ones made of metal, thick nylon thread as well as sealskin and narwhal sinews, and a thick cap of bearded sealskin for a thimble.

A sewing kit is as vital as a harpoon on a long dogsled journey. When members of the MacMillan Expedition broke off from the main team and forgot to bring along a sewing kit, they eventually died from exposure because they had no way to mend torn clothes. A hole in an anorak, pants, or a boot will eventually kill you with cold.

We continued on. There were no other sleds in sight. While Jens sewed industriously, Niels smoked and dreamed, and I let myself be overtaken with numbness. Not from cold, but from a free-floating unconcern. Once I had amnesia after an accident. That lost time was an empty frame, a brick wall of not remembering. It was a death box, a box of daylight forever unrevealed—claustral and unyielding—the opposite of what I was seeing now from the sled, which seemed only to open more and more.

Unfolding a topo map in my lap, I located Neqe, then Etah, Anoratoq, Inglefield Land, the huge face of Humboldt Glacier, and Washington Land—all places where Rasmussen, Freuchen, Peary, Cook, Nansen, and others had wintered or camped on their way to the topmost parts of the world. When I asked Jens how far north he had traveled, he told me in months, not miles. "Two months north in good weather to hunt polar bear," he said, which would have taken him halfway to Peary Land.

The icescape was wide, fresh, and adamantine; it stood for reality's reality and for indestructible emptiness untainted by human tinkering. Yet sun in the unmoving frozen north seemed paradoxical, if not redundant: light blasting down on entropy where nothing grew—what good was sunlight in such a place?

I folded the map and slid it under my thigh. The Arctic is no place for pragmatists. As we glided forward, new ice was being laid out in front of the dogs as if their visible breath had become an unrolling scroll. Glaciers pulsed, shifting back, grinding forward, collapsing their own icy pediments. Yet behind these razed columns new pillars kept revealing themselves as the snout advanced on its rupturing stilts. The sled, running smooth on frozen ocean, ironed all my thoughts flat until they emptied out behind me.

"*Ah ta ta ta ta ta,*" Jens sang to his dogs. Faster. Go faster. We glided in a trance. Jens loved ice and was indifferent to the open water that came with summer. "He is very strong," Hans Jensen had told me. "Not just his body . . . he is even stronger in his mind."

Our speed increased. To move was to break the trance, to travel beyond boundaries. "I am clearing the way, I am sweeping the path clean," a Yupik woman in Alaska once sang to me. Now I looked up and out: all was horizon, a silver pin laid at the edge of the universe, until even that disappeared.

A sled appeared in the distance. "That's Ikuo," Niels said. Everywhere I had traveled in Greenland people told me about Ikuo Oshima. He had come to Siorapaluk from Japan in 1972 as part of Naome Uemura's support team for the climber's solo attempt on the North Pole and had stayed.

His sled was moving so slowly it had almost come to a stop. In a few minutes we saw why: he had eight passengers and six dogs to pull them through deep snow. As we came up beside them, Ikuo leaped from the sled and greeted us with a comedic, wild man's dance. Small and wiry, he was all smiles, all enthusiasm. He poured hot tea into our cups from an oversized push-button dispenser—Japanese, of course. "Very modern, *desu ne?*" he said. The back of his polar bear pants were worn down to the hide from so many months sitting on a dogsled. His daughter and her Danish boyfriend waved halfheartedly—they were the young, amorous couple who had been stuck at Thule Air Base for five days with me.

Jens set the kitchen box upright on the ice and lit the Primus. Time for tea. He told me that the box had gone with him on his dogsled expedition to Alaska and served as a windbreak for the little stove set inside.

Niels broke off chunks of glacier ice and dropped them in a battered pot to melt for tea water. Danish cookies were passed between sleds. Ikuo chattered in Greenlandic to Jens and Niels and spoke Japanese and English to me. His good-naturedness was almost clownlike; I wondered what he was hiding. He was on his way home to Siorapaluk with his family—a wife, three children, and several friends from Qaanaaq. "That town makes me so tired," he said. The sun was in the north and the breeze was sharp. It was night, though what time, I didn't know.

After tea, Jens offered to take Ikuo's fat wife and one of their children on our sled to lighten Ikuo's load. Snow began again. "Too much *aput*," I said to Jens. Niels corrected me. *Aput* means snow on the ground, while *qaniit* means falling snow. "Okay, too much *qaniit*," I said, and they laughed appreciatively.

Our two sleds started off together, but soon Ikuo's lagged behind. We waved as we passed and headed for the wide mouth of Robertson Fjord. Behind, I could hear Ikuo singing a Japanese ballad to his tired dogs.

Two squadrons of dovekies—little auks—soared high above us as we entered Siorapaluk Fjord. They come to Greenland each year to breed, nest, and fledge their young on south-facing talus slopes. As we approached the village Ikuo's voice faded out and another sound took over: a buzzing, like something electrical. The vibration—almost white noise at first—grew louder and louder. Then I saw the auks, thousands of them, phalanx after phalanx flying over. The strange sound was beating wings. Up the fjord, the cliffs were steep talus slopes. Each rock served as a nesting ledge for a pair of auks. As we drew closer, the buzzing increased: the whole mountain was alive with birds.

Niels pointed to something on the far shore: a row of twenty-six houses and two children on a seesaw. This was Siorapaluk, the northernmost continuously inhabited village in the world. We made camp on the ice five hundred yards out from the village. All eyes were on us. Some were at their windows with binoculars to see who we were. Children played outside in the snow and couples walked from house to house visiting. In these all-light nights no one slept normal hours. Finally Ikuo straggled in. We had left Qaanaaq at noon. It was now ten at night.

Jens unhitched the dogs. With a long knife he scraped out notches in the ice through which he threaded the dogs' lines, separating them into three groups so they wouldn't fight. The dogs were quiet and alert, which meant they were hungry. We had not hunted that day and so had no food for them or for ourselves.

A thin canvas tent stained with seal blood was put up over the sled and three caribou hides were laid down on the slats. This was our bed; the floor was ice. I stood outside in a cold breeze. The sun—what I could see of it—was dead north and blurred by snow squalls. An Arctic fox cried, making a strangling sound.

We walked into the village to visit Niels's cousin. Besides the houses that climbed the escarpment, there was a tiny state-owned store and a red schoolhouse that doubled as a clinic when a doctor or dentist came through. We were greeted with coffee but no food. The house was large but nearly empty, no rugs, just a television set. The cousin's young son acted frightened—either of us or of his father—and didn't stay in the room long. Walter Matthau and Jack Lemmon were on the screen. The sound was off, since it was in English, and the actors, playing neighbors in a "hard" Minnesota winter, were vaudevillian. Attention soon waned and turned to local gossip: the Norwegian schoolteachers, a husband and wife with two children who had lived in Siorapaluk for three years, had quit their job and gone north to Washington Land to hunt polar bear. No one had heard from them and no new teachers had been hired.

After coffee, we visited the town's oldest hunter and his wife. They were both sixty. "That's not very old," I said. "It's a hard life," Niels reminded me. The man, bent over and toothless, looked eighty, and his wife, a skinny, nervous chain-smoker, looked almost as old. The conversation turned to hunting accidents and near-death experiences. He had once resuscitated a hunter from a distant village who had suffered a heart attack. "I gave him CPR," the man said. "When he came to, he started yelling at the icebergs. He thought they were his enemies. He never thanked me for bringing him back to life. Once he came here, but no one would talk to him. People were afraid of his voice because he had been dead."

The winter of 1970 was bad in Siorapaluk, they told me. A wind blew sleds and barrels of food away. The memory of the storm made the old woman's eyes light up: "Those barrels were never seen again. We always wondered what happened to them. Maybe if we traveled south a long way, we would find them," she said. But her husband shook his head. "No. Once they are out of this district, they are no more," he said with finality.

Once they did go south by dogsled to what they contemptuously called "Danish Greenland"—Ilulissat. Recalling the trip, the old woman began shaking her head: "Oh my, the sleds there were so small. We thought they belonged to the children!" She poured coffee. A polar bear had been in the village the week before. "I heard a noise out back and thought it was a dog, so I went out with my flashlight and it was a bear. He turned and looked at me. I just told him to go away . . . He ran back down the fjord."

The old man laughed, rubbing his arthritic hands: "My only regret is that I'm too old to hunt walrus. Now a younger hunter"—he pointed to a yellow house next door—"gets our meat for us when I can't go."

We went to the house of that young hunter. He was handsome and robust and dandled a baby on his knee. The tiny kitchen was crowded with neighbors drinking coffee, playing cards, talking on the two-way radio to friends camped out on the ice. Ikuo's daughter and her boy-friend visited. The baby crawled to me and fell asleep as I held her between my legs on the floor.

We still had not eaten anything except cookies. Back at camp, Jens lit his trusty Primus stove and boiled water for tea. Someone yelled out. It was Ikuo calling. He and Jens disappeared into the village and returned carrying a red plastic bucket of seal meat for the dogs. A month earlier Jens had given Ikuo two puppies and the meat was given in exchange.

Dogs were always the subject of conversation. Ten years before, almost every dog in Siorapaluk and Qaanaaq had died of distemper. Jens lost all but two. The local dogcatcher's job was to vaccinate the dogs for parvo and rabies, and also to shoot male dogs who got loose, went on rampages of fighting and killing, and were not claimed by their owners within a week. "The dogcatcher saves their lives and he also takes them," Niels said, smiling at the irony.

Jens's dogs lined up waiting to be fed. The "boss" and three others sat in the front row; behind them, two lines of six; and last, the four puppies. They watched intently as Jens hacked the seal meat into small pieces, then threw the chunks, one by one, into their mouths. His aim was as perfect as their patience. There was no fighting over food.

"I can't afford to lose dogs because of a fight," Jens said. "There's no reason for it. We need every dog we have and so we must think hard about them, what they are saying to us, and do what is right for them." He was always thinking about his dogs. They ate that night, we didn't.

Our kitchen—the floor in front of the sled, now our sleeping platform—was ice, and on it the Primus stove hissed and threw out heat. We hung our kamiks and our rabbit-skin socks on the line over our heads to dry, but as falling snow continued, the tent sagged until there was almost no place to sit. At two in the morning Niels's cousin came to our camp with his shy little boy, carrying a blue plastic tarp which they flung over the tent to keep the snow off. The cousin wanted to visit. Under his windbreaker he wore only a T-shirt despite the cold. Standing outside, he told Jens a long story about hunting near Dundas Village, where he and Niels had grown up. The northern dialect of Greenlandic replaces *s*'s with an unaspirated *h,* and the words have a soft sound. That night the men's slow-beat, velvety largo quenched in me an unnamable thirst. I lay on my sleeping bag like an island in the stream of their voices, happy not to know what they were talking about.

On the same day in 1917, Rasmussen made camp just north of Siorapaluk and wrote: "We sit here in an ocean of light which blinds our eyes, in the midst of the winter-white Arctic spring, with pure new snow round our feet, the sun-gilded horizon of the glaciers behind the russet mountains, and the cold, bound Polar Sea before us lonely, wandering explorers, with a whole world between us and our relatives and friends."

I closed the book and laid my head down. Jens and Niels were already snoring. We were sleeping on the bare skull of ice with only a skin and a few slats of wood between us and its cold brain. The village was quiet and the mountain was alive with birds. Much later, I was awakened by an animal's noise. I tapped Niels's shoulder. *Nanuq?* Polar bear? I asked. Niels opened his eyes and listened for a long time. "No, *qimmeq.* Dog," he whispered softly, then went back to sleep. We had made it through one day.

Much later the buzzing of birds came into my head. It lifted me from sleep like some solid thing. I stood outside and glassed the cliffs with binoculars. Individual auks were difficult to distinguish: the whole mountain was one quivering mass. Then one bird flew up and I could make out its thick black head and white underbelly. They are awkward fliers, like cargo planes lumbering into molasses-rich air. Their relatives, the great auks, once found on the shores of Newfoundland and now extinct, were altogether flightless, and even now, these heavy-bodied birds are unable to soar. That's why they have to beat their wings so fast, why the wings make so much noise. But there was one place they are all grace: under water. Auks are the penguins of the north—much smaller and less photogenic, but, like penguins, they dive for plankton and "fly" underwater as effortlessly as most birds fly through air.

Playful Mind. Joyful Heart. Those were the words stitched across Ikuo Oshima's red sweatpants, and no words could better describe him. We had gone to his house to visit. He was no longer the comedian dancing on the ice, but smart, quick, curious, kind, bold, joyful, and known by everyone in Greenland because he was such an oddity—an outsider who not only fit in but often surpassed the Inuit hunters who taught him.

"Sometimes you can be longing for something and you don't know what it is until you see it," he said. "Then it is yours. I've been twenty-five years here; I've found a place for myself."

His house stood apart at the edge of the village. He poured coffee, passed cookies, then sat crosslegged and barefoot on a chair as his eyes danced. "A fresh start, yes? We are all trying to make fresh starts, *desu ne?*" I smiled, yes, and he told me the story of how he came to Siorapaluk: "I had been studying mechanical engineering in college in Tokyo," he said, picking up a baby from the floor and looking into her eyes as he talked. "But everything was already invented, everything was done for you. You could only work on a small part of something, never make the whole thing. I hated that. It was terrible for me. I wanted to go abroad, just to see, so I worked for two years in a small factory to make money for traveling. I belonged to a Japanese mountaineering club and when the climber Naome Uemura came here to make an attempt on the North Pole in 1972, he arranged for me to fly to Thule and we came by dogsled to Siorapaluk." He, looking out the window, then directly into my eyes, leaning forward a little: "This hunting life . . . I knew immediately that it was something for me. It was a life I had been wanting."

He poured tea from his push-button thermos and served more cookies. "In Japan life is so tiring," he continued. "The people—too much stress—even to make a meal. Always in their faces is tiredness. Always in their body, running. Now you can see I am happy," he said, laughing. "I like this little village best."

The tiny house was full of things: a postcard from Japan, a piece of calligraphy on the wall, a small ax on the floor. Above our heads were two harpoons and an ivy vine strung all the way across the ceiling to the other side of the room. "This plant is nine years old. It is happiest over there by the window," Ikuo pointed out. Jumping up from his chair, he touched a leaf. "It took some time to get over there. And even now, sometimes we forget to water it. But still, it wants to live."

Leaning down he tossed up the neighbor's baby and nuzzled her fat cheeks, then poured more tea and coffee and replenished the cookie plate. A white fox skin hung from a line over our heads and moved, as if alive, when visitors came through the door. They removed their shoes (a Greenlandic as well as Japanese custom) and another baby crawled across the floor to sit contentedly between Ikuo's legs.

Ikuo's wife was silent. She sat sullenly, then moved to a pink couch in the back room, darkened by blankets over the windows, and ate candy from a box. Her lassitude accentuated Ikuo's nonstop activity. She was, as the Danes said, "special." When Ikuo found that she couldn't do the usual chores of a hunter's wife—preparing and sewing skins and flensing seals—he simply did them for her, performing both the man's and woman's work without complaint. He built sleds and sewed anoraks, made harpoons and fashioned mittens for the children, hunted foxes, made the bird nets and caught birds, gathered tern eggs, and cooked.

He took his walrus-hunting harpoon down from the rafters. Its shaft was inlaid with ivory. "I love hunting walrus the most," he told me. "Especially in the months when the ice is new—October and November. A walrus can weigh over two thousand pounds. When he comes, he makes a sound, *huff, huff,* and breaks the ice with the top of his head. Then I harpoon him. Sometimes the whole ice edge breaks off and the harpoon and everything goes, me too, into the water! But I always get out," he said, with a sly smile.

Jumping up, he peered out the window, a leaf of the long vine touching his head. The wind had picked up and it was spitting snow. "Usually this is the best month—strong sun and so beautiful—but maybe not this year . . ." I asked if he missed anything about Japan—the food perhaps. He wrinkled his nose and threw his head back. "Ah . . . I don't know. I can't think of such a thing. Food depends on the culture you are living in. If you are eating only vegetables, then green tea, *o-cha,* is good with that . . . but not here."

I followed him to a back room where he washed fox skins in an old washing machine adapted for that purpose. His hands were beautifully shaped, as if carved from hardwood. In the corner was a chamber pot with a cutout cardboard seat. "Japanese toilet," he said laughing. He had been back to Japan only once. "I'm from a poor suburb of Tokyo and I went around trying to find the apartment where I lived for eleven years. I asked many people but no one knew. Then I found the spot, but the building was gone and they had changed the name of the street. I was shocked. Nothing of the place I knew was there. No trace. I wanted to turn around and come home."

He went out to check on the dogs. "This female, she will soon be having puppies," he said. A packing crate laid on its side served as a doghouse. We looked over the fjord. It had gone gray with snow. Ikuo raised his arms and held his hands palms out to catch the snow. "It is like Hokkaido." He shook his head laughing. "But I like. There's nothing here I don't like." Something moved near his house. His wife was watching us from the window. Ikuo glanced at her, then tilted his head back. "It's different for me. They didn't choose to be here. I did."

Two years earlier, Ikuo hurt his back while hunting and had to go to Denmark for an operation. For the next year, the villagers hunted for him. He'd sold half his dog team to pay bills. He wrinkled his nose: "But I don't like that. I don't like asking for help. Now it's time for a fresh start, *desu ne?*" Walking back to the house, he hummed a Japanese tune.

Standing to leave, I asked if there was anything I could send from Japan or America. His voice deepened: "Ahhhh . . . sooooo." Then he shook his head. "Everything I need . . . it's out there," he said, pointing to the fjord. "No . . . It is better if I get everything myself. Needing things . . . that leads to unhappiness. And all the time, I need less and less."

The snow was wet and heavy and there was no wind. We climbed into our sleeping bags and slept fitfully. A thin crust had formed by morning, the kind that cuts dogs' legs. The birds were quiet because a peregrine falcon had been cruising around and a fox had come down from the region just beneath the ice cap and was looking for eggs. Jens busied himself making dog harnesses. They lay everywhere—piled on our sleeping bags, on the ice floor at his feet. "If we're snowed in too long, there won't be any room for us to sleep," Niels commented.

We went to the KNI store run by Niels's cousin. There was nothing much to buy—warm Tuborg beer, canned meat, and teabags. It was a quiet time in the village between seasons, between snowstorms. The dogs slept and children played outside regardless of weather, lured by the light. I went to Ikuo's house and watched as he taught his oldest daughter and her Danish boyfriend how to mend a bird net. They were going to Neqe to catch auks as soon as the weather cleared. "But that may not be until June," Ikuo said smiling.

That night Jens lit two Primus stoves—one for tea and the other to boil the chicken necks and backs he'd bought at the store—a whole chicken was too expensive at twenty dollars. Because we had not hunted for the second day in a row, the chicken would be our dinner. Steam from the boiling water whirled a dervish in the hole at the top of the tent, then snowflakes spit through. Jens and Niels ate without relish. Chicken was Danish food and they didn't like it. "In the morning, we'll give the soup from this to Ikuo," Niels said. "And tomorrow, we'll eat seal."

I stuck my head out of the tent. The *qaniit* is following us, I said. And indeed it was. We lay on our sleeping bags three across, our heads under the blue part of the tent—darkened to keep the sun out of our eyes. While Jens and Niels talked quietly, I thought about how Inuit communalism was an old necessity that had arisen from long and frequent bouts of famine. Now these men choose to be subsistence hunters in a modern world larded with Danish goods, where, in the event of a bad hunting season, the helicopter would bring food and supplies. Which in no way trivialized their pursuit; it simply moderated the consequences of failure.

Throughout the community meat was still shared as it had always been, but the oppressive edge of starvation and the rigorous societal rules that go with subsistence hunting had been relaxed. Part of Jens's work as a representative of all the hunters in the north was to keep those rules from being completely erased. Traditional hunting was the key: if dogs were traded in for snowmobiles, as they had been in Canada, dependencies shifted from oneself to paper money and the industries that produced machines and petroleum. "You can't get a can of gas with a harpoon," Niels said. And if there were no dogs to feed, there was no reason to hunt every day. Once the link to the world of animals was cut, the thread pulled loose and the moral compass began to bend, who knew which way?

The tent flap was tied back and the view out was of dogs lying in snow, and beyond, Siorapaluk's houses, sleds, dogs, and drying racks. In this last village at the top of the world, things had changed, and yet hunting with harpoons, kayaks, bird nets, and dogs still continued. I thought about Ikuo. He was a modern-day man of vision who could see into things because *qaameneq* had entered his body like a hundred flashlights whose batteries didn't fade. He could drop who he was supposed to be and go into another life unimpeded because he knew how to give himself in the same way. There were no obstacles except that his body was wearing out from such hard use and he would need a new one some day soon. Lying there, dreaming, I was suddenly seized by an unlikely idea: I wanted to get up, go to Ikuo, and have his child.

Wavelike clouds broke over the mountains, cold clouds that blew off the ice cap, gray and smoothed by wind. The sounds from the bird mountain crescendoed, then went silent, and the ice floor inside our tent began to melt. It was time to leave. Standing in front of the whole village, Jens yelled at the snow, "Go away!"

We broke camp and headed north up the coast toward the historic campsites of Neqe and Etah, which had been used by hunters for four thousand years. There, an elbow of ice pushed out into the frozen ocean and the rocky coast was broken apart by wedge-shaped fjords.

The Inuit people never had a written language. Now, the whip, trailing behind the sled, made marks in the snow that looked calligraphic in the loose, running style the Chinese call "grass script." These were ephemeral inscriptions on new snow telling old stories.

Now Jens used the whip like a baton, inspiring his dogs as they began to tire. "*Ai . . . ai . . . ai . . . ai,*" he sang. I'd thought before coming on the trip that I could stand anything except cruelty to the dogs—that I would jump off the sled and walk back to Qaanaaq if necessary. What a relief to find that Jens was a kind man.

The north wind blew colder and the snow increased. When I put on my Himalayan parka, Jens and Niels laughed. "Are you warm enough?" Niels asked. "It's like being inside a house," I reported. As snow deepened, the pulling grew harder as the dogs pushed into the wind. I looked over the snow-dusted backs of twenty dogs. They were black, gray, white, and brown—some of the females so small I wondered how they could pull anything. The dogs' private lives were played out in front of us, their love affairs and stomach problems, flatulence, vomit, shit; the females' menstrual blood or their quick squat to pee.

The dogs worked for Jens but were caught up in their own society. From the sled we observed the flowering and dissolution of friendships, feuds, power plays, and love affairs. Because of the way they were har-nessed—each dog with its own trace—they could move about at will, aligning themselves with whomever they pleased, and ducking under traces to get away—much like the group hunting life of the Eskimos.

"*Avanna!*" Niels cried out. We bumped through a patch of rough ice. One dog's trace snagged on a jagged edge, flipping him onto his back. Jens let him be dragged for a few seconds to see if the dog could right himself, but the traces only got tangled. Very casually, Jens stuck his foot out, snapped the line, and flipped the dog up on his feet.

A cold wind hit us like a fist. Jens got up on his knees as if in prayer. The sled still moving, he took his brown pants off, and his shirt and sweater. The sled had been our bed and now it was our changing room. Soon he had nothing on but his red union suit and he was laughing because it was so cold. Niels said, "Now you've seen an Eskimo strip-tease!"

Half-naked, Jens clucked to his dogs to keep them going. Snow flew past. He had delicate hands, high-arched feet, a barrel chest, a wide belly, and was shaped like a bear. "*Nanu*," he said, as he extracted a pair of polar bear pants from his dufflebag. "This bear I shot up near Wash-ington Land a year ago," he said, pulling them on. "Eskimo hotpants," Niels commented, because they came only to his knees and were held up by suspenders clipped to a wide seal fur waistband. Then came a thick sweater, and over that an anorak lined with fox fur. We glided on.

Next, Jens pulled on his kamiks—first the Arctic hare socks, then the sealskin boots rubbed yellow with polar bear grease to keep them dry. Over his green cotton gloves came sealskin mittens with long bear-mane ruffs at the wrist. "*Kinatit?*" I asked. "*Inuk* or *nanuq?*" Who are you? Human or bear? He smiled and pulled his hood up until it squeezed his round brown face.

I unfolded the topo map again. The land protruded here like knuck-les, and between were frozen inlets that received calf ice from Morris Jesup Glacier. On the tip of the knuckle was Neqe, used as a meat depot by every expedition that had gone up this coast. When Jean Malaurie, the French ethnographer who lived in Siorapaluk for a year, arrived at Neqe in 1951, he wrote:

> *At the edge of the ice field we came upon tents, root fires, and the smell of juniper. Harpoons and scraps of meat lay on the ground. This was living prehistory. Lying on the shore, men in animal skins basked in the sun,*

enjoying the arrival of the warm season. Half-naked children played in the spotted snow amid puppies and seal carcasses. As soon as they saw us, they began yelling: "Inussuaruna? Are you a spirit or a man?"

"Inussuanga. I am a man." (Malaurie, The Last Kings of Thule, *p. 374)*

Where the snow had drifted the sled bumped hard. The coastline scalloped in and out of sight, as did the edge of the ever-present ice cap. A wreath of fog lay like a feather boa across our path, billowing into animal shapes, then evanescing. Snow pierced through fog and the panting cadence of trotting dogs surged upward, piercing the shroud. "*A he, he, he, he,*" Jens sang out, the notes of his call descending gradually. We were going nowhere. The horizon was an indefinite place made of whirling snowflakes.

I folded and unfolded my legs on the side of the sled. To sit sideways for ten or fourteen hours with no back rest was normal for a hunter, but tiring for me.

"Have you ever been lost?" I asked Jens.

He blinked hard and didn't answer at first. Then: "On our trip to Alaska we could tell the direction by the way the snow drifted. The prevailing winds there are very strong. But every three days or so, we consulted our GPS to make sure. Coopermine was the coldest place on the whole trip." When I asked him how cold, he said, "You know, really cold, colder than Greenland in midwinter. The trip was very difficult. We don't want to do it again."

Sometimes I knelt to ease my back. At that higher elevation, I could study the signatures of dog tracks in front of the sled and the trailing whip's calligraphy, which seemed to write a story:

Once there were two young couples who had taken land together. The husbands were good hunters and the wives clever and beautiful, and they stayed together. One day, the men sat and talked together about many things, such as people do when they have eaten their fill and their thoughts can be of something other than food.

"The world is big," said one of them.

"Yes, but how big?" said the other. "No matter how long you drive your sled you can always see ice in front of you."

"Let us find out," they said as with one voice, and so it was decided that the couples would depart, going in opposite directions, and travel to where the world meets itself.

They prepared for the journey. The women cried when taking leave, for they knew it might be some years before they would see each other again.

Then they traveled. Every year when the ice broke up, they took to the land and stayed there over the summer. They always caught enough game to keep them going for the next winter. When the ice was firm again, they started out and kept traveling for the whole winter, on and on.

They went year after year. The children of both couples grew up and married people from the settlements they visited. They too grew old and their children married, and at last there was an entire tribe traveling in each direction.

At last, the old couples were weak. The men could no longer drive their own sleds, and their wives had to sit on the sleds instead of running alongside. But they never forgot their old idea, and they went on. After many years they grew blind and had to be led by the younger ones. But they could not die until they had met their old friends.

One day, each party spotted another group moving toward them very slowly. The two couples were finally meeting again. Very slowly they walked up to each other, and they recognized each other's voices.

They had been so long on their journey that their cups made of muskox horn, with which they had scooped up water from the river, were now so worn that only the handles were left.

They greeted each other and sat down.

"The world is very big."

"Yes, even bigger than we thought when we parted!"

Then all four of them died, and here ends the story. That's how big the world is.

Ice mountains and mountains of rock slid by, or did we slide by them? Does slowness times snow equal distance? The whole world was a moon waxing and waning with a fluctuating tide eating the underside of the ice. After this, were we still expected to believe the fiction of minutes going by, or was this how we learned to wallow in a single point of time eternally?

Radiant sun shone between bursting snow squalls; horizon gave way to horizon like tree branches snapping off. The sound of sled runners sinking down through snow to ice was like water striking the hull of a boat, mixed with the hissing sound of snow flying off the ice cap. Neqe was ahead, around a wide bend of rocky land, and Etah was up the coast another sixty kilometers. Was this the end of the world or the beginning, or was it something after and before those two things?

We feasted on ice, on sunless days and sun-gorged nights, perched on an ephemeral floor. There was no center, only fringe and more fringe, and there were no constants—only what Rasmussen called "the *chaussée* of tides" gliding back and forth under us.

"You can just sit down!" Niels yelled. As we moved out again, I studied the hand-drawn calendar at the back of my notebook and found I'd misnumbered the days. I couldn't tell if we had slid from April into May or May into June. When I asked Niels how many days there were in May, he laughed, then shrugged. Who cared? What did matter was the weather and the condition of the ice and when we would get a seal.

Jens stopped the dogs. A long way away, he had spied a black mark on the ice—a seal sunbathing by its breathing hole. Quietly, Jens pulled his rifle out from under the lash rope while Niels quickly assembled the portable gun rest with its white cloth sail used as a blind. Holding the cloth in front of him, Jens walked slowly toward the seal. The wind was right—the seal wouldn't smell him and he was half a mile away. The seal lifted its head and Jens froze in place. When the seal lay down again, Jens moved.

At a quarter of a mile, Jens did a belly crawl, the rifle cradled in the gun rest behind the white cloth. From a distance, the dogs watched intently. As Jens drew closer to the seal, the dogs stopped panting altogether. Niels caught my eye: "You can just sit down," he whispered. I didn't know why I should sit, but I did. As soon as the shot was fired, the sled jerked forward. Niels made a flying leap—I had to grab his parka to pull him on. The dogs weren't running away out of fear, they were running toward Jens. They had been trained to go to him; anyway, they had a special interest in the outcome of the hunt: this was their meal as well as ours.

The seal lay dead by the allu (breathing hole). Jens quieted the dogs as they came up behind him. He sat on the sled for a moment and sharpened his skinning knife.

It was a ringed seal—small, about three feet long, with claws in its flippers to scratch holes in the ice. Traditionally, a certain hospitality was shown toward captured or dead animals: songs were sung to them, fresh water was dripped in their mouths. In the case of a polar bear, the severed head was turned inland so the animal would be able to return home.

Jens's calmness spread to the dogs. They lay down as he rolled the seal on its back and made one slit from the throat down the belly to the tail flippers. Dark blood poured out, its warmth transforming the snow into pink crystals. The hide with its inch of blubber peeled back like winter clothing. I looked more closely: its heart was still beating. The old people say that if the meat of a seal is "alive"—still quivering— while it is being flensed, it means another seal will soon be caught.

With quick downward cuts of his knife, Jens separated the rest of the skin from flesh. "The skin's no good right now, it's the time of year when their coat is not warm, it isn't winter fur, so we just put it by the allu for the seagulls and polar bears to eat," he said. "Later, we'll keep the skins and make everything we need from it."

Now the seal was naked except for the clawed flippers and whiskers which were still intact. Jens dragged it to the sled and laid its pink body beneath the blue tarp. A ringed seal is so small without all its fat. "We'll need one more for tonight," Niels said. One and a half seals for the dogs, half a seal for us. It was to be our one meal of the day and, like the dogs, I was hungry. I looked back at the allu, where the seal had come to breathe and take in some sun. Now it looked like a drain for blood. We lashed the caribou skins down and continued on. Steam from the dead seal's still-warm body rose from beneath the tarp.

Halfway across the wide fjord, a wind blew down hard on us and a snow squall turned into a blizzard. We could no longer see the ginger-colored lead dog. Jens stopped the sled. He and Niels discussed something—no translation. The wind increased and snow caught in the fox fur ruff around my hood, which Jens's wife, Ilaitsuk, had sewn on before leaving. Jens gave the starting signal to the dogs, but suddenly we changed course.

"We will just go south now," Niels said. "I am sorry. It will be bad if we try to go to Etah." A month earlier a wind there had been clocked at 152 miles per hour. "It blows you down and you can't get up and the snow blows into your lungs. That could happen to us too, and to the dogs. We would not have time to make a snow house. We would be buried."

When Jean Malaurie made his way to Etah in a blizzard, he found the journey forbidding:

> *We made part of our return trip by taking a shortcut over the mountains. We crossed frozen torrents the position and dimensions of which I duly noted one by one—and with what effort! . . . There were outcroppings of rocks everywhere. The sledge scraped over the stones like a low-slung cart. We had to descend a talus 450 feet high that sloped at an angle of nearly thirty degrees. . . . At last we reached the ice field. All the snow had been blown away: it was like a skating rink, with blue glints and tiny iridescent white veins. The dogs' claws could not get a grip on the bare ice, and they were knocked down by the northeasterly wind. (Malaurie,* The Last Kings of Thule, *p. 298)*

We headed southeast for Herbert Island—Qeqertarsuaq. I longed to keep going north, all the way to Humboldt Glacier, but this was not a test of endurance but a hunting trip, and we went wherever the hunting was good. It would take another seven hours to get there. But seven hours on a sled goes fast even in a storm. I was disappointed not to see Etah, but my eyes filled with Arctic sights: changing planes of light, clipped turrets of stranded icebergs, drifting islands of fog, the under-song of the four-legged dogtrot, and the waltz of sequined snow across a universe of ice.

Jens gave the signal for the dogs to stop. We got off and stood in silence. To the west, toward Ellesmere Island, a silver thread of light marked the ever-elusive horizon as if to remind us that we are finite in an infinite universe. Sometimes the thread turned black, like a frame bent around the world. Later, it was colorless, the seamless floor curving up into an icy sky. That's when I wondered what I was really seeing. Was this an Arctic mirage, or the horizon's horizon? Then we saw the black spot on the ice: another seal.

Jens did his belly walk toward the animal, who was basking in inter-mittent sun. He shot it, skinned it, and laid the naked animal next to the first one under the bloody blue tarp. Now we had enough meat for the dogs and ourselves. If we had continued north, we would be approach-ing Etah by now. Jean Malaurie wrote:

> *At eight o'clock in the evening, attended by an escort, we reached the famous camp. It lay at the end of a long, narrow fjord dominated by the*

Brother John Glacier and its wind tunnel, and it was surrounded by massive scree slopes of pink sandstone over which towered twelve-hundred-foot-high precipices. Situated between the frozen seas and a small lake, clinging to its pebbly beach, Etah was a cold, gray camp swept by almost constant winds. Home of the blizzard. (Malaurie, The Last Kings of Thule, *p. 269)*

Halfway to the island Niels stepped from the sled and chipped ice off a stranded iceberg to melt for tea. With numb hands we fumbled at bread and cheese. Sometimes I had to look at my fingers to make sure I was holding something. I couldn't taste what I ate and wasn't hungry. Then Jens brought out a tiny white radio from a red bag, pulled up the antenna, and held it to his ear. The evening news was being broadcast in Greenlandic from Nuuk.

Niels looked at his friend admiringly. "He's the head of the Hunters' Council—it's like a union. He is responsible for keeping the hunting just the way it has always been," he whispered to me. We stomped our feet to get warm.

After the news we plowed through deep-crusted drifts and bounced over snow-covered ice hummocks. Frostfall glittered and black clouds fell through white layers, engulfing us with snow that blew upward like cut-up pieces of lace.

Sun at midnight. We had been traveling for twelve hours. The layered dacquoise of ice, mist, frostfall, and snow had flattened out. The dogs squinted against still-falling snow. Stiff from fatigue, I dozed, leaning against Niels. Under the lid of ice the broken sea writhed.

When my eyes opened, Herbert Island was directly ahead. We stopped and pried off a piece of glacier ice from a berg for meltwater. Jens held the glistening chunk in his lap like a deformed crystal ball. Could he predict our future? We lurched across rough ice to the shore.

We stayed in a dirty sheet-metal hut, sixteen feet square, that had come from Thule Air Force Base. Under the *illeq*—the sleeping platform—was a Danish porn magazine and two comic books. To the dogs, Jens fed seal ribs, backbone, flippers, and the ropelike white intestines, which they pulled from both ends in a tug-of-war until it tangled in the traces and snapped. We boiled what was left of the seal meat for ourselves. Jens found an onion at the bottom of his gear bag, cut it into three pieces, and dropped it in with the meat. That was our vegetable of the month. The only one.

On his tiny radio Greenlandic music played—soft country-western with lyrics about dogsleds and ice rather than cowboys, horses, and sunsets. There were no sunsets at this time of year, only sun glare and blinding snowstorms. Jens described a hunter's year: "In spring we hunt walrus and the seals that are lying out on the ice. In summer we hunt mostly narwhal and bearded seal between ice floes using kayaks. In autumn we start to catch seals again and when the new ice comes, that is the best time for hunting walrus. In winter, the dark time, we catch seals under the ice using nets.

"Before there were shops, we followed the animals. Now it's started to be modern so with my children and grandchildren, I try to get them to travel around with me so they know the life. Before, there was hunting together with your wife. Now, my wife has to work in town to pay the bills. We both hate that. Farther south in Danish Greenland, hunters are beginning to move into being fishermen. I think it's going to start up here too, which will be bad for the animals and the people too. It means they are dependent on the Danish-owned fish factories to buy their fish. That's how life gets its burdens and becomes broken. Can you see that? Then, pretty soon, no one remembers how to live the other way."

On paper plates we balanced a heap of seal ribs, the shredded meat steaming. Jens meted out the onion, one third apiece. It tasted ambrosial, but I kept my excitement to myself.

"Everyone is just trying to survive," Jens continued. "When the traditional guys found out that the fishermen were making lots more money, they stopped talking to each other. The old people say that before outboard engines there were many more animals. But we don't fish here in the summer. There are a few boats but if you see a whale— they breed and calve here—then you have to turn the engine off. It's only here in the northern part of Greenland that we are living with the old style, hunting narwhal and walrus with harpoons. If you look at Canada, you can see how fast the old ways can disappear. They shoot whales and walrus and use a hook. And they don't use dogs anymore. They go everywhere by snowmobile. So you see, everything is lost for them."

He looked out the filthy window. "Too much *aput,*" he said. Then he sat on the *illeq* and checked the dog harnesses he had been making to be sure his stitching held. After coffee and cookies, Jens and Niels went outside and adjusted their rifle scopes, using an old barrel for a target. I walked up a snowbound canyon, gunshots echoing behind me, for a few moments of privacy—not only to go to the bathroom, but to catch my breath and listen to whatever was in my head. But the wind came down hard and the snow was waist-high. I squatted, then quickly trudged back to the hut. Jens and Niels looked relieved when I popped my head in the door to say I'd returned. In Inuit society you don't go off alone in the snow for an evening stroll unless you're about to commit suicide.

I stood outside for a while. The sky was sunstruck and a line of silhouetted icebergs were like ships steaming toward open water. I could understand why Niels had wanted to become a merchant seaman: the floes looked like ships and they pointed in a direction away from the confines of his village, toward exotic places no one from Qaanaaq had ever seen before. Other icebergs were in ruins—the same deconstructed cathedrals I'd seen earlier—a spire here, a clerestory there, a nave somewhere else—their icy light spilling all over the place.

The dogs slept with their noses tucked under their tails. All except "the boss," the ginger-colored leader of the team, who busied himself burying a bit of meat under the snow with his nose. Perhaps, in saving food for the next day, he understood a concept of the future. It was hard to know. I thought of the seal we had eaten, how, when it was being skinned, I could see its vital signs: the carotid artery pumping, muscles twitching, and a slow heartbeat and wondered, when Jens pulled back the skin and blubber, if the spirit had had time to leave the body, or if, in eating that delicious flesh, we had eaten the seal's wandering, water-happy soul.

A cloud erased all warmth and snow continued. The worst part of the storm was still behind us, tucked up in a black knot at the head of a distant fjord. The wind had changed. It no longer blew off the ice cap. "We'll have sun tomorrow," Niels predicted. None of us could sleep. Curled in my corner, I tossed and turned. The longer we were out on the ice, the later we ate dinner and the less sleep we got: it was the body's circadian rhythm slipping from the conventional clock and sliding toward something more like a twenty-eight-hour day.

My sleeping bag was too hot. I looked over at Niels. He was reading a comic book. His grandfather had traveled with Rasmussen and had taken someone else's wife to go with him but never gave her back. She lived with him for the rest of her life and became Niels's grandmother. Three generations of his family, including his nine brothers and sisters, had grown up in Dundas Village and they had all been moved out by the Americans to Qaanaaq. When Niels saw me spying on him he began laughing. Then Jens's huge belly began to shake, and all three of us laughed until tears came to our eyes.

If we slept at all it was already midmorning by the time our laughter stopped and our eyes closed. When I woke, Niels was rubbing salve on his feet, ankles, and elbows. His skin was peeling off. I asked if he had eczema. He said no, that he'd been in the vicinity of the B-52 crash, and after, his skin started to peel.

In 1968, when a B-52 crashed in Bylot Bay just southwest of Thule Air Base. It was carrying four nuclear weapons. On impact, according to biologists currently studying the area, an undisclosed quantity of plutonium spilled. Had anyone done a medical survey and follow-up since the crash? Niels shrugged. No one had contacted him about it.

Morning brought sun. I went out to pee and a raven called in greeting. The dogs drank meltwater from little holes dug in the ice. They wandered around visiting, pushing their heads under another dog's long trace, exacting submission, begging for friendship, saying hello. We drank Nescafé and listened to the Greenlandic news, followed by Danish news, followed by an American song with the words "Drop all your troubles and let your wheels fly." "Wheels?" Niels said, and we all started laughing again: we were still traveling stone age style.

Niels's breakfast sandwich brought on more hilarity: ham salad, cheese, and shrimp on rye, followed by chocolate nougat and cheese on white bread. "What is THAT?" Jens asked. "That's chocolate—it's only for children!"

Niels looked abashed. "I don't know what got into me. I've never bought this before. Do you want some? It's good." We shook our heads, laughing. Meanwhile, Jens powered through a can of Spam, then one of liverwurst.

The conversation turned to sex, love, and marriage. Not long ago hunters traveled with their wives and children. Sometimes they were gone for a month or two, other times just a week. They might inhabit four or five camps a year, sheltering in stone-and-turf houses or, in summer, sealskin tents. The woman helped on the sled, holding the dogs back, flensing the seals. At camp or at home, she took care of the skins, made and mended clothes—fox and sealskin anoraks, birdskin underwear, hare socks, bearskin trousers, and kamiks. All the domestic chores—tanning skins, drying meat, making food—were hers, as well as fox hunting. "Now it's broken. Now it's pretty much the way the Danes live," Jens said.

"But before?" I asked.

In the old days a man never went hunting without a woman. If his wife was pregnant or away seeing her family, he simply took another woman. Inuit are tactful about these arrangements. No questions were asked. There was no onus to sexual desire or nudity, and having sex with someone other than your wife or husband didn't necessarily imply a betrayal, as long as the rules were obeyed. In the turf-and-stone houses, people had only one set of clothes and if it was warm, they went around naked or half-naked. There was no promiscuity, merely a nonchalance about matters having to do with the body.

When Peter Freuchen came north to hunt walrus, a friend, Tatianguaq, insisted that his wife, Ivalu, accompany Peter. Tatianguaq said she would help Peter find his way across the glacier and help set up camp. But his other reason for sending his beautiful wife off was because he'd been having trouble with her. She'd spent time on Robert Peary's ship when it was anchored at Thule and she'd become accustomed to "the white man's way of courting." She claimed she didn't want to go with Peter, refusing to get out of bed; yet she had new skins laid out for the journey. Finally she came down to the sled, but she still refused to get on. Peter had to pick her up and carry her. The dogs crowded around, curious. She despaired at this white man's inability to train them; picking up the whip, she swung it expertly, getting them to lie down. Then she sat on the sled and gave the starting signal. Peter just barely hopped on. They were lovers for the rest of the trip.

Greenlanders often traded wives, if not for a whole hunting trip, then for an evening. If the hunting had been bad, the angakok ordered an exchange in the hopes that the new arrangement would bring on more animals. Sometimes they played a game of "doused lights"—the dim light provided by burning seal oil in soapstone dishes. Villagers gathered in one house, all naked. The lights were blown out, and in silence, everyone moved around. At a given signal, a man would take hold of whichever woman was closest. After a time, the seal oil lamps were lit again amid much laughter.

The rule of thumb seemed to be full disclosure—sneaking behind your spouse's back was not permissible. If a man caught his wife doing some sewing for another man without his permission, she would be stripped, dragged outside the house, and beaten. Then he'd find the man and fight him.

On the other hand polygamy and polyandry were sometimes acceptable, though not common. There was a scarcity of women—female babies or children as well as the elderly were sacrificed when there was a chance of starvation in the village. Some women enjoyed having two husbands who were rivals for her love but best friends when out hunting.

In Inuit legends, trans-species erotics is commonplace. Women married dogs and bears and men married foxes and hares. Actual bestiality was not common, but because Inuit life was based on consensual tolerance, intercourse with animals—especially dogs—was allowed but with strict conditions. First, out of respect for the dog, she had to be in heat when the romance took place; second, if you wanted to fuck your dog, you had to do it out on the ice in front of the whole village.

Outside Jens surveyed the sky from atop a rock. "The weather and the hunter are not such good friends," he said. "Now is the time of year to start putting up stores of meat for the winter. If a hunter waits for good weather . . . well then, he may starve."

In the hut, Niels lay down again. When Jens came back in, he looked at his friend with surprise: "Are you tired?"

"A little," Niels said.

A long pause. Jens: "How can a translator be tired?"

Days went by. We slept, hunted, fed dogs, ate, hunted again. The complexities of ice and climate had just begun to sink in; I only knew enough to know that it would take a lifetime to comprehend them well enough to survive. In a rare talkative mood, Jens explained how the depth of the spring thaw would indicate what kind of summer would come—foggy and cold with almost constant ice, or else windy and clear with open water. The presence of *illeraq*, small fish, signaled the coming of the birds—the dovekies and guillemots—and these in turn would affect the abundance or scarcity of narwhal and foxes, and the coming of the cod would affect the seals. Farther north, beyond the last human habitation, where hunting success was crucial, the fluctuation in temperature by just a few degrees could make or break herds of reindeer and muskox—if it was too cold for summer grass, the animals and the people hunting them died.

As we soared along, I asked Jens what was most important for a hunter to know when living on the ice. He smiled and said, "Everything." Which meant the thickness and kinds of ice, variations in snow, the presence or absence of fog, wind direction, kinds of clouds, zodiacal lights and the phases of the moon, air, wind, and water temperatures, the changing shape of the shoreline, location of open water, numbers of birds, dates of migrations and of breakup and first ice, and the changes in routes of all land animals.

It's said that Inuit people have a pronounced paleocortex sharpened by keen powers of observation and memory for landscape. The shape of each island, inlet, and fjord is engraved in their minds, they can draw them in dirt or snow, scratching a safe route through open water on the palm of other hunters' hands, or outlining the coastline with fingers in the air. "This is an Inuit weather station," Jens said, pointing to his head. "And this, the map," holding his hand out.

Some days the frozen sea ice turned rough. We wove between icebergs, over drifts, bumping over and slamming down into troughs of snow. I listened for the hollow sound of bad ice but the percussive dogtrot and cadenced panting made a music that kept us safe. Two of the four young dogs began getting the hang of pulling a sled and stayed close to the team, but the other two, awkward with youth, still wandered, snagging their lines on rough ice.

At camp I watched how alliances between dogs were formed. A female would crouch, then lie submissively on her back while a single male stood over her for hours, lest some other dog in the team take his place. The young ones played, but the older dogs, attuned to long hours of work and hungry days between feedings, were serious-minded and cool-tempered, and slept as much as they could. Their behavior and the hunters' was the same. We were all packs of hungry animals moving over frozen seas, dreaming our dreams and looking for food.

"Which is your favorite dog? I asked Jens.

He studied each one carefully—the young black dog with the white feet, the shaggy-haired male, the three small females, the ginger-colored leader. Then said softly, "All of them."

That was the day we followed the ice foot—a belt of ice at the shoreline that forms between high- and low-water marks—to the southern end of the island. Our plan was to go to Kiatak and join the other hunters who were there catching auks, and later go to the ice edge together to hunt for walrus and narwhal.

The ice foot was narrow. Several times, the sled fishtailed, almost dropping off the cliff, but Niels and Jens stuck their feet out like rudders and kept the sled on course. We glided past a wall of broken rock hung with icicles. Surely the idea for chandeliers came from such a scene. Two Arctic hares—*ukaleq*—clambered up the mountain. "*Helloooo,*" Jens yelled to them. Patches of open water dotted with *puttoq*—frazil ice—looked like open sores. We stopped. Far out on the ice, beyond a wall of pressure ridges, a seal was sunning itself. It was too dangerous to take the sled. With the rifle in one hand and a tamping bar in the other, Jens walked slowly in the direction of the seal, shielding himself with his portable white blind and tapping the ice with the iron bar.

What if he falls through? I asked.

"He won't. He knows the ice better than the ice does," Niels said. The dogs were anxious. They watched Jens's figure grow smaller. Finally Jens lay down, aimed, and fired. "*Arretet, arretet,*" Niels whispered. The dogs wanted to run to him but it was too dangerous. They looked on helplessly as Jens dragged the seal a mile across the ice to where we were waiting.

Jens laid the skinned seal under the blue tarp and stowed his rifle under the lash ropes. He called to the dogs. Ahead, the ice foot narrowed like a waist, then widened again. Snow turned to sun; we slid from winter into summer. A glittering lagoon of open water came into view, packed with seabirds, ice gulls, and eider ducks. We stopped and gaped. The pond was a living sapphire and the birds navigated through blue glint, bumping from one beveled iridescence to another. What were we seeing? We drew in deep breaths; the burdens of winter dissolved effortlessly. A curtain had opened, pushing ice aside. This was an inner sanctum, a sudden blaze where everything was possible, where everything burned.

Then a cloud came down on us like a hat. "Summer" was over. The pond went gray and the ducks squabbled. "*Ai, ai,*" Jens gave the signal for the dogs to start. A sharp wind cut at my face. I zipped up my parka and pulled mittens on. Snow began again. Fog clung to white cliffs and the ice foot narrowed to nothing at the western end of the island. Ahead was Kiatak. We had no choice but to drop down from the elevated road-way to the expanse of frozen sea that had been shattered and squeezed between the two islands into an inpenetrable maze of pressure ice.

What looked impossible was not: the dogs climbed up an almost vertical slab of ice and disappeared down the other side. The long sled teetered on the top and bounced down hard onto another upended piece. Jens walked in front of the dogs, showing them where to go, leap-ing over chasms while Niels manned the back of the sled, holding the crossbar, trying to keep the sled from catapulting over a ledge.

Again we plunged, splashing through meltwater and lunging up the other side. "We" including me clutching wildly to anything that would hold—the edge of a reindeer skin, a lash rope. I was the ridiculous cargo on this flying bridge.

Up and down we went. We were on an Inuit roller coaster, steeper than any in the world. And the consequences of misjudgment were dire. On his trip north in 1917, Rasmussen wrote: "In some places we drove across awkward faces of old ice, similar in character to the edge of the inland ice. These floes have a rugged surface with deep holes, due to many summers of sunburn; they look like a high sea and the heavy sledges bob up and down on them as ships on waves."

A piece of sharp ice sliced open the ends of my fingers. The dogs scrambled and fell, caught up, hooked an edge, fell in a crevasse, scram-bled out again. To go three-quarters of a mile took five hours.

When the ice smoothed out Jens and Niels joined me on the sled. Behind us was the wall, the Hiroshige-style high sea of frozen waves. Jens looked back at me: I smiled and made a small gesture to say that everything was copacetic. Then I heard something breaking . . . like a goblet being smashed. Was it glass? No, it couldn't be. The sled began sinking. It wasn't glass but ice I heard breaking. The sled dropped straight down. I grabbed for something to hold on to, wedging my gloved hand under the lash rope. What happened next, I'm not sure. I saw dogs disappear, dogs falling through broken pieces of ice, splashing into water . . . then slabs of ice bobbing back up . . . but where were the dogs?

Niels crawled over me. "You can just stay there!" he yelled. I crouched as he reached for the back of the sled. He was unwinding something—I couldn't tell what, maybe a length of sealskin. In front, Jens had stretched forward, hooking his feet on the front of the sled, his huge body lying over the shank lines, pulling sinking dogs out of the water. With one hand he slung them over his shoulder onto the ice. But the ice ahead kept breaking, and the sled was slowly inching toward a gaping hole.

A dog landed beside me, then another. They were two of the young black ones. They looked confused. Water flew. They shook before they froze, spraying me. In back, Niels tied a line to an iron bar and jammed it into the ice to keep the sled from going down. Dogs scrambled, dogs were still in the water pulling us. The sled lurched forward. Niels steadied it: I saw the drag marks through the snow all the way down to ice from his heels.

All the dogs were out now. There was a *thuuunk* as the ledge of ice that held the sled dropped six inches into meltwater, then held. The dogs were wet but none had drowned. The sled held fast but pointing toward the open hole. Very gingerly, Jens stepped off onto a piece of ice, his great weight sinking down—I heard water gurgle and slush sliding. In one motion he lifted the front of the sled and turned it the other way. He sat quickly and clucked: undaunted by their swim, the dogs took off over snow-covered ice that was solid.

The past is fiction, the future is dream. I stopped trying to establish a firm floor under myself where there was none. We might die or we might live. Both were good. But I felt lost, like an eye that had flown out of a head, falling through the world, wondering what it would see. Was this constant gliding and falling a beginning or an end?

My eyes were drenched—not with snow or tears but with the refulgence, the blue glint, the shiver, the dove-gray snow flashing iridescence. Perhaps the place we go to at the end of life is not the primordial ooze but ice—layers and layers of rod-and-cone-shaking beauty. To see or not to see—that was the only worthwhile question.

Ice moaned under us and the dogtracks filled fast with water. Not a good sign. The sled clunked down. A whole slab of ice loosened where it had been fastened. "*Puquoq! Puquoq!*" Jens yelled urgently. The dogs struggled to pull us out and did. We traveled far out into the middle of the frozen sea, away from the island we were aiming for, in an attempt to avoid more drowning fields—open water hidden by snow. The farther we went, the more precarious it felt—there were no life rings, no safety nets to keep us from falling. Sky and ground were a sweep of gray that looked light but felt dark; I had gone into darkness with open eyes and had followed a dark road. "Are we going to drown?" I asked Jens, trying to sound chipper. He turned, smiled at me, and shook his head, no.

We drove in silence for an hour. I checked the dogtracks to see if they were filling with water. They were. No one mentioned the danger. "*Hikuaq,*" Niels finally said, by way of instruction. Thin ice. That was all. Looking away, he laid his gloved hand on my leg to comfort me. Somewhere out on the ice he stopped, unloaded our gear, and turned the sled over to plane the runners, which had been badly nicked by our uneven passage. Niels made tea; I walked in circles to keep warm. We loaded up again and took off.

Soon enough, new problems greeted us. We ran into more patches of open water obscured by fallen snow. Ikuo had warned us. "It's a good week to stay home," he'd said. Too late for that. We zigged and zagged, leaving a permanent wake of long S marks.

Then the dogs fell through the ice in slow motion, sinking slowly down in slush. Jens yelled something in Greenlandic. Again I crouched as the floor under us gave way; pieces of ice upended and the snow mortar that had held them together—the white veins—tore apart. Dogs went down scrambling and bobbed up. I let myself wonder if the ice on which we had traveled so euphorically would be the hatchcover under which we'd drown.

We approached Asugnaq on the island of Kiatak three hours later, stopping the dogs out on the ice and waiting, as is the custom when coming into a camp. Parked near the shore were six sleds and ninety dogs. There were eight hunters—friends of Jens's from Siorapaluk and Qaanaaq—and one woman, Robert Peary's great-granddaughter. Four tents were set up on the rocky shore of the island. Three of the sleds carried kayaks set on edge, and another had a skiff with an outboard motor. "We still need the old way to carry the new," Niels observed.

The hunters came down on the ice to greet us. They helped unload the sled, carry our duffles to shore, and put up our tent while Jens cut up one of the seals and fed the dogs. They had seen from a distance the trouble we'd had.

Four blond heads appeared: the missing Norwegian schoolteachers from Siorapaluk with their two young daughters. They were on their way home from a near-disastrous polar bear hunt in Washington Land and would soon be returning to Norway.

Our camp was at the end of a narrow, tiny valley bounded by steep cliffs and moss-covered talus with a trickling stream running down the middle. As soon as the talk quieted, I heard the birds: the same electric, humming, insect sound of a million fluttering auks whose nests were hidden in the dark recesses of the scree. These birds have provided the Inuit people with supplementary food during the difficult time between the ice breakup and open water.

I stumbled over a whalebone sticking out of the ground. Next to it was a chunk of turf that had tumbled down the slope and lay like a brown pillow at my feet. I picked it up: light as a feather. Turf, stone, and whalebone—original building materials for Greenlandic houses. Once all Polar Eskimos lived this way, making camps where the hunting was good, then moving on. In the 1850s, their bird nets, according to Dr. Elisha Kent Kane, were "purse-nets of seal-skin at the end of a narwhal's tusk." Peter Freuchen reported seeing a sled on Baffin Island made of whalebone and reindeer antlers lashed together with sinew. The runners were made of rolled reindeer skins that had been pushed through a hole in ice to get them wet, then shaped like a runner with a flattened bottom and laid out on the ice to freeze. The crossbars were sometimes made of frozen salmon or walrus meat cut to the right size. If things got tough, they could always eat the sled.

Even now, the hunters still made much of what they used—clothes, sleds, harnesses, harpoons, bird nets, and the slender, fifteen-foot-long skin kayaks. Only the rifle and the skiff with its outboard motor were strikingly modern.

The men sat together quietly, planing the long handles of bird nets, fixing harpoons, and discussing the ice that had become suddenly perilous. Their clothes were patched and they wore baseball caps under hooded anoraks. At the shoreline, the beach ice was broken—great uplifted slabs glistened in midnight sun. It was a wall that divided the human camp from that of the dogs. Looking south, I could see the domed peninsula of Cape Parry. Between our camp and that point, a million-acre field of ice was slowly becoming water.

Olaf and Petra sat with us. They were from Tomslo in northern Norway, and had just finished their third year of teaching school in Siorapaluk. Olaf was a carpenter by trade, but since the tiny school needed an extra teacher, he was hired along with Petra. Their two children soon spoke fluent Greenlandic and had acted as interpreters for their parents until they learned the language. In April the teachers quit their jobs and headed north to Washington Land to hunt polar bear.

The hunt had been difficult. They'd been stranded in bad weather with an old hunter who had hurt his leg, was hungry, and needed medical help. For five weeks they stayed with him, sharing their food, eventually running out of sugar, food, and fuel. The seals were breeding at that time and they tasted bad. The children refused to eat the meat. Now the ordeal was over and they were on their way home. "It's time," Olaf said. "If we don't go now, we'll never leave."

I helped Peary's great-granddaughter get water from the head of the spring. She was one of the hunter's girlfriends and had come along to cook. It didn't matter that she had American blood—she was an Eskimo through and through and didn't speak a word of English.

What a pleasure it was to fill our pots with running water instead of melting ice for tea. Downstream, a cake of soap and a small towel lay on a rock where everyone washed up for dinner. Water boiled on the Primus by the driftwood log where the men sat talking, and inside a small tent, the cook sautéed thin slices of seal dusted in flour in a frying pan smeared with imported Danish butter. At camp, all meat is shared communally. Even though the others had eaten earlier, an offering of food is never turned down. Dinner was served at one in the morning.

We had been traveling for ten hours and were bruised, bloodied, and tired, but no one talked about the ordeal. We drank tea and ate seal, though there was not quite enough. After, we were still hungry. Niels gave me a handful of cookies from his bag. By the time we went to bed, the remaining water in the boiling pot had frozen solid.

We lay in our sleeping bags listening to the Norwegians chattering in their tent. We had been alone for weeks and it seemed odd to be camped a few feet from other humans. The woman's voice was high-pitched and cheerless.

"Why does the way they talk sound so strange?" Jens asked. "It all goes up in the air at the end. Why can't they just speak Greenlandic?"

Niels and I laughed. Then Niels said, "I don't think she'll ever stop talking."

Sometime in the middle of the night the Norwegians did quiet down. Niels snored in my ear. A cold wind fluttered the tent walls. The tent's bloodstains were a waving Inuit flag saying, "For five thousand years we have followed the animals: seal, walrus, and whale, and we've survived."

In the secret language shamans once used, the word for "shadow" meant "man," and the verb "to ripen" meant "to arrive." Our shadows had ripened on this bleak shore at the edge of a scree slope where a million sleepless auks were hatching out their young.

Toward morning bird shadows flickered over the tent like black firelight. I got up to pee. It had snowed during the night but now the sun was radiant. Out on the ice the dogs were busy with their lives: some slept, others scraped at the ice for frozen bits of meat, and a few were hooked together in love bouts. Despite the broken edge of ice that separated us from them, nowhere had I seen people so completely linked to animals, their legends full of inter-species marriages, their shamans able to transform themselves into beings who were part seal and part bird, or part human and part dog, and who flew under the water like little auks to appease Nerrivik, the goddess of the sea, who lay naked on her *illeq* with long black hair flowing down over her shoulders onto the watery floor. From there she jealously watched for any wickedness or breaking of rules or taboos in the human world and when they were detected, she held the sea animals inside her house and let the humans starve. My question was, that morning, Where do the gods go when there are no more shamans to appease them and tell their stories?

It was cold, despite the sun, and we warmed ourselves by the Primus. Though we had come together to hunt walrus and narwhal at the ice edge, the hunters made a group decision: best to wait a few days until the storm passed if it hit us at all. After, the ice would harden. In the meantime we would catch birds.

Carrying their fragile, long-handled bird nets, the hunters scaled the nearly vertical talus slopes as if climbing stairs, rising up a crumbling chimney, never grabbing at handholds, just stepping effortlessly to the top. From below I could see their nets swing—like brooms sweeping the sky—as squadrons of birds spiraled down toward the cliff from great heights as if caught in a hurricane.

As I climbed the slope behind the hunters, I entered a symphony. Curds of brown turf fell away from my feet as I stepped up and up into the auks' thick hum. Birds whooshed past my head. Near the top, I perched on a rock: hundreds of little auks landed around me. In a moment of quiet the melodious song of the snow bunting filtered across the canyon to me. Far below, a dog, chained up alone by a rock wall, began to howl. Its melancholy chant uncoiled, echoed; then the other dogs joined in and their group song pierced the snow buntings' twitter. The auks flew up, soaring this way and that. I thought of the old woman, observed by Peter Freuchen, who, on just such a morning, swept her igloo clean with a single gull's feather.

One by one the bird catchers returned to camp, their bags full—all except Jens. "I caught some but when I swung my net up, they just flew out again," he said laughing. The hunters sat on the drift log. Their hands were busy, plucking auk feathers, sewing torn clothing, mending bird nets. Kane described the young men in a bird camp as being boisterous: "Rudest of gypsies, how they squalled and laughed, and snored and rolled about! Some were sucking bird-skins; others were boiling incredible numbers of auks in huge soapstone pots; and two youngsters, crying at the top of their voices, '*Oopegsoak! Oopegsoak!*' were fighting an owl."

Jens and a hunter named Peter talked quietly about ice conditions, the coming storm, snow depth, the dogs, and the whereabouts of the walrus and narwhal. As they talked, Peter fastened a sealskin thong to a detachable old-style point of ivory. The six-foot-long shaft was perfectly planed. When the seal is harpooned, the shaft falls off and floats (it's retrieved later) and the point sticks into the animal.

Two younger men were making *kivioq*: burying whole skinned seals stuffed with auks under mounds of rock. "We bury them now, guts and all, and come back in July to eat them. You should be here then. Eating *kivioq* is like eating candy!" one hunter told me.

Another hunter turned his sled upside down and planed the hard plastic runners while another sewed his torn anorak with long pieces of sinew from a whale. In the tent I rubbed Swiss-made sunscreen on my face twice a day—only because I'd promised my mother I would—and hung the sheepskin liners, kamiks, and sealskin mittens over the tent line to dry.

The Norwegian children came to visit. They were shy and we sat quietly on the platform, our heels making dents in melting ice. I brought out a small bag of nuts and dried fruit from California and offered it to them. They looked at me, and I nodded, yes, for you. They ate voraciously—not from greed, but hunger. They hadn't eaten fruit of any kind, dried or fresh, for a year.

In the afternoon, when the ice had hardened, Jens and Peter climbed a hill and glassed the Arctic plain with binoculars, trying to find a safe route out to the ice edge. Their hand gestures cut through air like knives, with a little flourish at the end, drawing the precise geography of land, hard ice, polynyas, and dangerous patches of soft ice.

When they came back to camp we loaded our sleds with kayaks, harpoons, rifles, and spare clothes and took off—six abreast—due west toward Canada's open water. "*Puquoq, puquoq,*" Jens sang to the dogs to get them going. The teams raced each other and the hunters yelled and whooped. The ice smoothed out and we picked up speed. Auks swooped up and over us like Ferris wheels, spinning, gaining altitude, then returning to Bird Mountain. To the north, clouds that had lofted across frozen valleys of ice between the peaks of Kiatak evaporated, and mist hung from the underside of shadowed cliffs like silk banners.

In brilliant sun we peeled off clothes—another Eskimo striptease: hat, gloves, bearskin pants, anoraks, and parkas. The ice was glass. It mocked the idea of solidity, but for a moment I didn't care. Everywhere I looked there were vistas so majestic my eyes felt tired. Niels and Jens peered down into the dogtracks: if water rose up in them, we were on *hikuaq*—thin ice. But whose life wasn't always teetering there?

So far, so good. But farther out, near the ice edge, the ice gave way when a hunter harpooned a narwhal, and his dogs fell in. To save them he'd had to cut his line. After the commotion, a long discussion ensued: more knife-cutting hand gestures. Then we headed back to the island for the night.

Jens dried his kamiks on the upturned ends of the sled. We ate seal cooked three ways and tried to talk to Ikuo Oshima in Siorapaluk by two-way radio. The static was so thick we couldn't hear. Then his voice did come through. He said the storm was bad and to be careful. In the morning, we would check the ice edge again.

Jens and Peter walked to the head of the valley and stood on a ridge to view the storm's progress. It had been stalled somewhere north of us on the strait. If the storm caught us we would have to move out on the ice and build snow houses—igloos—to protect ourselves from drifting snow. I hoped the storm would arrive soon. But Jens didn't. He said the Canadian Eskimos were much better at making igloos than Greenlanders, and had heard of one built for drum dances that was big enough to house sixty people.

Igloos, typically twelve feet in diameter, are built with progressively smaller wedge-shaped blocks cut with an ice knife. Freuchen described the process:

> *The base circle consists of about fifteen large blocks. As the walls get higher, and the rings narrower, he cuts the blocks smaller, and he has to step inside to put them up, while somebody may help him by handing the blocks from the outside. The last circle has five blocks in it, and he closes the top hole with a block in which he bores a small hole for warm air to escape. A well-constructed igloo will never collapse, only sag in the middle, but the rising heat from the people and the blubber lamp would eventually melt it completely if it were not for the little airhole in the top which is regulated with a whisk of dried grass.*
>
> *When the igloo is completed the man cuts a low arch for an entrance, then builds a long passageway which not only serves to keep the direct impact of the cold away from the igloo when somebody enters or leaves, but which also becomes storage space for hunting gear and other things they don't want to leave on their sled.*
>
> *Meanwhile the wife and children have been tightening the cracks between the snow bricks with snow, and they throw snow over the whole construction. As soon as the igloo is finished, the wife takes her skins and cooking gear and goes inside to arrange the bunk and make the igloo livable. The construction takes about an hour and is usually used only overnight, but sometimes it is lived in for several days while a storm exhausts its fury.* (Freuchen, The Eskimo Way of Life, pp. 56–57)

Freuchen also noted ruefully that the drafty entryway to snow houses was where orphans were often forced to sleep. He had employed one such boy, named Qupagnuk. "He was so full of lice nobody liked to have him sleeping in their house, and he usually slept in the tunnel of an abandoned house. He was happy, though. He played with the other children, and he looked well fed. But he was always hungry, so when the hunters were feeding their dogs he came running to get his share of the walrus hide or meat. He jumped in among the voracious, battling dogs, who often bit him in the face and on the hands, and he saved himself a bite or two."

When Freuchen protested the boy's treatment, the hunters said he was the lucky one, that his treatment hardened him to a better life. "Look and you will see that all the chief hunters living here have been orphans," an elder told him. They could live without food and sleep, track animals, raid the foxes' food caches, and never tire on long dogsled trips.

"We aren't that strong anymore," Jens commented.

That night I dreamed of the tiny langoustines I'd eaten in Paris and the sips of champagne I'd taken, birdlike. Like an orphan I was stealing food, from other people's plates.

In the morning we went with other hunters to the ice edge and came back discouraged. We saw narwhal, but couldn't get to them because the ice kept breaking off. We followed the ice edge first one way, then the other, but couldn't find a place where it was firm. That's when we began to turn for home. Jens followed a circuitous route mapped out in his head and chosen by group decision about how to avoid bad ice. "*Attuk, attuk,*" Jens yelled, trying to keep the dogs moving to the right, away from what they knew was the direct route home.

We heard voices behind us and looked: it was the Norwegians. Jens blinked in exasperation. "Not them again," he muttered. They needed our help finding the way. We traveled due south into the middle of the sound before turning east toward Qaanaaq. Patches of rough ice alternated with long straightaways that were smooth. Here and there eyelets of open water blinked at us.

When the Norwegians caught up, they came alongside too close and the two teams of dogs started fighting. Jens tried discreetly to change directions. "*Attuuk, attuuuk.*" Olaf, the Norwegian, used his whip on his dogs unmercifully and we had trouble getting untangled. As we pulled away the end of Olaf's whip hit my face. I was glad I was traveling with a gentle man.

"Please, go very slowly," I pleaded with Jens. "I don't want to go home." He pointed at bulging black clouds over the northern coast. The wind had changed direction again and blew off the ice cap. The barometer dropped but the sun felt warm. I tipped my head back, senselessly happy, and let it heat my face.

We stopped to hunt when we saw a seal. In no time the animal was tucked under the sled's blue tarp. By then the Norwegians, whom we thought we had lost, had caught up. While waiting for us, Olaf had trouble controlling his team. He hit a dog in the face with the butt of his whip handle. Niels turned away in disgust. The dogs were whipped every time they moved. It was not their fault: they didn't understand what was expected of them. "You have to teach them with your voice, not your hand," Niels said. I looked at his kind eyes. "Men only act like that when they're afraid," he said.

The next seal was the Norwegians' to hunt—according to Inuit etiquette. There was a look of exasperation on Jens's face. Olaf took one of his girls with him. After a very long wait—long enough for Jens to take out his needle and repair two harnesses—we heard a gunshot, but the Norwegian returned empty-handed. "I was letting her shoot and she missed," he said flatly. Niels whispered to me, "He must think hunting is a game. He doesn't understand."

Gray clouds lifted up from island ridges like smoke. In a canyon where there had been an avalanche, shadows stretched across the couloir like white shutters. We traveled due east toward Qaanaaq. It was two days' sled ride away. The Norwegians were far behind. Far out in midstrait, I wondered if we would drown.

Before being Christianized, East Greenlanders believed that a human being had many small souls that resided in every limb and joint, all over the body, and were shaped like miniature people the size of a thumb. The souls in the throat and groin were larger than the others: they must have known that singing and sex were demanding human needs. When death came, the souls had to unify in order to depart and find another body to inhabit. Death by drowning, tradition said, meant going to the underworld of the sea where the dead were happy and the hunting was better than on top of the ice.

Death was taken in stride, as was life. Babies were routinely born during hunting trips. While crossing a glacier with Peter Freuchen, the wife of a hunter announced that she was about to have a baby. How inconvenient, Peter told her, and asked if she couldn't wait until they got down from the glacier, which she did. On the shore, they quickly built an igloo; she went in and came out an hour later holding her baby. They continued on their journey the next day.

Sometime later, Freuchen's own wife, Navarana, came home early from a party, saying she had a stomachache. A few hours later she was in labor. In his excitement Freuchen went to bring Rasmussen (who had also fathered a child with an Inuit "wife") over to the house; by the time they got back, Navarana had delivered a son.

Life was difficult. Therefore, death did not come as an insult or a surprise. Since weather and ice shaped every aspect of society, life and death were an easy come, easy go proposition. Greenlanders thought the aurora borealis represented the souls of stillborn children kicking their umbilical cords. When life "got heavier than death," suicide occurred; when there was nothing to eat, children were drowned, left behind, or else eaten—though not without a great sense of shame. An old hunter who could no longer provide for himself would sometimes ask his oldest son to throw a party, and at the height of the festivities the son would put a rope around the father's neck and "hoist him to his death" as the angakok shooed out evil spirits. Old women preferred to be stabbed in the heart with a knife.

An old angakok told Rasmussen: "I know nothing; but life is continually bringing me face to face with forces stronger than I am."

We came to a patch of rough ice and the traces snagged, pulling dogs this way and that. One dog flipped over and was dragged on his back. When the sled almost ran over him, Niels and Jens held the dog away from the runners with their feet. They wanted to see if he could get up on his own, but he couldn't. Finally Jens snapped a line: the dog came free and resumed trotting.

The dogs were as strong-minded as the people. It was the conditions that made them that way. Jens had raised this team after a disastrous outbreak of distemper in the 1980s. "I had one left. Fortunately it was a female," he said. From her he began all over. "I'm always bringing up young dogs and putting them into the team."

Ahead was something long and dark. We approached: it was a crack in the ice too wide to cross. Jens stepped off the sled cautiously, using an iron bar to test the ice. He shook his head: "No good here," he said.

Niels and I smiled victoriously. We were delighted by the delay. "Take us anywhere, but not back to town," we sang.

We followed the lead north, in the direction of Herbert Island. The crack went on and on, sometimes widening, sometimes growing a little narrower, always a dark ribbon dividing two fields of white. Sometimes I thought we had found an Arctic equator, a never-ending crack in ice that circles the whole polar north. I wanted to follow it, at least until we got to Alaska. "What do you do if we can't find a place to cross?" I asked.

"We cut blocks of ice and drop them in the crack, like stepping stones," Niels said. "But that takes all day."

The island looked close but was not. Four hours later, the lead was still on our right. Ahead, on the shore's ice foot, we saw tents. We had already been traveling nine hours and there was nothing to do but spend the night. Half an hour later the Norwegians arrived. I heard Jens's sharp intake of breath. As they approached, I turned my head away. I could not look the whip-wielding Norwegian in the face again.

The cliffs that rose above us were made of decomposed granite with bulging outcrops of black rock topped by rock that had eroded into purple-and-gold filigree. Through it, I could see the storm clouds coming. The camp was traditionally called Avataq or Avatarpaussat, because the rock formations looked like a seal bladder or harpoon float attached to the harpoon line and used to keep the dead animal from sinking.

Jens fed the dogs and we hoisted our battered tent over the sled. An old man who was camped out on the ice with his wife greeted us. He was the former head of the Hunters' Council—now Jens's job. He explained to Jens about a place where, in the morning, if the ice hardened during the night, we might be able to cross safely. I put ice on to melt for tea. Nearby, the Norwegians were having trouble securing their tent. Instead of carving out notches, Inuit-style, they tried to pound metal stakes into the ice. Their dogs were hungry; the two girls played contentedly on the snowy slopes above camp.

The children were hardened to Arctic life—they were agile and confident on the ice and on the sled. I wondered how they would fare back in Norway. Between handfuls of nuts and dried fruit, they told me their life plan: after university they would come back, marry a hunter, and live in Greenland happily ever after.

Later, we offered the old man a cup of coffee and he told Jens about a Danish vicar who loved hunting so much he wore his skins under his robes. One Sunday, too impatient to conduct a whole service, he recited the opening and closing prayer, stripped his robes off, and ran down the aisle and out the door to a waiting dogsled. It turned out he had a Greenlandic girlfriend and a child stashed away in a distant village.

As the old man left, he winked at us: "Be good. Go to sleep." But we couldn't. The Norwegians were making too much noise with all their talking. Exasperated, Jens told them to go to sleep, but their voices were so loud, they didn't hear him. We began to laugh so hard, our commotion finally quieted them.

I lay in my sleeping bag with a scratching sensation in my eyes. Closing them did not relieve the pain. Earlier, when the dogs were being fed,

I had walked down the ice foot away from camp and realized I was having trouble seeing. Was the ice rough or smooth? My lids were swelling. It felt as if my eyes had been smeared with ground glass. I squatted and pressed snow to my face but it didn't ease the pain. No one said anything about how I looked. Back at camp, I rummaged through my dufflebag and found the ophthalmic salve I'd grabbed out of the veterinary kit at home—salve I'd used on one of my horses when he'd had an eye infection. I knew the horse hadn't had the corneas of his eyes burned by ultraviolet rays—he'd had a fly-borne infection—but what the hell. I squeezed the salve under both eyelids, reducing what eyesight I had into vision that could only be described as gooey.

So much in the Arctic has to do with blindness and seeing: we go snowblind when the sun is too bright, as if too much exposure to what is real exhausts us. We let ourselves be fooled by Arctic mirages—the Crocker Land discovered by Robert Peary, for example, turned out to be not land but a frozen sea. There is ice blink and water sky; there are shadows miraging shadows, cloud layers that shroud snowfall, and ice through which you can see water. And in the dark months the mind's troubled eye opens wide, a cerebral lens that allows the imagination to blossom.

The pain in my eyes kept me awake part of the night. I thought of the horrendous expedition of April 1912, when Freuchen and Rasmussen ascended the Clements Markham Glacier, north of Etah, to go to Peary Land via the ice cap. Among many disasters—near-starvation, sickness, accidents, and having to belay down a wall of ice at the bottom of a glacier—Freuchen wrote: "The worst calamity of all was that I was falling victim to snowblindness. Unless a person has experienced it, he cannot appreciate the torture. Your eyelids feel as if they are made of sandpaper. Knud Rasmussen, who had much dark pigment in his eyelids, was not troubled, but I am rather light. . . . All I wanted to do was crawl into my sleeping bag and get away from the everlasting glare."

Morning. No *qaniit*. But the clouds were cold and low. For breakfast we ate fried seal steaks, liver, intestines, and a loaf of Danish bread. Snowstorms ringed us with a hoop larger than the one made by the circling sun. The mountains rose up purple. We left the Norwegians behind. As usual, they had talked late into the night. Every time there had been a moment of silence, Niels would say, "Okay, we sleep." Then the talking had started again.

Now we traveled in shadow. The ice was a pane of emptiness that had slipped under our sled. Ahead were islands of ice—transparencies merging into drowning fields. The light was flat and so was the mood. We didn't want to go back, but the ice had hardened during the night despite the sun and we crossed the gaping crack with no trouble.

As we headed toward Qaanaaq, the bottoms of black clouds split open—a dark shade falling to its knees—spewing out milk, ash, void. Snow was carried horizontally into our faces on a ferocious wind. We put on parkas and mittens; snow caught in our fox fur ruffs. The dogs were almost too tired to pull, but Jens, ever-patient, ever-persistent, encouraged them. *"Puquok, puquok . . . A ta ta ta ta ta."* By the next morning, three feet of new snow had fallen. It was the middle of June.

On the way home Jens and Niels shot three seals and I kept my eyes averted from the light. I had been blind from sun, blind from snow. Jens's deep tenderness toward his dogs carried me, even though I dragged my foot off the side of the sled to slow our progress. The salve I'd used from my vet's kit eased the scratching pain under my eyelids. At home, my mother was going blind and I felt linked to her. In going back to Qaanaaq, to town, it felt as though we were heading toward some kind of blind zone. Out here, almost everything the hunter seeks is hidden and the way to it is constantly obstructed by ice. As he is unable to see his prey,the hunter's hearing is enhanced, and his eyes become sharp enough to see where a seal might have been.

The dogs struggled in deepening snow. Or was it just depression? Home for them meant being tied up and left outside. Once when Jens went hunting near the village of Savissivik, a spring storm had blown in. "The snow was up to my chest; we were almost out of fuel. What usually took three days took a month. Finally, I put all the dogs on the sled, made a harness that went around my waist, and pulled the sled and the dogs myself."

I shoved my hands under the lash ropes. We snagged traces, bumped over plates of ice soldered together by sun. Ice was the mirror under which the tormented, broken sea writhed, and snow was coming fast.

The dogsled had been a bridge over chasms, across leads in ice. It had been our sanctuary for sleeping, our tiny island of safety in thin ice, our platform for seeing out, going blind, seeing in. Before I knew it, we were zigzagging through the rough ice near shore and sliding by a glacier that had disgorged its contents like laughter onto the still-frozen fjord.

The village of Qaanaaq stood rigid on its lonely hill. We had gone back into whiteness, into winter, into the opaque cataract of civilization. Was it a poison or the inevitable inflorescence of human activity? The closer we came to town, the more cigarettes Niels smoked. Far ahead, we could see Jens's wife and grandchild waiting at the shore. Jens showed no emotion but made a beeline for them. Ilaitsuk and the child were waving. Then, as we bumped toward them, a snow squall took them from sight.

The Fifth Thule Expedition, 1923

In March 1923, Rasmussen and his Greenlandic companions, Qavi-garssuaq (Qav) and Arnarulunguaq (Arn), said good-bye to Peter Freuchen and the others on Danish Island and started off on the last leg of their trans-Arctic journey. They would travel back over the migration route the first Inuit hunters had taken to go east from Alaska, following the game and looking for new places to live. Much like the silk roads of Asia, these "ice roads" had been used by the Eskimos for ten thousand years. It was only in the mid-1800s that this route became known as the Northwest Passage. Clearly, it was the only feasible way to traverse Arctic America.

Rasmussen and his two companions set out to retrace those steps. Along the way Rasmussen found ruins of winter settlements made by Eskimos several thousand years earlier—proof that they were on the Inuit migration trail. And in the process, Rasmussen took down the life histories and ideas of people who had been living there, so isolated that they had never seen human beings other than nomadic hunters and the rare and almost always starving foreigners whose ships had been crushed in winter ice as they sought the Northwest Passage to Asia. Those sailors died from racism and arrogance. All they had to do was ask the Inuit hunters which way to go and how to eat, dress, and live along the way. But they were too proud and they died.

Freed from the cumbersome logistics of a large group, the second part of Rasmussen's journey was lively. "In number we were as few

as possible," he wrote. "And I was to be accompanied only by two Eskimos from the Thule District: Qavigarssuaq and his female cousin Arnarulunguaq. Our outfit too, had been made as spartan as the long journey demands."

Rasmussen and his friends traveled with two six-meter Hudson Bay–style sleds, each pulled by twelve dogs with a load of 500 kilos per sled. Their supplies consisted of dog food, tea, coffee, sugar, flour, tobacco, trade goods, extra clothes, and guns. They would spend seven months, from April through November, living among the five main groups of Netsilik Eskimos in the central Canadian Arctic, in the area of Somerset Island to the north, Victoria Island to the west, King William Island and Adelaide Peninsula to the south, and Boothia Peninsula to the east, using the frozen straits between to travel from one village to another.

Rasmussen described the mind of the Netsilik as being like the surface of a lake—quick to be stirred and just as quick to regain its equanimity. They were people who met hardship head-on with no complaints; serious adversity was taken in stride. He especially admired their treatment of women. Men and women among the Netsilik were comrades and equals. As a result, the women were lively and outspoken, often dominating the conversation and making jokes—something he had rarely seen in northern Greenland.

This was 1923, the year Yeats won the Nobel prize in literature, Freud published *The Ego and the Id,* Miró and Kandinsky were painting, and Bartók was writing string quartets. By contrast, Rasmussen was traveling by dogsled among ice age peoples whose year was mostly winter and whose isolation would have been complete for at least another hundred years if it had not been for the search for the Northwest Passage, a European quest that culminated in the mid-1800s.

John Ross, the English explorer who had made the first sighting of Greenland's polar people in 1818, overwintered in Lord Mayor's Bay, Northwest Territories, in 1829. By the time his ship was crushed by ice and sank, the cargo had been unloaded and local Netsilik hunters were given their share of wood, iron, nails, knives, and iron hoops from barrels. Using the iron hoops as saws, they cut the masts off the ship and used the wood (a prized possession) to make sleds, kayaks, and harpoons.

The Netsilik had other contacts with outsiders. They remembered John Rae's visits between 1847 and 1854, and earlier, near King William Island, they came upon the starving stragglers of John Franklin's expedition. A detailed memory had been passed down:

> *The white men were very thin, with sunken cheeks, and looked ill; they wore the clothes of white men, and had no dogs, but pulled their sledges themselves. They bought some seal meat and blubber, and gave a knife in payment. . . . There were already many caribou about at that season, but the strangers seemed to hunt only birds. The eider duck and ptarmigan were plentiful, but the earth was not yet come to life, and the swans had not arrived. My father and those with him would gladly have helped the white men, but could not understand their speech. . . . They pointed toward the south, and it was understood that they proposed to return to their own place overland. Afterwards no more was seen of them, and it was not known what had become of them. (Rasmussen, Across Arctic America, pp. 172–73)*

The landscape through Rae Isthmus was full of streams and lakes, low mountains, and rounded knobs of gneiss. The fish-shaped chalk concretions at the edge of Committee Bay were thought to have been created when a giant, Inugpasugssuk, splashed water with his hand, causing a tidal wave to wash fish up on the shore.

Rasmussen made camp near a river that flowed into the bay. The caribou had begun migrating and they wanted to hunt. It was there, in a snowstorm, that they met Orpingalik, a shaman who brought the strangers home with him. His village consisted of two snow huts with a passageway between. Unlike the Caribou Eskimo huts, these were well heated with blubber lamps and padded with thick caribou skins. Rasmussen and his companions were given salmon and hunks of caribou meat. By the time they finished eating, the other men had built a large snow house for the visiting Greenlanders.

Orpingalik and Rasmussen got on well and within a week Rasmussen had gone through one hundred tales, comparing those of the Netsilik with the Iglulik, the Caribou, and the Greenlanders. Orpingalik was notable for his songs, which he called "comrades in solitude" and "my breath." When Rasmussen asked how many songs he had composed, Orpingalik responded, "I keep no count of such things. There are so many occasions in one's life when a joy or a sorrow is felt in such a way that the desire comes to sing; and so I only know that I have many songs."

When hunting caribou he sang:

> Wild caribou, land-louse, long-legs,
> With the great ears
> And the rough hairs on your neck,
> Flee not from me.
> Here I bring skins for soles,
> Here I bring moss for wicks,
> Just come gladly
> Hither to me, hither to me.

He composed his Whitmanesque "Song of Myself," he told Rasmussen, during a fit of despair that came on after a long illness:

> I will sing a song.
> A little song of myself.
> Sick have I lain since autumn
> And have turned weak as a child.
> Unaya, unaya.
> Sorrowful, I wish that
> my wife were gone to another house
> to a man who can be her refuge,
> secure and firm as the thick winter ice.
> Sorrowful, I would she were gone
> to a better protector,
> now that I have no strength myself

The Fifth Thule Expedition, 1923

to rise from bed.
Unaya, unaya.
Do you know your fate?
Now I lie faint and cannot rise.
Only my memories are strong.

(Rasmussen, Fifth Thule Expedition, *vol. 8, pp. 14 and 15)*

On April 5 Rasmussen broke camp and reluctantly bade farewell to his new friend Orpingalik. He then set out northwest to Pelly Bay, where he met the Arviligjuarmiut, a group of Netsilik Eskimos totaling fifty-four people who were living in three settlements—two out on the ice and one on the west coast of Simpson Peninsula. This area was dubbed "the Land of Great Whales," but it was rich in caribou, muskox, seal, and fish as well. Unlike in the Barren Grounds, there was rarely any starvation here. They hunted with bows and arrows, made skinning knives from yellow flint, harpoon shafts and tentpoles from the shafts of caribou antlers, harpoon heads from the shinbones of bears, and sewing needles from the legbones of seagulls.

Sneaking up on caribou was difficult when the snow creaked under their feet. That's why, in midwinter, the Arviligjuarmiut could be seen stalking herds of caribou barefoot, and if that wasn't enough, they sometimes went completely naked so as not to make any noise.

Rasmussen traveled here and there among various groups. He met a man named Uvdloriasugssuk, big-boned, black-bearded, with a deep, slow voice, who had just completed a "mercy killing" of his own brother, who, he said, was deranged and had killed several villagers in a mad rage. He'd told his brother of his mission and offered him his choice of how to die. The brother, knowing that he was a menace to society, chose the bullet and Uvdloriasugssuk shot him on the spot.

Another evening two men crashed into Rasmussen's snow hut. The visitors, brothers named Qaqortingneq and Angutisugssuk, were from the Magnetic North Pole. They invited Rasmussen and his companions to join them on their trip home. As usual, Rasmussen accepted. It was the beginning of May; en route, they spent idyllic evenings sitting around a campfire with plenty of caribou to eat, listening to the brothers talk.

The brothers thought that inside the earth—all of which was sacred in the summer, including grass, stones, and turf—very large eggs were stored. These were called *silafat*—something that will become Sila—though some of the eggs were transformed into muskoxen.

There were stories of giants who could crumple up flat ice and smooth out pack ice, of a woman who bit a black bear to death by becoming, momentarily, a polar bear. One female angakok made herself into a man, using a piece of willow for a penis. She scooped out her own female genitals and employed them to make a sled. With a clump of snow which she had used to wipe her behind, she made a white dog with a black head. From then on she hunted like a man, killing seals at breathing holes.

Rasmussen, Qav, and Arn made their way to meet up with Qaqort-ingneq's fellow villagers, who had moved since he'd left home. They crossed Shepherd Bay in a snowstorm. Just as they reached the Magnetic North Pole, they came onto a narrow path lined by seal skulls. Qaqort-ingneq told Rasmussen not to disturb them, as they were compass marks showing the way to the new village site.

The seal skull was thought to be the locus of the soul, and because the soul is reborn over and over, the heads were pointed in the direction of the new hunting ground so the souls could find their way there. "That's how we kill the same seal over and over," Qaqortingneq explained to Rasmussen.

The sled dogs had scented the village from an hour away. Falling snow was so thick everything vanished. By following the line of skulls, they reached the village—a small group of snow huts.

There, Rasmussen encountered people who hadn't seen a white person since Roald Amundsen had come through twenty years before. Angutisugssuk shouted, "We've got white men visitors!" waking everyone. The man's mother jumped up from a sound sleep; by way of welcome, she lifted her skin clothing and gave her breast to her son. This was the traditional mother-son greeting when they had been separated for a long time.

The people were dirty. By blubber lamp Rasmussen wrote: "Only then did I really see the naked bodies. Here it was not dirt, it was layers, and the short-clipped hair was miry with oil. My first impression was that ears and brow at the roots of the hair and the neck were full of sores, but this too proved to be deposits of dirt."

The villagers walked in single file around the sleds. The circle of footprints would confuse the bad spirits and hold them prisoner so they could not invade the snow huts, they explained to Rasmussen. Then a snow house was built and the sleds were unloaded and the feasting began.

As usual Rasmussen sought out the oldest man in the village. He was the shaman, Niaqunuaq, who received the stranger lying on his sleeping platform, his face glistening. On closer inspection, Rasmussen saw that the inhuman shine was actually seal blubber smoothed onto his skin—his version of cleaning up for the occasion.

Caribou skins were laid on the ice platform over a mattress made of ribs. Windowpanes were made from slabs of freshwater ice. The huts were positioned so as to keep out the prevailing northwest winds, and the insides were kept warm with soapstone blubber lamps that threw a low, flickering light on ice walls.

After the feast, Niaqunuaq broke into Rasmussen's snow house and began screeching in a falsetto about how Qaqortingneq had eaten salmon entrails—a taboo—and now misfortune would befall them all. Rasmussen quietly got up, lit the Primus, and put on a pot of coffee while the old man railed on. But as soon as Niaqunuaq smelled the fumes, he came out of trance, sat down, drank a cup of coffee, and admitted that with a small gift from Qav, the bad spirits could be whisked away.

In the next days, Rasmussen set about collecting whatever amulets the villagers could spare, since they were worn to ward off sickness, misfortune, and bad luck in hunting. He had brought trade items: sewing needles, knives, thimbles, nails, matches, and tobacco. In this way, he was bringing in the new in order to learn about the old ways. Soon there was a steady stream of people wanting to make an exchange.

As the villagers laid out their amulets, they explained their uses: the swan's head was to produce a male child; a ptarmigan's head gave swiftness in hunting caribou; the tern's head helped to catch enough fish; the foot of a northern diver made a man good in a kayak. There were caribou teeth, bear teeth, plus bits of dried flounder for protection against strange tribes; a raven's head and claws ensured a good share of the meat during a hunt (meat was shared communally). A bee with its progeny, sewn into a piece of skin and fastened to a hood, made the head strong; a fly gave invulnerability; a water beetle gave strong temples; and a thin strip of salmon skin caused women's stitches to be strong.

Magic words and songs were also sung or whispered early in the morning for the purposes of healing people and pacifying storms, using the special language of the shamans—words that had been passed down from father to son or bought from a shaman:

> *Land earth-root,*
> *Great land earth-root,*
> *Here is the*
> *Song-text's master.*
> *The world's pillars*
> *They pale,*
> *They turn white.*

> (Rasmussen, Fifth Thule Expedition, *vol. 8, p. 283*)

When it came time for Rasmussen to leave, the shaman objected. He claimed Rasmussen hadn't given the villagers enough. He must also give away locks of his own hair. Against Rasmussen's protests, a man named Itqilik hacked off the visitor's locks with a dull knife. They had never heard of or seen scissors.

The next day it was decided that Qav would travel west across Queen Maud Gulf to Kent Peninsula, where he would ship off their collections from the Hudson Bay Company post. In June he was to meet Rasmussen and Arn on King William Island with fresh supplies. By now Arn and Rasmussen had become lovers—not unusual in Inuit society, where a companion on the ice might be different from the one at home. The practice, when it existed, was tolerated. Discretion was urged but there could be no secrecy involved. Children were never considered "illegitimate" in Inuit society. Rasmussen's "legal" wife and children were in Denmark, but he spent very little time there. Arn was his Eskimo wife—his partner on this three-year journey across Arctic America.

It was the end of May when Rasmussen and Arn reached the mouth of the Great Fish River (now called the Back River) and proceeded on to Itivnarjuk, a village near Lake Franklin, named after the explorer John Franklin. Every route Rasmussen explored in the area was strewn with the bones of ships and men who had fared badly in these narrow straits as they attempted to find a way to Asia.

One day he met a man and his son preparing to eat raw liver at the breathing hole where they had just killed a seal. The hunters knelt down around the dead animal as a narrow incision was made and the liver was pulled out. As soon as the opening was pinned closed to keep from wasting the blood, the liver was eaten. Rasmussen described this as almost a religious feast: "There we were, quite close to the breathing hole, all on our knees in the wet snow, silently eating a seal's raw liver with small squares of white, swelling blubber; a strange hunting reminiscence that seemed to me like a Thanksgiving and a homage to the daily bread."

Rasmussen wanted to go inland one last time to meet the Utkuhikhalingmiut, the least known of all the Eskimos, a tribe no white people had seen since a visit of a few hours in 1879. In fact, the nearest white settlement was three months away by dogsled.

Rasmussen found the people to be quiet, dignified, handsome, and extremely fit. They wore a band of white caribou skin tied around their foreheads. They had never seen anyone like Rasmussen—a white man who spoke their dialect. As soon as Rasmussen's charm worked on them, they helped him and Arn unload and settle in for a day of conversation.

The Utkuhikhalingmiut said they didn't believe in anything; they were fearful—of ghosts and of the dead, and especially of Nuliajuk, the giver and taker of all the animals on which they subsisted. Freewheeling spirits could be as small as bees or as big as mountains. When people died, the moon carried them up to the land of the dead, where the windows of the houses showed as stars.

People lived on after death. Shamans knew this, and ordinary people did too, because the dead appeared to them often. There were three places dead people could go. The first was Anerlartarfik—"the place one can always return to." Far up in space, it was a land of pleasure where the houses stood in long rows and people were always playing. Clever hunters went there, as did women who had allowed themselves to be tattooed so they would be beautiful. It was said to be a great plain with huge herds of caribou grazing and berries growing.

The second place was called Nuqumiut—"those who always sit huddled up with hanging head." Their land was just under the earth's surface. All the lazy hunters went there, as did the women who could not endure the suffering of being tattooed. Slothful and idle when alive, in death they sat with their heads hanging. They were always hungry and their only food was butterflies.

Finally there was Aglermiut—"a place that is deep in the bowels of the earth." This place, like Anerlartarfik, held famous hunters and shamans and the hunting was always good and the people joyful. They could move at will out of a tent by spitting upward and flying through the spit as through an open hole. They could change into seagulls and fly. The only difference was that the seasons were reversed—as if the entire realm of the dead were divided hemispherically.

The river ice had begun to break up and Rasmussen had to move on. He left in the middle of the night, since travel on spring ice is fastest when undertaken during the coldest hours. He and Arn were on their way to spend the summer on King William Island. He described their leave-taking as especially cheerful:

> *Amid a chorus of farewells from our friends we struck out over the great water. One might almost say through it: for a mush of sodden snow and water came threshing up over the sledges, and we ourselves were soaked through at once, having to go down on our knees in order to heave the sledges clear when they stuck fast. Altogether about as wretched going as one could wish for the starting of a journey but we took little heed of it, and laughed as we plunged into the ice mess through which we had to toil that day. The snow-broth seethed about the runners, and we drove through it singing. (Rasmussen, Across Arctic America, p. 200)*

On June 13 they arrived at King William Island, expecting to meet there with Qav, who would be bringing new supplies. Spring was at its height (summer, as we know it, doesn't occur in the Arctic until July). Rasmussen was happy with the prospect of spending the whole summer in this lovely place:

> *The country rises as one moves inland, in terraces marking the site of earlier beaches, with long narrow lakes in the hollows between, fed by small streams from the melting snow. There are a few ranges of hills, but as soon as one gets away from the sea, the country at this time of year presents the appearance of a grassy plain. Spring was at its height, and the earth on every side was bursting into life. Geese, duck, and waders were gathered in thousands on the lakes and marshy ground; red patches of saxifrage glowed among the rocks, the first flowers to greet the light and warmth of the sun. (Rasmussen, Across Arctic America, p. 202)*

Instead of traveling by sled he now walked, always taking a few dogs with him. "They gambolled to their hearts' content over the plains and waded out into the lakes to cool themselves."

For several days he had a feeling that he would see something he had never encountered before. Then he came on a ruined village of ancient Eskimo stone houses. They were the first permanent winter houses found in the central Arctic. Rasmussen and Arn put up their tent among them, in what the Eskimos called "the Many House Ruins" (also called Malerualik) to start archeological excavations there.

Summer was waking. The ice on the lakes had begun to melt and flocks of swans had arrived for the nesting season. On the tundra snowy owls stood waiting for lemmings, and a few straggling caribou trotted northward. They met a hunter with a handmade wooden leg carved from the old cross slats of a wooden sledge lashed together around the knee with caribou skin as a cushion for the stump. The foot of the wooden leg was made of muskox horn in the shape of a hoof.

Seals and caribou were scarce, as was ammunition. Rasmussen set a net he had brought from Repulse Bay into the river and caught two or three salmon a day, but that was not enough food for themselves and seventeen dogs. By the third week of July Rasmussen and Arn found it necessary to move to the interior of the island, where they hoped the salmon catch would be better.

On what turned out to be the last day in their beloved summer camp, they caught three seals; for the first time, they were able to give the dogs as much as they wanted to eat and still have enough for themselves. The day had been calm with a soft gray sky. "All this loveliness was short-lived, however," Rasmussen wrote. "The next day there was a violent thunderstorm followed by pouring rain." The ice became so watery that hunting seals was no longer possible.

On July 25 they set off with others from camps nearby, traveling Netsilik-style, using individual dogs as pack animals, since there was no snow for sleds. At first the dogs protested. Some tried to rub the packs off and others ran into the meltwater. One dog, whom they dubbed "the secretary," assumed "a nervous air of responsibility" as soon as the pack was put on her back. She stayed close to Rasmussen at all times. Later he entrusted her with carrying his voluminous diaries.

The long procession of pack dogs and humans started off at midnight in bright sun, tramping alternately on muddy trails and over lakes whose mirrored surfaces were dissolving. "King William Island is very monotonous to the eye," Rasmussen wrote. "The plains seem to be endless and as we never kept to any straight path but cut off to right or left after game, the impression of immensity grew upon us with every day that passed."

They had long since run out of tobacco, tea, coffee, and sugar—"the luxuries that add zest to life," especially in a diet mainly of raw or boiled meat. But Rasmussen was no stranger to starvation and he was grateful for any food at all.

On August 1 they pitched camp by an enormous lake. In the evening a solitary swan glided by. Rasmussen and Arn delighted in its presence. Five days later they came to Amitsoq, famous for its abundance of fish. There were already five tents and many families there. Though the weather was horrendous and it was too early for the fish, nobody cared. It was summer and the Netsilik were in a festive mood. Even in pouring rain and bad hunting conditions, the people were "gaily starving, cheerfully freezing in ragged clothing."

To catch fish, the Netsilik built a stone dam and put a weir in the little stream that connected the large and small lakes. Rasmussen observed that the river trout that swam into the trap could easily get out, but the salmon, swimming upriver, never turned around once in the weir and were easy to catch. There were rules about the time of day for fishing. The fish needed to rest during the off-hours, the hunters contended. And those hours were taken up with play.

The children's favorite amusement was "the spirit game," in which they imitated and parodied shamans' seances. Magic formula were spoken, the child playing the shaman imitated the trance, enemies were fought off. When Rasmussen inquired whether it was safe to mock such serious ceremonies, the hunters assured their guests that the spirits understood a joke.

He was told then about things of the spirit, about life after death: "The world is not only what we can see. It is enormous and also has room for people when they die, when they no more walk about down here on earth."

When Rasmussen was preparing to leave, he wrote:

On the 12th of August I had, with regret, to leave this place, where every single day had given me the impressions of the enviable lightness of the primitive mind. If thoughtless abandonment to the moment were really a blessing, I had actually been in the 'Land of the Blessed.' The fishing was still quite poor, the caribou remained in quite other parts of the island, rain and wind were merciless, and often there was not sufficient to eat to satisfy one's hunger. But it was summer still; there was still a chance of their hunting luck turning; so why think about the morrow? And besides, an old tribal tradition said that the spirits never helped the anxious and dismayed! (Rasmussen, Fifth Thule Expedition, *vol. 8, p. 69)*

The Netsilik believed that luck followed misfortune. It was already the end of summer, and on the trip back to Malerualik Rasmussen and Arn came across migrating caribou. They hunted with a man named Qupaq, who had been helping his stepfather on the other side of the island split a rare and precious piece of driftwood into sled runners, kayaks, and tentpoles. Soon they had more meat than they'd had all summer. Rasmussen and Arn were returning to the site of the ancient houses to continue excavations and also to meet up with Qav, who had been gone for two months and was now overdue. Back at the camp of ruined houses they found that the caribou cached by Qupaq had been eaten by foxes, but they had enough meat for the time being, and Arn caught two trout.

Rasmussen remembered that night as romantic. Arn fried the trout over a cassiope fire, and they lay outside under the stars. A small herd of caribou descended from a ridge near their tent. "They kept to the plain just before us, turned in toward the interior, and before long they disappeared in a cloud of dust just as suddenly as they had come. We felt as if we had seen an apparition, and the dogs, unable to control their disappointment at not having been allowed to hunt, did not settle down again until far into the night." Perhaps it was that night that Arn became pregnant with Rasmussen's child.

On August 25 a storm froze the ground and ponds. Where was Qav? A shaman had a dream about him: he was on the way and had killed two bears, but was having difficulties. In the meantime, Rasmussen and Arn began building a Greenland-style stone-and-turf house where he could finish compiling his notes in collaboration with the Netsilik in the area.

Three old friends from the previous spring came by and looked on in astonishment: they had never seen a house made that way. But soon they lent a helping hand cutting turf and before nightfall, Arn and Rasmussen held "a roofing supper" of salmon, caribou, and dried meat as they completed the house.

"Hospitality is a law among all wayfaring people," Rasmussen noted. Arn spread skins on the dirt floor and they crowded together to sleep, illuminated by a moss and caribou fat lamp. "Our talk was becoming languid when Itqilik began to tremble all over and started shamanizing. He had seen sparks coming from his inner coat, and it must have been because he had worked with soil and stone at a time when it was forbidden."

To avoid a disaster, Rasmussen quickly interrupted the seance and assured everyone that he was "superior to all taboo" because he had only followed the customs of his own country, and therefore no one had to fear bad luck in their hunting. "Then the rushlight was blown out and the general signal for sleep was given."

Soon it was September. They were almost out of matches and ammunition. On the 3rd, the weather was "a calm frost"—sunshine and a clear sky. Arn gazed out over the water: "Oh! Look there! I thought the tide was out and now there is a rock I don't seem to know. Look, look, it's moving!"

They saw a kayak—tiny on the horizon—coming toward them. Which was odd, because in the central Arctic, kayaks are used only on freshwater lakes, never on the sea. It was Qav and his companion. An hour later they arrived. There was a joyful reunion tempered by disappointment: they had brought little ammunition and no tobacco, tea, coffee, sugar, or flour. "But we are alive and kicking and that hasn't always been such a natural thing as you might think."

They had been accosted by groups of hostile Kitlinermiut and had had to tie their dogs up around their tent to warn them of an ambush. The collections had been safely delivered to the Hudson Bay's agent on Kent Peninsula, but the shelves at the store there were bare. The river ice melted in early June, so they left their dogs at a camp along the way and traveled by borrowed canoe. They passed a migration of caribou so vast it took three days for the animals to pass by. Then the pack ice moved in to shore as autumn approached and travel became difficult and slow.

The sled journey to Nome, Alaska, resumed. The caribou were gathering and moving down toward the coast of Simpson Strait, then across to

Malerualik, where Rasmussen and his friends were camped. Inevitably, the animals would be followed by people:

> *The eleventh of September we were surprised by an invasion of Hivilermiut who put over Simpson Strait on ferries of the most original kind. They consisted of caribou skins sewn together. They were about two skins in length and a good skin's width; they were stuffed with platform rugs and old clothing and then sewn up all round. Their pairs fastened together or made fast to a kayak that had special stays, one of the wide skin handles being on each side of the kayak. In this manner about thirty people had ferried themselves over the strait and now joined in as serious competitors to our hunting. (Rasmussen,* Fifth Thule Expedition, *vol. 8, pp. 77–78)*

By the fifteenth of that month, there were a hundred people. When a large herd of caribou came through, panic ensued. Guns began firing. Rasmussen and Qav figured that when the killing was over, fifty animals were dead. But in the process, they had expended five to seven rounds of ammunition per animal—a poor result in Rasmussen's mind, as he was dangerously short of ammunition and each shot counted. But for people who were used to reckoning according to bow and arrow, the result was a good one.

Snow fell. The caribou, frightened by the recent slaughter, hid out. Local sled travel became possible; Rasmussen and Qav went off to hunt and returned with seven fat animals. A week later there was another commotion in camp. Everyone was running to Rasmussen's tent. "Look there!" they said. Rasmussen turned and saw a ship under full sail heading toward them.

The hunters had never seen such a thing before. "How could it float? Where could they have got all that wood from? And it swam over the water like a big bird, the sail spreading out from the hull like great white wings," they said.

Rasmussen ran the Danish and Union Jack flags up a pair of skis in front of his hut, and soon a launch from the ship came toward the settlement. A Swede and a Dane appeared. They were on their way to establish a new post for the Hudson Bay Company on King William Island. The ship was the *El Sueño*—built in San Francisco and now old and worn out. The two seamen had made it through the most perilous part of the Northwest Passage with no navigational tools or charts. "We are not Vikings and Norsemen for nothing," they said.

Autumn weather came swirling in with blustery winds and cold sleet. Thin ice formed on the lakes, melted, and froze again. But just when it seemed winter had come to stay, snow and rain set in and the ice melted away. As Rasmussen, Arn, and Qav continued their excavations at the Many House Ruins, he noticed that the approaching darkness began to affect the nerves and minds of the Eskimos. Every evening marauding spirits were said to swing through camp and had to be combatted by the three resident shamans.

One night a shaman came to Rasmussen's window and shouted that the angakok Niaqunuaq was fighting four ghosts and everyone had to go to their tents to protect the children and dogs from the spirits. Later, the shaman Samik came by and said he had met a fifth ghost, who had torn his clothing.

By mid-October winter came on hard and the caribou passed the camp in big herds—one hundred to two hundred at a time. Meat was plentiful again. On October 27, a hunter named Oqortoq sent a message around that he wanted to have a feast because his foster son had taken his first steps that morning.

A snowstorm raged, but the festival took place out from the snow huts on the lake ice. There were contests of strength between men and women and a boisterous game using a piece of caribou fat for a football. Then there was nose rubbing between a line of men and women so vigorous that nosebleeds resulted. As the festivities concluded, Rasmussen noted, "This was one of the most amusing and most original festivals I have ever witnessed; and the severe weather contributed its share to give the performance the true Eskimo spirit and character."

Rasmussen's party had stayed with the Netsilik for seven months. One of the shamans reminded Rasmussen that their word for "entrance" also meant "road." Both were openings to new understanding. Now the ice was coming in and travel could begin again. It was not easy to say good-bye. But it was late in the year 1923 and he was less than halfway across the Canadian Arctic. On November 1, Rasmussen and his companions hooked their seventeen dogs to the sled and set out west across the Queen Maud Gulf.

New Ice, 1923–1924

In autumn, cold weather and new ice can be a traveler's helper—the ice is smooth and the going is fast and a distance that might have taken ten hours to traverse takes only two or three. But darkness comes fast. The days grow dimmer and dimmer until there is no light, and unless there is a moon and cloudless days and nights, travel and hunting are almost impossible.

The trio from Greenland—Rasmussen, Qav, and Arn—drove west following the ice foot along the shore of the Queen Maud Gulf. Rasmussen wrote:

> *Great caution is necessary. The uninitiated will often be unable to see the difference between the thick, safe ice and places where it is only a few hours old. This may be fatal, for it is always extremely dangerous to fall through thin ice where there is no snow. On breaking through the water washes over the unbroken edges and softens them, so that one continues to fall through: unless there is really old ice close by, it is impossible to clamber up again.* (Rasmussen, Fifth Thule Expedition, vol. 9, p. 8)

Accompanying them were the Hudson Bay traders Peter Norberg and Henry Bjorn, plus a companion sledge carrying much of their ethnographic collections, driven by two Netsilik men who were good hunters but whose dogs were poor. Rasmussen often left them behind and went on ahead to establish a camp on land, since the ice was too

dangerous. He built huge driftwood fires as sentinels to light the way: "In those dark evenings those bonfires glared with entrancing beauty: all around us was the waste and gray and when we stood still we could hear the grating moan of the ice out in the open sea which was never very far away."

The Copper Eskimos had a reputation among other Inuit as being violent and hostile to outsiders. Rasmussen paid little attention to these warnings and proceeded north toward Melville Island. They traveled on a fifteen-mile-wide river and camped on a tiny island so populated by foxes that all the snow was trampled down smooth. The barren expanse of the eastern Arctic began to give way to islands with ragged, rocky coastlines and more luxuriant growth of alpine grasses and flowers. In a two-day blizzard, they followed the coast with such expedience that by November 15 they had their first sighting of a Kitlinermiut, between Queen Maud Gulf and Arctic Sound.

Rasmussen wrote: "I had clambered up a hillock to reconnoitre when suddenly I caught sight of a young man jigging for cod on the ice. Scarcely had he seen me when he hauled up his line and disappeared at a run round the point. A moment later he reappeared, this time carrying a brand-new Mark 1920 repeating rifle, evidently ready to let it speak if I did not come around as a friend."

Rasmussen was a master at overcoming differences with others. "The misunderstanding soon dissolved in laughter," he recalled. They were invited home with the hunter. The man's village bore the influence of the nearby Hudson Bay post. The people used shiny tin lamps instead of soapstone blubber lamps, enamel dishes instead of wooden trays, aluminum pots rather than stone pots, and wool blankets that had been laid on top of caribou skins on the *illeq*. The hunter's wife wore a calico overall that covered her caribou-skin jacket. She smoked Lucky Strikes.

The Kitlinermiut were nomadic groups who lived in the vicinity of Victoria Island (the Inuit name is Kitlineq). There had always been communication among all the tribes of the Northwest Passage, and the Copper Eskimos were the westernmost of these. All trading and exchanges went east from here. What was known of people to the west was, simply, that they existed.

Before arriving, Rasmussen had heard from the explorer Vilhjalmur Stefansson that there was a group of Inuit living on Victoria Island known as the blond Eskimos. Many of them had gray eyes and light brown beards. There had been much controversy over whether they were related to early Norsemen. However, when Rasmussen inquired, there were no memories or legends of any such European connection. Rasmussen would soon find such fair-complexioned types on nearby islands, but no stories of outsiders known to have intermarried there.

Rasmussen chose to stay among a group who'd had the least amount of contact with European culture. Off he went to find the Umingmaktormiut—the Muskox People—who had settled for the winter season on the island of Malerisiorfik near Kent Peninsula. Instead of hostility, Rasmussen found that these people had "a great, inborn hospitality that did not wear off all the time we were among them."

A year earlier, writing from Repulse Bay in 1922, Rasmussen had asked his supporters at home in Denmark to send out a film photographer to accompany him on the last leg of the journey. Leo Hansen made his way to this meeting point via Copenhagen, New York, trans-Canada railway to Vancouver, then by schooner past Point Barrow and Herschel Island to Tree River in Coronation Gulf, and from there to the Hudson Bay post on Kent Peninsula.

One wonders what conflicts the sudden introduction of a movie camera into Rasmussen's ethnographic studies might have caused. Rasmussen was, in every way, leading a double life. He was Eskimo as a hunter and traveler with Arn, his Inuit "wife"; at other times, funded by Danish backers, including his Danish wife's family, he was thoroughly European in his ethnographic pursuits, collecting amulets from around the necks and waists of villagers and recording his travels on film. Perhaps because he was born in Greenland, not Denmark, and grew up in a colonized Inuit society, he never seemed to get bogged down by the conflict—if there was one. In fact, he used it as fuel: the stirrings his double existence caused was dealt with by leaving. He kept going across the polar north—by dogsled—as if to outrun the confusion when it surfaced.

Now it was November and the light was fading, and Hansen was eager to get to work. Rasmussen, Hansen, Arn, and Qav arrived at the Umingmaktormiut village in a blizzard. "It was some time before they could discern us through the billows of snow that washed over our sledges," Rasmussen noted.

The villagers lived in snow huts crowded together in the shelter of a mountain, and once Rasmussen moved into his own abode, they crowded inside, all talking at once so that it was difficult for Rasmussen to write anything down. The people were fearful of Leo Hansen's hand-cranked movie camera. Rasmussen dispelled these fears by having himself filmed first to prove that the process would not kill them. Soon enough, their self-assured and wild spirit dominated. Rasmussen said of them that they were the most poetically gifted of all Eskimo peoples, that their minds were "inflammable," that "they had a tongue that was enough to take one's breath away."

Land, sea, air—all were filled with humans, animals, and spirits. Up in *qilak*—the sky—the stars were all people who had died an inexplicable or violent death and who in death had become shining spirits. The aurora borealis—*arharneq*—lent a helping hand to the angakok. The aurora was alive: if the shaman whistled, the pulsing colors came closer; if he spit at it, its colors ran together.

Rainbows with steep sides meant happiness for all, but a rainbow with a flat arc meant disaster—that someone would die. *Qilauta* was the ring around the sun—frequently seen in the Arctic. It was called "the drum of the sun," like the drum used in the shaman's dances. A half-ring near the sun meant someone had died. Lemmings lived in the sky and occasionally fell. When a man named Ilaitsiaq was out walking on the ice, a sky-lemming dropped onto his neck and he instantly became a great shaman. Shooting stars were a star's excrement; meteors were fire. Thunder—which rocked the central Arctic frequently—was caused by small birds singing a thunder song. The sky suddenly darkened and lightning flew from their beaks.

The spirits of the air were attracted to the shining body of the shaman and entered via the navel, resting in the breast cavity around the heart. Ordinary people were "like houses with extinguished lamps; they were dark inside and did not attract the attention of the spirits." Shamans received their helping spirits from the earth's surface as well as its interior, and from space as well as from the border between earth and sky.

Most spirits were much like the ones all Inuit people knew of. Added to them were the following: the chinless one, who killed people; *nighilik*, the hook, who could cause whole passage walls in snow huts to crumble; *hilaq*, a monster in the form of a black bear; a one-eyed giant who was very dangerous; and a giant with no eyes at all. If a house was visited by spirits the dogs barked and the inhabitants got up, put lighted wick moss in the windows, and waved hand-carved wooden knives in the air to chase the demons away.

The secrets of how animals like the wolverine and the wolf turned into humans and how a human changed into a polar bear had all been lost by the time Rasmussen arrived.

Whenever taboos were broken, the woman at the bottom of the sea—called in this tribe Arnakaphaluk—hid all the sea beasts under her sleeping platform so they could not get out. She was a punishing presence who made hunting fail. But among the Umingmaktormiut she had a compassionate side too—rare in Inuit beliefs. When people were in need and sat in darkness because they had no blubber for their lamps, her lamp went out too and she felt their pain and was moved to help them.

A shaman invoked the sea goddess by gathering the villagers in a *qagje*—the dance hut far out on the ice. Inside, a hole was made in the ice resembling a seal's breathing hole which the angakok covered with a caribou-skin jacket. He then got on his knees under the jacket and peered down into the hole while the villagers sang:

> *Great woman down there*
> *Will she, I wonder, feel a desire to move?*
> *Great woman down there*
> *Will she, I wonder, feel a desire to move?*
>
> *Come out, you down there!*
> *Those who live above you, it is said,*

Call you
To see you, savage and snappish.
Come out, you down there.

(Rasmussen, Fifth Thule Expedition, *vol. 9, p. 25)*

Then the sea goddess Arnakaphaluk entered the body of the angakok by riding a seal that opened a way up to the surface of the sea and kept the way open like a tube. When she entered the shaman's body, he writhed in pain. The villagers held his head down: the air of human houses was thought to be too weak for a spirit and mustn't be inhaled. If the shaman lifted his head for air, Arnakaphaluk would retaliate in anger and smash the *qagje* and cause severe storms. The angakok held his breath: the pain left his body and the noise of wind subsided. Then he lifted his head from the hole in the ice, out from under the skin, and told his neighbors that the lamps had been relit and good hunting would resume.

In another Copper Eskimo group, angakoks were chosen literally at birth. The placenta was held up as soon as it was expelled and the infant was lifted up to look through it, a ceremony meant to give the child second sight. These children were later called *tarakut ihilgit*—those who have eyes in the dark.

They were fond of composing songs. Their "Magic Prayer When One Gets Up" was sung to Rasmussen:

That house I shall use,
That breathing hole I shall use.
One comes back,
One comes back again.
First I quickly removed the rime.
I bobbed up [through the passage entrance, the
breathing hole].
Was it not lovely!
Was it not lovely!

(Rasmussen, Fifth Thule Expedition, *vol. 9, p. 113)*

About songs, they said: "When a man's thoughts begin to turn toward another or something that does not concern him: without his hearing it, one makes magic songs so that there may be calm in his mind—for a man is dangerous when he is angry."

Good advice, since, as Rasmussen noted, they were willing murderers. Out of fifteen families, every male had been involved in a killing of another—cases of jealousy, the desire for someone else's wife, a vendetta, or infanticide.

Yet Rasmussen lived at Malerisiorfik almost a whole month with two of the wanted murderers with no problems. "We got to know them as pleasant and extremely helpful men who were very devoted to us and left with us only the best of memories." Rasmussen wrote. He had often observed their volatile tempers and saw "how quickly a storm between two minds can rise and disperse again."

Infanticide was common practice, as elsewhere in the Arctic. Too many mouths to feed, not misogyny, prompted it. It was the consequence of a people who were hungry much of the time. This was a hunting society, not a hunting and gathering society. There was nothing to gather except for a few eggs in June and some berries in August. Any creature whose usefulness was diminished was killed or left behind, including dogs, old people, children, female babies, the disabled. Women who had no children to look after might have taken up the harpoon and hunted. But that rarely happened, even in modern times.

Sometime during their stay there, Arn gave birth to a boy fathered by Rasmussen. The two travelers had been together since 1921. It is said that no special house was built for her as her time drew near. She simply kneeled on the platform, supporting herself with one arm and leaning against another woman until the child came out. After, she tied a piece of caribou skin between her legs and rested for a day. During that time she had to wear the hood of her anorak. Knud came in. She immediately leaned over and lit the fire under the cooking pot. Doing so meant the child would learn to walk quickly.

Rasmussen helped tie the umbilical cord with a piece of braided caribou thong. Then one of the women cut it with her *ulo* (knife). A bandage of caribou skin was applied. When the end of the navel fell off, it was sewn into his inner coat as an amulet. The *ulo* with which it was cut was also given to the child and saved.

Arn gave the boy his first "bath" by wiping him with the forehead skin of a caribou, then the soft skin of a northern diver (duck). Before she nursed him, the angakok came and sang a song. Then she gave the child a piece of meat to suck, to ensure that he would never go hungry. It was then time to give the child a name. Rasmussen held the boy up in the air and said, speaking for the boy, "With strength from the one I have been named after, with strength from the one I have been named after, I who am insignificant myself, may I soon be allowed to hunt." Then the child's name was uttered, though in Rasmussen's notes that name was not recorded.

On February 15, Arn put the infant in her amaut—the hood on the back of her anorak in which children are carried—stepped onto the sled, and, with Rasmussen and Qav, bade the Eskimos of the Northwest Passage good-bye. There had been a twenty-four-hour farewell party of singing and dancing, which Rasmussen and the others left with heavy hearts. They had spent seven months with the Netsilik and the Muskox People and parted from them with great reluctance.

The Greenlanders were about to begin the final stretch of their long journey during which they traced (backwards) the ancient migration route of the Inuit to Alaska. Little did Rasmussen know that the Copper Eskimos represented the last subsistence hunters who were still wild and free. As they pulled out of the village on their heavily laden sleds, their friends yelled after them, "*Inovaglutik nunanuaminut uterpaglik.*" May the living return to the land they hold dear.

Qaanaaq, 1997

For a week after hunting with Jens and Niels, I was the lone guest at Hans and Birthe's hotel. It was June and the middle of the night when I arrived and there was no dinner for me. In the kitchen I helped myself to whatever I could find. I'd been longing for vegetables, but there were none. Instead, I made soup, rice, and toast. I hadn't seen myself in a mirror since leaving and did not recognize what I saw. It's not that I had "the look of the ice cap or starvation" on my face, as Rasmussen did at the close of his Second Thule Expedition, but I did look as if I was wearing a mask. My face was blotched tan, almost black, my lips had peeled, and the skin around my eyes was puffy and white.

In the communal shower room my Polartec union suit stuck to my skin—I hadn't taken it off for the entire trip. Naked now, my skin was all red bumps and the water coming off my body ran brown.

After a long hunting trip, everyone is tired. I lay low for a few days, as did Jens and Niels. For hours I stood at the windows in the guesthouse and looked down at the village and the fjord. Village life is said to be a reflection of the busy hell inside us, but compared to the excitement of life on the ice, it seemed stagnant. The white nights were placid. The village dogs were sleeping and the strait was frozen white.

During the daytime hours I watched the daily parade of front-end loaders driving out past the sleds to get ice for the town's domestic water supply. Near the shore the Kommune offices and stores were busy: the post office–bank–ticket office, the tiny grocery store complete with its

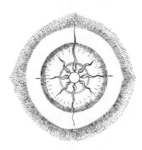

Danish bakery, the clothing store, the power plant and ice-melting facility, and the community carpentry shop, open to all, where sleds were made in the winter. The town owned two or three trucks that were available for use by anyone in need. Jens met his guests at the heliport with one of them. Keys were left in the ignition. If you needed the vehicle, you just climbed in.

Qaanaaq's houses were laid out in a grid on a single slope. It had the feel of a "new town," which it was, having only come into existence in the 1950s after being moved here from Dundas Village. There was the usual Arctic clutter of dogs, children, toys, sleds, drying racks, boats, and harnesses. Hunting cultures have no premium on neatness. Why should they? The neat-as-a-pin farmstead look came with agriculture, and has no redeeming qualities for far-ranging, seminomadic hunters on the ice.

In the days to come I ate more soup and rested. I missed our seal meals. *Sinikpoq.* I grew to love that word. It means "He (she) is sleeping." I slept often and long. Icicles fell from the eaves of the hotel. Summer was coming, winter was melting, spring was rocking on rotting ice under continually bright skies.

To pass the time I read Peary's journals from 1891 to 1909. His grandson's house, painted a garish purple, was just down the path from the hotel. As Robert Peary traveled the same stretch of coast from which we had just been turned back by a snowstorm, he wrote:

> *May 16, 1892. At 3 p.m. after getting into several cracks and getting wet to my waist, we find open water reaching in against the land. Go ashore over a shaky bridge of floating cakes and follow along the land to the north point of Wolstenholm Sound and Granville Bay. . . . Part of the time we were storm-bound, buried in drifts at the base of the wild shore cliffs. Then*

we were struggling at a snail's pace through deep slush, intersected by hidden cracks and wide leads of open water. The disintegration of the sea ice had proceeded so rapidly since our downward trip that we were repeatedly compelled to take to the shore, climb the shore bluffs, sometimes carrying sledges and outfits on our backs, and make the long detours overland. In one place we were obliged to scale a nearly vertical curtainlike drift, the crest of which rose 1,050 feet above sea level. Up this we carried the sledge loads on our backs, along zigzag steps cut into the face, then pushed and pulled the sledges and dogs after. (Weems, Peary, the Explorer and the Man, *p. 145)*

Now Kaalipaluk, Peary's Inuit son, born during one of his late expeditions, was ninety-one years old and lay dying in the local clinic. I went to visit him but he was asleep. His face looked like carved ivory on the pillow. The shadows between the creases near his eyes and alongside his mouth were black. I waited and came back several times, but his niece told me that his mind had no more need to talk.

Qaameneq. How does light enter the body? That's what I was wondering when I glassed Ikuo Oshima's dogsled rattling down Politiken Glacier onto Inglefield Sound. Sun glinted on his sled: he looked like a sliver of light coursing down the mountain. Two sleds followed him, both carrying a Japanese crew that had been filming segments for a TV show about the life of a Japanese hunter at the top of the world.

Late in the evening Ikuo and the TV crew made camp on the ice in front of Qaanaaq and I went down to visit. A mishmash of Japanese, Greenlandic, and English was being spoken. They were brewing green tea, eating potato chips and seal jerky.

As they filmed, Ikuo read a few selections from his book, published in Japan, about his life. It begins with a description of taking a shit on the ice: "If there isn't a blizzard, you can go outside, but don't stay out too long or you'll freeze your fingers and penis," the book warns. "And the dogs are always starving, so be careful that they don't bite your ass." He goes on to describe his meeting with the Japanese climber Naome Uemura, who was in Siorapaluk preparing for a solo journey to the North Pole. "My first feeling on seeing him again," Ikuo writes, "I thought he looked like an Eskimo." They ate raw seal meat and *kivioq,* which made Ikuo sick. "It gave me a strange feeling on my tongue," he writes. "Naome was eating seal intestines and his face was covered with blood. I tried to eat it, but it came up. I swallowed again and it came up again. I was almost crying; I was fighting with my stomach. Later, I learned to love these things."

Ikuo had met Naome at a lecture sponsored by the Alpine Club at Nihon University. "He wasn't a very good speaker," Ikuo remembered. "I asked him if I could help on his trip to the North Pole and he said I could." "That was the end of November 1972. By February, I could speak pretty good Greenlandic and had my first dogsled." By March he had shot his first seal at the breathing hole. "But when I went to skin it, it slithered away. It wasn't dead, only dazed by the sound of the bullet. All the Greenlandic guys were laughing." Soon he began learning how to hunt. "I made many mistakes. I fell through the ice, I lost my dogs, I missed my aim, but that's how you learn. And when you get hungry, you learn even faster."

Coincidentally, two North Pole expeditions started out at the same time. One was Naome's solo trip with dogsled. The other was Nihon University's Alpine Expedition, for which Ikuo was hired as a translator.

The university expedition began disastrously. A large team of Japanese alpinists and eleven Eskimos flew from Thule Air Force Base to Alert at the north tip of Ellesmere Island; 116 dogs died of asphyxiation in the back of the plane. Ten days later, another 100 dogs were sent but they were untrained, so there were many difficulties. The Japanese and Eskimos didn't get along because they couldn't agree on food. The Eskimos ate through the food supply too quickly, without regard for what they would eat the next day. The Japanese fed food scraps to the dogs, which made the Inuit furious. The Inuit wanted more money when the going got rough. They couldn't have cared less about getting to the Pole. This was just a job for them. So some returned to base camp; the rest continued on. "I was getting a bad stomach from all this fighting," Ikuo wrote, "knowing too that Naome was traveling absolutely alone with his dogsled." They were racing against each other with no contact between them. The University team won. They were fourth in the world to get to the Pole. Naome was the first to succeed in a solo trip and the fifth to attain the Pole.

In 1974 Ikuo met a young Greenlandic woman from Siorapaluk. Anna was living with her father, and Ikuo often ate dinner with them. While on an expedition with a Japanese film crew, Ikuo heard on the CB radio an old man from Siorapaluk who was arranging Anna's marriage. "Three men were mentioned as possible mates. My name was one of them. I asked myself, 'What is happening?' Then I asked the stars in the sky. Everything said yes. I felt it was my destiny, so I married her." By January they had the first of five children—a baby girl.

Ikuo's life was never easy in Siorapaluk. When drinking became a problem in the village, he moved his burgeoning family to Herbert Island to get away. But two of his boats sank there during a storm and he had no money. "I fixed old things so I could continue hunting and provide for the family." Later he moved back to Siorapaluk. Hunting walrus became his favorite activity. He made dogsleds and harness, harpoons for hunting walrus, bird nets to catch dovekies in the spring. Soon he not only hunted but did the women's work of preparing the skins and sewing as well. There was nothing he could not do to perfection.

Some chapters of his small book give recipes: to make *kivioq* you have to put 700 dovekies into a seal intestine, sew it up, cover it with seal fat to keep the flies off, stash it under a stone cairn, and leave it for two months. Ikuo laughs about his former distaste for the delicacy. Now his Greenlandic friends say he makes *kivioq* better than they do. He even gets orders from what he calls "hungry spirits."

He likes autumn hunting the best, when phosphorescent bugs are scurrying around the water and when the ice comes, the walrus break through with their heads. The sun goes down on October 24 and by mid-November the ice is solid. "One day you look out and nothing is moving," he writes. "It looks like a mirror big enough to reflect the galaxy."

Winter is very long, Ikuo told me, and he asked if I knew the word for winter. I did. It is *ukiuq*. "That word also means 'a year.' " He smiled.

Then he said that bad things are happening to them up here. Greenpeace came and got the prices for sealskins slashed to almost nothing. "They did not understand that we hunt to live, not to sell skins. It is our necessity. Eskimo never take vitamin or eat vegetable. We get all that from liver, brain, and fat of the seal, walrus, and whale. We eat the meat, use the hides, make clothes from them. Then, if we have some extra skins we sell them—but it's a very small number. But in 1983, the selling of sealskins in Europe and America was banned. All our extra income— money we need now for telephones and other bills—disappeared and

there is no way for full-time hunter to make money. We can feed ourselves, but we can't exist in the modern world. Greenpeace thinks they
know it all, but there are seven million ringed seals in these waters,
and we, who live on what we hunt, would never harm the population
because we would be the first people to die. When what you hunt is all
you eat, you do not make mistakes. We decide among ourselves how
much, how long, and how many animals we shall take. And we take
only what we need."

He looked out the tent door across the ice toward Ellesmere Island.
"It looks so clean here, but do you know we have some of the worst pollution problems in the world? Yes, it is so. The pollution of America,
and Canada goes up into the Arctic Sea and enters the polar bears' and
seals' bodies. We can measure the PCB and DDT in them and in us. The
contaminants in the mother's milk of Eskimo women are five times
higher than in America. So we are taking on their pollution problems,
the ones they create but don't solve. Only the peaceful Eskimo tastes it.
That's why I am unhappy now."

Ikuo pulled the hare socks from his kamiks, inspected them, found a
hole, and began mending it with a needle and seal gut thread. When
he was finished, the film crew refilled his cup with *ocha*—green tea—
brought from Japan. He held the cup with two hands. Steam grazed his
sun-darkened face. At fifty, he had begun to go gray.

"I am a hunter and I live the Eskimo life. It was not mine, but I made
it so and now they don't remember that I am Japanese. I miss Japan
sometimes, but it is very far away from me. Eskimo life is very busy so I
don't have time for homesickness. Everyone should live in the place
were they want to be. I chose this place, not Hokkaido, Kyushu, America, or France, but by chance, Siorapaluk in Greenland. My parents
understand my way of life and say, 'Just do it,' because I was very weak
when I was young and they did not expect me to survive. That I am still
living is enough for them.

"I was very shy as a child. Now I'm interviewed all the time by television people and by many magazines. Actually, I'd like to be left alone.
When I look up at the night sky I see satellites. Now I hear about the
ones that are so strong, they can see a car license. But I still read by
kerosene lamp and listen to the radio. I live as a hunter and do the oldest
job. I still get my food with a harpoon, same as the hunters a thousand
years ago. This makes me wonder what that satellite sees: on one side of

the world it sees Tokyo and on the other side it sees me standing at the ice edge dressed in polar bear pants and holding a harpoon. What does this make the satellite feel? Maybe confused and broken.

"After living in nature for so many years I understand that we are just a small dot. We are very small beings. But I want to say that this small life has the same importance as one in Tokyo. There is a soul in every sentient being—in the ant, the walrus, the businessman, the baby, the farmer, the hunter, the seal. Each one counts. That is what my life as a hunter helps me to know."

I thought of the old shaman who had warned Rasmussen against "living brokenly." To live "wholly" in the late twentieth century was almost impossible. At best, it meant stitching together an almost random piecework, and doing it precisely. Too many people in the developed world now come into comfort and riches with no intermediary apprenticeship in the natural world. They are hardened neither to the lushness of existence nor to the rigors of enlightenment.

Later I walked to Jens's house in the middle of the village to return the cup and knife I'd borrowed from him. Ilaitsuk, his wife, offered me a beer and a shot of Gammel Dansk, which I accepted. I'd suffered a bout of loneliness since returning from our trip. It had less to do with the absence of company than with the cessation of movement. Waves of restlessness swept over me: I hated living indoors. Out on the ice I was conjoined with ice, dog, wind, sled, and snow. Everything else was superfluous, and anything less was poverty. Any town, even Qaanaaq, meant consuming with no consummation, mobility without movement, communication without comprehension. Who needed it? To the south were towns where the speed and fracture of modern life ate you.

In Rasmussen's time, less than eighty years ago, weather and the movement of animals controlled every aspect of life. The hunting life required emotional strength, physical agility, and a keen intelligence. Those who were weak-minded and physically awkward didn't last long in a place where one or two mistakes or missteps meant death.

Now, Jens had to cultivate a strong, unified mind to counteract the disparate landscapes, societies, and conditions. He jumped from a monthlong spring hunt to a helicopter that would take him to Nuuk to testify in front of Parliament. On behalf of the Hunters' Council, he was working hard to ban the use of snowmobiles and prohibit fishing boats in Inglefield Sound, where the narwhal calve and breed in summer. Jens lived by the harpoon, which meant he could feed himself and his family by hunting. He and Ilaitsuk could tan hides, sew skins, and cook, train, doctor, and care for dogs; he could see in the dark, fog, and snow; he could build snow houses (though reluctantly), read ice, water, and weather, go sleepless, and defy death by meeting all adversity with a hard hand, a calm mind, and a belly shaking with laughter. "Snow storms, bad ice, going hungry—that's easy compared to fighting for the right to live this way," he told me.

Ilaitsuk's shoulders were like those of a swimmer—broad and strong; her hair was tied back in a topknot—the traditional hairstyle for Inuit women, though she wore lipstick and Ray-Bans. She was used to Jens being gone for weeks and months at a time, because she had descended from a long line of traditional hunters. Her grandfather had traveled with Rasmussen partway across Arctic Canada. Now, in her kitchen, she cut slivers of raw whale for me to eat. She was surprised that I liked it and set a whole plate in front of me, laughing. The flesh was gray with a pink tinge and tasted fresh the way caribou do. Strong-faced, savvy, and bold, she preferred to go out on the ice with Jens, but had been forced to take a job in Qaanaaq to pay the bills. That was the reality of a hunter's life these days.

Sometimes good work gets mixed with the bad. Greenpeace activists had changed the hunters' lives. They failed to understand the needs and interests of subsistence hunters, and pushed legislation to ban the sale of extra skins outside of Greenland. The prices of sealskins plummeted. Now sealskins didn't even bring enough money for groceries, much less electricity, heating oil, and the phone. "The best thing would be to get those Greenpeace guys to go out with Jens on a dogsled trip. Then they would see how we live. They would see that we don't kill to get rich. They would see how we are trying to preserve the same things they are trying to save," Ilaitsuk said, and I agreed.

Thanking Jens for the trip, I stood up to leave. I told Ilaitsuk that during the hunt we had come on bad ice and had almost gone down, but that Jens got us out of trouble and I was grateful to him. Jens shyly rubbed his short hair with his meaty hand, then reached for something and handed it to me—it was white and smooth: a carved, polished walrus tooth. "Thank you for traveling with us," he said in Greenlandic. "As soon as the weather gets better, I will take you out again."

I walked back through falling spring snow to my room and hoped for clear skies. A dog followed me, a large male sled dog who had broken his tether. At the door to the hotel I kneeled down to see if he would come to me. He sniffed, but held back; then, catching the scent of a canine female, he trotted away.

I lay on my bed. The next time I went out with Jens I would insist that Ilaitsuk come with us so that we would live the traditional way. She could teach me to flense (skin) a seal and sew a fox skin, and at camp they could both tell stories.

That night I dreamt the sled dropped through ice, down and down, but the abyss was white, not black. We had been traveling for years. Our cups made of muskox horns were so worn down they no longer held water, and we were thirsty. We came upon cracks too wide to cross and stood staring, mesmerized. The sun shone hard in my eyes as we were falling and the corneas broke like glass. Water that had seeped upward from dog tracks was shunted behind my eyes; the rounds of ice we cut to make a path to the other side kept sinking. I woke crying; again, I had dreamed about my mother.

The weather at Qaanaaq did not moderate, nor did Jens go out again. An Arctic low hung over us and wouldn't budge. Snow deepened. I could not gauge how deeply my tiredness went. After a while, fatigue began to equal loneliness and I couldn't tell which was which or if one spawned the other. I wandered from one end of the village to the other, breaking through waist-high drifts. Eskimos believe that solitude is a sign of unhappiness. The *pulaar*—visit—is a ritual and a habit. Blood relatives visit relatives, hunters visit hunters, birthdays are celebrated, old people are listened to, neighbors talk until a complex web of obligatory visits mounts up in every tiny village. Even an outsider like me had people to see.

Hans arranged a meeting with Torben Diklev, the curator of the town's local museum, Avernersuup Katersugaasivia—open only by appointment. It was once the house Rasmussen had built and lived in at Dundas Village. The building had been moved to Qaanaaq in 1984 for the sake of preservation and was used to house artifacts of the paleo-Eskimos that Rasmussen and his scientist friends had collected.

I took off my boots and knocked. A tall, improbably handsome Dane greeted me at the door and smiled. "I know you. I've read all your books. You look too small to be a cowboy," he said in perfect English.

Earringed, silver-haired, blue-eyed, he was dressed in brown leather pants and a bright Guatemalan shirt—the kind of man, I thought, who uses his good looks to cast spells over women. Nevertheless, I succumbed. I had been out on the ice with men whose reserve was a point of pride; Torben's effusive greeting came as a shock. Speechless, I walked through the museum—two small rooms—with glazed eyes.

Lithic raw material utilization. That's what I'd been told Torben's specialty was. My gaze passed over neat rows of churt, agate, and flint blades and microblades, and harpoon heads made from iron, bone, and ivory. I studied the blades made from the chalk cliffs of Washington Land and the ones made from the meteorite at Save Island, a large chunk of which Robert Peary carted off to a waiting ship and sold to the American Museum of Natural History in New York, where it remains today.

Torben had launched his own archeological trip to plot Thule village sites along the northern coast at Inglefield Land. His was the first systematic mapping expedition since the Danish archeologist Eric Holtved roamed the area in the 1940s. Torben unearthed several large paleo-Eskimo structures; his findings were so important that the National Museum in Copenhagen took over. Being an independent operator, not an academic, Torbin found himself excluded from his own discoveries.

I walked around the little room. There was too much to take in. My mind was distracted with images from the sled trip: breaking ice, the percussion of dogtrot, the slide of sled runners, steaming meat pulled from boiled seal ribs, the sleek elegance of kayaks turned sideways and carried to the ice edge on dogsleds.

Torbin pointed to a blade of the late Dorset period. "These people had very specific standards about how things were made, how things had to look. They were not a very adaptable people. If their spearheads had to be made of flint and they didn't have flint, for example, they didn't improvise. They went without. But in a place of great harshness and scarcity, inflexibility could lead to extinction." Indeed, by the tenth century, a climate change brought on the takeover of the Dorset people by the Thule people, who were very adaptable, using makeshift materials, testing new ways of making things.

My mind wandered. I stood in the center of Rasmussen's room and tried to conjure up his presence. Torben looked perplexed. "Don't you have any questions?" he asked.

I said I wanted to live in the house, lie on its *illeq,* and sleep long *siniks* . . . In answer to his question: No. There was too much to ask and no way to begin.

Torben smiled and took pity on me and guided me to the back room where we drank coffee and talked. He understood my incapacity. Sometimes he stopped in midsentence and sang a bit of a song—a 1960s song, maybe Bob Dylan, or something from the 1970s like Jackson Browne. He ate his breakfast—an Eskimo Pie—with hearty enjoyment. We talked about angakoks and the disappearance of the ceremonial life in Inuit culture.

"But we still have dreams," he said, his eyes sparkling. "Our dreams are as real as our waking life. They understand that up here. It's natural that the spirit life is part of the equation of the material culture, of the hunters' society. It is the other side of nature—it represents the dreams that nature would have about itself."

More coffee was poured. He had lived in Qaanaaq for fifteen years and spoke Greenlandic. As he learned the language he realized that in Greenlandic thinking there was no way to discuss abstractions or ideas. "We Europeans talk about concepts of togetherness or economic policies, or a philosophy of the environment, but it's impossible to talk that way here. It's not in the language and not in the thinking. So teaching Greenlanders to take on the big jobs, like running a large organization, for example, presents obstacles—not because they aren't clever, but because they don't believe in top-down organization. You can't get them to come in to work in the morning and tell them what to do." He mused for a minute, smiling. "It's quite wonderful, isn't it—that there are still people who can't be co-opted. Yes, in Greenland, it's very hard to make a plan for the next day."

Torben claimed he'd had woman problems but knew how to dig deep into a culture, drive a dog team, and make dovekie stew. For three summers he and his Greenlandic wife camped at the edge of bird mountains like the ones Jens, Niels, and I saw, and documented the lost art of bird skinning and sewing. "We made birdskin socks and underwear, and cooked the birds many different ways. We still have this knowledge in our minds and hands, and maybe someone will learn to do it again. I hope so."

His mind was acute but his dashing looks betrayed him. His Inuit wife had left him for another man. "It's a strange thing to see your wife coming out of a house with another man," he said. That was the difficulty of village life. There was no getting away from what pained you. Now Torben worked for the home-rule government as the trader buying and selling the Greenlanders' carvings for the local co-op. "Carvings represent the power to bring an animal into existence in a magic circumstance," he told me. "A carving occurs because the Eskimo knows how to think like an animal. They would say, animals exist because they think them, and the animals would say the same thing about people. That people exist through the lives of animals."

Morning. A dead dog lay in the path. It was the dog that had followed me the day before. I saw the frayed end of the green nylon line where he had broken loose and the hole in his chest where he'd been shot. Stepping over him, I said a quiet blessing: "Please take this dog and give him lots to eat and a warm place to sleep and friends to run with wherever he wants to go." Then I made my way to a row of bachelor shacks at the shore to find Niels.

I noticed that all the red-and-white flags in town were at half mast. An old man had died, someone told me, and the whole village was in mourning. No, it wasn't Kaalipaluk, Peary's son, but Naasooq, the last person to live in a turf house in the village of Qerqertoq, refusing adamantly to move into a wooden one. "Wood I don't know. Trees I don't know. I would be a stranger in such a house," he'd said.

His father had traveled for a year with Rasmussen on the Fifth Thule Expedition, and like his father and grandfather and those who came before him, he had been a subsistence hunter all his life. "When a man gets old, then the young ones have to do his hunting for him. I don't like to sit inside. I go out in the spring to shoot seals."

Once Naasooq and Niels had been in the local hospital together. Niels said: "He saw shadows come toward him and kept yelling at them to go away. He thought I had taken all the nurses as girlfriends and he wanted to fight me. He was crazy with jealousy. Then, near the end, he asked to see his parents. He wanted me to dig them up from their graves so he could see them. They were buried by the side of the little turf house where he was born and where he lived his whole life. That's where he'll be buried today."

It was midnight when the sun came out from behind a mountain and the stranded icebergs gave way to solar weeping. My head felt as if it had been filled with helium and was about to burst. Maybe this is how Rasmussen's "polar headaches" felt, and Olejorgen's. The mask across my cheeks had started to fade. I imagined my eyes had reddened not from snowburn but from the excesses of Arctic beauty and now had to be healed with salve. I felt skinless and exposed. Up and down the coast were ice-eaten beaches and push ridges where pack ice had been driven against the island by wind. Polynyas were the open sores of sea ice, and needles of light dropped out of the sky's radiant vacuum to become the silver sliver of the horizon.

Walking up a hill behind the village, I gazed at the place where five glaciers had tumbled ice out onto the fjord. It looked as if the glaciers were trying to get down to where the seals and dogs and people were; they were wheels churning in place, endlessly turning—verbs with no nouns to push around—and could get no purchase on *nuna*—earth— or whatever was below the white floor, if anything. No wonder that the Polar Eskimos who lived here in isolation for five thousand years thought the whole world was made of ice.

Torben and I met at the museum for early morning coffee and conversation, something one can starve from the lack of as much as from a lack of food. The mind of the Eskimo is like nothing else, he said. He remembers exact coastlines, every detail of a tool, he has perfect recall. "I met a ninety-year-old hunter who said, 'I haven't really forgotten anything in my whole life. I remember everything I've learned. That's because we didn't read or write. We had no choice but to remember.'

"Their stories about life are intensely detailed, and in the retelling of them they have to use the exact same words. The Inuit have rules about learning because the harshness of the environment calls for special conduct. There are no other possibilities or options, as in a temperate climate. No, here you have to learn and do things right the first time or you die, and the genes of a stupid or awkward person will not be carried on. The Eskimos accept that they can't win over nature. Nature is the stronger power and they have to work with it, not against it. That is why they are so precise in everything they do."

By comparison Torben saw himself as an overeducated drifter. Sometimes he felt perplexed. "When a Greenlander feels this way, he just goes out hunting. But for us, it's different. We brood." I mentioned my polar headaches and wondered if the magnetic pole was affecting our metabolic and neuronal traffic. He shrugged. "Up here, it could be anything—one of the spirits who lives on the glaciers, or sunspot activity. Who knows?" Then, "I'm all confusion today," he said smiling.

The attraction between us was so strong it was hard to part. He was packing to go to see a grandchild in the Faroe Islands whom he had never met. He didn't know how he should feel about anything or anyone and wondered if there might be a remedy. To which I could only respond, "More living." In a week, he would be fifty years old.

Niels called and asked if I was feeling lonely. I said yes, and he said, me too. We visited his sister, who worked as a nurse's aide at the local clinic. She and her husband had a big house at the edge of town looking in the direction of the heliport and, beyond, the Politiken Glacier. She told me that when she went to school in Denmark she didn't feel right. "I hated the trees. They made me feel as if I was inside all the time."

Later, I had a midnight feast with Connie Poulsen, the school's vice-principal, a confirmed expatriate Dane who had taught in Botswana, China, Australia, Denmark, and southern Greenland, preferring Africans to all other people. Stocky and nearsighted with a gleam in her eye, she said she took every fifth year off and traveled somewhere new in the world.

In her freezer I discovered vegetables. She had bought them at Thule Air Base the last time she came through from Denmark. "Could we?" I asked. I held the small packet of green beans in my hands like a sacrament. We ate them, along with rice and Arctic char, and split her last fresh apple for dessert. Nothing had ever tasted so good.

She talked only of the dark side of this northern Arctic society. If village life was the tight linking of every citizen by family affiliation, hunting practices, and pride in being a Greenlander, then its dark side resembled a boa constrictor that took away one's air. In the school Connie saw all the consequences of wife beating, child abuse, and alcoholism, but also the astute cleverness of people weaned at the back of a dogsled who had in their bellies a memory of starvation. Still so isolated they had never been farther than they could go by sled in one season, they were, like Jens Danielsen, struggling to maintain a subsistence culture in a splintered, dissociative, market-driven world.

How is it possible to hold to village life in this century? What kind of lures does it take to keep traditional hunting alive—with dogs, sleds, kayaks, and harpoons—in a world hungry for things—snowmobiles, for example, which had already desecrated hunting life in Arctic Canada and Alaska? How does one weigh the speed, ease, and expense of petrochemical power against dog power? How does a young man or woman find dignity when money is at the heart of things, and when living the life of a subsistence hunter ensures a life of poverty? How does someone turn down welfare money from Denmark when it adds up to more than you can make in a year of hunting? How does a young person breathe and nurture intellectual curiosity or creative genius in a town where there are no expectations for worldly success, and where all eyes are on them? Prison or sanctuary? That was the question I kept asking about living in this town.

During dinner a blizzard blew. After, we listened to music. By the time I stood to leave, the door was blocked by drifted snow. Finally we were able to push it open, but the wind blasted me so violently it was hard to stand. No one in the village was stirring, but I knew I was being watched. Slowly and carefully, I waded through soft, powdery drifts—some more than waist-high—down the long path to the hotel, humming the Japanese tune I'd heard Ikuo sing.

In the morning Hans asked why I had been walking around in a storm. Did you see me? I asked. He said no, but someone had called him, worrying about whether I'd gotten home. I asked what he thought about the violence and drinking in Qaanaaq. He looked pained for a moment, then said, "It would have been better if alcohol had never been brought here, if outsiders had never come. Now, we have to try harder to be ourselves."

It was Wednesday, the day the government offices were closed to the public so the workers could catch up on their work. "But, of course," Hans said, slightly amused, "everyone just goes home for the day." It was true enough. Sled after sled took off across the ice to go seal hunting.

Hans and I walked down the hill to the shore ice. Summer was still a month away. "It lasts for two weeks. And the river runs very high through the middle of town. Oh, it is so beautiful," he crooned. "There are flowers all over these hills all the way back to the edge of the ice and the sea is open water and the icebergs float by, and every day and every night there is new scenery."

The ceiling lifted, the snow stopped, but the sun was still obscured. The whole ice prairie shone, a *mer de glace,* an ocean of ice of limitless dimensions.

On a path below the hotel we met up with an old man named Uutaaq, who invited us to his home. His father had gone to the North

Pole with Robert Peary and he wanted to tell me the story. His house was cozy, though he complained that it was cold in the winter when the wind blew. "Not warm like a turf house," he said. His wife, wizened and wiry, never sat still. Both in their eighties, they had spent a lifetime outdoors and their hands were gnarled with arthritis.

His wife lit the traditional candles on the coffee table before the stories began, as if their wavering light would summon the thread of the past into the room. Between the two families much of northern Greenland's history had been covered. The photographs on the wall showed his wife's father, Mitsok, who traveled with Rasmussen, and Uutaaq's own father, who went to the North Pole with Peary.

Uutaaq was born on the island of Kiatak, where we had just been bird hunting, but in those days, he told me, families moved every two or three months, following the game. In the summer months they lived in sealskin tents and traveled south to Savissivik to hunt walrus. He took two harpoons from the wall with their long sealskin lines and showed me how a walrus was killed. The first harpoon to stun him, and the second to kill. A balloon—an *avataq*—made of a seal bladder kept the dead animal afloat. "There were many more animals then because there were no motors or guns," he said, puffing on a cigarette.

As the sun slid to the north the room cooled down and his wife handed him a blue oxford shirt to put on over his T-shirt. "The doctors say I should stop smoking, that it's dangerous." He paused and looked out the window. "But the life of traveling in the north with many changing weathers and sometimes not enough clothes or food to eat, and hunting walrus from kayaks with harpoons—now that's dangerous . . . And you see, I'm still alive!"

Uutaaq's eyes twinkled as he began recalling his childhood. He tucked his right leg up under his left, the way one sits on a dogsled. "When I was a child my parents and I traveled to Canada to visit relatives. That is what is good about the hunting life. You can live anywhere and travel while you hunt. You don't have to stay home to get your wages." He looked in the direction of Ellesmere Island, which was only thirty-seven miles away, but between here and there was open water even in the winter. "So we had to travel all the way up the coast to Cape Alexander, then go across and south again to Grise Fjord. If we had good ice from here straight over to Canada, we could get there in three days. But this other way takes a month if the weather is good. Better plan on one and a half months or two."

They called Robert Peary "Puilissuaq," and the North Pole, the "Poli." He began coming to Greenland in 1891 and made his successful attempt on the North Pole in April 1909—there had been eight trips in all. He had been a mama's boy raised in Maine. As a child he had read the Arctic adventures of Kane and Hayes. His natural curiosity, intellect, and ambition had fueled in him what Jean Malaurie calls "the quiet madness" that finally drove him to the far north. After becoming a civil engineer attached to the navy, he married the bright, adventurous daughter of a Smithsonian scientist. Then he finagled one leave of absence after another from the navy to embark on a series of expeditions to Greenland.

"Peary had an ego the size of the inland ice," Torben had said earlier. Now Uutaaq continued. "When Peary lived, those were different times. Anyway, what else would drive someone to look for the North Pole? There's nothing up there but ice and more ice."

He pulled out a map of the Arctic and showed me: to think of Greenland as a distinct entity is an illusion. Attached to Peary Land is a topknot of ice—the frozen Arctic Ocean—that extends all the way over the pole to Siberia.

In a letter to his mother, justifying an early trip across the ice cap, Peary wrote: "Remember, Mother, I must have fame, and I cannot reconcile myself to years of commonplace drudgery and a name late in life when I see an opportunity to gain it now and sip the delicious draught while yet I have youth and strength and capacity to enjoy it to the utmost."

Peary's objectives were vague and varied at first. He only wanted to be first and best. It was not so much a love of the far north that drove him as the fact that it had yet to be "conquered." Bumptious, unlucky, vain, persistent, he learned about weather and ice the hard way, suffering snowblindness in the process, a broken leg, and eventually the loss of eight toes to frostbite.

Yet after being turned back from an initial exploratory trip on the inland ice, Peary wrote rapturously in his diary:

There is no bluer, softer, fairer, brighter summer sea in all the tropics than this Sea of Baffin and this Bay of Disco on such a sunlit August afternoon. . . . Pale blue, distant mountains gird the bay, icebergs fleck the sapphire waters, the murmur of the sea comes faintly to the ear, and everything is, blue sea, white bergs, brown and red cliffs, and emerald

moss and grass-grown slopes, bathed in brilliant sunshine. (Weems,
Peary, the Explorer and the Man, *p. 82)*

Josephine Peary, his wife, accompanied him on the first two major expeditions, against all advice from friends, family, and crew members. If she didn't share his lust for fame, she was willing and adventurous, and gave birth to her first child in a hut on the slope of what is now named Bowdoin Glacier just as winter was setting in. She noted in her own journals that after six months of darkness and lamplight, the child tried to grab and hold the first ray of light that passed through the window of their winter house.

Back and forth the Pearys went between New York and western Greenland. Peary was distraught to find that a Norwegian, Fridtjof Nansen, had successfully accomplished a crossing of the ice cap, forcing Peary to rethink his goal.

Rethink it he did. The youthful references to "conquering the North Pole" found in his college letters became a serious ambition; with his usual intensity and intellectual vigor, he thought of nothing else. A third expedition ended in disaster. Peary lost all but his two little toes while seeking refuge at Fort Conger on the Canadian side of Smith Sound, where the American explorer Adolphus Greely and his starving men were finally rescued after the tragic expedition of 1883–1884.

General Greely and twenty-five men had established the Fort Conger base camp where they had been dropped off by the ship *Proteus* with a three-year food supply. The ship was to return in two years for the men, and if it failed to appear, they were to go south and live on the rations that the ship would cache along the way. The ship returned on schedule in 1883 but was crushed in the ice before reaching the fort. Greely and his men went south but found almost no food at all. In May 1884, a relief ship came for them and found the seven survivors nearly dead, having lived off the flesh of the men who died before them.

Fifteen years later, in January 1899, during the dark of the moon, Peary and his men, also sick and starving, groped through darkness on a shore he had never seen and came upon Greely's base camp. The food left behind by Greely saved Peary's party. They munched on biscuits and drank weak coffee. Then Peary discovered he had no feeling in his leg. His toes were frozen beyond repair; surgery to amputate them was performed on the kitchen table before the warmth of the room allowed gangrene to set in.

After, Peary described himself as a "helpless cripple," unable to walk or stand. On the wall by his bunk he scrawled the words "*Invenium viam aut faciam*—I will find a way out or make one." A month later, the return trip by sled to the ship where he would receive better medical care was torturous. The temperature was 64 degrees below zero and every time the sled bumped against rough ice, the pain in Peary's feet was almost unbearable. His Eskimo guide's response to being alive was "I have got back again, thank God!" But Peary noted in his diary: "To think that I have failed once more; that I shall never have a chance to win again."

That was February. In August, when the ice came free, Peary, his right-hand man Matt Henson, a black sailor who had served with him in the States, and a doctor were left off at Etah. The ship sailed home. More trials were to come. Peary's wife Jo discovered that Peary had fathered a child with Aleqasina, an Inuit woman who accompanied him on his expeditions; Peary's mother died; and Jo and Peary's second child died. Several more attempts to get to the pole failed.

Eight expeditions and eight years later, Peary set out again for the North Pole. His ship, the *Roosevelt*, named for Teddy Roosevelt, who had helped send Peary off from Oyster Bay on Long Island, dropped the team at Etah in August. They overwintered at Cape Sheridan. Several groups—consisting of 133 dogs, twenty-two men, and nineteen sleds—took off for the pole on February 28, 1909. The temperature was 50 below zero with a hard east wind blowing.

As usual, the guide, Uutaaq's father, accompanied Peary. His son elaborated: "When Peary first saw my father he liked him. After that, he never went anywhere in the Arctic without him. He was very clever. He learned English fast. Between Peary and my father there was a very good feeling. They just worked together well. Peary loved my father because he helped him so much and they spent many good and many hard times together. Peary said, 'If I don't have Uutaaq, I won't have a successful expedition.' "

The going was difficult as usual, but this time luck was with Peary. Leads of ice closed, allowing them to cross, and more often than not the weather held. Peary, Matt Henson, Uutaaq, and two other Inuit hunters reached the North Pole, by their reckoning, on April 6, 1909.

But another piece of bad luck lay in wait. Peary's victorious homecoming was tarnished by the fact that Dr. Frederick Cook's announcement that he had already reached the pole. Rasmussen was on the boat with Cook as he sailed from Greenland to Denmark. Rasmussen was a believer at first, but after examining Cook's records, he knew the claim had been falsified. Peter Freuchen's response was "Cook is a gentleman and a liar; Peary is neither of these."

When I asked the younger Uutaaq what he thought about the controversy, he replied, "There is bad talk about Peary. Some say he lied too. But from what my father said, I think he got to the North Pole. I looked at all the maps and went through the calculations. Yes . . . my father wouldn't have said so if it hadn't been true."

Uutaaq talked of another disappointment faced by Peary. "My father told me that Peary had expected to start a community here and raise the American flag. But when they came back from the North Pole, they found that Rasmussen had already arrived and raised the flag of Denmark. Rasmussen beat Peary to it. And frankly, we were glad the Americans didn't settle here."

His wife clucked her teeth: "You're being rude. She's an American."

Ignoring her, Uutaaq continued: "We were afraid that with the Americans, the Inuit would disappear. Peary started taking Greenlanders to the States and they never came back. The Americans found out that we are very clever and wanted to use us. The Danes were better—they let us live and do what we do here." There was a long pause. "Of course, soon I learned I wasn't as good at some things . . . I never could learn English like my father."

"So they wouldn't have taken you anyway," his wife said, smiling wryly. She stood and wound the clock that had stopped. Her watch had stopped working too. "When I was young we didn't have these things," she said, tapping the watch face. "We didn't even have calendars. You don't need them when you live outside. We hunted when we were hungry. We didn't care what time it was, or what day, or even what year."

Uutaaq was still thinking about his father. "Most of the Inuit who went to the pole with Peary weren't really paid when they got back. Peary just thanked them. He gave my father some carpenter's tools. It's hard to know how people thought then, but without the local people here, Peary would never have had any success."

The next few days the weather was all sun, all glare, all scintillation, and my eyes tired easily. I checked with Jens to see if he was going out, but he had to work in the mayor's office while the mayor was gone. I stood at

the shore and watched two hunters take off. The parallel tracks behind
the sled were the lines between which music is written—a Webern string
quartet for example, whose slow and fast tempi, brief outbursts, and
tremolando were a form of cerebral intimacy described in Greenlandic
only as Sila, consciousness, or Arctic weather.

I stood at the windows of the hotel for a long time. "Always changing, always beautiful," a voice behind me said. It was Torben. We made
tea, then directed our gaze shyly at each other. He pointed toward a
green house down the hill. "You must visit Sophie. She lives just down
there. She is famous in Greenland for her drum dancing. They fly her all
over to teach the young people the traditional singing and dance."

I asked Niels to come along to translate. We found Sophie sitting
outside on a hard-backed kitchen chair leaning against the wall of
her house in the sun. She was eighty but still had the signs of great
beauty: an aquiline nose, high cheekbones, and a beautiful mouth. Her
hair, pulled back into a knot, had gone gray, and her mischievous eyes
sparkled blue.

She squinted at me. "When the weather starts to be like this, the
birds arrive. We use this time to welcome them back. Sometimes there is
sun, sometimes snow. It's always this way. That's what spring is, a time
when the weather is fickle. Please . . . ," she said, motioning us past the
slop buckets waiting to be emptied into the sewer truck.

Inside the house we drank coffee and ate fresh pastries from the
bakery. The room was bright and sparsely furnished. Family photographs hung on the wall. One showed the profile of a beautiful woman
standing in front of a dog team out on the ice. A wisp of hair had blown
across her face and she was looking toward the sun, which was low on
the horizon. Who is that? I asked. She laughed and said, "Oh, that's me
when I was thirty. Much had happened by then. My son had disappeared under the ice, and I had been doing the drum dances and had
been stopped by the village priest."

She bent down and lifted a small hand drum from the floor. She held
it like a fan, tapped it, then put it down. "When I was young I saw people making hand drums. They were down on the shore. The drums were
made of bone and reindeer skin with an antler for a drumstick. After, I
felt music here," she said, clasping her heart.

"I saw someone making a dance and heard her sing. The song was
about a woman who fell in love with a hunter but he went away with

someone else. That's the first song I learned and I've never forgotten it," she said. When she rose to her feet her knees swayed and the song she had learned seventy-two years before filled the room. A cloud-veiled sun lit her face.

Later we drank coffee. "In those days drum dances were forbidden by the priests," she told me. "But I danced anyway. Even my husband and son didn't know. So many songs came into my head. I sang them silently."

Like most of the older people in Qaanaaq, Sophie had been born in Dundas Village at the current site of Thule Air Force Base. I spread a photograph of the village in front of her but she didn't want to look. Tears filled her eyes. The house in which she grew up no longer existed. "They let some of the houses go to ruin," she said, then brightened: "I remember seeing Rasmussen and Freuchen around there when I was a child. You see, our village was the center of the world. Being moved out was more than anyone could comprehend."

When they arrived at the present site of Qaanaaq, there was not much there. "We were put in thin canvas tents in this place, where we are now. That first September it started to be cold. We never took our clothes off. Some old people died. That was a hard time. It was just an open slope. Nothing like the old village with the long valley full of foxes and reindeer. We lived in those tents for four months. There are not four months in the whole year in Greenland when it is not cold. But they didn't care. Finally, a ship came with lumber and carpenters. That was our reward: they built little wooden houses for us. We only wanted to go home."

The sound of a gunshot made me jump. We went to the window. "It's the dogcatcher," Niels whispered. We knew what that meant—a stray dog had been killed. Sophie put a Danish coffee cake in front of us and filled our cups with strong coffee.

She continued: "When I was young we all lived together in one house. I'm missing that life now. We used to cut turf and gather stones and make little houses that we could use for a while. To keep warm, we harvested grass and put it in our beds. For windows we used bearded seal intestines. We'd clean them, scrub them, and lay them in water, then blow air through them and let them dry. After, we'd cut the skin and stretch it to make windows. We'd sew it to frames made of bone, leaving one small hole at the top to look through.

"The best life is to be happy. Happiness is traveling. Now I call airplanes 'flying dogsleds.' When the bad weather comes, I get sad, so I sing and dance. Later, after sleeping, I wake up happy again. I think love is the most important thing in life. I was married to a hunter, but before that, I fell in love with a Dane. He came around for the Danish government villages. We weren't allowed to stay together. When someone looked at us, we stood apart. We didn't speak the same language so we used our hands. I can't remember now when I stopped seeing him. The Americans started to arrive at Thule and we were moved away and I never saw him again."

Sophie threw her head back and a song came out—a song about her son who disappeared under the ice and her husband who died, and another song about the man she truly loved. Her bell-like voice ululated.

"Sometimes I see people who are dead," she told me. "I was sitting here and I saw a man walking around and around the house. He had a beard and a mustache and wore a jacket. He left no tracks. He came into the house walking backwards and I recognized him. He had just died. Then he vanished. Another time I saw a man who was still alive. He didn't even live in this part of Greenland. He walked through a locked door and stood here looking at me. I don't know why this happens to me. I ask people but no one knows."

She looked out the window. Pale light touched her aquiline nose and a wisp of gray hair fell against a cheekbone, just as in the photograph taken fifty years before. She was beautiful then and she is beautiful now. Snow was falling. Her blue eyes were disturbed bodies of water. She spoke softly: "Sometimes everything is clear when there is nothing to see."

A week later Birthe cooked dinner for me and two new guests—middle-aged Danes who were designing the airport to be built at Qaanaaq the following year. "This isn't the top of the world, it's the end of the world," they said more than once. Yet they seemed content with their laptop computer and knitting projects, waiting for the helicopter to come. I was still expecting to go out with Jens and wondered if Sophie was singing or sleeping or seeing ghosts. I watched two dogs roll and cavort in love games under Uutaaq's window, then went looking for Torben.

From behind snow clouds, the sun came out and the northwestern coast of Greenland turned gold. The icebergs were sphinxes, stranded in the frozen fjord, holding their secrets from the polar bears who hid behind them from hunters. In the village only the dogcatcher was up, patrolling for strays. I walked past Torben's house but the lights were out. I hesitated, then decided not to go in.

At the edge of the village I stood in front of Rasmussen's old house—the museum—and tried the door. I wanted to sleep there. Unable to get in, I turned and walked toward the shore. On the path I ran into a woman I had met who spoke a little English and she invited me to a gathering of hunters. They had resurrected a turf-and-stone hut at the far edge of the shore. It was tiny inside, lit only by a candle, and one fading flashlight stood on end on a dirty windowsill covered with a towel. There were beer bottles all over the floor. A woman in a corner held a drum made from a reindeer skin pulled tight around some animal's bent rib, and she was playing it, sometimes with the side of her hand, sometimes with her forehead or with an antler.

It was hot inside. I thought of Rasmussen's and Freuchen's long nights in such houses in Thule. The hunters had stripped down to their bearskin pants and their brown bellies shook in the candlelight when they laughed. A radio was playing Greenlandic country music; a hunter was singing a traditional song: "*Aja . . . aja . . . aja . . .*" Sweat poured down the sides of his body. After a while, he took his pants all the way off, then lay on the floor gnawing on a seal rib. The woman playing the drum was naked from the waist up; her white kamiks shone in the candlelight. Then I saw that the intricate embroidery on the top was torn and smudged with dirt.

I sat down by her, filled with all kinds of conflicting thoughts. I was still mesmerized by Torben's bold beauty and Ikuo's bright internal spark—how I would have liked to have Ikuo's child if I'd been younger. Late in the night I felt faint because of the suffocating heat, and took my shirt off too. The woman held her arm next to mine and laughed at the contrast of my dark brown face and white chest. Then her tremulous voice rose up, quieting the room.

I thought of Rasmussen's seance with the shaman Unaleq: "The spirits spoke now in deep chest notes, then in a high treble. Between the words, sounds of trickling water, rushing wind, a stormy sea, snuffling walrus, a growling bear."

Everyone started moaning, growling, and chanting variations on the *aja* tune. Some sounded like seals barking, or dogs. I thought of the two dogs outside the hotel rolling over and over, mounting each other while I had been on the phone. The woman handed her drum to me and told me to sing. Sweat poured down my chest . . . *aja* . . . *aja* . . . *aja* . . .

Toward morning I walked up the hill to the hotel. Along the way I saw Birthe, Hans's wife, standing alone on a snowy path in a long skirt, turning around and around. *Nani Hans?* I asked. Her black hair flew out from her shoulders and her feet stomped a flat pad in the snow. She shook her head, grinning: "*Sinikpok.*" He is sleeping. A cigarette hung from her lips and her eyes lit up mischievously. "Where you go tonight?" she asked me. I shrugged. Her eyes flashed again. The light on her cheekbones looked like bars of gold. She opened her arms and began spinning. "Isn't it beautiful!" she said looking up. *Hikiniq,* I said. Sun. She turned around and around like a globe tethered to the North Pole. She was dancing.

As the days went by, the ice did not melt but a moat of open water began to form at the edge of town. I watched Jens stake his twenty dogs farther out where the ice was still thick. I waited for him to give me the word that we could go hunting again, but unseasonable snows continued. "Usually the sun is strong now," Hans Jensen kept saying. "I've never seen it like this."

Niels teased Jens about having to run the mayor's office while the mayor was out of town. Jens hated deskwork, but by necessity, he had become a political man in order to preserve his tradition. It took a lot of work and a tolerance for paradox: "I'm not asking for money, a new house, or food," he said. "I only want to be able to go out on the ice with my family to hunt. Everything we need is right here. We're asking, almost, to be allowed to be poor. You would think the world would be glad to have us. No handouts, no snowmobiles, no petrol. We have petrol." He pointed to seal meat hanging on a line to dry. Then, patting his large belly and grinning, he said, "And this is my bank account."

More *pulaar* was in order: I stopped at the bakery, bought some sweet rolls, then went by to see Uutaaq and his wife again. They were happy to see me and complained that none of the young people ever visited them to hear their stories. Uutaaq's wife rolled two cigarettes, handing one to her husband, then put a lump of sugar on her tongue and flooded it with coffee.

I asked them about the future of Greenlanders. Uutaaq answered:

"We can't live like we did. Civilization is going very fast and everyone can see what the future of this district is. Most of the animals will disappear. They'll go north to get away from people and noise. When I started living here there was lots of walrus, seal, and narwhal, and we hunted only by kayak. We just stepped out the front door. But not now. You have to go much farther away."

I passed the rolls around and Uutaaq's wife poured more coffee. "In the future people here will be hunting birds, not marine mammals," Uutaaq said. "But dogs will continue because it will be easy to buy dry dog food. The outboard motors are here to stay. It's too late to stop them now. But that's added to the problem of there being fewer and fewer full-time hunters."

Wind blew a door closed, startling us, then Uutaaq resumed: "And then there's the weather. It continues to change from the old days. So it's impossible to use only the kayak for hunting. It's much stormier now. Much more wind especially in the summer and when the ice comes, the wind breaks it up. You can't use a kayak in water like that. And so, things keep going that way. As for the weather, I don't know why it keeps changing." Then he smiled. "Maybe it's because, like me, the weather is getting old."

The Mackenzie Delta, 1924

In order for Rasmussen, Arnarulunguaq, and Qavigarssuaq to reach the Seward Peninsula in Alaska while there was still ice and snow, it was necessary to travel fast to the Mackenzie Delta. Anyway, the country between had already been studied by two ethnographers, Diamond Jenness and Vilhjalmur Stefansson, on the Canadian Arctic Expedition of 1913–1918.

The distance was 2,200 kilometers, but Rasmussen's dogs were well rested and fed. "One is apt to give second place to the kindness shown to oneself; the man who feeds his dogs wins one's heart," Rasmussen commented in his journal.

It was a cold January day, 42 degrees below zero, when they departed from Kent Peninsula. The sled runners had been shod with peat meal and water, which then froze and was rubbed smooth. Arn sat behind Rasmussen on the sled and carried her baby in her amaut, while Qav went on his own sled to hunt. They first headed to their old camp at Malerisiorfik to pick up the belongings they had cached. There they slept in Ma Kanjak's "boarding house"—a huge snow house where the dogs were kept inside to save on food. (The dogs require more food if left out in the cold.) Leo Hansen joined them there and would continue with the Greenlanders to Alaska. They were snowbound for two days. On March 18 they set out again, following the smooth ice of the Kungarssuk River.

On the Atiaq Peninsula they camped out on the ice for three days. Heavy snow fell. They kept their snow knives out, ready to make an igloo if necessary.

The snow deepened, burying their food and sleds. The dogs, lying outside, were "little hummocks," Rasmussen reported. A total whiteout enveloped them; only occasionally could they see the steep cliffs of the peninsula. There were a few lucid intervals, then they were "smothered in a white surf." To go outside was to become instantly disoriented; breathing was almost impossible.

On the third evening of the storm, villagers came by and invited Rasmussen, Arn, Qav, and Leo Hansen to the shaman's snow house. There the visitors were told the ancient legend of the giant's son who sought revenge for his parents' death by flying through the skies and turning into bad weather. Now the local shaman wanted to know why the boy was angry and had brought this storm.

The wind and blowing snow were so intense they had to walk three by three, arms linked, to make their way to the dance house where the seance would be held. "The wind took such hold of us that sometimes we had to stand quite still and cling on to one another to prevent being blown into the pack ice that towered round about us. Tremendous gusts from the shore lashed us like whips, and after three or four strokes we were able to proceed until the next gust, followed by the screams of the storm. . . . I think that half a kilometre took us a whole hour."

The angakok had a reddish beard and blue eyes. His "helpers" were a giant with claws so long he could cut right through a human being with one scratch, a figure made from soft snow, and a red stone that he'd found while hunting caribou.

"Baleen," as the angakok was called, protested that he was unable to speak the truth, to call up invisible forces. Slowly he went into trance.

He began dancing wildly, flailing his arms and legs and grunting like a caribou bull in rut. He grabbed an onlooker by the neck and shook him the way a dog does until he "died." Then the onlooker was revived and shaken again. "The sky is full of naked beings rushing through the air. Naked people, naked men, naked women, rushing along and raising gales and blizzards," Baleen shouted out. "Don't you hear the noise?" The storm raged. Someone let the dogs inside to keep them from suffocating in the snow.

"Suddenly it was as if nature around us became alive," Rasmussen recalled. "We saw the storm riding across the sky in the speed and thronging of naked spirits. We saw the crowd of fleeing dead ones come sweeping through the billows of the blizzard, and all the visions and sounds centered in the wing-beats of the great birds for which Kigiuna [the shaman] had made us strain our ears."

The next day they were able to travel "in dazzling sunshine and hardblown drifts." Light from the newly risen sun drew them west. "With light the desire to be on the move returns," Rasmussen noted. "Our faces quite pale—one stands the cold because the goal is in sight."

In the Dolphin and Union Strait they reached the western limit of the Eskimo people of the high Canadian Arctic. In the evening, the travelers stopped in a village of twenty snow huts whose blubber lamps made them glow in moonlight, each block "a scintillating pane." They were having a feast to welcome the sun. "What these people can get out of this cold land in the shape of festivity and happiness," Rasmussen said, "is remarkable." A large dance house of snow blocks was hastily erected on Rasmussen's arrival and by ten in the morning the dancing had begun. The "leap dance" continued until ten at night. Later, a female shaman bit an evil spirit from between Rasmussen's legs, then rose up with a blood-smeared face and a set of bear's teeth protruding from her mouth.

Their travels continued. In mid-February, on the Inman River, Qav scouted out a unique shelter in a cave so far up a cliff they had to use an upended sled as a ladder; in another place they had to make a raft of an ice floe and propel themselves across open water with a driftwood pole. By the beginning of March they began seeing Point Barrow–style houses with gutskin windows in the roof, though they were still far east of Alaska.

Blizzards so strong they couldn't stand up in them gusted through, but then warm winds began to blow. On March 6 they found willow shoots in a frozen stream—a sign of spring. Other changes were noted: a mercenary attitude among the Eskimos surprised the Greenlanders. On the Horton River, which drains into the Amundsen Gulf, Leo Hansen fell sick. When they tried to hire a driver for his sled, no one would go. "This is the first place I have seen where people would not help a sick man, even for money," Rasmussen noted bitterly. The influence of the American market economy had infiltrated here.

They passed "Smoking Mountain" north of the Horton River, where a pocket of subterranean coal had caught fire years before and had not stopped burning. On the Anderson River an American man who had sledded all the way from Fairbanks, Alaska, brought the first news of the world Rasmussen had heard in several years: the explorer Frederick Cook, whose North Pole conquest had already been proven fraudulent, had been sent to prison for fifteen years for a bad business deal; the explorer Roald Amundsen had begun a balloon expedition in the Arctic; and the former American president Woodrow Wilson was dead.

It was mid-March by the time they reached Baillie Island, where the Hudson Bay Company had a station. Here the Mackenzie Eskimos couldn't have been more different from the people among whom Rasmussen had been living for the last three years. He was shocked to find that subsistence hunting wasn't the only source of income: "The pursuit of gold and money values had revolutionized everything," he wrote. Yet their names, which Rasmussen noted down, reflected the full range of human quirks, flaws, and possibilities, reminding him that they were still human beings, Inuit, like him: there were Makuaq, the rejected one; Qunujuna, the smiling one; Huvuijaq, the one like a knife; Ihumataq, the one who resembles a thought; Qomeq, the knock-kneed one; Arnajaq, the womanlike one; and Qigsimik, the shy one.

On the Mackenzie River there were more surprises to come. Rasmussen found Eskimos living in log houses built from the immense quantities of driftwood that floated by. The landscape had changed from ice to tundra. There were willows on the banks and rich soil supported alpine flora in the summer months. Rasmussen had dropped down to 70 degrees north latitude; by the time his journey ended in Alaska on the Seward Peninsula, he would find himself well below the Arctic Circle. By comparison to the glacial fjords of Greenland, much of Alaska was temperate. There was diversity not only in the flora and fauna but in the human population as well: the Inuit of northern Alaska and the Yupik Eskimos of the wide delta regions of the southwest lived side by side with Indians—both Athabascans and Aleuts—toward whom the Inuit had a deep enmity. Rasmussen heard countless stories of Athabascans killing Eskimo men and stealing their wives.

As Rasmussen proceeded west, Eskimo settlements became few and far between. Instead, the Greenlanders met up with trappers, trading post managers, missionaries, and Alaskan characters—Americans, Danes, and Swedes. When they came across Inuit villages once again, Rasmussen found that the western Eskimos' wealth consisted almost entirely of "white men's goods"—not just Hudson Bay Company blankets, but schooners, typewriters, cameras, safety razors, and kerosene lamps. "I felt myself something of an old fossil at first, among all these smart business folk," Rasmussen wrote. He had been living hand to mouth Eskimo-style for many years, his movements dictated by weather and season, his heart given over to Arn and their son, born while traveling. Now he felt himself a man from the past, set down among twentieth-century Eskimos.

The usual helping hands and informants who offered themselves to Rasmussen now charged for their "services." The ravages of Western civilization had already taken its toll: the population of the Mackenzie Eskimos, once 2,000 strong, was now reduced, through illnesses introduced by outsiders, to 400. Rasmussen despaired of ever finding an uncontaminated Inuit culture again.

Yet, on Liverpool Bay, east of the Mackenzie River, Rasmussen met a storyteller, Apagkaq, who had come from Kotzebue. Rasmussen had to pay him fifty dollars for five days' work as an informant. To his surprise, Apagkaq turned out to be one of the best storytellers he had ever met. Maybe there was more to these people than he thought; perhaps those first appearances were hiding a rich cultural resource. Rasmussen felt the stiff veneer of so-called civilization peel away as Apagkaq told his creation story:

He was squatting in darkness.

He was quite alone on earth, when suddenly he became conscious and discovered himself. He had no idea where he was. Nor did he know how he had come there. But he breathed and there was life in him. He lived!

But who was he? A being—something living. More than that he could not comprehend. All about him was dark, and he could see nothing.

Then he groped about with his hands. His fingers brushed over clay wherever he felt. The earth was clay; everything about him was lifeless clay.

He let his fingers slide over himself. He knew nothing of how he looked, but he found his face and felt that he had a nose, eyes, and mouth, arms and legs and limbs. He was a human being—a man!

He felt across his forehead—and found a hard little lump. What was that for?

He had no idea that one day he was to become a raven, and that the lump would grow out to become a bill.

He fell into thought. He had understood that he was a separate being, not grown fast to all that surrounded him. Then he crawled over the clay, slowly and cautiously. He wanted to find out where he was. But suddenly his hands felt only empty space—an abyss—and he dared not go. . . . (Rasmussen, Fifth Thule Expedition, *vol. 10, no. 2, p. 61)*

Alaska, 1924

On May 5, 1924, Qav, the filmmaker Leo Hansen, Rasmussen, Arn, and their child crossed the line of six-foot-high stakes in the snow that marked the boundary between western Canada and eastern Alaska. This would be the last leg of his trans-Arctic trip. Rasmussen had traveled 800 kilometers along the barren coast of the Mackenzie Delta, gliding on iced-over lagoons formed by coastal sandbars. Ahead lay flat, featureless land all the way to Point Barrow, the first real town Rasmussen and his Greenlandic companions had seen since leaving Greenland in 1921.

Point Barrow had 250 Inuit residents, a few white people, some stores and warehouses, a hospital, a church, and a school. Everyone came out to greet Rasmussen's party. After all, Alaska's first white visitor, in 1741, was Vitus Bering, a Dane. Rasmussen spoke neither Danish nor English to the onlookers, but Inupiat, his Greenlandic dialect matching theirs almost perfectly.

The villagers at Point Barrow were whale hunters. Sometimes as many as twenty whales were caught in a single spring, which afforded them the luxury of time, and time translated into a material and cultural richness Rasmussen had not expected to find. Whales were thought to be human beings who were susceptible to women.

The night before a hunt, the chief invited his harpooner—a young, strong man—to sleep with his wife: it pleased the whale to be killed by a man who had just come from the bed of a woman.

Whales were hunted from skin boats—umiaks whose sealskin covers had to be changed every year. The harpoon heads were made of flint or slate, though by the time Rasmussen arrived at Point Barrow in 1924, the harpoon had been given up in favor of "darting guns with explosive bombs." Rasmussen observed that during a hunt, the chief's wife stayed inside her house, sitting on her *illeq* with one boot removed. This pose enticed the whale to her home. Once the whale was caught, the woman filled a pail with fresh water, went down to the shore where the dead whale had been beached, and gave it a drink of cool water.

In Point Barrow, as in every Eskimo community, there was a constant interchange between humans and animals. A young angakok became known in his community because he was the poorest hunter: any animal that came near him turned into a bush, stone, or tree, and was rendered invulnerable.

One young angakok went mad for a while. He lost himself when a spirit entered him and he was no longer able to recognize anyone. An older shaman was then sent to teach the young one. First the novice was sent through a hole where worms ate all his flesh. It was a ritual death, after which he became light and "shining." Then the novice learned *ilimarpoq*—to fly through the air with his hands tied behind his back and his ankles bound. A heavy stone was tied around his neck. Finally, a spirit entered his chest; the chest was the spirit's house and from it a special language came.

An angakok could make any of the spirits in the world dangerous; not all shamans had the well-being of humans in mind. Some were evil, ambitious, and greedy, and could strike down people with sickness. They were most dangerous in the autumn. That's when they turned themselves into fireballs that could be seen rushing through the sky. They could also do good if they wanted. They could see into people's suffering and heal anyone they chose, but they were demanding: to stay on their good side, villagers had to give them presents all through the year.

Sometimes death could not be avoided even if the angakok intervened. After death, it was said, life went away into darkness that could not be seen through, even by a shaman.

In June, Qav, Rasmussen, Arn, and their child started down the west coast of Alaska. Leo Hansen stayed on in Point Barrow to film the festivities that were about to begin there. From the terseness of Rasmussen's account, it appeared that he was happy to leave the photographer behind.

At Wainwright—Ulruneq—the snow was so deep all the houses were buried. The Greenlanders arrived at Qajaerserfik—Icy Cape— on June 8. Its Eskimo name means "the place where kayaks are lost" because it is built on a sandbar and often floods during onshore gales.

A feast began two days later: hunting had been bad, but one whale was finally caught. Neighboring villagers from inland camps sledded down the huge, iced-over rivers—the Noatak, the Utorqaq, and the Colville—to take their share.

They assembled in the *qaagsse*—the dance house. First the whale's tail was cut up and distributed. Then everyone played "tossing in the blanket," which meant using a walrus hide like a trampoline to fling someone up into the air. The feasting continued all night and all the next day amid loud, festive singing.

The inland Eskimos, the Utorqarmiut, often came via the Utorqaq River to the coast to buy whale blubber at Icy Cape. They were known for their hunting expertise and used twenty different ways to catch caribou and wolves.

A successful wolf hunt carried with it many rules. When a hunter returned with the skin of a wolf (the meat of this animal was not eaten, perhaps because it so resembled dog), he had to walk

> *sun-wise round his house, kicking his heel four times against the outer wall; he had to wear the skin over his shoulders; he had to urinate on it and take off all his clothes and stand naked in the snow and rub his body with caribou skin, light a bonfire and allow the smoke to waft past his bare skin; he had to sit inside his house and invite others to hear his stories, not for their entertainment, but for the wolf's; he had to rise at dawn and send the wolf-soul away by getting on his knees and grunting out a song that sounds like howls; he had to give a feast afterward and promise not to kill more than five wolves in a year. (Rasmussen,* Fifth Thule Expedition, *vol. 10, no. 3, p. 130)*

At the end of June, Rasmussen and his companions continued down the coast. The ice had gone and travel by sled had become impossible. The dogs and their progeny who had come all the way from Greenland

and had taken them across the polar north were left behind now. With a heavy heart Rasmussen gave all but four of them to a trader at Icy Cape. From that point on they traveled by boat through the newly opened lagoons between narrow, sandy islands. The four remaining dogs were tied on long lines, running on the beach and pulling the boat.

On one side of the sandbars was the tundra, already blooming with summer flowers; on the other side was a moving mass of rotting ice. "Romantic at the lagoons—only ten paces between summer idyll and winter ice," Rasmussen noted in his journal.

Point Hope lies on the coast at the western end of the Brooks Range. Its Eskimo name, Tikeraq, means "the point that runs out like a forefinger." It was once an ancient Eskimo village site where several thousand people lived—"as many as there are now along the entire Northwest Passage between the Magnetic Pole and Herschel island," Rasmussen noted.

In early times there was no finger of land sticking out and the people had to live on top of a mountain. But Raven paddled out into the water and speared something dark. Blood oozed from it. It was not a whale, but some enormous mass with no beginning or end. Raven towed it to shore. The next day, it had lost all its life and had become rigid—no longer massed flesh, but land. The hole where Raven speared it can still be seen.

The Eskimos at Point Hope used masks in their ceremonies called *kinaroq*. The masks were only made after the shaman had journeyed to the land where spirits live and had returned with fresh impressions of their faces. He would then begin to carve.

Each mask had a life; it came with its own songs and these were sung by the wearer of the mask in the dance house. There were wolverines with human heads and a tail at the top of the head. The wolf mask had a sea horse in its mouth; the *eitje* (the dangerous one) was half-human, half–red fox, but could turn itself into a polar bear. The *juktora-niaq* was worn outside because it helped moderate the weather. The *anisut* was worn by a female shaman in male dress and had fox ears.

The songs they sang while making and wearing the masks came directly from the mask's *inua*, and so, when they sang the wolf's song, the sea horse's song, or the polar bear's song, they were giving expression to things that came directly from that animal's heart.

When Rasmussen asked one old man how many songs he knew, the man said, "I cannot say. I have not kept count of them. I merely know I have many, and that everything in me is song."

On the last day of July Rasmussen, Arn, the boy, and Qav left Point Hope and went by boat to Kotzebue. The seas ran heavy and gales blew down on them, forcing them into half-sheltered natural harbors and summer fishing and reindeer camps on the way. The winds felt cold to them, these Polar Eskimos who had easily endured 40-below days on a moving dogsled. To their snow-hardened skin, the temperate coastal weather—blustery, humid, and wet—felt colder.

It was difficult traveling with a small child in rough seas. Arn kept checking her amaut to make sure the child had not been thrown from her protective hood into the raging sea. Despite the weather, Rasmussen did not fail to see the beauty of the coast, the green, luxuriant slopes, stippled with streams and rivers, all flowing into the sea. As was his habit, in every settlement, Rasmussen met with old men and women and continued taking down their stories. One story, called Qajartuarungner-toq, traditionally took a whole month to tell.

They reached Nome on the last day of August. It was a bustling town, a real town, and they wandered around in a state of shock. When they entered a restaurant, they were refused service. Horrified, Rasmussen reported, "The race-problems crop up at our first meeting with civilization!" and quickly sought out another establishment.

The first step away from his Eskimo life had already been taken. That evening he and Arn talked. They could stay in Alaska or Arctic Canada and raise their child; they could all go back to Greenland and live in a village—Siorapaluk, perhaps, or Savissivik; Arn could stay behind in Alaska with the boy. Or they could give the child away and return to their respective homes and lives—Arn to Dundas Village and Rasmussen to Hundstead outside of Copenhagen.

To protect himself from gossip, Rasmussen wrote in his diaries that the child was Qav's. Nothing could have been farther from the truth. In the first place, Qav had promised himself to a woman on Herbert Island. Before leaving he had taken a pebble from the beach in front of her house and put it in his pocket. He said that if he came back and presented the stone to her, that would mean he still wanted to marry her. When Qav and Rasmussen made the rough crossing to Little Diomede Island and were searched by Russian authorities, Qav was so worried that he would lose the stone that he held it between his teeth all the way. That's how determined he was to marry the Herbert Island woman.

When they returned, Rasmussen and Arn had to face the gravity of their domestic situation. It was all right for her to have had a child during the trip, but not if Knud was the father. He was married and famous. They had already left their beloved dogs at Icy Cape; when he returned from Little Diomede, Rasmussen decided that they should leave their child with the Inuit couple who had hosted them in Nome. That child is now an old man, still living as a hunter in the Arctic.

At the end of October, Rasmussen, Arnarunguaq, Qavigarssuaq, and Leo Hansen boarded a ship that took them to Seattle. There they split up, Rasmussen and Hansen boarding one ship, Arn and Qav another. Their epic journey, comparable in scale to Lewis and Clark's, was ended. By December 1924, they had all returned to their respective homes.

The Line That Ties Us: Leaving Qaanaaq, 1998

In the middle of June I moved out of "the world's northernmost hotel" with great sadness. Hans escorted me to the heliport. We walked in lingering sunlight, joining the slow processional of those who were leaving. I was on my way to Illorsuit on Ubekendt Ejland, where I had stayed two summers before to see Marie Louisa. It would soon be the solstice, the longest day of the year, but how could a day be any longer than this one? I asked. Hans only smiled. I hung on to his arm: "I don't want to go," I said. He suggested I stay, but I had made a promise to Marie Louisa . . .

I spent the requisite nights at Thule Air Base. This time, there was no community of Greenlandic women to tell me stories. Only Imina and his mother were there—Imina to go to Denmark for a back operation and his mother to return to Sisimiut. The other passengers were Danes: a male nurse and a geologist, but I wasn't in the mood to talk to them. I visited Thyge and Steen, the Danish friends I had made during my previous stay, and cooked dinners in their barracks.

On the third day I was arrested again. Steen and I had driven to the edge of the ice cap to collect rocks. Out there the drone of the Twelfth Air Command faded to absolute silence. The caterpillar that I had seen on my way north was now a butterfly. It stood on a rock facing the ice

cap, opening and closing its wings. One snow bunting sang. A cliff of ice shouldering dirt rose up before us and snow blowing off the top of the ice cap sifted down.

The flat rock I collected there was studded with garnets. It was heavy—perhaps fifteen pounds. Later, I boxed it up and lugged it to the U.S. post office on the base, but the windows were closed. I left it on the counter for a moment and stepped outside to see if someone could give me a ride back to my barracks. In those few seconds a worker spied the unattended box and called the bomb squad.

Three dark blue Ford pickups drove up, blocking the roads; seven uniformed men—military police—got out, holding machine guns. Sirens blew and didn't stop. I looked around—should I duck? Was something going on behind me? I turned back: they were walking toward me. The dining hall across the road was evacuated. My Greenlandic friends stood on the steps and watched. The MP's stepped closer, forming a tight circle around me. These were Americans, I kept reminding myself. One of them, young and blond with a Texas accent, asked for my papers. I didn't have them on me and had to be driven to the barracks to get them. Then they drove me back to the post office, passport in hand, to open the box.

It's just a rock, I kept saying, but they didn't seem to believe me. How am I supposed to open this? I asked, looking at the sealed-up box on the counter. "You'll see, it really is just a rock. I'm a rockhound." Loudspeakers were going off. Thyge Anderson was being called—I'd used his name for a return address on the base. I wanted to put my ear to the box as if listening for ticking, just as a joke, but I didn't. The guns were still pointed at me.

I had to borrow a knife from one of the MP's. See, I said, opening the lid and lifting the rock up into the light. Just a rock. I tried to hand it to the Texan but he shook his head. They stared at the specimen with disappointment in their eyes.

I was taken to a room and interrogated. They had information about me from my first visit: illegal entry onto the base and no transit visa, no ticket to Qaanaaq. They already knew I was a writer. Again, they suggested I might be a spy. I told them I had trouble figuring out Agatha Christie mysteries. They didn't smile. Finally, the attending officer sent the other men away. Alone in the room, he admitted that perhaps they had overreacted, though he still couldn't understand why I had entered the base illegally on my way north. I tried to explain how the Danish embassy told me explicitly that I didn't need a special permit to transit through Thule, and in most places in the world the embassy is where you go to get visas. He looked bewildered. He'd never traveled before. "So you're not a Russian spy?" he asked again. This time, I started laughing. Thyge had been arrested too and released: he was a Birkenstock hippie with a security clearance. The Texan drove me back to the barracks. On the way, he asked me out on a date. I declined.

That afternoon I took a walk, even though I knew they were watching me. Already the rivers were beginning to flow and the snowdrifts that separated the valley from Dundas Village over the hill had begun melting. The image of being surrounded by soldiers with machine guns kept looming. I started shaking from the cold. Back at Thyge's barracks, I sat alone on the floor of his room, hunched over, sipping tea. Thyge had gone back to work, but a friend of his, a Dane I barely knew, opened the door and in a gentle voice said, "I'm so angry for the way they treated you today. It happened once to me, and after I felt a little sad and empty inside. Please don't take it personally. They treat everyone like that. I'm sorry it happened to you."

I hadn't known how frightened I had been until he left: then I burst into tears.

Pituffik, the name of the valley here, means "a line that ties us to something." Like a dog harness, or an infatuation, or a religion. What was tying me to this place? In Thule I saw how easily a valley can be defiled; in Siorapaluk and Qaanaaq I saw how a culture could be sabotaged by cutting the binding thread of the spiritual life of a people.

The jet was supposed to come the next day. I made one last loop past the Knud Rasmussen Library to the shoreline. Looking out at North Star Bay for the last time, I wondered how much plutonium had leaked into these waters, how long the skin on Niels's arms and ankles would continue to peel, and for how many centuries the marine mammals here would be contaminated.

In the morning First Air took off for Kangerlussuaq on schedule at 8:00 a.m. The military police were there to make sure I left the base. At the top of the steps I turned and waved to them, Nixon-style. You won't have me to push around anymore, I wanted to say. To rise up from that valley and head south was both exhilarating and sorrowful. The unexpected intimacies of the sled, the village, and the barracks vanished, as did the horrors.

"Going away and seeing each other again is all part of the same thing," Steen had said the day before. He knew; he was a veteran of good-byes. "They go together. They have to. And tomorrow, without you here, it will all be so feeling empty."

From the plane I looked down on land from which glaciers had retreated, land that had been disburdened and was rebounding. One moment I longed for night and trees and passionate embraces—the realm of human entanglement—and in the next moment I wanted only dogsleds and ice—clarity and cerebration. The landscape of the northern district, in all its iciness, stood for the panoramic view, for time without end or beginning, for the blindness of birth and the brightness of death, and the solipsism of the sun's relentless shining. My chest heaved; the air felt light.

Farther south we came into another season. Not the way we had on the dogsled. This "coming" resembled the speed and fracture of modern life: the ice floor had splintered where a guillotine had slammed down. My tie to the north had been severed. Where Smith Sound gave way to Baffin Bay, pieces of floating ice—*kassut*—were rotting and had turned a deathly gray. Before the season of open water came, the ice had to die. The long tail of a ruptured iceberg unspiraled.

Olejorgen, Ann, and their children Ludwig and Pipaluk met me at the heliport in Uummannaq when I flew in from Kangerlussuaq. After the open vistas of the north, Uummannaq's rock-walled beauty startled me. The sun was hot and the fjord's open water glittered. We walked up the steep hill to their house, stripping down to short sleeves. Warm air on bare skin felt luxurious. Olejorgen looked darker, leaner, stronger, and had the beginnings of a hunter's mustache. It had been five years since he had seen Uummannaq for the first time. Now he had just returned from a monthlong dogsled trip up the west coast of Greenland. As usual we had missed each other: he had left Qaanaaq just as I was arriving.

As we walked to Ann and Olejorgen's yellow house on the hill, Olejorgen spoke to their daughter Pipaluk in Greenlandic, Ann used Faroese and Danish, and Pipaluk replied in a baffling mixture of the three languages. Born in Uummannaq, Pipaluk had weighed only 1.7 kilos at birth. The doctor at the local clinic had no incubator and didn't know if she would survive. Now I saw that she had Olejorgen's dark skin and hair and Ann's defiant nature: she wriggled out of her father's arms because she wanted to walk.

Ludwig, Olejorgen's ten-year-old son from Denmark, looked Greenlandic, though when he arrived from Copenhagen three years earlier he had spoken only Danish. Smart and handsome, he was now fluent in Danish, Greenlandic, English, and a little Spanish, effortlessly picking up any language spoken in his presence. I asked him where he wanted to live when he grew up. He looked me straight in the eye and said, "California."

My baggage was thrown into Ann's Russian car, driven by the Greenlander, Duppe, who had given us our midnight ride around the town years before in the dark of winter. As we climbed the steep hill, Ann insisted I stay in their small house even though I had reserved a room at the hotel. One more didn't matter, she said. There were already ten people sleeping there.

Hans Holm called from Illorsuit and lamented the bad ice conditions that separated us. It was too thin for a dogsled, too thick for a boat, and despite warm days the ice was holding tenaciously. "You have come at the in-between season. I don't know if you will get here or not," he said.

I talked to Marie Louisa on the phone. By talk I mean I grunted out syllables of languages neither of us knew very well. The excitement in her voice was enough. I was determined to get there. "I think there's a helicopter scheduled to come. Call Arne and find out," Hans said.

Arne Fleischer recognized my voice right away. After all, I was the odd, lone American woman who kept reappearing in Uummannaq, and he had been Aleqa's boyfriend years before. The helicopter schedule was uncertain, he told me. Also, it would be the last one of the season. Once I got out there, I would have to return by dogsled or boat, and, depending on the weather and ice, passage back to Uummannaq might be a month away. I made a reservation for the next day.

Ann insisted that we go next door to the Children's House for a rehearsal of the drum dances the children were learning. She was the director there. "Change that to dictator!" she said as she scurried from room to room, greeting children, cleaning up messes. "But a good one."

The building was modern, homey, and cheerful. "The kids don't want to leave when they turn eighteen," Ann told me. "And we have kids with no problems who want to come live here, because they see how much fun we have."

In her office a pile of faxes lay waiting on her desk. She was preparing to take seventeen children to Denmark and Paris the following week. A tireless fund-raiser, she was still looking for sponsors, soliciting the queen of Denmark, the Danish embassy in Paris, the airlines, and clothing companies.

Ann's degree in sociology from the university in Copenhagen didn't come easily. "They told me that I could never be a good social worker because I had come from a good family. But how can you give love if you've never gotten it?" she asked. Buxom, bespectacled, and sometimes overbearing, her dictatorial whims were tempered by openhanded generosity that sometimes made the rest of her family feel left out.

"No one runs things like Ann. She is the best, taking the kids on her own holiday, staying up all night when new children come in," Poul Karoup, her brother-in-law and the editor of one of Greenland's daily papers, said on the phone. He had called to say he was coming to visit in a few days. "She gets things done. She's had a hard go of it too, good family or not. She watched her boyfriend go down in a helicopter right out here. Then she had a bout with cancer, and almost lost her first child. And she has a sister who is handicapped. Her family comes from the old fishing community of the Faroe Islands. There isn't an ungenerous bone in their bodies. They have always believed in taking in whoever needs help."

When I asked Ann why she was the way she was, she said simply, "My family has always been like this. We like lots of people around."

A seven-year-old girl ran into the office and out again, screaming. Her parents in Upernavik had kept her in a box for five years. They didn't know how to handle her because she was autistic and was always running; sometimes she ran out on the ice and they were afraid she'd drown. Ann said, "They weren't mean people. They just didn't know where to ask for help. Finally, someone in the town saw the child and brought her here. Now her father has come to visit. But she's frightened of him and fearful of what will happen to her. She doesn't want to go back to the box. That's why she's been running all day."

The sound of drumming and singing filtered into the office. I wondered if Sophie from Qaanaaq was around. "No, it's a young man from the high school who is teaching the children," Ann said. She led me to the living room, where the man stood in front of the kids, knees slightly bent, beating a skin drum high over his right shoulder, then his left. After the song, he summoned three teenage girls to try. They were shy at first, so Ann stood up with them. Together they performed an awkward rendition of the dance. "See, you don't need to be shy. No one will be as bad at it as I am," Ann said to the children amid much laughter.

While awaiting their turn two girls combed something dark through their hair. Earlier in the year they had dyed their hair pink and green. Now they were dyeing it back to "regular Eskimo color"—black—so that when they traveled in Europe performing traditional Greenlandic drum dances, they would look like who they were.

Olejorgen's favorite word is "Eskimoic." He had been bursting with pride since the completion of his dogsled trip to Thule. Unrolling a new map of Greenland that showed every village, ruined house, and hunters' camp, he pointed out the Danish names that had been changed to Greenlandic. "It is important to have all these things right because we were colonized so long ago, we can't remember what we forgot," Olejorgen said.

He traced the route of his trip to Qaanaaq taken in April. There were five sleds and eleven people. Accompanying him were several hunters, including Kristian Moller from Illorsuit, and five teenage boys from the Children's House.

"I traveled alone on my sled. The five other hunters carried one person each: four boys and one worker from the Children's House. We didn't hunt along the way, but bought halibut at the fish factories at a cheap price. The first day we traveled to Illorsuit and stayed with Hans Holm. Then, with Kristian Möller along, we went north to Sondre

Upernavik. It was cold and dark—about minus twenty-five Celsius—and took four days. At Proven we had to go overland because the ice was bad. Getting off the glacier on our way to Aappilattoq took fourteen hours and was quite tough and cold. Then on to Innaarsuit, where we stayed three days. It's a very energetic place, but there's one sad thing: people there have begun using snow scooters to transport fish. We feel this is very bad. At Nuttaarmiut there were four ice-bear skins drying at the place where we stayed. The boys who came with us had never hunted polar bears or been out on a long trip. We hoped it would give them a taste of what they could become. I think it did that.

"At Kullorsuaq we began eating narwhal and beluga too. Then we entered Melville Bay. It took eight days to get to Savissivik. It should have taken only four, but the snow was deep . . . More hunters joined us. We didn't have the long Thule sleds. Ours were shorter and we soon found out why that was a mistake. Short sleds don't work as well in the north. Our sleds are built for going across the mountains; Thule sleds are built for hauling large loads and crossing crevasses and leads in ice.

"We passed the Devil's Thumb, a big high round rock, two hundred fifty meters high. One hunter went out to shoot a seal and came back eight hours later with a polar bear. So we ate bear from then on—curried bear, bear with rice, boiled bear, bear with pasta.

"Savissivik and Save Island, where Peary got the meteorite, are very isolated. The snow is always deep and there are many bears. There are black Eskimos there too—descendants of Matthew Henson, Peary's first mate. They are very good hunters. Being an Eskimo is not just race and nationality, it's also how you live. Three more days and we reached Dundas, then we spent a night at Moriussaq, up the coast from Thule Air Base. Matt Henson's grandson runs the KNI grocery store there. In another two days we reached Qaanaaq. The dogs and the children and I were very tired. But these boys had lived on the ice for fifty days."

I heard an "Ooh la la" from the other room. It was Ann, getting into the swing of drum dancing. From her college photographs pinned to the wall, it was clear she was once a "looker," as Ludwig said. More matronly now, she still had fun. "Ooh la la," she piped out again, joining the kids in their dance and banging a hand drum. "We're going to Paris! Come on, dance!"

During the rehearsal, the autistic child darted in and out screaming. Her father, a thin man with a mild, weather-beaten face, was waiting patiently on a straight-backed dining room chair. Every time his child whizzed by, he held out a hand and said, "*Kutaa*," Hello. But she rushed past. That's all the contact the child could stand.

Ann surveyed the room. The children looked healthy and happy, but the stories of how they ended up in Ann's care were hair-raising. "Things can look calm in a village but be very bad behind the scenes. Nothing can describe the hell underneath. Some of the parents might as well have given these kids to the dogs to raise. The dogs would have taken better care of them."

When the dancing slowed Ann shouted out encouragement. Everyone laughed; no one was frightened of her. "I take these kids to Europe because it teaches them that they are first-class citizens. It shows them how to live with other kinds of people. Many of them have already seen and tasted violence. Now they will learn how to live without hurting anyone."

Back at the house we began cooking dinner. A teenage girl knocked at the door. "Yes, yes, come in, come in, you can stay," Ann said. When the girl went into the bathroom, Ann whispered: "She tried twice to kill herself, first by cutting her wrists, then she shot herself in the mouth, only it didn't kill her. She's pregnant—probably with her own father's child. She used to live at the Children's House but the Kommune—the local government—kicked her out. She could have had an abortion— you only have to go to the clinic on any Wednesday morning—but in revenge, she kept the child. And now we have her like this. She must be crazy in the head after putting a gun inside herself and then not dying.

"She went back to live with her parents. There was nothing we could do. They live in a ten-by-fourteen-foot room. Six people live in there and all she says to them is 'I am a good girl.' She says that to please her parents. Why? Because she's so scared. I say to her, 'I don't want you to be a good girl, just be yourself, then we can help you, then you have a chance to be happy.' Now it's too late. Too late for an abortion and maybe too late to be happy. All the time I give these children a choice. You want the baby, we will help; you don't want it, we will help then too."

Olejorgen appeared in the kitchen with a sack of new red potatoes. "Look, they're fresh, just off the boat. The first of the season." He dropped them into boiling water. At dinner we set the pot in the middle of the table and stuck our forks in. Olejorgen held a half-eaten potato in the air. "You can taste the earth in its skin," he said. There was no earth to speak of on Uummannaq Island.

We ate voraciously; Olejorgen continued dreaming. He leaned over a map of the entire circumpolar north: "I want to travel, maybe from Svalbard to eastern Greenland, and also to Washington Land and Peary Land—anywhere by dogsled. Also, I would like to spend a winter in Siorapaluk, if Ann will let me." He smiled boyishly.

"Ya, ya, ya. Sure." Ann said. "But there won't be any red potatoes there."

Two teenage boys burst in with Ludwig. They wanted to spend the night too. "Yes, okay, you are welcome," Ann said. "Go upstairs." In Greenland children are often handed around: if one family can't take care of a child, then someone else in the village will, and the exchange is not considered a big deal. No legal papers are signed. There are no lawyers here, only in Nuuk.

We counted heads: there would be twelve people sleeping that night in Ann's 900-square-foot house. By morning the compost toilet would be full.

Shortly after dinner, Olejorgen went to bed. "He's been very tired since his trip," Ann said. "But it's okay. He is different from us. Greenlanders have a lot of silence and do-nothing time inside them. That's the way they are. They don't have to be busy all the time like the Danes. That's good, don't you think? Maybe they learned it from their dogs, who sleep for days and weeks between hunting trips. It's how they survive."

Late in the night the talk was about raising children and bettering society. Sven, a middle-aged Danish dentist, had stopped by, one of many doctors who rotated through Greenland from Denmark. "The paradox of Danish socialism," he said, "is that its ideal is to give people their basic needs so they can get on to more important things. But we've found that giving is a complicated matter. Part of the animal survival mechanism is to be opportunistic. It's very easy to make parasites out of perfectly healthy, clever people. But if they're not healthy . . . well, there are problems. So it's always a matter of how much to give and to whom and when . . . It's very difficult indeed to know these things. Perhaps some ideals can't be fully enacted. They must be held inside, in the heart, but not put into the government. We are always looking at ourselves, trying to solve the puzzle of how to be human."

I woke up midday, aswim in the split rivers of homesickness: one for the far north and the other for my own home. I also longed to see Marie Louisa. Arne Fleischer called from the heliport to say there would be no helicopter to Illorsuit that day. While we straightened up the house, Ann played a CD of country music. I twirled around the room to George Strait with little enthusiasm.

Ebbe, a sweet-faced wunderkind in his early twenties, came to take me on a hike to the other side of the island. He was staying with the prime minister's brother, Severin, who lived up the street. Tall and strong, he set a pace I had difficulty keeping up with. Just beyond the Children's House we heard a whistle, then a small explosion. They were dynamiting rock to make room for a new addition. Half a mile farther, we skirted a lake and scrambled up granite walls, traversing a ledge. Chest pains traveled down my left arm to my elbow and clouds of mosquitoes—not seen in Qaanaaq or Siorapaluk—hovered around us. We climbed up behind the village. All the houses were built on one side. The rest of the island was uninhabited and was referred to as the sheep's heart that stood upright as if in a human's body.

My aching heart climbed to the top of the island's rock heart. On the other side we descended to a small hut and rested in hot sun. From there I could see across the end of the fjord to Ubekendt Ejland and Illorsuit. Halfway across the mouth of the fjord, ice began, opaque and crumbling, a flattened wall that kept me from getting to my friends.

A helicopter burst into view from the other side of the island, the noise of its mixmaster blade percussing against island rock. Down to the end of the fjord it went, then veered north up Illorsuit Strait. Could it really be going there? I waved my arms helplessly, then shielded my eyes to see. "I'm supposed to be on it," I told Ebbe. But it was too late. The helicopter had already gone from sight and would soon be there.

We tried to get back to town in case there was a second flight, but the exertion caused more chest pain. I had to stop and rest. None of my decisions about when to go, where, and why seemed to be right. As we climbed over the top of a rock wall, the helicopter returned. But by the time we made it to the heliport, it had gone again. I called Arne. He said the second flight was going not to Illorsuit but to Ukkusissat. And that would be the last flight of the year. The helicopter would not leave again until spring.

That evening I called Hans Holm again. He sounded hurt. "Marie

Louisa thought you were coming so she walked by herself all the way up to the heliport. Along the way she picked flowers. When the helicopter landed, she was waiting for you. She ran to the door, but you didn't come out. Then, the villagers said, she sat down on the ground and cried."

I resigned myself to whatever came next, willy-nilly. Nothing else but seeing Marie Louisa mattered. How could I explain my absence to her? What was the use? We didn't even speak the same language. A hard sun shone its argentine foil on the inky fjord water. Chest pains continued, spurred on, no doubt, by abject guilt. My attention had lapsed just when it was needed, and nothing I did would make up for my mistake. It was not enough to notice that the days were long in summer; they were also saying, "There is no escape." Infinity is constantly mocking us by giving us summer and twenty-four-hour-a-day sun—or is it immortality that has the last laugh?

Ann worked nonstop getting ready for the tour to Europe, faxing airlines, the queen, friends, and embassies asking them to help—a free meal, a free pass, an audience, a visit to the House of Parliament, anything to show the children how the rest of the world lived. Olejorgen stayed in bed, slept, and read.

Later in the day Olejorgen got up to do chores, looking professorial. He fed the dogs dried halibut and kitchen scraps wearing a blue oxford shirt, khaki pants, and a cardigan sweater. Remembering his dogsled trip, he said, "Sometimes when we were traveling, eight days felt like one, and near Savissivik the fog was so thick I couldn't tell the difference between heaven, earth, and ice. I couldn't see. I don't mean just in front of the sled. I was lost . . . Sometimes I felt as if I was flying upside down." He pointed to his heart. "I was lost out there on the ice, and also, inside myself."

He offered each dog water from a pail. They had no shade and no other source of water. "Just now one of my dogs died," he said flatly. "I guess from the heat." I asked if the dog had had water that morning and he shrugged. "Maybe not." He still had a long way to go in his understanding of what made a good hunter.

We walked down to the harbor, looking for someone to help fix the outboard on his small boat. "Tomorrow we will sail to see the place of the mummies on the other side of the fjord," Olejorgen said. Across water the great walls of the adjacent island ran black with meltwater and the fjord shone like clean hair. Olejorgen didn't seem to be bothered by the fact that he'd lost a dog. On his trip to Qaanaaq, he had lost four, he told me.

A fine-featured young man walked by and Olejorgen called to him. We were introduced. "This is Jacob, Rockwell Kent's and Salamina's grandson," Olejorgen said.

Jacob was pale-skinned, black-haired, and handsome. Behind elegant wire-rimmed glasses his eyes sparkled with intelligence. "Yes, they say Kinte was my grandfather. Of course, one never knows about these things. But I think so. Yes, I feel him in me." Then he rushed off to teach school.

The outboard motor was fixed. We would go across the fjord the next day. That night and every night, I talked on the phone to Hans Holm and Marie Louisa. He suggested that we watch the film his father, Mogen Holm, had made in the 1920s; we could get it at the museum. "He was the first doctor to go to Qaanaaq. Everyone was dying of TB then and he diagnosed the disease and treated all the people there and saved many lives. So you see, I got my ideas about coming to Greenland with my baby food."

In the morning the skies were clear and the water was smooth. Our "family" sailing trip turned into an all–Children's House expedition—seventeen children, ten workers, and friends. Four boats crossed the fjord. On the other side we met up with Mogens, the Danish vice-mayor of Uummannaq, whose enthusiasm about the prospective oil boom in Greenland had been quelled: there was no boom.

Mogens and his wife invited us on board. His fancy cabin cruiser had an interior cabin and galley and slept four. While the children fished and leaped from rock to rock, we sipped white wine and basked in sun sheltered from wind on this patch of open water.

The place of the mummies, on the north slope of the Nuussuaq Peninsula, was called Qitsaliq. The perfectly preserved bodies of two women and four children had been found by two Greenlandic boys out hunting. No one believed them at first. They took pictures and showed them to the police, who finally went to the place and saw that what the boys said was true.

We clambered over smooth-sided, glacier-scoured granite past a tiny meadow with its evidence of four house sites from the 1800s—stone-

and-turf shelters used seasonally by hunters. On hands and knees I peered down into the cavernous holes where the bodies had been found and taken away. Olejorgen told the story: "It was an autumn day and the new ice was moving in. The women must have been caught rowing an umiak. Their boat was overturned by drift ice and the people drowned. Since then the sea level has lowered and so they were preserved up here in the rocks by the ice and cold."

In the afternoon we rowed the dinghy back to the boat and formed a long processional with other boats to the far side of Uummannaq Island, to a high grassy knoll bounded on one side by a thousand-foot-high rock wall. Olejorgen, Ebbe, and the teenagers picked dry heather for our "Eskimo barbeque." Tall stones were set in place with flat rocks laid on top, griddle stones on which meat would be cooked. Food was unpacked and carried up from the boats, the children singing the drum dance songs as they worked. After the meal three teenage girls, the best dancers, stood on a high perch of rocks to perform: A slow drumbeat began, and their Inuit chants, sung for hundreds of years all the way around the polar north, echoed back and forth across the canyon.

Ann and I rode home with Mogens. Half a mile from the harbor, the boat bumped up against something. We slowed to a stop. Over the side we saw black ice. Mogens proudly assured us that the hull was doubly thick. We proceeded slowly and broke a path through the ice. I looked around. All water had been stilled. There was no pulse. The fjord was a blindfold, a black solid. The bow was fracturing dark mirrors that did not give back reflections. The other boats fell in behind us in a stately procession. At the entrance to the harbor a dead dog floated under the ice.

At the end of the week a red ship, the *Disko,* pulled into the tiny harbor carrying Poul Karoup, Olejorgen's brother in-law, and Lars Emil Johansen, the prime minister of Greenland. Poul and I embraced warmly (he and his family had visited me twice in California) and then stood aside as the prime minister walked by. Known as Lars Emil, he was not much taller than me, wore a black T-shirt, black jeans, and Nike running shoes, and was attended by a handsome young Greenlander with whom Olejorgen had gone to school in Nuuk.

The night before, Ann, Olejorgen, and I had shared a midnight feast with Lars Emil's brother, Severin, who belonged to a different political party. When we mentioned Lars Emil's impending arrival, Severin made a face and said, "He doesn't listen to me. I'm taking the morning helicopter south."

We lunched with Poul and Lars Emil at the Uummannaq Hotel. Shrimp, seal, and Danish meatballs with gravy were served. Lars Emil was born in the village of Illorsuit. When I told him I had spent a summer there to see where Rockwell Kent had lived and painted, he said he remembered Kinte well, even though he had been a little boy. He asked me to extend his greeting to everyone in the village.

Lars Emil mentioned the toxic waste dump he was negotiating for Greenland; his brother had gone to Nuuk to protest it. When I tried to tell Lars Emil that Greenland didn't need that kind of money, he ignored me and smiled. "Do you want to come on the ship with me tonight?" he whispered. I smiled and declined.

After lunch, Lars Emil jumped into a red Toyota pickup and sped up the street. He didn't bother to ask if he could borrow it—he was the prime minister. He careened between houses, dogs, sleds, and children, stopping now and then to visit old friends.

Late in the day, he stopped at the Children's House. Crowded together in a small room, we watched the children perform the dances they had been rehearsing all week. Bending knees and swaying hips, they beat the small drums with the flats of their hands. Their slow, sweet voices cast a spell over us all, even the impenetrable Lars Emil.

"There is no other Children's House in all of Greenland of this caliber," Poul Karoup whispered as we watched the dancing. "Ann is the best, taking the kids on her own holiday. She can be a little overbearing, but it's never for her own sake, it's always for the children."

The ship's whistle blew. It was time for the visitors to leave. Lars Emil and his aide jumped in their borrowed truck and sped toward the harbor. We followed in the Russian sedan with Ann's driver Duppe at the wheel. The dock was empty. No one had come to wish the prime minister farewell. Was it because the people in Uummannaq didn't vote for him? Ann shook her head. "They still don't believe that they can make their views heard, that they have a say in the government."

Poul nonchalantly lit his pipe and hugged us good-bye. He climbed the gangplank two steps at a time and disappeared inside the ship. Lars Emil stopped to talk to me again. "I had a special nickname in Illorsuit.

Ask them to tell you what it was and what it means. You'll like it," he said. Then he leaned closer. "Are you sure you don't want to come?" I shook my head and thanked him, kissing his fat cheek.

Up on deck he stood alone. The ship's whistle blew again and the gangplank was raised. A truck roared up: it was the children. As the ship pulled away from the dock, the kids waved and shouted greetings in three languages.

Lars Emil looked tiny. Like many Greenlanders of mixed ancestry, he had dark skin and blue eyes and his gaze was piercing. He beckoned to me as the ship backed slowly away, as if I might be able to leap aboard.

"Look how lonely he is," Ann said. "Everyone who visits Uummannaq wishes they could stay."

We piled into the Russian car again and asked Duppe to take us on one more "round trip" tour of Uummannaq, like the one we'd had two years before, only this time it was under the bright glare of the sun. Up the hill we raced, swerving to avoid hitting two teenage girls who were walking arm in arm to Rema, a little grocery store. From the top of the village we descended to the far side of the island. New houses were being built overlooking the fjord and beyond to Baffin Bay. We stopped at the blue house Olejorgen had wanted to buy. It was still for sale. Just as we got out, the red ship carrying Poul and the prime minister came into view. It sliced through black water on its way toward Baffin Bay.

The blue house was empty. "Something wrong with the way the roof and the floors were built. Now it's very cheap," Duppe said. Olejorgen looked at it longingly. It represented a reprieve from the close quarters of village life—a perfect viewing site from which to dream. But Ann would have none of it. She had to be in the middle of things.

Ann called to Olejorgen to get into the car. Sometimes he still looked like a child scholar—innocent but stooped, his long fingers more fit for turning pages than flensing seals. But he was stronger than he had been, and though he wasn't a full-time hunter yet, he had pledged to learn what he could of his own hunting culture.

The ship, getting tinier as it neared the horizon, blasted its whistle. I wondered aloud if Lars Emil was on deck enjoying the view. Ann snorted: "He's probably on his cell phone with the Americans trying to close the toxic dump site deal."

The next night a friend and I ate dinner al fresco—fish, potatoes, and cabbage. Halfway through the meal the food froze to the plate. I could see out over the town of Uummannaq. A dog howled in the bright midnight sun. I wondered if the moon—invisible to us in daylight—was full, and if the dog could see or sense it.

The fjord was flattened again by black ice. Fog spread like smoke; the fjord, the village, the harbor—all gone, erased from the white blank on the map that was Greenland.

When I woke on my last morning I felt nothing. Does emotion come from the same place as ice? I stood at the window. Maybe it was out of fog that ice is made. I saw things: a snow house appeared, dissolved, then a string of ice mountains. When Arctic fog rises, it does so from water—rarely from land—as if trying to become ice again. Soon the helicopter would come, the thump and strobe of its blade ticking. My mother told me that a blind person's night is white gauze and the days are like dirty glasses. I had been snowblind and sunblind, and now I was fogblind. Then I remembered that a blind in duck hunters' lingo meant a place to hide, a place from which to see.

Arne came for me and drove me to the heliport. Fog had risen from the head of the fjord and snaked past all the villages—Saattut, Uummannaq, Qaarsut, Niaqornat. It lay down below the heliport—a safety net for a soft landing. In the helicopter, an old Sikorsky, we labored up above the dark, flickering and luminous headwalls of Uummannaq. I saw Ann, Olejorgen, Ludwig, and Pipaluk waving good-bye.

Flying south, we crossed water, moved over mountains. I stared down into the jewel case of a crevasse and saw blue sapphires. In a narrow canyon, a cracked cornice hung from a russet ledge, then dropped. Where snow fell, clouds lifted up as effortlessly as smoke. We crossed the long interior lake of Nuussuaq Peninsula. It was over this water that the February sun had performed its six-minute peep show. Now the sun was an incinerating dot above our heads piercing the wandering eye of the fog. How many times had I taken this ride? It was like leaping over the back of a horse. Who knew what I would find on the other side?

Near Ilulissat we thumped over Baffin Bay's frozen geometries and augured down just beyond a half-thawed, vaginal-shaped pond whose shores were lined with diamonds. This I'd learned: the blind man's night is white; the fog is a trail I follow home.

Lost . . . we were all lost. That's what I was thinking when, in the crowded waiting room at Kangerlussuaq, filled with southern Greenlanders and Danish businessmen, a familiar head unexpectedly popped above the others: Torben's. He waved and smiled. "What are you doing here?" he asked.

"Going to Copenhagen," I told him.

"So am I."

After takeoff he left his seat and sat by me. Mistakenly we'd been put in "Polar Class"—Greenland's version of first class—and, taking advantage of the luxury, we ordered extra wine and salads with our dinners. "I haven't been out of Qaanaaq for a year," Torben told me. "But I never feel deprived. In fact, it's the opposite. The farther south I go, the more penalized I feel."

We flew east over Greenland's ice cap for two hours. At its summit the snow turned dove gray and seemed to sink. Was this the umbilical? Or just a melting mass of ice? We talked about how the world ended up being the way it is, how it twisted into this alien place decked out with experts, monetary currencies, and global economies. Might not it have been a place of generalists—hunters and gatherers? Couldn't we shift the balance from a corporate, bureaucratic mode of control with therapeutic overtones to a natural hierarchy based on food-gathering and home-caring skills and on natural intelligence, talents, and proclivities?

Replace money with seal; replace bureaucracy with natural hierarchy, the most skilled hunters rising to the top; replace thought control and marketplace conformity with eccentricity and geographical-tribal identities. What do you get? More or less fulfillment? But then you must ask, What is it human beings need to be fulfilled?

"The word 'primitive' means 'first,' not 'backward,' " Torben said. "The Inuit are modern-day stone age tool users who are born clever and smart. We Europeans are becoming more and more primitive in the bad sense of the word. We don't know much about how to live well, as the Inuit do. The Inuit have always been clever. The Arctic weeds out the dumb ones. A hunter just can't make a mistake or he'll be dead.

"On the other hand, no one in the world is better at communal living. They have to be both things: individually tough and smart, but also communal-minded. I'm afraid we have a long way to go to get that good at living."

We looked down at the white-capped ocean and the long arm of northern Iceland curving gracefully around a blue lake. The light began to change. Night was coming. Fading sun was like an intoxicant wearing off. Torben put his hand on mine. In silence, we watched the North Atlantic's rolling swells subsume themselves.

We sat with our shoulders touching and our hands clasped. "I don't know how I feel," Torben said. "Or how I'm supposed to feel. Do you think something is wrong with me? Tomorrow I'm going to be fifty. I'm going to see a grandchild in the Faroe Islands whom I've never met before, and I don't know if I will love him or if he'll love me."

Lost. In the last hour of twilight, Norway's west-facing mountains humped up ahead of us in the middle of the sea and the sun's mad burning finally faded. Torben seemed stunned. What would he make of night's devouring oblivion, I wondered, or of the city's faded mornings in the days to come?

At the airport, we were separated at customs. Later, I saw him standing at the baggage claim staring at his suitcase going around and around. Civilization is impatience; Torben was having trouble getting the hang of it again. "I can't remember what I'm supposed to do," he said amid choked-up laughter.

There was no possibility of spending the night together. He was catching another plane to go see one of his ex-wives and his grandchildren. I smiled at him. "You'll figure it out. And happy birthday." Then I passed through two sliding doors into Copenhagen's soggy night.

The pale walls of Ann and Olejorgen's capacious flat in Copenhagen were hung with paintings of Greenland. Ann's mother, Maria, poured tea. She was tall, red-haired, soft-spoken, with a squinting, faraway look as if trying to call back the exact tenor of her early days in the Arctic. Everyone in Ann's family had spent time in Greenland. Now I was gulping tears. The farewell at the airport had torn something. I felt bereft. Everything seemed superfluous: bedrooms, heaters, umbrellas, decor. On the other hand, I was lonely to the point of wanting extinction.

Maria gazed at me pityingly. She stopped pouring mid-cup and looked into my eyes: "It's too bad for you when you visit Greenland, because then you have to keep going back. When you have been with those people—with the Inuit—you know that you have been with human beings."

Winter to Spring, 1998

Between hunting seasons, during the dark time, Torben began writing letters to me. Like Rasmussen, he was a man caught between two cultures, not sure where he belonged. But he did not have the good fortune to be born in an era when Arctic exploration was prized. He had worked in Europe and Africa, but Qaanaaq had become his true home.

Dear Gretel,

> *It's January first and I have taken out my beautiful Parker Duofold fountain pen for this letter. Then I'm going to send it to you on my new fax machine. Funny world. I'm up here freezing my soul out yearning for inspiration. I've been working on exhibitions for the museum and feel alone. Of course I can perform the tasks but the joy of two minds working together is lacking.*
>
> *Next month we welcome the sun back. Traditionally, this must be done with a bare head and hands held out, palms up to feel the first rays of sunlight. It was believed that you would not survive the year if you refused to welcome the sun properly; the sun was known to be a great source of life.*
>
> *The sun itself came into existence during a lamp-*

*extinguishing game when the soapstone lamps were put out
and the partygoers found partners for intercourse in the dark
by touch, not sight. During one of those games, a brother
happened to pick his sister and slept with her. When the lamps
were lit again and they saw whom they had made love to, the
sister was ashamed. She grabbed her torch and fled. Her
brother pursued her, but his peat torch did not burn well. When
the sister came to the edge of the world she jumped into the sky.
Because her torch burned brightly, she became the sun. Her
brother became the moon, a fainter light still trying to catch
up with her.*

January 11.

*In December a meteor fell onto the ice cap in southern
Greenland. In the pitch-black day, there was a tremendous
glare. People in Nuuk said they thought the sun had come back
suddenly. Then it vanished and they still haven't found where it
can have gone. The last one hit 2,000 years ago near the village
of Savissivik. It's the one Robert Peary found on one of his
failed journeys to the North Pole. He took chunks of it on his
ship back to New York. That meteor revolutionized Inuit
hunting: they used the meteorite to make harpoon points and
all kinds of tools because it didn't break like agate or bone. I
can tell you from experience that there's nothing worse than
harpooning a narwhal and having the point break in half when
it hits the skin, because then you are attached to a live, wild*

animal. Yes, these things falling out of the sky have been good for Greenlanders.

February 10.
Last week a hunter found dog bones in Disko Bay which date from the late Dorset period. It's not known how dogs were used then—they didn't pull sleds, but were perhaps used for burden carrying. The Dorset people were priggish: they set such strict standards for themselves in how and what they made and how things looked—material and aesthetic standards—that they ceased to thrive. The Thule people were the opposite—and maybe they learned the hard way. They were like Californians, always using new materials, testing new ways of doing things, so theirs was a makeshift society, but one full of adaptive behaviors: they were always becoming someone new.

This evening I was thinking about memory. Those weren't the skills he needed to survive, but knowing where he was at all times, having a map of the entire coastline or island in mind was absolutely necessary. My ex-brother-in-law, who is Inuit, has an amazing mind for physical detail—for places and objects. Today a ninety-year-old hunter said he hadn't really forgotten anything because he never learned to read or write. From that point of view you and I are doomed; you could say that literacy has been our downfall.

March 18.
There's light in the sky, not the sun yet, but secondhand light is good enough for me at my age, fifty-two. You ask for excerpts from my journal. My memories would be like instant coffee: brief and dark and with the inevitable physiological results. I came to Greenland twenty years ago. I'd long since finished my studies in archeology. I was tired of reading about Eskimo artifacts. I wanted to see some. There was an opening at the museum here so I took the job. This was the house built by Peter Freuchen and Knud Rasmussen when they lived at Thule, so I thought I'd get good inspiration here.

It's a tough event to find yourself in middle age a complete stranger in an Eskimo village. But of course I had worked in other such places before—in Africa. I knew all along that I should be keeping a journal, but writing is too slow; talking is my trade. I prefer to be freewheeling in speech rather than on paper. The odd brainspin gets lost as soon as I try to capture it. Like love.

Eventually I married a Greenlandic woman. She was very clever—smart and capable. She and her brother and I made many expeditions to the far north coast—Washington Land where we found some old house sites of the Thule people. But something went wrong. I was standing by the kitchen window one morning and saw her coming out of a house with someone else. There's no way to describe what that felt like. I'm somewhat of a failure in this area. I'd been married to a schoolteacher in the Faroe Islands and had two children with her, and there was another wife, much earlier in Denmark. So you see, it's better that I just stay here.

Meanwhile, I've been married to the honey bucket all day. You are kind to ask what you might send me from the U.S. A tape of Dylan or Jackson Browne would get me through to spring.

You asked about Rasmussen. He was a spellbinder and a troubled man. Always a stranger, having grown up in two worlds. He was religious, always looking for the lost world of the angakok.

Evening.

I invite you to come and spend some weeks with me before your trip to Humboldt Glacier with Jens Danielsen. Could you alter your plans? Only by spending time together will we get to know how we get along. This appears to be as good a chance as they come. Unfortunately I do not have the time to travel north with you later in the month, as I will be busy with tourists exactly those weeks. But if you decide to spend a number of weeks with me before going north we could make some trips around the vicinity, granted my dogs survive in sufficient number. Only last night did I need to shoot the last of my seven beautiful six-month-old puppies. They all came down with distemper. We have not received the result of the analysis from Denmark. But the one made in Greenland did not show the otherwise-expected Parvo virus. Therefore I think it must be distemper. Could turn out to be some other disease. Anyway, the dogs are dying. But do come to my house—okay?—and we will see what may be done about it.

P.S. You will need to get permission to transit through Thule Air Base, so I've written to the Danish Foreign Office to tell them of our plans. Because it is the off-season, you may not come as a tourist but shall be an ethnographer helping me. You must write them as well, by fax immediately.

March 30.

I've been undercover all day. That is, in bed with a sore throat and sinus pain, but feeling rather better since I've been able to read in peace all day—Shackleton's Arctic expedition. Base at Etah, expeditions across Smith Sound, Kane Basin to Ellesmere Island. No news from the Danish Foreign Office. I shall call them. But this leaves you missing your scheduled flight and so we must book another.

Later. I've just contacted Gronlandsfly and the rebooking would cost an extra $2,000, which makes it $4,000 round-trip. That's more than I have to spare right now and I'm sure it's the same for you, after so many trips here when it has been so expensive. I understand your disappointment. Have no sorrow. Regardless, I still plan to call the Foreign Office in the morning to see about your permission. Could it be that when you got into trouble there the last time that they have your name down? I hope not.

March 31.

What a deplorable state that again they denied you permission to transit through TAB [Thule Air Base]. It makes no sense at all. You say you are frustrated. Momentarily for me too. About missing you—I can't figure this one out either—

*geography, distances—Well, it seems we can make continents
shrink in a fax machine, and that's all we have for now, and
now is all we have.*

Love, Torben

Days later a fax came, not from Torben but from Hans Jensen at the
hotel. He confirmed Torben's suspicion that distemper had broken out
among the dogs in Qaanaaq and Siorapaluk. The hunters had put their
trip to Humboldt Glacier on hold until they knew how widely the disease was going to spread. It's a long trip—a hundred miles north of Siorapaluk, it would take a month to get there and a month to get back.
Jens Danielsen, Ikuo Oshima, and Mikele Kristiansen were set to go and
others would undoubtedly come. The glacier comes right to the edge of
the ocean at Kane Basin. Its massive face is seventy-five miles across.
Then two dismal notes arrived from Torben:

April.
*Everything up here is ridiculously bad, in case you haven't
heard. The dogcatcher is drunk. He was supposed to vaccinate
the dogs for distemper and give out the serum to hunters but he
forgot. Now distemper is spreading though the villages and
there's no way to stop it. Jens doesn't think he can take you. In
fact, nobody will be going to Humboldt Glacier now. It takes a
month just to get there and even if the dogs were well enough
to make the trip up the coast, they might get sick and not be
able to get back and you would all surely die.*

April 6.
*Twenty dogs died last night in Qaanaaq and eighteen in
Siorapaluk. I have eleven now. Then I watched two more of my
puppies die. I have only four dogs left. Jens has lost half his
team and so has Mikele. The dogs were dying last week and this
week and they'll keep dying. Soon, we won't have any left and
no way to go hunting. A hundred years ago this would have
meant sure starvation for all of us. But now, we can get fat on
Danish cheese and cookies which the helicopter has just
brought while our dogs perish and spring hunting season goes
by and we sit immobilized.*

Aliberti's Ride, 1998

I did what I always do when things go wrong in the Arctic: I called my old friends Ann and Olejorgen in Uummannaq to see if they had any spring trips planned. Their dogs were too far south to be in danger of contamination. They had already heard about my trip being canceled. "So, you must come with us!" Ann said. "Take the Wednesday helicopter. We are going visiting around the District with some of the children and three hunters from Ikerasak. There will be six sleds. We have an extra sled for you."

Ice pulled back like a sheet to reveal the crumpled body of Davis Strait, the unsteady southward journey of turreted icebergs, and on the south Greenland coast the lonely wake of a single kayak moving behind a whale. In front of the Nuussuaq Peninsula an iceberg had come apart, its white splinters floating like a scattered picket fence. They speared the front of a motionless floe, crossing its meltwater moat. The turquoise of this moat was a blue so still and clear that it carried a reflection of the coastline like a necklace, deforming it to fit round the icy neck, then drowning it every time the wind blew.

Over the mountains the shuddering helicopter fanned the half-frozen water of a lake and slid down a brown canyon so narrow it caused intimate acts to erupt: the couple in front of me began caressing

one another's faces. The fjord opened before us and the island of Ikerasak appeared. Three sled tracks started out from its one village. They were the hunters who were part of our "sled-about" party, with whom I would travel. We followed their tracks to Uummannaq.

No one met me at the heliport, and once again Arne Fleischer offered to give me a ride. He told me that Aleqa was in town with a new boyfriend, a Danish doctor who had come to Uummannaq to work for six months.

Ann and Olejorgen's house was in chaos, filled with children. There were mounds of winter clothing on the floor: mittens, boots, polar bear pants, anoraks, hats, half-filled dufflebags, sleeping bags, caribou skins, and food boxes. Ann carried a screaming child, Pipaluk, on her hip.

Time slid. At two in the morning the children were finally asleep upstairs, but we were just finishing dinner. When Olejorgen insisted that we get an early start, everyone laughed. "Eskimo days have more hours in them," he explained laconically, then trudged upstairs to bed.

Despite five years out on the ice learning to hunt, Olejorgen still looked like a scholar, with his long, graceful fingers and slightly stooped shoulders, bent from reading books. He could talk about paleo-Eskimo Saqqaq and Dorset sites, about Rasmussen's expeditions, about Tunit Inland ice dwellers and angakoks' flights under water to visit the goddess of the sea, but he had never yet harpooned a narwhal or a walrus, and had shot only a few seals. Nevertheless, he was leaner this year, his skin darkened from months in the sun, and he sported a hunter's sparse mustache. Out on the ice, harnessing dogs, his pace was measured and slow and his gaze wandered. Still a dreamer? I asked Ann. She smiled.

We went to bed at three. I felt at home in this house, where I had visited so often, and slept on the couch by an open window. The middle of the night was my favorite time in Uummannaq. The town was quiet and only the dogs and a few insomniacs were awake. The evening light in April at 71 degrees north latitude is a pale, reddish glow. The sun had barely set; for two hours it shimmered under the western horizon, then rose again. A lone hunter went outside to check his dogs. He was tying up a young dog for the first time—puppies are left to run loose until they are about ten months old. No longer free, the dog sat, head down, back hunched up like a Halloween cat, eyes half-closed. For the rest of the night he moaned softly, dejectedly. I fingered my knife—I wanted to cut him loose—but it would do no good. Like him, we have all been subdued.

The shit truck's chained snow tires awakened me. It had taken only a day for all of us to fill up the toilet. The door opened. Two young men slipped in, emptied the bucket, returned it, then disappeared down the narrow street. It was a good job because it paid well and they were finished with their work early, so they could go out hunting in the evening. I thought of the Buddhist monks who asked for the job of cleaning toilets in cities to help "ground" them, bind them to what is actual during a long course of otherworldly practices. But how much grounding does a subsistence hunter need?

The household woke slowly. We dressed for frigid weather and carted loads down the steep hill to the ice where the dogs were staked out—food, sleeping bags, fuel, stoves, warm clothes, presents for friends. Our route would take us from Uummannaq to Ukkusissat, to Illorsuit, north to Nuugaatsiaq, back to Illorsuit, then to Niaqornat, Qaarsut, and home.

The ice at the base of the town was a Coney Island of hunters, sleds, children, and six thousand dogs all yipping, howling, barking, screeching, and yapping. Children played tag between sleds while hunters harnessed their teams. One team was being fed frozen halibut. They yelped and yapped as the chunks were tossed into their mouths while the other teams looked on silently, knowing there would be no food for them. After a long winter, the dogs had spring fever: females in heat ranged freely among chained-up males, causing yowls of sexual union and longing. Everywhere I looked, dogs were fucking, getting stuck together, crouching, sitting, biting, and yapping. One male grabbed the trace line of the female he wanted, jerked it tight, then jumped on her from the rear. A dog that had been left behind sat up on his hind legs, a lone figure pawing at a world of ice and air.

Our party consisted of sixty-six dogs, six children, and seven adults. Aliberti was the hunter with whom I would travel, as his only passenger. It was his sled and those of two other hunters—Jacob and Unatoq, or "Mr. Warm"—that we had seen coming the night before from Ikerasak. The other adults were Ann, Olejorgen, and an Inuit woman from the Children's House, Louisa.

At fifty-eight, Aliberti's face was weathered, making him look older than his years. He had the small, tight build typical of Inuit hunters and moved like a cat. A cigarette dangled from his mouth. When I laid my duffle and sleeping bag on the sled, he smiled, and the cigarette stuck to his lower lip. He was nearly toothless—just a few black stubs. Standing face to face we could look straight into each other's eyes. He slipped my parka and duffle under caribou skins and lashed them tight.

Seven cigarettes were stubbed out on the ice; we had been waiting. Olejorgen's dogs were tangled and fighting. One female got loose and ran away through the midst of six thousand other dogs chained up on the ice or being harnessed, and a collective howl rose, echoing. The young sled drivers—Ludwig and Aliberti's son—were having troubles too: their trace lines had broken and two more dogs got loose and ran off with another team.

Aliberti looked on coolly. It is not the Inuit way to give help unless there is real danger, otherwise no lessons will be learned. He tightened the lash ropes on our sled again, blew his nose, secured his mittens under the lines—until finally he couldn't stand it anymore. Shaking his head, he hooked the trace lines to the sled. The dogs lurched forward and with one flying leap we landed side by side on the sled. He looked back at the chaos behind us and laughed. It would be some time before the others could follow.

I thought of a story told to Rasmussen by Inaluk in 1902: "There was once an orphan boy who drifted out to sea on an ice-floe, and arrived among strange people. They took him into their service at once and used him for all their menial work. But he had a brother who was a great magician and who, when the little boy did not come back, began to look for him in soul-flights. . . ."

Now, almost one hundred years later, Aliberti had his own story.

Three days before Christmas in 1959, Aliberti, then nineteen, went out to get a seal. He lived on the island of Ikerasak. A warm wind, a foehn, blew and the fjord ice began to break up. Before he knew what was happening, Aliberti was adrift with his dogs on an icy slab. He had no food, no stove to melt ice for water, no extra clothes, just his rifle—he hadn't been planning to stay out very long.

Aliberti's ride lasted five days. At night the temperature was 20 below zero. He drifted past the village of Uummannaq, then north up the coast past Niaqornat. He had gotten wet trying to jump to shore and his clothes froze stiff. There was no way to get dry or warm. It was December and completely dark, with no light at all in the sky. That week there wasn't even a moon. Up the coast he went, pushed by currents and pulled by tides. No one saw him drifting.

His parents waited. By Christmas Day he was presumed dead. Perhaps he had slipped under the ice, as so many had done before. His obituary was read on the radio. But he was alive and still drifting. "I remember seeing the candles in people's houses at the villages. Christmas came and went. I could hear singing. No one could see me. I didn't think I would live."

The currents took him north into the Illorsuit Strait along the east coast of Ubekendt Ejland—Unknown Island. He had already drifted seventy miles. "Things got worse. When it's that cold and you have no food or water, *sila* becomes stronger than you are. My dogs died one by one and I pushed them over into the water. I just lay on my sled and waited. On the fourth day I noticed that the ice floe had gotten smaller. Then it split in half and I had to jump from the bad part to what was left of the floe. The ice didn't look like it would hold. I wondered what my family was thinking. They couldn't come look for me because there was too much ice to go out in a boat and not enough to travel by dogsled. My clothes were wet on the inside and frozen on the outside. You get pretty cold. On the fifth day something woke me. I had been drifting in my mind too, but I heard the ice bump against something. I looked up: I had come to a stop a hundred yards from the village of Illorsuit.

"For a moment I thought a miracle had happened. I could see people in their houses with candles burning. They would see me and rescue me and I would live after all. I lamented the fact that all but one of my dogs had died. I allowed myself to think about eating and drinking. I lifted up on one arm and yelled and waved. But no one came. Another day passed. I was telling time by the rising and setting of the moon.

Sometimes I called out with what strength I had left, but the wind was blowing the wrong way. My last dog died.

"A villager came outside to pee and he saw me. He yelled out and I lifted an arm. Then he went back inside his house. He was gone a long time. I gave up hope. I think I fell asleep. The sound of voices jarred me awake. I didn't know if they were human. The man I'd seen on the beach and another hunter were making their way toward me in a skiff, pushing big pieces of ice aside with an oar. When they got close they looked like giants. I wasn't right in the head by then. They took me to shore.

"The hunters thought I was a ghost because my death had already been announced on the radio. My hair was coming out in handfuls and my teeth were loose. When they carried me ashore, people ran the other direction.

"The hunter took me to his parents' house. There I was fed and kept warm. They got through to my parents on the two-way radio and told them that I was alive but my mother didn't believe it. After a few days, the weather improved and the hunters took me home to Ikerasak. And as you can see, I am still alive."

Bright sun, clear skies, a slight breeze, the temperature about zero. The ice was smooth and fast. With our light load, the sled fishtailed and the dogs' panting became the only sound we heard as we slid from the noise of town. The smoke from Aliberti's cigarette snaked back across his cheek as we glided forward. He turned and smiled. There was no need to talk. To be alive and on a dogsled in Greenland was enough and I was happy.

Far out in the middle of the fjord, the dogs slowed to a trot. My whole body worked like an eye, watching the world scroll under and over us. Aliberti and the five others headed straight north, gliding between the uninhabited islands of Abut and Saleq, then veered northwest toward the village of Ukkusissat on the thumb's tip of land that extended from under the ice cap.

Cool, alert, and relaxed, Aliberti sat sideways at the front of the sled with his legs sticking out straight. Seagulls and eider ducks flew overhead in flocks—a sign of spring. From shoreline—ice line—everything looked mathematical. We glided through its permutations. If water is time's shapeless infinity, then ice is time's body, inhabited by light and shadow, tormented by sun and cold.

A row of stranded icebergs was a giant slalom course leading out to sea. We glided by, staring at their outsize beauty. Icebergs are lessons in geometry: they give and take light at will, changing a shined, chrome side into a dull fastness, then back to a sizzling angle of vitality, with a fine, thin, razor-sharp ridge cutting winter out of the sky.

Jacob and Unatoq came up behind us on their two sleds, carrying Ann on one and Louisa and a boy from the Children's House on the other. Finally the others—Olejorgen, Ludwig, and Aliberti's son—caught up. Ann zinged by, whooping, then Louisa and the boy. They shouted something in Greenlandic I couldn't understand. The teenage girls rode with the teenage boys and they were always last. This was an Eskimo–Danish–Faroe Islander–American laughing, gossiping sled party heading north. First stop, Ukkusissat, where we would celebrate the birthday of a friend.

Between Uummannaq and the mainland the ice was rough. We bumped over small waves, their topsy-turvydom frozen in place, then stopped and waited again for the others. Olejorgen pulled up beside us and whistled his dogs to a stop. With his movie-star looks, he resembled an Eskimo pasha reclining on a bearskin rug and wearing polar bear pants. His hair had grown long and he wore dark glasses. I imagined a remake of *Doctor Zhivago,* set in Greenland rather than Russia. As he tried to settle the dogs, he promptly ran over one of them. The animal screamed in pain. We lifted the sled up and Olejorgen held the injured animal. He wasn't sure what to do next, so Aliberti told him to carry the dog on the front of the sled until we got to the village. The others showed up and we continued on.

Seagulls flew over: there must be open water somewhere. A slow-moving sled pulled by five skinny dogs passed us going the other way. The hunter looked comatose, lying flat on his back and gazing skyward, his dogs wandering. When we stopped for lunch, Jacob said that during his monthlong sled trip to Qaanaaq the previous spring he had developed stomach pains. He stopped in Upernavik and the next day he was operated on there. While the others continued north, he rested. When they returned three weeks later, Jacob drove his own dogsled home.

On the way, Jacob was lucky and got a polar bear—he was in need of new pants for the next winter. "Not only did he get an ice bear," Olejorgen exclaimed, "the bear fell over dead on Jacob's sled, almost killing him!" Laughter.

Jacob quipped: "We call this story 'How I almost died twice in one springtime hunting trip.' "

Rounding a bend, we saw a long arm of rock pushing out into the fjord. On its tip was Ukkusissat. As we approached, litter blew across multiple sled tracks—beer bottles and plastic bags. Ann insisted on stopping and picking up every piece, indignant for her beloved (though not native) Greenland. "We must not be so dirty," she exclaimed to no one in particular. The hunters smiled. Her garrulousness amused them, but she also held their respect for the fine job she did with the children.

Ukkusissat consisted of a few small houses set in stepping-stone fashion up a hill. Behind the last building a towering wall of basalt lay crumbled in ruin, as if an older village had once been sited there. Birthe ran down the hill to greet us. Fine-boned, strong-willed, and skittish as a colt, she was joyous at having company. She was the only Dane in this village of one hundred people and she drove her own dogsled. "I just barely know how to do it," she said apologetically. "But it's transportation between here and my friends in Uummannaq." After the dogs were unharnessed and fed and the duffles and sleeping bags had been unloaded, we sat on the empty sleds and basked in the evening sun.

An old man came to inspect the injured dog, who had been laid on the snow. The dog's back was broken. The man told Olejorgen: "After you have gone, I will shoot him for you."

The birthday celebration began at Birthe's house that evening. We cooked seal ribs, potatoes, and onions, and drank warm Tuborg beer. How quickly and effortlessly food for twelve was prepared. At midnight the sun hovered, then began to slide behind the mountains into the northern part of the sky. One by one the others went to bed. Ann and Olejorgen appropriated Birthe's bed, so she and I stayed up late, talking.

There was no night, no darkness. I trudged down to the ice. Aliberti had pitched a canvas tent over his sled, blue canvas at one end to keep the sunlight out. Inside, a Primus stove was lit to keep him warm. I unrolled my sleeping bag next to his on the sled and slept. At three in the morning gold and purple stripes of light lay across the ice. The sounds from the village subsided, but the dogs, staked out everywhere in a vast slumber party, talked for the rest of the night.

When we woke there was no sun and the dog whose back was broken was still alive. He lay unattended in the snow covered with rime frost. A fog had come in and sealed itself to the ice. The dogs sat hunched and waiting. As the fog lifted, an eerie yellow light shone through.

I helped Birthe move her dogs from behind her house to the ice. She had decided to accompany us to the next village. One by one they pulled us downhill—that's all they know how to do. After, we carried the toilet bucket from her house and poured the contents into a pipe that emptied into the fjord. City living, she said with a grin, because on hunting trips any piece of rough ice served as a bathroom.

Aliberti broke camp, harnessed the dogs, and loaded the sled. The flying *S* of his whip snapped: we were on our way to Illorsuit, the village where he was saved after drifting for five days, where Rockwell Kent lived with Salamina, where I spent a summer with Marie Louisa. Again we took off before the others were ready. All was lost behind us in fog. We drove in a white shroud, a white darkness, continually breaking through a crust of ice that had melted and refrozen.

"*Sumiippa?*" I asked. Where are we? Aliberti smiled but said nothing. We were dressed in skins: sealskin pants, sealskin anoraks with fox-fur ruffs around the hood, sealskin kamiks, and sealskin mittens with dog-hair ruffs at the wrist. His whip straightened out above the dogs' heads like a thought coming apart. Sun shone behind mist; now we traveled in a brightening cloud. "*Uatsi,*" I said. Please wait. I got off the sled to pee. When I looked down, I found that I'd unexpectedly gotten my period.

In the Arctic there is no privacy: Aliberti walked over, looked at the blood on the ice, and laughed. "This is good! It looks like we killed a seal! They will think I am a very good hunter to find a seal in this fog. And also, they will be able to find us."

Soon Jacob, Louisa, and the little boy pulled up and together we waited for the others. Hot tea and a bag of frozen shrimp were passed around. The boy started a game of tag. He was short for his age, as though stunted, and had come to the Children's House from a family where sexual abuse was epidemic. He ran around the circle of adults, then tagged me so hard that I fell, stood, and fell again. We were five people slipping and sliding, playing tag 700 miles from the North Pole in the middle of a frozen ocean with no land in sight. When Louisa was tagged and turned to tag the boy, he vanished into thick mist.

Another hour went by. The horizon's seamless wall of white frayed. I sat on the edge of the sled as if it were the edge of the world, with my hands over my eyes, trying to locate myself; my body was still, but my eyes tumbled around; my head was a goblet of ice. Is ice a form of indifference or is its intent to obscure? How absurd we must have seemed to the marine mammals swimming below, to the walrus with its colossal appetite and backward stroke, feasting orgiastically on shellfish, and the narwhal with its mysterious white tusk needling the ocean floor for food.

Aliberti dozed on the sled. We were not really lost, just living under the thumb of weather and it was pressing down on us hard. Good time to sleep, he said. But I kept trying to see. My eyes wandered . . . I was looking at a world that had overflowed its outlines, where everything had grown into invisibility.

Finally the others came. Birthe's dogs had gotten loose in the village and she had to start the harnessing process all over again. By tacit agreement, Aliberti took the lead once again. He was still honored in Ikerasak for having survived his five-day ordeal on the drift ice. "*Meeeeuuww, meeeeuuuw,*" he called out, and we took off, seven sleds abreast amid dogfights, tangled trace lines, and laughter. Then the dog-pant, dogtrot rhythm began again.

We drove through a flock of thousands of Arctic gulls. One bird's foot had frozen to the ice. As we approached it struggled to escape. The other gulls, seeing an easy meal, attacked and killed him. Aliberti watched impassively as we slid by, then turned to see if I'd seen. My eyes went from the cannibalized bird to him. He flashed a look that said, yes, it's tough up here. To the north, icebergs sprouted clouds, then fog closed in again, more tightly than ever, hiding my trail of blood.

Mist constricted and freed us simultaneously. Our slip-and-slide dealings with our psyches were never more evident: we long for solitude, but as soon as we have it, we are desperate for friends. I contemplated the shape of Aliberti's head, wondering what a PET scan might reveal about his ability to draw perfect maps of this coast from memory. Plato thought that vision was "a stream of fire or light that issues from the observing eye and coalesces with sunlight." But there was no sun and a hard, glasslike crust slowed down the dogs.

Gliding blind, I lost my bearings, wondering what life must be like for my mother, who was going blind. "The worst part of it is not being able to drive," she told me. Olejorgen's sled passed us, then fell back. I blinked: a rock wall shot up in front of us spangled with ice crystals and new snow. "*Takurngaqtuq!*" I yelled. "I feel as if I'm seeing [something icy] for the first time."

Aliberti turned and smiled. "It is called Apaat . . . this rock."

The way to Illorsuit was silvered, the top sift of snow blowing across our path as if swept by a giant broom. We cut through long-tailed drifts that pointed north like arrows toward the open end of the fjord, which gave onto an entire ocean paved with ice. Where snow had blown off stranded icebergs, exposed walls had been fired by sun and refrozen into glass—all glint and glaze and broken crust like crème brûlée. The snowed-on, fog-sealed ice in front of the sled revealed only the toes of things—icebergs whose drift toward the sea had been postponed by winter.

A headland loomed topped with crosses: Illorsuit's cemetery, which doubled as the heliport. Around a bend the village appeared, the same ramshackle houses lying in the arc of a half-moon bay. Seeing and smelling other dogs excited our dogs. Our seven sleds raced each other to the edge of the village. I took a deep seat and hung on to the lash ropes: we flew through the uneven middle of a decapitated iceberg and lurched down onto flat ice. Aliberti was in the lead, but at the last moment, when we had to go around a piece of rough ice, he was beaten by Mr. Warm.

I saw a young girl weaving between sleds and dogs lying in soft snow, noses tucked under tails, others yowling while being fed, and children pulling handmade toys on a string. She walked toward me, then sat on a sled nearby and waited. *Kina una?* I asked tentatively. Who are you? She smiled. I was still puzzled. *Kina una?* I asked again. Then I knew it was Marie Louisa.

She had grown. Her black hair hung down in a long braid, her cheeks had fattened, and she was four inches taller than she had been two years ago. Then someone grabbed me from behind and spun me around: Hans. We all laughed and hugged. He was grayer and thinner and immediately launched into a litany of grievances about village politics: "Last week they passed a bill allowing snow scooters in this district. Nothing will be the same. Now they say we need a truck in the village. All these hundreds of years we've walked and used a wheelbarrow and in winter a sled to transport our supplies. Now we will have to worry about our children and dogs getting run over."

"Where is your sled?" I asked as he loaded my duffle onto the back of the town's one snowmobile.

He gave a disgruntled shrug. "Last week they began selling Coca-

Cola in Greenland. The helicopter brought it and it was sold out within half an hour." He told me to get on the snow scooter.

"This is against my religion," I said.

He laughed ruefully. "Yes. Those are my feelings too."

"*Takuus!*" I yelled to Aliberti as we sped off. See you soon. The others dispersed: Ann and Olejorgen went to the schoolteacher's house, the children and Louisa to the clinic (used for extra housing for visitors), the hunters to the house of the family who had saved Aliberti's life forty years ago.

Hans's house had not changed. The walls were pale blue and yellow, the rug was red, the clock still gave the time as noon, and the photographs from his hippie days in Christiana were still on the wall. Snow sifted through the broken skylight and left a perfect white pyramid on the floor. Because there was no word in Greenlandic for pyramid, we referred to the invading snow as "the igloo of Egyptians." The living room was still empty except for the foam pad—my bed—on the floor. "I haven't moved it since you left two years ago," Hans said.

Only one thing had changed: Arnnannguaq was not there. "I told her she was not to come to the house when she was drinking," Hans said. What had been a minor problem had escalated. Now she was drinking all the time. Hendrik and Marie Louisa burst in the door and jumped on the pad, burrowing under the covers. We hugged and wrestled and spoke our usual jumble of Greenlandic and English which only we understood.

In the middle of the night I found myself at the small window where I had kneeled sleepless so many times before. The view across the fjord was marked indelibly on my mind: the rock-faced mountain with two glaciers spilling out on either side like grand stairways, and the gleaming fortress of the ice cap looming above. Dogs howled, the diesel generator chugged, and the weather worsened. Blue sky fused with white, its porcelain fracturing into frostfall.

The children woke and joined me in the living room. We watched the sun droop in the west and bounce back up to circle the northern sky. Despite the sun, the living room started to feel frosty. We looked: the heater was off and the thermometer had dropped to 16 below. The children huddled under my sleeping bag until Hans fixed the heater again.

Much later Marie Louisa awoke and was upset. "*Anaana, Anaana!*" Mother, Mother, she cried out, nuzzling my breasts like a baby. But she was eight years old. I held her tight. Things had not been good for her here.

We slept huddled together during the two hours of twilight in the middle of the night. As soon as the sky lightened again, it began to snow. Marie Louisa looked up and asked if the world was really round. I said yes, but realized that I was only repeating received information, that I hadn't actually laid my hands on the rounded fender of this planet. I asked how she thought the world was made and she said, "Big flat pieces of ice pushed together." She still didn't understand how we stayed attached to a sphere. I said, "Gravity—a kind of glue."

In the morning Hans played "Mr. Tambourine Man" while I made pancakes for the children. Marie Louisa played the electric piano that Hans had given her for Christmas and tried to keep up with the song. Later, when the children went off to play, Hans told me his troubles with A.: "She is drunk most of the time now; she doesn't give love when the children need it, only when she wants it. This is no good. But what can I do? Where can I go? I'm fifty years old with an unfinished education and it's too late for me to go home to Denmark and get a job. I didn't think about these things when I was young. Now the children need more education, which means I have to go somewhere else. The law isn't in my favor because we are not married, the law will want to give her the children. But I have been feeding and dressing and taking the children to school every day for years. But how can I prove that to the Greenlandic social worker in Uummannaq? Who will believe me?"

When Aliberti, Olejorgen, Ann, Jacob, Louisa, Unatoq, and the children packed up the sleds and continued north to the village of Nuugaatsiaq, I stayed behind to help Hans. A foot of new snow fell during the week, then another. Arnnannguaq came home, sober. I helped her get water. Two years earlier we had collected water from a spring behind their house. Now water was fetched from a huge red tank on the hill. "Progress," Hans said.

The Arctic geometries began to soften. Sky and ice turned powder blue and the glaciers on the far side of the fjord bent up into a white nothingness. All afternoon the north-facing village rested in shadow, but at night it was bathed in bright sun. Kristian Moller, who had brought me to Illorsuit on his boat two summers before, stood on the beach and looked at his dogs while Marie Louisa and I played catch on the ice with a pink ball. Later, I watched her pounding up and down the hill behind the village on short red skis. I told Hans that I would take her to live with me and go to school if he found he couldn't leave the village. She trusted me and I loved her and I would bring her home to him for the summers. He agreed. The next night she slept curled up against me. Her face shone in the midnight sun. A tremendous wind howled.

We climbed the steep mountain behind the village, kicking footholds in ice and snow. Near the top we stopped to rest. From above I could see that the way was swept clean. The grooves the glacier had made on the rock were free of snow. Across the fjord two glaciers flanked an immense rock wall, their gashed roofs carrying debris like dark hats to the sea. Above the crumbling snout and the stretched *seracs,* the castellated masses of the glacier, the ice mound was aswirl in blowing snow.

We descended, following a track made by a rolling stone that led us under the thin spray of a frozen waterfall where, in summer, we had bathed daily, then came down to the shadowed crescent where the houses were. The beach was all gravel laced with ice. The lines made fast to skiffs went slack and taut, slapping the open water and leaving marks that looked like arrows pointing toward another season.

Our heels had pushed down through snow, then scree. We jumped over the boggy grass around a spring and landed on the beach where chunks of ice caught on pebbles. In the summer, Marie Louisa liked to take off her clothes and swim in the frigid Arctic water. Now it was a white floor on which she danced, tossing the pink ball, then skate-skied as fast as she could away from where I was standing.

The fjord is six miles wide but looked narrower. The brown wall we had descended was a soft amphitheater into which the sounds of collapsing icebergs would soon be gathered. Behind us the village lay in shadow. Out on the ice Marie Louisa grew smaller and smaller. Come back to me, I wanted to yell, but did not. I suddenly sensed how forbidding solitude could be here, how effortlessly death could occur—just a slip through the ice. Then I did yell, and Marie Louisa turned laughing, then went farther until she was no bigger than an ant. Finally she skied toward me.

The next day Olejorgen, Ann, and the Uummannaq bunch returned in snow that was so deep, it came up to the middle of the dogs' chests. They could barely move; the hunters had to walk in front to break trail.

While they rested for a few days, the wind began to blow. Snow stuck to brown rock behind the long string of houses. The light shifted and the sky came apart as frostfall, glitter from the Land of Day.

The last night the children climbed into my sleeping bag with me—a slumber party, I said—but they didn't understand. Framed in the window was a pyramid-shaped iceberg. An eerie twilight filled the room. Toward morning, a ring circled the sun, which meant bad weather.

The sleds were packed. As Aliberti took off in the lead, Marie Louisa ran after us calling "*Anaana.*" The sky cleared and it was deeply cold. We pulled our sealskin anoraks on. From the numbness beginning in my feet, I knew it must be zero.

On our seven-sled procession out of Illorsuit, sharp bits of ice flew in our faces. We bowed our heads in the face of Sila as the dogs' fur grew thick with snow. "Sometimes spring feels colder than winter," Aliberti said, pulling his hood up tight around his face. We were dressed head-to-toe in sealskin pants and anoraks with fox-fur ruffs. "We eat the inside and wear the outside," Olejorgen said, passing us as we left the village. Marie Louisa stood in the ice storm watching. I wanted to take her with me right then, but she was still in school. Hans said he would call me in Uummannaq. I knelt backwards on the sled, waving until she was out of sight.

Where pieces of ice stuck up like gravestones, snow had drifted in long inverted V's and the wind broke these apart into scudding curds that slid on ice. The rest of the ice was clear. Beneath us a tormented ocean heaved, while continually pushing up against the lid of ice, the topside was smooth and mirrorlike, reflecting only calm. The poet Muso Soseki wrote "No clarity can flatten torment, no fragment can undo clarity. . . ."

Aliberti cracked the whip in a circular underhand motion and the dogs ran. A cloud bank grayed the horizon and sun lit the place where the fjord gave way to the whole of Baffin Bay. We veered southwest toward the village of Niaqornat. Wind howled out of the west and blew from distant headlands all the way across the frozen sea. When we passed behind an iceberg, we were shielded from wind, but the snow grew suddenly deeper where it had drifted, almost bringing the dogs to a standstill. Between stranded floes, the ice was blown clear. The dogs speeded up and the sled fishtailed on what looked like a thousand-mile-long mirror.

Halfway down the flank of Unknown Island, the weather worsened: a ground blizzard stirred. Bits of ice, like tiny continents, blasted our eyes. Aliberti motioned to me to lie down behind him on the sled. He laid his right hand on my hip and I draped my left arm over his shoulder. The sled tipped and bumped: we held each other on. Wind-driven ice tore at the dogs. Their feet and legs were bleeding and their muzzles were encrusted. The fog lifted but still we couldn't see. I looked down at my body and Aliberti's. Dressed like seals we slid over seals: thousands of pinnipeds, with only a thin sheaf of ice separating us. If they could see us, would they think we were seals?

Ice flew. We slid closer together and pulled our hoods down almost over our eyes. Once in a while I saw one of the other sleds in the distance, then it disappeared. Where the ice under us was smooth, we could almost doze. Then we hit a rough patch and had to hold on. Ice cut us; snow blinded us. So much in the Arctic attempts to obstruct vision: fog, snow, darkness, ice. But each element has its built-in clarity, an opaque shine. Another ancient theory of vision went like this: "An eye obviously has fire within, for when one is struck, this fire flashes out."

We bumped along lying close. Seen another way, we were fake seals, like decoys, trying to attract the seals under the ice, as we made gestures of intimacy, my feet in his hands, his back against my chest, my hand on his sealskin shoulder: seal love with no thought of possession. All I knew was that the seal body in front of me was blessedly blocking the wind.

We traveled for eight hours without talk, chastely intimate in a bond of blood, snow, and fur. Yet I knew that what I was seeing was transient: glaciers, human love, sea ice, dogs, humans, and my own perishable body and his—Aliberti's. Too often we confuse what is happening in the moment with notions of permanence. The intimacy would not last.

My feet hurt with the cold. Even on a simple trip such as this one, things could go wrong. Jorgen Brönlund, who had traveled with Rasmussen up this strait, wrote in his diary of the 1908 Denmark Expedition: "Perished on 79th Latitude North after attempt home—journey round the inland ice, in November I came here in a waning moon and could not continue because of frost-bitten feet and the darkness. Hagen died on 15 November and Mylius about 10 days later."

A few hours later we came to a hut. Two sleds from our party had reached it before us. Aliberti stopped the dogs. We stood up and looked at each other: we were both blasted white with snow. I stumbled when I walked: my feet were completely numb, but I said nothing since I hadn't brought an extra pair of kamiks. Inside, tea and coffee were being brewed. I passed around nuts, raisins, and figs from California. When Aliberti saw me wriggling my toes, he quietly removed my boots and socks and began massaging my toes.

Years ago in a Wyoming winter, two of my toes were frostbitten; a neighbor who had lived through seventy winters helped thaw them out. Now they were white and painful again. Aliberti held them between his knees while he drank coffee. Nothing was said. Then he signaled to one of the young boys and said something in Greenlandic. A moment later he was slipping a different pair of boots on my feet.

It was time to go. Aliberti motioned to me and I followed. We were two seals who had sprouted legs. Untangling the traces, he hooked the dogs in and the lines pulled tight. We flew off the lip of a cornice and slammed down onto the ice, hooked together on the sled. My feet were warm again as we clattered, bumped, tipped, and shuddered across the frozen sea toward the village of Niaqornat.

Sunday morning. Complacencies of the anorak and the doubletime contrapuntal panting of dogs. Nothing moved but my eyes. All beauty stayed behind only to give way to more—not the green freedom of the cockatoo, but the liberation of the diamondlike ice and Arctic sun that, after ten days of traveling, no longer went down, but only lingered at the eastern and western extremities of the sky, enticing us forward.

When the dogs' paws bled because they were trotting through glass, we stopped to put sealskin booties on their feet. A northwest wind poured across the fjord like cold water. Earlier, the Greenlandic radio played Marilyn Monroe singing "Diamonds Are a Girl's Best Friend." We drove over wind-drifted humps of ice blown free of snow, a rocky road paved with shining, beveled diamonds, then stopped to hack off a piece of young ice to be melted for drinking water. Its faceted interior was a blue wilderness. At its base, droplets of dog blood stained the snow.

Snowy polka dots dappled the sled track in front of us. They looked like eyes. Who was watching? Could Sila see? Fog was snow-flecked. Was it possible to draw eyeballs on chaos?

When the storm cleared two ravens flew in front of the sled, one on top of the other. Aliberti pointed at the double-decker birds and made a quick gesture to indicate "fucking." He laughed and his black teeth showed. A dog got tangled in the loose trace lines. Aliberti jumped off the moving sled, ran alongside, plunged into the middle of the dogs, snapped a line, tied a knot in another, jumped back out, and leaped back on.

We traveled close to the brown flank of Ubekendt Ejland. The island was brown, copper, and slate—all mudstones piled vertically and opening out at the bottom in fluted vaginas cut in half by ice. Ahead the way was silvered, the top sift of snow blowing across our path and sweeping it clean, then refilling it again.

Where Illorsuit Strait flooded into Baffin Bay, a sweep of ice filled my eye, stopped by the hammered silver at the horizon. We turned and headed into Uummannaq Fjord. I dozed until Aliberti shook me awake to show me an eider duck flying by. Then we lay on the sled as we had become accustomed to doing, hooked together: we were two seals moving over a world of seals with only a thin sliver of ice between us. I felt the weight of his hand on my thigh; my hand rested on his shoulder. Palisades of rock strobed by. We slipped across sea ice that had no end.

In Niaqornat, a village of one hundred subsistence hunters, we stayed in an empty house. Neighbors brought pots and pans and toilet paper. Private property is not something drilled deep into Greenlanders' psyches: whatever they have is used and passed around. Since there is no ownership of land, there is little sense of territoriality beyond what is practical.

My roommate was the teenage girl who had gone to the Children's House seeking sanctuary after being raped by her father. In her suicide attempt, she had misaimed and shot a hole through her cheek. The visiting Danish dentist and the local surgeon sewed her up at the Uummannaq clinic. Now she seemed content to flirt with Aliberti's fourteen-year-old son and write in her diary.

The village was U-shaped and faced inward, as if village life were not already intimate enough. Five or six hundred dogs—including ours—were staked out on the frozen bay in the middle. The houses were built close together, ten or twenty feet apart, and placed irregularly as if wind-pitched. The paths between were all mud, melted snow, discarded seal intestines, and dog shit. Sealskins and fox furs flapped on clotheslines and tall racks were covered with bloody slabs of walrus and seal flippers, with pieces of each cut into thin slices for jerky. Other racks had nothing but halibut flapping. Packing crates were used as shelters for sleds. Dogs lay in the dirt. Howling, screaming dogfights erupted; stacks of lumber were covered with billowing plastic tarps; skiffs, frozen in ice, were tilted every which way; red gas cans were tipped on their sides; and beyond was a white ground and a white sky.

As the wind blew and the temperature dropped, we gathered in the kitchen while Louisa started dinner. Ann, in a pink nightgown over white tights, played cards with the hunters, her huge breasts pressed like bumpers against the table. Olejorgen mended harness, Unatoq hung kamiks on a line to dry, and the kids came and went, borrowing money to buy candy at the store. Out the window I saw an elderly woman too elegantly dressed for this village: dangling silver earrings, an ivory bracelet, a black sealskin anorak. She was feeding hunks of fresh seal to her dogs. Then I recognized her: she was the woman I had met on the ferry coming north five years before.

The card game resumed in the kitchen after dinner. Louisa, Jacob, Mr. Warm, and Aliberti slapped cards down hard on the table. Everyone laughed except Jacob, who wasn't winning. Stories flew around the room: Aliberti told how his father-in-law died in a kayak that was attacked by a walrus. "He didn't have time to do anything. He just went down."

Maassannguaq, the twelve-year-old boy, sat on Louisa's lap, rubbing his eyes because he had been crying. Ann explained. "He watched his mother kill his father. His father had been abusing him sexually for years. There's so much black put into the white of a child's life, and so my job is to put as much white back in. There will always be a lot of gray, but we have to try."

We walked up to the cemetery on the headland overlooking the fjord. Aliberti's son smoked a cigarette and cracked his whip in the air. From there we could see the entire district. The butt end of Ubekendt Ejland was a dark mass shrouded in white. Our sled tracks led from it, the marks covered here and there by drifting snow. Evening sun stretched our shadows until they were enormously long. Village sounds rose to the top of cliff: dogs howling, children screeching. It was the one noisy point on the map of an area otherwise gripped by silence.

Late in the all-light night, the dogs started what became a five-hundred-dog howl that sometimes jarred me awake and at other times drove me into a deep sleep. Before anyone else got up in the morning,

Louisa washed the kitchen floor. Her long braid had unraveled and raven hair swung over her solid body. She sang quietly to herself as she polished the floor with rags tied to her feet, skating over linoleum as if it were ice.

When the dogs had rested, we packed up the sleds and headed for home.

It begins with ice and ends with ice. What looks like open water is ice cleared of snow, or else ice blink caused by the shadow of a cloud making frozen water look blue, or sky's reflection of open water turning clouds dark. Sun shone down like a flashlight illuminating a path through pressure ice, a way that had been cleared. Up on the ice cap, the *innerssuit* (beach spirits) and *inorsuit* (glacier spirits) cavorted, coming down to play with our minds. The glacier groaned, its castellated face splintered and calved out thousands of icebergs; the chunk of glacier ice we brought into the tent to melt for tea water exploded.

A wave of mist washed over us and as it receded, we found that we had turned into seals. The air glinted with frostfall. The Copper Eskimos treated cataracts by fastening a louse to a hair and letting it walk to and fro across the bad eye. Now circling sun augered light down like an arrow of time, pushing us across the great expanse because there was nowhere else to go.

Ice is time solidified. As we flew off a cornice at the edge of the bay and rattled away from Niaqornat, I tried to see back into time, to the old sleds made of whalebone and caribou antlers pieced together with sealskin and whaleskin thongs, the rolled skins frozen into the shape of runners. The houses were made of peat and stone with bone roofbeams. Long and narrow passageways led into them. Their sealgut windows and sputtering whale oil lamps lit the half-naked bodies of hunters and children inside. Sometimes a shaman was seated there, half hidden behind a hanging sealskin; as he slipped into trance, a loud noise woke the dead. He sloughed his body as if molting and swam down to the goddess of the sea to comb the lice from her hair, which then rose up slowly to become seals.

The sled rattled. We moved against time, which had stacked up into pressure ridges, then lay out flat again like a tongue with no words. Our going looked effortless but wasn't. We passed a man sitting on top of a tall iceberg with no dogsled in sight. Aliberti said he must have missed getting on the sled and the dogs ran home. We yelled something to him; he said that a helicopter was coming. "He should walk," Aliberti grumbled. We continued on.

The whip cracked. Clouds broke over the bay. We paralleled a copper-colored cliff. On the other side of the sled the glass stairways of a dozen glaciers descended the mountain. We lay on the sled and bumped across what Rasmussen liked to call *la mer de glace*.

"Look," Aliberti said, pointing upward. I looked. There was a ring around the sun, a lens zeroing in on us. What did it see? Seals or humans? Who were we?

We stopped to chip off bits of ice to melt for tea. It was like hacking at an eyeball. I held a small chunk up as if it were optical glass and scanned the horizon from Davis Strait all the way around to the ice cap. The chip bent what is straight into fractals and upended mountains into angular cubist plinths. Nothing was identifiable. We're lost! I told Aliberti. He laughed and I gulped back tears.

Yupik shamans in Alaska who were diagnosing illness or trying to determine if someone was going to die practiced *tangrruarluni,* which means, "pretend seeing." To do this they stared into a bowl of water or oil, or into the eye of an animal. I had no oil or water and no animal eyes. I was only a passenger on a dogsled moving fast.

Snow fell straight down and the temperature rose. Our bodies relaxed in the warmth and proximity to town. Now we were lounge lizards, fake seals enacting gestures of intimacy: my feet in his hands, his back against my legs, my hand on his furred shoulder. How odd that this camaraderie carried such deep meanings: sexual but not carnal, mutual but not proprietary.

When the other hunters caught up we slalomed between icebergs, stopping again to make tea. But the wind picked up so suddenly we decided to go. As Aliberti's sled pulled out, I missed getting on, and ran behind it in my two-sizes-too-big boots, much to the merriment of the hunters. Aliberti took pity and looped back around for me, clasping my forearm as he whizzed by: I jumped; I was on. Later, Aliberti said he had decided to have his teeth fixed. I said good idea, and wondered if it was this loop to Illorsuit where his life had been saved forty years ago that had prompted his decision.

On the last leg home the usual feeling of dread filled me. The red fin of Uummannaq Mountain wavered in evening sun. Where was the mist that had swallowed us earlier? Couldn't it take us now? Leave-taking and homecoming brought on feelings of apprehension as well as relief. I never knew which was stronger, whether to come or to go.

The sled rode sun-smoothed ice, then a blast of wind thumped us. Snow came like artillery, boring into our faces and the dogs'. When Aliberti turned to look at me, I wiggled my toes to show him that, despite the barrage, my feet were still warm. He smiled. Then we lay down one last time, my hand on his shoulder and his hand on my thigh, clutching each other tightly as we bounced and banged down again. These intimacies of the sled were partly due to the jarring obstacle course that was our path and partly to a tender habit inspired by traveling together in bitter cold—a closeness that we'd grown accustomed to and enjoyed, but would have to abandon as soon as we arrived home.

Palo's Wedding, 1998

Early evening. Coming to Uummannaq was like coming into a canine city. The dogs were all staked out on ice. I tried to count them but couldn't—perhaps two or three thousand, maybe more. Polyphonic howling greeted us plus the hustle and bustle of hunters and their wives packing sleds, sorting fish, flensing seals, harnessing dogs, and mending tracelines. Puppies, females in heat, and children roamed among the harnessed dogs. We pulled around to the back side of the island near the heliport, a long way away from the others who had traveled with us. Aliberti unhooked the dogs, a cigarette dangling from his lips. I returned the boots he had given me and pulled on my own kamiks. There were no good-byes. Only a smile. Then I shouldered my duffle and walked alone across the fjord, up the steep hill to the house.

Ann was already in the kitchen catching up on the news from a worker at the Children's House. Since we'd been gone a Russian priest had parachuted onto the North Pole and planted a cross there. Birthe made it home with her unruly dogs through deep drifts back to Ukkusissat. A photographer, Robert van der Hilst, from a French magazine was staying at the hotel, as well as a ragtag Roumanian rock band—the only gig in the world they could find was to tour Greenland.

I walked to the grocery store to buy food for dinner. While perusing a two-week-old Danish newspaper, I discovered to my dismay that the glorious Mexican poet Octavio Paz was dead. *"El corazón es un ojo,"* he wrote. The heart is an eye.

At the end of the checkout line I saw a familiar face. It was Lars Emil, the former prime minister. He recognized me from the year before and smiled. He'd given up running the country, and was now involved in international business. He still wore a black T-shirt and black jeans; his blue eyes were piercing. He began to say hello but his assistant ran up just then, whispered in his ear, and the two men disappeared out the door.

Back at the house Aleqa came by. She was living in Uummannaq again for a few months with a new boyfriend, a Danish doctor who was doing a rotation there. Arne Fleischer (her former boyfriend) called and said they were unloading fresh potatoes from the helicopter if we wanted some. Olejorgen and I ran down, bought a sack, brought them home, and cooked a potful. Everyone joined in with a fork. We couldn't stop eating. I took a nap and dreamed that four polar bears were chasing me. I ran from them with no boots on.

Outside snow fell softly in gauzy light. The ice had gone gray and someone rode his bicycle out on it, going nowhere. Ikerasak's rock *usuk* (penis) stuck up in the distance, snow-swirled. A raven flew by carrying someone's sandwich in its beak. Simon came in from being on call at the clinic and gave an update: a fight had erupted at the hotel bar and a woman was bitten in the face by a man; a child with a high fever was brought in with convulsions; a girl who was raped crawled into the clinic on all fours.

On hearing all this, Aleqa opened the window and breathed in and out: "It is so beautiful here but there is so much hell inside these villages." Then she spotted Lars Emil on the street. "Come up for tea," she yelled down to him. He smiled. "I will, I will, but just now I must go to a meeting."

Later we watched *Palo's Wedding*, the 1936 dramatic film made by Knud Rasmussen in East Greenland. It is a reenactment of an old Greenland story: the love of two men for one woman. She lived in a sealskin tent with her two brothers in a summer camp on the rocky coast. She flensed the seals they had harpooned from kayaks, dried their wet clothes over a blubber lamp, listened to their hunting stories, cooked for them. Palo and Samo were young men in love with her. When they fought, it had to be done according to tradition, in a drum dance. The villagers decided who was stronger. Palo won. But Samo went out and harpooned a polar bear off a drifting iceberg and towed it back to the village with his kayak. The girl's sympathies swayed between the two men. Autumn was coming on.

The seas got rougher and the two brothers decided to move to a different camp for the winter. The girl was bereft. Now both men were lost to her. Dutifully, she helped make the winter house, cutting peat and carrying stones. Palo got into his kayak to find her. On the way, Samo sneaked up behind him and threw a knife, seriously wounding his rival. Bleeding badly, Palo returned to his camp but nearly died. The shaman was called. He went into trance and became a bear. On all fours he chuffed and grunted, then leaned down and sucked at the young man's wound. The blubber lamp flickered. The shaman moved wildly. After, Palo revived. In the midst of a violent autumn storm with high seas he arrived at the girl's camp in his kayak, carried her down to it, tied her on so she was sitting with her back against his, and paddled away. They were bound together for life.

The next night more visitors came. I declared Ann and Olejorgen's house the northernmost "salon" in the world. There was Simon and Aleqa; a painter from Nuuk; Robert Van der Hilst; Sophie; a magazine editor; Manfred Horender, a German photographer I'd met with Aleqa in 1993; and Aliberti.

I helped Olejorgen pour coffee and pass chocolates. Aliberti was clasping his hand over his mouth and his cheeks were swollen. "He just had all his teeth pulled. The dentist is making new ones for him. He didn't know it was going to hurt," Olejorgen told me. I gave Aliberti two Advil. When the pain began to subside he laughed with the others amid tangled translations of French, Danish, German, Faroese, English, and Greenlandic.

Late at night, after all the guests had gone except Aliberti, I asked the question I had been asking during all my visits to Greenland: Could 16,000 years of deep beliefs and spiritual practices disappear in 300 years? Then I heard about Pannipaq.

"They say there are no more shamans, but there are still people who can do things," Olejorgen said. "Pannipaq is about my age—in his forties. He's a hunter, but also he can harm you or help you. The day I met him he was fishing. I was on my way up the coast to Thule. Beside his hole there was a pile of fish taller than he was. Everyone else just had a few. He always gets as much or more than he needs without trying and gives it all away. He can bring narwhal to you, or else he can make you drown.

"In his village, one of the women on our trip visited Pannipaq's mother. We had just passed through a difficult section with bad ice and she was afraid. The old woman told her to look for a raven's help. 'If you see a raven on the way up to Melville Bay, then the ice will be good and you will be okay.' We continued on. That night when we stopped to make dinner, this young woman discovered that in place of the Danish chicken she had bought in Uummannaq was a snow bunting. This was an amulet from Pannipaq and his mother, and the chicken was the payment for the amulet.

"The next day the ice was good. The storm had passed and the rest of the trip went well. When we got to Qaanaaq a few weeks later, the young woman called on Pannipaq's mother to tell her that we had arrived safely. The old woman said she already knew it because the raven had returned to her village looking happy.

"On our way home I tried to find him again, but could not."

At the end of the story I asked if we could go see Pannipaq. "Yes, yes," Olejorgen said enthusiastically. Aliberti nodded in agreement. "We will go soon," I said, though it was already too late in the year. The ice had begun melting. Aliberti leaned close to me on the couch and took my stockinged feet in his hands. "Are they warm?" he asked. "Yes," I said. "Good. Then we will go." Olejorgen stood at the map of Greenland ogling the ragged coast. He traced with his finger north from Uummannaq, past Upernavik and Proven. "We will go when the ice allows us," he said. "And maybe the next time, Pannipaq will let himself be seen."

Nanuq: The Polar Bear, 1999

An eyelid had been drawn down over Greenland since December and now it had lifted, revealing a puzzle of ice whose floating pieces—*kassut*—had been knocked apart by sun and sea currents and welded back together by wet snow. The ice had sheared off from a tangle of frozen rivers, fjords, and oceans, then thawed, the many becoming one until its threads were picked up again and turned back into separate waterways.

The ice had come in mid-October and now, in April, it covered the entire polar north. Like old skin, it was pinched and pocked, pressed up into hummocks and bejeweled by old and young calf ice rising here and there in beveled outcrops, hacked at by thirsty travelers such as ourselves in search of something to melt for drinking water.

Six hundred miles to the north, the rotating umbilicus of the North Pole was still sloshing around, held by its collar of continents, each body of land separated from others at its northern extremes by more frozen seas and straits pinched up into corridors of pressure ice. Now scientists were preparing to put a long line 2.6 miles down into that polar navel, not to catch halibut, but to read the currents, water temperature, salinity, and thickness of ice, to catch the rhythms of the ocean-atmosphere exchange.

Jens, Ilaitsuk, their five-year-old grandson Meqesuq, and I drove out onto that white puzzle of collisions and annealments and headed north in search of polar bears. Their friend and brother-in-law, Mikele Kristiansen, joined us. We were on two sleds, thin splinters moving across

ice. The *iparautaq* (whip) snapped above each team of fifteen dogs and ice unscrolled beneath us as Greenland's mountains sailed by.

Since my last visit, Jens had begun getting gray at the temples and had gained weight. He now rued his "Eskimo bank account"—his potbelly—wishing he could find a good diet, and despaired over the struggle required to keep northern hunters from losing their traditions. He also worried about climate changes, how the spring months were colder, the summers rainier, the autumns stormier, and the thinning of the ice. Jens's friend Mikele, younger, thinner, and more agile, was at the height of his prowess—a keen intelligence that allowed him to get almost any animal he hunted. He joined us because he needed new polar bear pants for the coming winter. As we slalomed between jutting pieces of rough ice, his brown skin and high cheekbones shone in the pale transparency of spring light.

Meqesuq had crawled up to the front of Jens's sled and sat in his grandfather's lap. The frigid wind blew in his face but he didn't care. He wanted to know if I'd come all the way to Greenland from California by dogsled. He didn't know there was any other way to travel, had never seen a car, a train, a field, a tree, or a highway. Even at the close of the twentieth century, he still belonged to the Polar Eskimos, who shared an ice age culture that began thousands of years ago and had flourished in relative isolation.

We churned through fresh-fallen snow and skidded sideways on ice. I rested my hand on Jens's rifle laid on caribou skins and tucked under a blue nylon lash rope. "*Issiktuq* [it is getting cold]," Ilaitsuk said. Even though it was April, it felt more like February or March. Ilaitsuk and I had already changed into winter clothes: *annuraat ammit,* skins; *nan-*

nuk, polar bear pants; *kapatak,* anoraks; polar bear *kamikpak,* boots made of polar bear skin lined with Arctic hare; and *aiqqat,* sealskin mittens with a dog-hair ruff at the wrists. We were headed north in search of animals whose skins we could make into more clothes.

By chance we were following the track of a sled that was carrying a coffin. Two days before, a young hunter had shot himself on the ice in front of twenty schoolchildren and his body was being taken home to Siorapaluk. Accident or suicide? Nobody knew for sure. "There are troubles everywhere. Even here," Ilaitsuk said, clasping the shoulder of her tiny grandson.

"*Harru, harru*" (go left), Jens yelled to the dogs. We swerved around a flat slab of ice that looked like a gravestone. "*Atsuk, atsuk*" (go right). We corrected our course. When his grandson mimicked his commands, Jens turned and smiled.

Wind belted out of the north, covering Jens's whiskered face as well as the muzzles of the dogs with rime ice. The dogs were still recovering from the outbreak of distemper that had killed half their numbers in the northern villages. Jens's and Mikele's teams had dwindled to three or four dogs. Friends from west Greenland sent replacements and those youngsters were still being trained.

One of Jens's dogs was sick and kept falling behind. Jens jumped off the moving sled and, at a run, picked the dog up, threw him into the midst of the pack, then hopped back on. The dog was gaunt and his gait was uneven; he quickly fell behind. Sometimes he was dragged alongside the sled by his trace line, other times he hobbled, never really pulling. Finally, Jens stopped and lifted the dog onto the front of the sled. We set out again, now five instead of four on the sled.

We stopped to make tea. The old kitchen box was set on end and the Primus stove was lit and placed inside the box to shelter the flame from wind. We hacked at a piece of young ice with an iron pole, stuffed the chips into the pot, and melted them for tea water. A whole frozen halibut was stuck head first into the snow and Mikele, Ilaitsuk, and Jens began cutting off chunks of "frozen sushi." The dogs rolled in the snow to cool themselves while we stood and shivered. When the water came to a boil, tea was made. "Is this the same box that went all the way to Alaska with you?" I asked Jens. He nodded.

The closer we got to Siorapaluk, the colder it got. The sled carrying the coffin made deep tracks, as if the finality of death was weighing the sled down. Jens untied the crippled dog from the front stanchion of the sled and threw him into the pack with the others. He hobbled along with less trouble. Appearances count: it wouldn't look good to arrive in a village with an injured dog. We slid around a bend: Robertson Fjord opened up. At the head of the fjord, three glaciers lapped at the sea ice with white tongues and the ice cap rose pale and still behind snowy mountains. Where one began and the other ended was hard to tell. Then, on the far, east-facing side of the fjord, the village of Siorapaluk came into view.

We made camp as usual on the ice in front of the village, pushing the two sleds together to serve as our *illeq*—our sleeping platform—and raising the canvas tent over the sleds. When I looked up, something caught my eye. The funeral procession had already started. Six men were carrying the coffin up the snowy path above the houses. The singing sounded faint. Wind took the strains of music and blew them out the end of the fjord away from us. Mourners gathered in a knot as the casket was set down on the snow, blessed, then pushed into a shed where it would stay until the ground thawed enough for burial. My eyes moved west: on the horizon a mirage shimmered, compressing the roots of the mountains and lifting them above ice and mirrored light, an errant stripe of geography, or a human life that no longer fit earth's puzzle.

As soon as the sun went behind the mountains the temperature plummeted. It was well below zero. All of us crowded into the tent. Shoulder to shoulder, leg to leg, we were bodies seeking other bodies for warmth.

Later. The sound of three hundred dogs crooning woke me. I looked across the row of bodies stuffed into sleeping bags, at Jens's barrel chest and face pressed wide by cold and wind. He was holding his grandson. They both opened their eyes: two moon faces smiled at the canine chorus. There were gunshots.

Mikele stuck his head out of the tent, then fell back on the *illeq*, grunting. "They shot at something but missed," he said.

"At what?" I asked.

"*Nanuq, imaqa*" (Maybe a polar bear), he said, smiling mischievously.

Bright sun, frigid breeze. It must have been midday. We sat in silence watching ice melt for tea water. "*Issi*," Ilaitsuk said again. We broke

313

camp quietly. The crippled dog was tied away from the others, since he wouldn't be coming with us, and the tent was taken down. The pace was deceptive: it looked laid back because Inuit hunters don't waste energy and work quickly, with the utmost efficiency. Before I knew it, Jens was hooking the trace lines into the *urhiq,* to ivory hook that tied the dogs to the sled. I grabbed Meqesuq and made a flying leap as Ilaitsuk and Jens jumped aboard the already fast-moving sled. Jens laughed at his grandson for not being ready and the boy cried, which made Jens laugh harder. Mikele raced past us grinning. That was the Eskimo way of teaching children a sense of humor and the necessity of acting with precision—lessons that would later save their lives.

As we glided away from Siorapaluk on ocean ice another mirage appeared. This one lifted a band of cloud, and beneath it a light shone. We slid from a deception resembling a mirror. It seemed to be taunting us: could we see anything, could we even see ourselves? After eight years of traveling in the Arctic, I knew less and less. The complexities of ice would take a lifetime to learn. It was one thing for one moment, and quite another in the next. Now, as we moved, the mirage moved: the mirrored ice was not something in which you could gaze at yourself nor an instrument of self-knowledge. Instead, it only saw us—specks on ice, smaller than the *uttoq*—the seals that hauled out in the spring to bask in the sun when there was any.

Snow began pelting us in the face. "The weather and the hunter are not such good friends," Jens said. "If a hunter waits for good weather he may starve. But he may starve anyway. That's how it is here and always has been."

When we stopped to rest the dogs rolled in snow, then slept. We drank and peed. I laid out my topographical map. North of Siorapaluk the details stopped. There were no more human habitations but only seldom-visited places: Inglefield Land, Humboldt Glacier, Washington Land, Hall, Nyeboe, Warming, Wulff, Nares, Freuchen, and Peary Land, all the way over the top of Greenland at 83 degrees north latitude to the east side of the island, most of which was also uninhabited.

Snow deepened and the four-mile-per-hour dogtrot slowed to a walk. On our right brown cliffs rose in sheer folds striped with avalanche chutes, crisscrossed by the tracks of Arctic hares. "*Ukaleq, ukaleq,*" Ilaitsuk cried out. Jens whistled the dogs to a stop. "There, there," she pointed excitedly. The rabbits meant food, and their hides provided liners for kamiks. We looked: they were white against a white slope and hopped behind boulders. No luck. On the ice, there were no seals. What would the five of us plus thirty dogs eat that evening?

Rounding a rocky knob, we saw a large bay open up; we crossed its wide mouth. Looking inward, I saw a field of talcum powder, then a cliff of ice—the snout of an enormous glacier made of turquoise and light, carrying streambed debris like rooftop ornaments. I glassed it with binoculars: my eyes darted into caves, bumped over pinnacles and fractures, traced the sensual, inward deformations of ice, the overturned folds and the weathered foliations that told the story of a glacier's life: its contortions, fractures, movements, birth, and rebirth; how it appeared to be static but wasn't; how its fins and flippers of ice were bent up by canyon walls; how, in summer, its snout, on touching sea water, lifted up, floated, and calved enormous icebergs—its life almost human.

Above the terminus, the glacier was curvaceous; its seeming motionlessness was in reality a slow coming apart. Its surface was fractured and crosscut—a grid for a city that had not yet been built. Bands of color revealed the rhythm of ablation and accumulation for what it was: the noise and silence of time. Above that was the ice cap. At its edge, rows of twenty-foot-long icicles hung like beaded curtains in front of caves, obstructing entry and exit as if to say: give up now, it is too big to know.

At the last minute we changed course. We were hungry and followed a lead in ice. We veered out into the frozen ocean looking for seals. Snow came on hard as the cowl of a storm approached, rising from behind the mountains of Ellesmere Island. There were breathing holes all along the crack, but no *uttoq*—no seals basking on the ice. We went west toward the storm. Then it closed over us and all afternoon and evening we traveled without being able to see.

Once a hunter told me about getting vertigo: "Sometimes when we were on our dogsleds and there was bad fog or snow, we felt lost. We couldn't tell where the sky was, where the ice. It felt like we were moving upside down."

Two ravens appeared out of the white, jeering at us as we zigzagged from one frozen-over crack in the ice to another. We hadn't eaten meat for two days and our hunger was a kind of group ache. All was white. We stopped for tea, pulling the two sleds close together and lashing a tarp between them as a windbreak. We scrounged through our duffles for food. I found a jar of peanut butter but was dismayed to see the words "reduced fat" on the label. Never mind. I spread it on a cracker, then drank tea, and split a bittersweet chocolate bar with Ilaitsuk. Bittersweet was what I was feeling that day: happy to be in Greenland again among friends, but getting hungrier with each bite I took.

It was easy to see how episodes of famine could sweep through the Arctic; how quickly hunting could go bad, how hunger dominated. Before stores and helicopters, pan-Arctic cannibalism was commonplace. When the food ran out, they ate their dogs and boiled sealskins to make soup. When that was gone, eating human flesh—the remains of those who had already starved—was the key to survival, repellent as it was.

We headed north again, crossing back over a large piece of frozen ocean. The sound of the sled pushing through snow was oceanic. Rabbit tracks crisscrossed in front of us but we saw no animals. The edge of the storm frayed and light flooded through. Everything was made of chipped crystal: snow, ice, air. Meqesuq asked his grandmother for his sunglasses. It had become a ritual: on, off, on, off, and we adults were the caretakers of the precious things. He put them on and turned to us: he was pure Hollywood and he knew it.

How wonderfully relaxing it was to travel with another woman. Ilaitsuk and I tipped our faces up to the sun. Its warmth was a blessing, and for a few moments we closed our eyes and dozed. A yell shook us awake. Ilaitsuk scrambled to her knees. Far ahead, Mikele's sled was moving fast and he was half standing. "*Nanuq! Nanuq!*" he cried, pointing. A polar bear and her small cub were trotting across the head of a wide bay.

"*Puquoq, puquoq,*" Jens yelled, as his dogs took off in that direction. Mikele had already cut two of his dogs loose and they chased the bear. He released two more. The snow was deep and the little cub couldn't keep up. The mother stopped, wheeled around, and ran back for her baby, but Mikele's loose dogs caught up and held the bear at bay.

Now our sled was between the cub and the she-bear. Repeatedly, she whirled around to go back to her cub. The dogs closed in, not harming her, just threatening. She pawed, snarled, and ran again. Ilaitsuk told me that because the bear had a cub, she would not be shot, that Mikele would soon release her. Then something went terribly wrong: one of the dogs spied the cub. Before we could get there, the dog was on the cub and went for its jugular. We rushed to the cub's rescue, but the distances were so great and the going was so slow that by the time we got there, the dog was shaking the young bear by its neck and had been joined by others. Mikele and Jens leaped off their sleds and beat the dogs away with their whip handles, but it was too late. The cub was badly hurt.

When the dogs had been dispersed, we stayed with the cub while Mikele caught up with the mother. The cub was alive but weak. A large flap of skin and flesh hung down from the neck. If I'd had a tranquilizer dart, we could have sewn him up, but we had nothing. Dazed and weak, he was still feisty enough to snarl and scratch. Jens approached, throwing a soft loop around the cub's leg to hold him close to the sled and keep him away from the loose dogs.

We let the young cub rest. He was whiter than his mother and his button nose and eyes were black holes in a world of white. Maybe he would recover enough for us to send him back to his mother. Far ahead, the she-bear started to get away, but the loose dogs caught up with her again. Near the far side of the fjord, the bear darted west, taking refuge next to the wall of a half-crumbled iceberg. Mikele caught up as his dogs began to tire. The bear stood in her icy enclosure, coming out to charge the dogs as they approached—not so close that they would get hurt and not so far away that she could escape. She no longer looked for her cub; she was trying to survive.

The sun was out and the bear was hot. She scooped up a pawful of snow from the ground and ate it to ease her growing thirst. The slab of ice against which she rested was blue and shaped like a wide inverted V, its sides melting in the spring sun. The dogs surrounded her in a semicircle, jumping forward to snap at her, testing their own courage, but leaping back when she charged them.

Five hundred yards behind Mikele, we watched over the cub. If we got too close, he snarled. Sometimes he stood up, but he was weak and began panting. His eyes rolled back. He staggered and was dead.

Jens tied a loop around the cub's neck and dragged it like a toy behind the sled. Its skin would be used, and maybe the meat.

Mikele turned as we approached. "Is the cub dead?" he asked.

Jens said that it was. I knew what was going to happen next and begged Jens to spare the mother even if her cub was dead. She was young and beautiful and she would have more babies. "It's up to

Mikele," he said. Mikele, whose polar bear pants were worn almost all the way through, considered, then quietly loaded his rifle.

Meqesuq and I sat on the side of the sled. Tears streamed from our eyes. Jens looked at us and chuckled—not at our softheartedness, but our naïveté. To think that they could pass up a bear for what he considered sentimental reasons was absurd.

The loose dogs continued to hold the bear at bay. I got off the sled and walked closer to her. She could have attacked me, but she had eyes only for the dogs who taunted her. After a long time she rested against the cool wall, licking its ice. Then she turned and looked toward Ellesmere Island. Standing on her toes, she laid her elbow on the top of the berg and scanned the frozen sea, searching for a way out. I rooted for her: "Go, go," I whispered loudly. These were the last moments of her life and I was watching them tick by. How was this possible? Did she know she was doomed? Of course not. But she knew enough to be making plans.

Once again I pleaded for her life, but only got questioning stares from the hunters. Again, she peeked over the top of the ice, but slumped back halfheartedly. She was tired and there was no escape.

The dogs began to lose interest. They turned away from the bear and licked their small wounds. She stood alone in her icy chamber, waiting. Ilaitsuk covered Meqesuq's ears as Mikele slowly raised his rifle. The boy was frightened. He had already seen the cub die and he didn't want to see any more. Standing in deep snow, I felt like a witness to an execution.

The bear was now close enough to jump forward and get me in one swipe. I don't know why she didn't. At the same time, I understood how important it was for a hunter to kill a polar bear. She would be a source of food and her skin would be used for much-needed winter clothing. I looked down at my own body: I too was wearing polar bear pants and boots and it was solely because of them that I was warm.

The bear bent forward, half standing, half sitting, exhausted and bewildered, then slouched down and sat. Did she wonder where her cub was? I wanted to carry her dead baby to her. But she couldn't know any of this and it would make no difference if she did. The world, for her, held no clues about human ambivalence, and she gave me the same hard stare she would give a seal. After all, I was just part of the food chain.

It was the same stare Mikele gave her now, not hard from lack of feeling, but from the necessity to survive. Predator and prey. In the Arctic, you never knew which side of that coin you'd find yourself on, and you lived by your wits, as did the bear and the seal, the dog and the fox, the raven, dovekie, and hare.

The bear's fur was pale yellow and the ice wall was blue. The sun was hot. Time melted. What I knew about life and death, cold and hunger, seemed irrelevant. There were three gunshots. A paw went up in agony, scratching the ice wall as she went down. Then she rolled on her back and was dead.

An Iglulik shaman once told Rasmussen that "the greatest peril lies in the fact that to kill and eat, all those that we strike down and destroy to make clothes for ourselves, have souls as we have, souls that do not perish with the body, and therefore must be propitiated lest they revenge themselves on us for taking away their bodies."

I knelt down by the young bear. The fur was thick between her claws. I heard something gurgling. It was too early in the year for running water. Then I saw it was her blood.

Mikele tied his dogs back in with the others. Tea water was put on to boil. We rolled up our sleeves in the warm afternoon sun. Ilaitsuk glassed the ice for other bears; Meqesuq sat on the snow beside the bear and put his tiny hand on her large paw. The snout of the glacier that came to a halt just behind us was a wall of living sapphires.

The bear was laid out on her back like a woman about to have sex. Jens put the tip of his knife on her umbilicus and made a quick upward cut to her neck. The fine tip traveled under her chin and through her black lip as if to keep her from talking.

Soon enough she was disrobed. The skin was stretched out on the snow and after the blood was wiped off, Ilaitsuk folded it in quarters and placed it carefully in a gunny sack on the sled. Then the ursine body was dismembered and the pieces were stowed under the tarp, so that when we put away our teacups and started north toward Neqe, she lay beneath us, and we were riding her. According to Inuit legends, bears could hear and understand everything human beings said, even after death. Which is why we traveled in silence for the rest of the day.

In 1917, a shaman told Rasmussen about the souls of bears: "The bear is a dangerous animal but we need him. We may hunt him, but if we do we have to take certain precautions that the soul may not come back and avenge itself."

Because bears know everything and hear everything people say, every action after a bear hunt is prescribed. When the bear hunter returns from the chase, the flayed skin is brought into the house and placed in a *qimerfik* (a box for dog food). If it is a he-bear, they hang the snout over the hunter's thong, together with a harpoon point and a harpoon, a little blubber and meat, and a few pieces of skin, all of them an offering to the dead bear. The fragments of skin will later be used to patch the hunter's boots; bears walk around so much. If it is a she-bear, they hang up a piece of the dressed skin of a seal over the skin, a little meat, and a few bits of skin to patch with. The sealskin and offerings remain undisturbed for five days.

Also, it is necessary to collect all the bones as the meat is eaten and put them in a heap on the windowsill. The head should be turned inward. "This is done so that the soul of the bear shall not have too much difficulty in getting home."

At Neqe we pushed our sleds up through the hummocks. A historic cabin, used for one hundred years as a jumping-off place for expeditions going north, rested on a hill at the tip of a long thumb of land sticking out from between two tidewater glaciers. Its windows looked down on Smith Sound. Out front there were meat racks crowded with walrus flippers, dead dogs, and bits of hacked-up seals. The place was half sanctuary, half charnel ground; in the Arctic, where famine is always lurking, the two are the same.

Our dogs were unharnessed, the sleds were unloaded, the *illeq* was covered with caribou skins, and water was put on to boil. We sat outside on the sleds facing west and caught some rays. Maybe spring was coming. *Imaqa.* Tufts of last year's bunch grass peeked out from under the snow and seals began to appear on the ice, basking in fresh, sweet, warm air.

After a hunt there is no boasting. Greenlanders are modest and reverent. The better hunters they are, the less attention they attract to themselves. Living on the ice, they bow down to the unknown every day and freely admit they know nothing. This is survival after all, not vanity.

We talked hardly at all. Later we threw our dictionaries in a pile and enjoyed a feast of words. I tried to memorize such useful phrases as *nauk tupilaghuunnguaja*, which means "you fool"; and *taquliktuuq,* "dark-colored dog with a white blaze over its eye." But often I failed, which made for even more merriment.

Something about the cabin at Neqe made us cheerful anyway. The walls were covered with Greenland's weekly newspaper. I saw pictures of friends: Olejorgen Hammekin on his sled while traveling from Uummannaq to Thule, and Lars Emil, the ex–prime minister, visiting villagers from the red-and-white ship on which he had once invited me to travel.

More than one hundred years ago a ship called the *Polaris* was lost near here, and the survivors found themselves adrift on a four-mile-wide ice floe. They drifted 1,300 miles and were rescued off the coast of Labrador in April of the next year.

Rasmussen recalled "killing time" here on his way to Peary Land in the Second Thule Expedition:

> *We dived into the very extensive library of the Crockerland Expedition, visited the Eskimo families which were all old friends of ours, and every evening ended with a ball which lasted into the early hours of the morning. The Americans had a wonderful gramophone, which entertained us greatly with its varied and select repertoire. There was something for everybody's taste, so that at times we heard songs from all the operas of the world, sung by Caruso, Alma Gluck, Adelina Patti, etc. and at other times we abandoned ourselves to musical debauches, for a change, indulging in tangos and one-steps. (Rasmussen,* Greenland by the Polar Sea, *p. 43)*

We danced no tangos but stood on the ice terrace in front of the cabin with our anoraks pulled off, gazing out at the wide expanse of frozen ocean. We saluted the rarely seen sun. Its warmth penetrated us and for the first time we relaxed. Ilaitsuk wore a festive red sweater and dark glasses. I put on new long underwear. A hidden beer emerged which we all shared.

The strangled cry of a fox floated out over the frozen bay where we shot the bear. Now, a band of fog rose from that place. It covered the marks of the bear's death dance—where she stopped, wheeled around, attacked, and retreated—the hieroglyphics of blood and tracks, and the hollows in snow where the dogs rested after the chase. I was glad I couldn't see.

A Primus was lit. We cooked the rest of the frozen halibut we'd hacked at for hor d'oeuvres, not polar bear. No one mentioned the bear or the cub or the chase or the reward of the skin to make next winter's clothes. We simply ate and went to bed.

In our sleeping bags we lay in a row on the *illeq*. It was still warm and no one could sleep. Jens and Ilaitsuk held their grandson between them as Jens began a story: "A long time ago when shamans still flew under water and animals could talk, there was a woman named Anoritoq who lived on that point of land north of Etah. The name Anoritoq means 'Windswept One.' This woman had no husband and her only son was killed by a hunter out of jealousy because the young boy had no father but was becoming a great hunter anyway. After her son died, a hunter brought the woman a polar bear cub, which she raised just like a son. The bear learned the language of the Eskimo and played with the other children. When he grew up, he hunted seals and was very successful. But she worried about him. She was afraid a hunter might kill him, because after all he was a bear, and his skin was needed for clothing. She tried covering him with soot to make him dark, but one day, when some of his white fur was showing, a hunter killed him. Afterward she was so sad, she stopped eating and went outside and stayed there all the time and looked at the sea. Then she changed into a stone. Now when we go bear hunting in that area, we put a piece of seal fat on the rock and pray for a good bear hunt."

Morning. Everything was slow, effortless, almost lazy, but not really, because nothing in Inuit life is slothful. On the other hand, nothing macho goes on either. Any such mockery of real strength would be laughed at, just as failure is laughed at, and accidents—bumping up against obdurate reality—because it's all hard surfaces here. The mixed shyness and contempt Jens once showed me when we first met was gone. Now he treated me royally, as if I were an aging child incapable of caring for herself on the ice. He called me "the boss" because I asked to accompany them on the trip, but he knew that I was happy to go along with whatever he wanted to do.

Suddenly Jens and Mikele started preparing to go. That's how it always was on these trips. Languorous hours floated by, then there was a flurry of activity and you'd better be packed, dressed properly, and on the sled when they hooked up the dogs or you'd be left behind.

We followed the coast north to Pitoravik. It was not a long trip.

From there we would determine our route to Etah—either up and over part of the inland ice or following the coast if there was no open water or pressure ice. A wind began to blow as Jens and Mikele took off to investigate the trail over the glacier. They were gone several hours and when they came back they shook their heads. "The drifts are very deep and the crevasses are wide and the snow hides them," Jens said. "Down below, the ice is badly broken with open water. Too dangerous. We'll wait until morning. If the weather is good, we'll try to go over the top. If not, then we'll go to the ice edge out there, toward Canada, and hunt walrus and narwhal."

In the morning the weather was cold but clear. We hooked up the dogs and headed toward the glacier. The day before had been easy and they'd been fed, and now they pulled vigorously. Jens walked ahead of his dogs. In some places snow came to his waist. But a little farther ahead, the drifts were wind-blown and hard-packed and the dogs could get a purchase on the ice and pull hard. Mikele yelled wildly and jumped on his sled as he roared ahead. A crevasse yawned on his right and he slowed the dogs. I peered down into it as we passed: the center of the earth is blue.

The slope steepened and the dogs struggled upward. Ilaitsuk and I got off and pushed. Even though we had pulled off our anoraks and mittens, the sweat still poured down our faces and backs, which meant we'd be cold later. At the top we stopped to rest. I looked out over the frozen sound and thought of how many times Rasmussen had made this trip going both ways, and wondered if, like the wagon ruts on the Oregon Trail across Wyoming, his sled tracks could still be seen. But this was ice and all that lasted up here was memory.

Down the other side Jens put a loop of rope under the runners to slow our speed and traded places with Ilaitsuk, so if the sled threatened to overrun the dogs he could hold it back. We swerved, just missing boulders, and bumped over loose shoulders of hard snow. Chasms opened and closed but we managed to stay between them.

Getting off the glacier was more difficult. We jumped the sled over a wide space between the shore and the ocean ice. The sled was just long enough to bridge the gap, though the back right side fell slightly. At just the right moment, the dogs surged ahead and we flew down onto the white sea floor.

Etah. Not a village but a piece of history. It was here that the last group of migrants from Baffin Island touched Greenland soil in 1862, led by the shaman Qidlaq, who had dreamt of the place; here, too, Rasmussen's expedition to the top of Greenland began and ended.

History caused us all to sleep well that night, or maybe we were just tired. In the morning a continuous, mesmerizing snow fell. Ilaitsuk, Meqesuq, and I stayed in the cabin while Mikele and Jens went off to hunt. Our food was dangerously low, and as usual the weather was worsening. Ilaitsuk sewed overboots for each of us. She drew patterns on old newspaper, laid seal and caribou skins on them, and cut them out. Her cutting and sewing were swift and sure; in a few hours we had new footwear. Then she mended three or four pairs of sealskin mittens, all the time trying out what little English she had with my poor Greenlandic. We managed to talk in a very limited way about food, sex, children, and husbands, and she told me the plot of the old Inuit story that she and Jens were telling her grandson.

Jens and Mikele returned with one seal. Not enough for all of us plus thirty dogs. We knew who would get fed first—the dogs. What remained, Ilaitsuk made into soup, a thin, salty broth with a few bits of meat floating around, which we gave to the men because they had been outside hunting. Then the storm hit and we huddled inside for another day.

When the sky cleared, Jens and Mikele spent the morning on a hill behind the cabin discussing our next move. A foot of snow had fallen and the way north was a blank, though we knew that a few miles north white slabs of pressure ice rose sharply like the upended sidewalks of a city.

A decision was made not to continue north. Another storm was coming and the snow was deep. "There's nothing to eat," Jens explained. "We might get too hungry. If we get stuck on this side of the ice and can't get back for a while, it will be bad."

I wasn't happy but said nothing. We humped over the top of the glacier again and sidled down the steep mountain back to Pitoravik, where we rested. Another seal was caught and another evening we drank broth.

In the morning we followed the ice foot toward a small glacier. It was a carnival ride of bumping, tilting, lurching, and twisting that made us grab fast at the flapping edges of caribou skins. Meqesuq and I fell off once and rolled against a slab of standing ice. Jens wasn't amused. We scrambled to our feet and jumped back on as if nothing had happened.

Then the ice flattened out and we slid onto a wide expanse of smooth snow. We headed west and south for the island of Kiatak, where two years before we had gone to catch birds.

The storm approached in pieces: wreaths of black clouds undulated over the mountains and islands, dragging across the ice cap. Jens made a smashing gesture with his fist, demonstrating how the storm would hit us. Ahead were broken clouds with sun piercing through. Sudden warmth meant snow: we shed our winter anoraks and passed an ice floe shaped like a crystal ear. "*Ai, ai, ai, ai,*" Jens called to the dogs. Faster. Behind us, the snout of the Neqip Sermia—the Morris Jesup Glacier, where we shot the bear—was a receding fresco full of interrupted shapes that looked both bearlike and human. A light snow fell blurring the glacier's top edge, but the ice wall remained translucent, all precision facets—fused diamonds that hardened into turquoise.

Beauty causes joy; snow or no snow, I was happy. I tried another new word: *qirngaqtuq*—calling up good weather by incantation. I asked Ilaitsuk if I should try a weather song and she nodded, yes. I belted one out, over the rattling sled and dog panting, but the weather worsened. By late afternoon, we were hungry again. We followed a lead in ice looking for seals. But there were none, nor were there any walrus, whales, birds, or rabbits. The storm played tag with us, darkening the sky and throwing snow, then hanging back and spilling sun onto the ice.

The crack gave nothing. The dogs hadn't been fed and they'd need food soon, as would we. Finally the storm did catch up, and behind us and before us all icebergs, mountains, and glaciers disappeared in every compassless direction.

For days we traveled in bad weather. Once, when we stopped to rest the dogs, Ilaitsuk, Meqesuq, and I played tag on the ice to get warm. The child never complained. When his feet got numb he merely pointed to his toes, and Ilaitsuk slipped on the overboots she had sewn for him three nights earlier. He sat at the front of the sled, wind-blasted and happy, echoing his grandfather's commands, snapping an imaginary long whip, already becoming a man.

Patience and strength of mind are the hunter's virtues, along with flexibility and humor. Jens shot at a seal and missed. Another one caught his scent and dove down into its hole. He returned to the sled laughing at his failures, explaining to Mikele exactly what he had done wrong.

We continued on, lured by the promise of walrus and narwhal. "*Hikup hinaa,*" Jens said. The ice edge. My stomach growled and I thought of the legend of the Great Famine, when winters followed one after the other with no spring, summer, or fall between. When everything had been eaten—dogs and things made of sealskin—then people ate each other to survive. Jens said that this winter and spring had been the coldest in his memory. Ironically, colder weather in the Arctic was thought by some climatologists to be a side effect of global warming: as pieces of the ice cap melted and calved into the ocean, the water temperature cooled, which in turn cooled the air. If this were so, would global warming cancel itself out? Jens didn't understand my "Greenglish." "*Issi,*" is all he said, rubbing his arms. "Maybe we will have to eat each other like they did in the old days."

We bundled up and kept going. Midway across the frozen ocean, snow, ice, and sky merged. An hour earlier a jet had flown over, its belly glinting far above us. We joked that it must be a nonstop from Tromsö, Norway, to Barrow, Alaska. Ahead, a raven perched on a piece of ice and made a noise I'd never heard—not an avian woodwind sound but a mammal's strangled cry: a raven's imitation of an Arctic fox. Then it flew out of sight.

For a long time there was nothing. What notation designates soundlessness? There were sounds, of course—the rattle of the sled and the panting dogs—but these sounds occurred in a vacuum. Listening more closely, I heard a hum: it was the smooth-working machinery of my own body ringing in my ears.

A piece of ice toppled as we passed a stranded floe, then a snowflake struck on my shoulder. One of the two made a thunking sound, I didn't know which. There was no breeze. Yet shadows lengthened. What blew them this way and that? Was it Plato's fire issuing from an eye? The paleo-Eskimo carving of something half-human and half-bear bounced up and down in my mind. Thoughts floated on the dog team's slipstream. Nothing grew in the Arctic except the imagination. Lacking a pharmacopoeia or any kind, the Inuit ingested the icescape whole. You could grow wild on it, they said, get happy, or go mad. *Perleroneq* was the word meaning Arctic hysteria, and it could infect people as well as dogs. "But not much anymore," Ilaitsuk said. "Now in the dark time, we watch TV."

The reason bears could hear and understand everything that human beings said was that there were no obstructions, there was no extraneous noise. That's how life seemed to us that day. The *ha, ha, ha, ha, ha, ha* of the dogs was the only sound around. If we asked for silence, then listened, anything was possible. We, who were tiny dots riding a wooden splinter across infinity.

Did days go by or hours? We were fur-wrapped, rendered motionless by cold. We searched the ice for food. Shadows made by standing bits of ice looked like seals. Then we did see one, a black comma lying in the alabaster extravagance. Jens and Mikele stopped their dogs. The world went silent whenever their panting ceased. Jens mounted his rifle on a small stand with skis. A white sailcloth hid his face. The snow was shin-deep but the wind was right. He crept forward, then lay on his belly, sighting in his rifle. All thirty dogs sat at attention with their ears pricked. As soon as they heard the muffled crack of the gun, off they went, running to Jens.

The seal lay dead by its breathing hole. Jens skinned it with quick efficiency, cut into its belly, and pulled out the liver. He cut off a piece and ate it, then cut pieces for Ilaitsuk and me. The seal's blood pooled in the snow, thinning it to pink water. Jens cut a notch in the back flipper to use as a handhold and dragged the furless seal onto the sled.

All evening we traveled in the storm. At tea, there was no view, no coastline, no islands ahead, no ceiling, no floor. We ate sandwiches, a candy bar, and a few cookies. Jens flipped the caribou skins over, inner side up, because the snow was wet and it caught in the fur, making it wetter. We moved out, turning in what felt like the wrong direction, and proceeded in what may or may not have been a straight line toward Herbert Island.

At 10:30 in the evening the storm broke. Gray came apart, clouds split in half, the lower portion moving in one direction, the upper half pulsing toward Ellesmere. Clots of mist peeled away like calf ice, dropping down to reveal huge areas of sky. Then the dark edge pulled past, a black bumper receding, and unrolling in its place was a seamless scrim of midnight blue.

Clear skies meant plummeting temperatures. It was now May, but 18 degrees below zero. Sunlight streamed through clouds in long yellow stripes. The red walls of a distant island appeared.

For the first time, cold penetrated my layers of Polartec and polar bear. Near the island, soft snow hardened into undulating wind-packed drifts. The sleds flew. Jens took a shot at a seal from the moving sled and missed. Then he did get one, and hurriedly cut it up and stored it under the load on the sled. A raven led us. We sped over smooth, hard ice. Jens called to the bird. *Caw, caw,* he cried out, and the raven leapfrogged, perching on a triangular piece of ice, then flew up suddenly and raced ahead.

At midnight we reached the hut on Herbert Island—the same one we'd used in 1977. It was still filthy, the sheet-metal walls splattered with seal and walrus blood, the floor three inches thick with dirt and grease, and the same pornographic magazines were lying on the sleeping platform. I'd had nightmares when I stayed here before and I dreaded the coming night, but Ilaitsuk covered everything with fresh newspaper and lined the *illeq* with caribou skins, making the room seem bright and fresh. Then she lit the Primus and set water on to boil.

As Ilaitsuk and I unloaded the sleds, Jens and Mikele cut up seal meat while Meqesuq practiced snapping the whip. I knew I was cold and dehydrated because for no reason his antics irritated me, and my urine was dark brown. The dogs lined up in rows waiting for food with avid attention. It had been two days since they'd eaten their fill of fresh meat. A chunk was flung through the air, then another and another. Jens's and Mikele's aims were so perfect, every dog got its share, and the faster they ate, the more they got. They chewed, swallowed, then waited eagerly for more.

Jens cut up the rest of the seal for our dinner; we watched as lumps of meat churned in brown water. Sitting on the caribou skins with her legs straight out in typical Eskimo fashion, Ilaitsuk softened Jens's frozen kamiks on the rounded wooden end of the whip handle, then hung them up to dry. As the hut warmed up, we stripped down. Meqe-suq's tiny T-shirt read "I Love Elephants."

Bedtime was 3:30 a.m. We were up just before noon. The weather was bright and breezy but the Primus wouldn't light. It took a long time but no one complained. Ever patient, Jens sat on the floor, the stove's many delicate parts scattered on newspaper in front of him as he pieced it back together. The boy wanted a story. Ilaitsuk lay on the platform next to him and in a smooth, low voice continued the saga of the orphan boy. Then it was time to go.

When hunting at the ice edge in spring, it's best to travel in the evening, when the ice is firm and the edge doesn't break out from under you. We bumped down to the ice foot and turned left, traveling around the edge of the island. Off to the west was the polynya—a perennial patch of open water. Its effect was to vanquish winter for a few moments while seagulls swooped and rode pans of ice, white on white, going wherever their little boats took them. Water rippled, sun shone, and all that had been transfixed by ice now moved. Ilaitsuk smiled and lit a cigarette for Jens. We were temporarily becalmed by the sight.

All is illusion: we had been walking on water, flying across time, whose white face had no hour hands. Now the water was liquid, not ice, a floating season that lured us into thinking we had gotten somewhere and found summer when we hadn't.

Between this island and the next there is often a rough, almost inpenetrable barrier of ice. But this year, there was hardly any. Once it had taken us seven hours to make the passage. Now we glided freely. The world was a mirror; we flew across a checkerboard of cracked platelets, blue tiles chinked with soft snow. We passed the cliffs where the birds came to nest, but it was still too cold, Jens said. "They will wait and come when it is warm enough, *imaga.*" They were due on May 10 at the latest, in a few days. Ahead, on the ice, there were seals hauled out everywhere, but the wind was wrong. It came from behind us, sending our scent forward as we approached, and they disappeared.

Late in the evening we saw a sign of spring: two Arctic gulls mating in midair ahead of the sled. Jens made a motion with his hand—like revving a motorcycle—meant to indicate a sexual act. The more he did it, the more we laughed. Eskimo spring fever we called it. We made camp at Nazsilivik on the edge of Steensby Land in a sheltered bight.

While the dogs were being unharnessed, it was obvious that Pappi, Jens's dog, was unhappy. Every male dog in the team pounced on her together, each one trying to have his way with her. She lay crouching and squealing until Jens got the dogs off, then he staked her out with his lead dog away from the others where they could take their pleasure in peace. I taught Jens the word "honeymoon."

Mikele repaired harness while Jens trimmed his whip (it was too heavy, he said, and didn't fly fast enough through the air), singing the high-pitched bearded seal's song. The whip's long thong was made from the skin of a bearded seal. He showed me a wide scar on the palm of his hand where it was caught in a rope when he tried to pull a bearded seal up onto the ice. The line cut all the way to the bone. One of the other hunters came over and helped him, then sewed his hand up while they were out on the ice. "It hurt when he did that—a little bit. When I got home, the doctor said the suture was so good, he didn't have to do anything."

Another night we stayed in a hut on the south side of Kiatak Island. It was spacious and well cared for. The last occupants left a family picture and the name of their village tacked to the wall. Because I was the oldest one of the group, Ilaitsuk insisted that I have the softest pad on my part of the group bed, despite my protests.

After unloading the sled we relaxed. It was the first time we had not traveled half the night and the reprieve from cold and tedium was welcome. Hunting had not been good but it would take an all-out famine to douse our spirits. And tonight we were to have a special meal.

Jens brought the polar bear meat inside and cut it up with a small ax. We watched as it was put into the pot to boil. We were cold when we arrived but soon the room was warm. Our mittens, hats, kamiks, and hare socks hung overhead, drying. The boiling bear meat mesmerized us.

Jens passed plates. "*Nanuq. Nanuq,*" he said in a low voice. "We have to eat her in a special way. We boil her like the seal, but we pay special respects to her, so her soul shall not have too much difficulty getting home." After twenty minutes, chunks of meat were doled out. It steamed on our plates.

"*Qajanaq,*" I said, thanking Mikele, Jens, and most of all the bear.

"*Mamiqtuqtuq,*" Jens said quietly. Eat the meat with pleasure.

Ilaitsuk cut the meat into tiny pieces for Meqesuq, who dunked each chunk into salt. We used our pocket knives and fingers. The meat was tender and good, like buffalo, I told Jens. He smiled and opened his jacket to reveal a sweatshirt with a picture of a buffalo on the chest.

A loaf of bread was passed. We each had a slice, then drank tea and shared a handful of cookies. After, Ilaitsuk set a piece of plywood in a plastic bucket and stretched the sealskin over the top edge. With her *ulu*, a curved knife with a wooden handle, she scraped the blubber from the skin in strong downward thrusts. When the hide was clean, she used a *kiliutaq*, a small square knife, to scrape the brownish-pink oil out of the fur. The skin was then hung on a line to dry.

Just as I thought it must be time to go to bed, Jens and Mikele reloaded their rifles and went outside. I threw on a parka and followed. "We're going hunting for *ukaleq*," Jens said. Up the scree slopes we went, straight up—Jens in one direction, Mikele in another. Mikele stepped up the face of the mountain as if he were climbing a ladder, moving effortlessly, his rifle slung over his shoulder and the earflaps of his red cap slapping his cheeks. Ilaitsuk, Meqesuq, and I followed, scrambling over rock, glissading across snow chutes. Sometimes we saw the long floppy ears of a hare dashing between boulders, then a shot, then another scramble. Soon Mikele was far above us, almost lost to sight, and we went home.

Lying inside my sleeping bag, I listened to the wind. In one day we had prepared a sealskin, eaten polar bear, and hunted Arctic hare. When Jens came back empty-handed, he told stories about the woman who adopted a bear, the hunter who married a hare, and the man who went behind an iceberg and came back out as a seal. I touched the fur of my polar bear pants as I listened. We lived with, ate, and wore the skins of these animals. Jens's voice went soft and the words droned, putting us into a sweet trance. He said he sometimes dreamed about an animal that he would kill the next day, and in doing so, "ate his soul," the words translated literally. I didn't know if I would ever be able to sleep again without that voice and those stories. Maybe I would begin having those dreams too. Hours later, Mikele returned clutching two rabbits. "*Ukaliqtuq*," he caught a hare, Ilaitsuk said, turning to me. Even in the middle of the night she tried to teach me new words.

A seal's *agluq*, or breathing hole, is made in the autumn when the new ice is forming, because seals need to come up for air every fifteen or twenty minutes, regardless of the weather. Ring seals have claws in their flippers to scratch holes in the ice. They do this when the ice is still quite thin. Later, as winter snows come, they keep scratching to keep the hole open. As the ice thickens, the agluq begins to take on a funnel shape, reaching twelve or thirteen inches long, topped by an air-filled dome covered and camouflaged by snow.

The storm that passed us returned, or else a new one descended. The bright, crisp night that we had spent climbing scree slopes had turned gray. "Today we will just go *uttoq* hunting, then tomorrow we will find the ice edge," Jens said. He and Mikele harnessed the dogs and we took off, only to come to an abrupt stop. Pappi, the female in heat, yowled as she was mauled by the male dogs in the team. They were piled three thick on top of her. Finally, Jens jumped into the middle of them, pulling them off. As soon as the dogs were sorted out, we took off, but to no avail. Again he had to untangle the dogs.

We went farther and soon saw that there were no *uttoq*—no basking seals. That's when Jens reverted to winter seal hunting, called *aquiluktuq*—hunting seal at the breathing hole. Jens got off the sled and instructed us to drive in a wide circle around him: the sound of the sleds would fool the seals into thinking the hunters were way out there, and push them toward the center agluq, where the hunter was waiting with a harpoon.

Now Ilaitsuk was driving the sled, but because of Pappi she was having trouble controlling the dogs. Off we went, the sled zigzagging, banging up and over rough ice. No shouted commands got their attention: their only interest was jumping on Pappi. We hit another piece of ice and almost tipped over. The circle was broken: we'd gone too far out from where Jens was standing at the agluq to do any good. Then, totally out of control, we rounded a large piece of year-old ice and the dogs headed toward home. Qaanaaq was days away, but they didn't care. They'd chase Pappi until they got her.

A dogsled out of control can be dangerous when the ice isn't smooth. Dogs broke their traces and we careened over rough ice. Ilaitsuk yelled, but they weren't listening. Finally, little Meqesuq crawled up to the front of the sled and, imitating his grandfather's commands, got the dogs to stop.

Stopped but hopelessly tangled, they soon took off again. One dog got his hind leg completely bound up in a loose trace and ran on three legs. Loose dogs were running everywhere. Finally we brought them under control and turned back toward Jens. Our plan to deceive the seals was now a joke. Who was fooling whom? we wondered. The humans were not coming out on top.

Jens looked at our mess and shook his head angrily. "*Uluuq!*" He shouted at the dogs to come to him, then chastised Ilaitsuk for failing to keep control.

She returned his fury: "It is impossible to do anything with this dog in heat," she said. "Why did you bring her?"

Jens threw his harpoon on the sled, snapped the whip over the dogs until they cringed, and set to work untangling and making new traces.

Four hours had gone by and still we had nothing to eat. The dogs continued to misbehave. As we moved out, they piled up on Pappi again: "*Aquitsit, nuiliqaa-nauk, aulaitsit,*" he yelled. The dogs lay still; he turned to Ilaitsuk and began laughing—at the dogs, at her ineptness, at himself for getting mad, at our failure to get any food at all. Ilaitsuk laughed too. Then Jens cut Pappi loose and the dogs went smoothly back to the cabin.

Hunting seals at the agluq is an art of patience . . . and quiet, Jens said later. He told how Rasmussen, when he was staying with the Netsilik, was one of fifteen hunters who spent twelve hours standing at breathing holes and only getting one seal.

In the next days the hunt was not for seals but for the *hikup hinaa*—the ice edge—where we would hunt walrus and narwhal. We packed up our things and camped on the ice wherever we found ourselves at the end of the day (usually the middle of the night by the clock). The ice edge was where all the game would be, Mikele promised, smiling. We traveled due west from the tip of Kiatak out onto the frozen ocean between Greenland and Ellesmere Island. We came to a long column of enormous icebergs and stopped. Mikele and Jens climbed an iceberg and glassed the frozen ocean beyond with binoculars. Then they came down and we continued. Hours went by and Ellesmere Island looked no closer.

Mikele trained his young dogs all during the day, first urging them to go fast, then slow down, then go to the right and the left in a slalom. Jens was helpless to do much with his young dogs because of Pappi. Instead, he taught his grandson voice commands and how to use the whip without touching the backs of the animals. Would Meqesuq be a hunter too? I asked. Jens said, "I am teaching him what he needs to know. Then the decision will be up to him. He has to love this more than anything."

At a second line of icebergs, Jens and Mikele clambered to the top and glassed the entire expanse of ice ahead in search of open water. We were already halfway across Smith Sound. Once Rasmussen and Peter Freuchen killed a polar bear on top of an iceberg. The bear's warm blood created a fissure; the iceberg exploded and they were almost killed, and the bear disappeared down a crevasse.

Jens came back to the sled, shaking his head in disbelief. "I have never seen it this way in my whole life at this time of year. There is no open water," he said. "It is ice all the way to Canada." But there must be an ice edge somewhere, he and Mikele decided later. We turned south and at Cape Parry, we met two hunters coming from the opposite direction. As usual, there was a long silence, then a casual question about open water. They shook their heads: no ice edge that way either. The hunters couldn't remember when such a thing had happened. It was May 8. The little auks that migrated up this coast by the millions, supplying Eskimo families with needed food in the spring, had been stalled below Cape York more than one hundred miles away.

More storms crowded in from the north, funneling out of Smith Sound, scouring Anoritoq, Etah, Cape Alexander, and Neqe. We pulled up the hoods of our anoraks as we traveled. What direction should we take? It didn't matter. A ring of fox fur encircled my face and the polar bear fur on my legs caught snowflakes. Up on a steep red slope, a fox made its harsh, strangled sound as we passed. Were we animals or people? it must be wondering. More snow fell on ice that would not break up and the ice cap at the center of the world grew taller.

That night I lay in my sleeping bag, squeezed tightly between Mikele and Ilaitsuk. Soon, the hunters would be harpooning narwhal in Mac-Cormick Fjord from their kayaks. "I feel as if we are stuck in winter," Mikele said, looking frustrated. He had a big family to feed. We lay awake listening to wind. The tent was a lung panting and puffing, its heaving sides throwing off new snow.

Early in the morning before the others were awake, I went outside to pee. The light was a flame—white hot and stinging cold. At midday we climbed an iceberg that was shaped like the Sydney opera house to look for the ice edge. Jens shook his head, no. As we climbed down, Mikele yelled and pointed: "*Nanuq.*" Far out, a polar bear danced across the silvered horizon, blessedly too distant for us to hunt. A mirage took her instead of a bullet. An illusory band of geography made of white light and mirrored light floated up from the ice floor and enveloped the bear: her dancing legs turned into waves of spring heat still trying to make its way here.

By the time we began to get tired we'd traveled halfway to Ellesmere Island. Coming back, the westernmost end of the island was laced with leads in the ice that had refrozen. The foot of the island looked like an icetray that had been dumped: white blocks lay tumbled at cliff bottoms. Snow came down, a piece at a time in brilliant sunlight.

We camped for a night, then finally headed for home, crossing the wide, monochrome monastery of ice. The Arctic functioned like a monk's cell, without need for walls. The ice floor and the ice mountains invited inward liberation and deterred escape and frivolity.

We traveled along the east side of Kiatak. Walls of red rock rose in amphitheaters, Arctic hares raced across snow-dappled turf and grass. A raven swooped by, and a fox floated its gray tail along a steep hill. Near the bottom of the cliff, icicles hung at odd angles from beds of rock. We passed back over the area of broken platelets; they looked like mirrors that had been tossed down and broken, their uneven edges making the sled tip this way and that. Some pieces of ice were so exquisite I asked Jens to stop so I could stare at them: a finely etched surface overlaid with another layer of ice punctured with what looked like stars.

All I could think about was getting something to eat. I had been dreaming about food, and in the middle of the night I ate a teaspoon of peanut butter while everyone else slept. Now, sitting hunched on the sled, I swung between pangs of hunger and the oblivion of perpetual ice which required no food. Looking at the ice cap, I understood how glaciers got fat and humans got thin: snow fell on ice, fell on itself, melted, and turned into ever higher mountains of ice. And below, people starved.

We crossed through a line of icebergs as through a city on a plain. It served as both gathering point and barrier between the end of the fjord and the beginning of the frozen ocean; it was both confluence and obstruction. Ice came to seem like a source, the see-through crockpot where life first brewed. Things had not begun with chaos and darkness, but with a translucency. Ice was the glass slide on which we could choose between the window and the mirror, enlightenment or narcissism.

Pappi wasn't happy that last morning. She was constantly hounded by the male dogs, who fought in a circle around her. She was at the height of her estrus; the other dogs could think of nothing else except getting to her. Again, Jens made the revving sign with his hand, meaning sex, laughing as Pappi slunk behind the other dogs, clamping her tail down and refusing to pull. Then the males fell back too and the sled came to a stop. Jens untied her and fastened her in back, but that didn't work either. She fell and was dragged and couldn't get up. Finally, he cut her loose. There was a moment of relief; she ran along in front of the other dogs. She was free, but not wild; she was happy. Jens urged her to go on ahead, which she did—not too far and not too close, a useful dictum for any happy romance. Ilaitsuk looked at me and smiled, her strong face beautiful in the sun.

The snowpack was hard and icy and the sled careened as the dogs gave chase. Once when we were airborne, flying between icy moguls, Meqesuq got on his hands and knees and squealed with delight. The cold and hunger and terrible hunting conditions were behind us. As we approached Qaanaaq, the dogs, ever optimistic, ran very fast.

Spring to Summer: Qaanaaq, 1999

Smith Sound remained frozen, its white shutters of ice firmly closed well into May, with the blue ruffle of Ellesmere Island vaguely visible. I tried to pinpoint the knob of land where the last immigrants might have crossed over to Etah, led by Qidlaq in 1862, but a white cloud descended on the distant island, blotting out the view. Town life in Qaanaaq, with its half-empty shelves of imported Danish food, proceeded as usual despite the bad hunting and intense cold. People were eating meat that had been frozen all winter—walrus and narwhal—and a battle with alcoholism was still being waged. There was a parade to celebrate the end of a weeklong period of abstinence, followed by a cake-decorating contest, though Hans Jensen pointed out sadly that as soon as the week was over, the store filled with people buying warm Tuborg beer.

It snowed softly and the sun shone. Walking the pathways, I spied Jens in his yard, bending the first long piece of wood to make a kayak because he had outgrown the one from the previous year. When I first met Jens he had patted his belly proudly and called it his "Eskimo bank account"—a hedge against hunger. Now he and Ilaitsuk wanted to go on diets and I promised to send them a good one from a California spa. While Jens pieced together this most elegant of watercraft, Ilaitsuk sewed tiny kamiks for a new grandchild on the way. This would be their daughter's third child without a husband. They were already raising Meqesuq, and now there would be another one.

I asked if young people here were likely to become hunters and stick with what was left of their traditional life. "We tell them the stories, we take them hunting, we teach them how to handle dogs, we give them a whip and a harpoon and a gun when they are old enough. That's all we can do. The decision is up to them," Jens said.

Close to midnight Torben called and invited me over for pancakes. They were thin and delicate. I watched as he spread them with jam and rolled them into tubes. His back had hurt all winter and the museum was in disarray—half remodeled and the entire collection in boxes. He was no longer working as a trader, though no one knew why. The daily faxes he had sent two winters before went unmentioned. He was going on with his life. He was now living with a young Danish woman who was handy with dogs. Staying put in Qaanaaq was extolled as a virtue. But he seemed troubled and there was nothing I could do.

When I asked about the continuum of Eskimo life into the twenty-first century, he said, "We're in a long transitional phase between traditional hunting life—just a step away from the stone age—and something else. Who knows what it is? Only a hundred years ago people were living here as they had lived for thousands of years in the polar north. Not that there hadn't been any contact with outsiders—they had plenty of that, starting with the Vikings, the English, and the Dutch in the nineteenth century. But they still lived very much as they always had because it's the only thing that works here, the only way to survive. The stone and bone age persisted with modern elements incorporated. Wood was brought by the whalers so that harpoon shafts ceased to made from narwhal tusks. Rifles were given to hunters by Robert Peary to shoot polar bears and seals. The last bows and arrows crafted from antlers and baleen had been made in 1930."

Torben had been visiting Qerqertoq, a village on a low-lying island on the east side of Inglefield Sound. There, an old man showed him how to make string figures—an art and a game known to Eskimo peoples for thousands of years. "People in all the villages across the polar north once knew them. Rasmussen recorded the same images when he visited the Copper Eskimos. Now they are being forgotten. It seems to have become preferable to look at Brad Pitt on a video."

String figures were made with sinew thread or thin seal thong. Each figure possessed an *inuk* (spirit) who decreed when the figures could be made. Some villages made them only in the dark time, others only in the summer. Some figures were animals, others were body parts, such as arms and legs, a penis, a vulva, or an anus. One might represent a hunter at a breathing hole, a man long dead, a piece of ice, fire, a mouth, or a bird. When Torben arrived the old man configured forty-seven images; just as he was leaving, the man suddenly remembered forty more. A few figures were of animals that no longer existed. "A collective, atavistic memory was at work," Torben said. "One image was of a woolly mammoth. The last one died six thousand years ago. That's a long string of history to keep unwinding."

We drank tea as Torben continued: "But culture keeps going and going. What's fascinating is how the same ideas occurred all over the world before there was global communication," Torben said. "Who needs it? We're in sync anyway." Now he was smiling. I kissed him good night.

Outside the window a dull gold light lay on the fjord. The village was quiet, and the bulldozer that all day had been pushing boulders out of the stream bed that had flooded the summer before was still. The phenomenon of global warming was being felt here.

Hans and Birthe were still up and I went by for a visit. Last summer, he told me, it rained almost every day in August; usually there was almost no rainfall that month. Spring storms were wilder and brought more snow, and in the fall, the normally placid weather turned stormy, its turbulence breaking up the ice.

Hans prided himself on being traveled and multilingual, but he remembered when he went to Denmark as a boy: "The first time I got close to a tree I was expecting snakes and monkeys, but instead, I saw an apple. It was so exciting. I had never seen anything like that in my life. I had no idea how apples grew. Then I saw a horse. I was so afraid. I touched his head. It was so hard. I hadn't expected it would be that big."

Because both he and Birthe had been born in Dundas Village, the talk always returned to Rasmussen. Hans's parents were schoolteachers in Dundas, and for a while they lived in Rasmussen's house—the building that now served as Qaanaaq's museum. Birthe's grandfather was Qavigarssuaq (Qav), Rasmussen's companion on the Fifth Thule Expedition. "He was twenty when Rasmussen chose him. He wasn't married yet, but had fallen in love with someone in the village named Pipianne. He knew he would be gone for years, so the day he left, he picked up a small stone and showing it to her, said, 'This piece of stone I'll keep with me all the way across the world and will think about you every time I feel it in my pocket or hold it in my hand. When I get back, if I show it to you, we will get married.' "

Qavigarssuaq took it all the way to Siberia and halfway back around the world again. When they were crossing to Little Diomede from Nome, he was afraid the Russian police would find it and take it away, so he put it in his mouth when they searched him and held it there all the time he was in Siberia. Then he put it back in his pocket. When he got back to Dundas, he showed the rock to Pipianne and they were married the next day. "We still have that stone. It is in the museum. He had been gone for three years."

Later I called Torben and asked if I could see the stone. In the museum, he opened a case and held it in his hands. "This is the ultimate love stone," he said. "Here, hold it. Maybe that will do it for us," he said, laughing. But nothing did.

As often happened, Torben, like other anthropologists and archeologists before him, was helping to preserve traditions. He recorded stories that went with the making of string figures, and knew the history of every tool used by Eskimos for four thousand years. The demise of his marriage to a Greenlandic woman had stymied him. But his mind was alive.

"The tradition of sharing is what is left of ceremonial life here. When a whale is caught everyone who was on the hunt shares the meat. Widows are given food, the less able hunters always get a share, equipment and dogs are traded around, huts are used by everyone. No one owns land here."

We walked down to the shore where the ice was beginning to break up. A bit of water slapped the beach. Torben reminded me that the beach was where the shaman would rub a *tupilait* against his genitals, then lay the object in the water. It would swim out and be mistaken for a seal. When it surfaced it had to be harpooned. If it failed to kill the intended, it came back and killed the creator. Or, if the man in the kayak was strong enough, he could turn the *tupilait* around so it would go back and kill the maker.

Walking home to the hotel at 2:00 a.m., the town was quiet, though there is always someone awake in an Arctic town when the sun is out. Outside my bedroom a man in his twenties and three teenage kids were making a snow sculpture. I watched as a pillar began rising up from between their hands. As the night went on, the column became taller and taller. Finally, near breakfast time, when they stepped back from their creation, I saw that it was not a column at all, but an enormous penis, its perfectly shaped head glistening in the morning air.

Summer: Qaanaaq, 1999

A narwhal's corkscrew tusk opened the day. It was summer and light gave way to an undefinable lucency. I walked up a slope that over-looked the fjord to watch Jens and Mikele hunting narwhal from kayaks.

"The Greenland kayak is perhaps the finest craft that mankind has devised. It is less a boat or canoe than an extension of man him-self to be amphibious; the kayak and the man are one," Rockwell Kent wrote in his memoir, *Salamina* (p. 106). The mountains on the other side looked close but weren't: the kayaks were splinters float-ing on water. The men's bodies looked halved, as if they had lost their legs.

I'd read about the discovery of exoplanets—planets that are still hidden from sight but write their signature in galactic dust. There is a planet ten times the mass of earth orbiting 6.9 billion miles away around the star Beta Pictoris. Those kinds of dimensions are imaginable only up here, where the scale of things is unencumbered by airborne pollution, where the immensities are set off by the tininess of the human being hunting in order to survive.

A Greenlander's kayak rests low in the water, narrow and long, covered with canvas or skins, the harpoon attached on the top right side like an arrow of time pointing into the next day. Jens and Mikele paddled slowly, each dip stirring a cosmos of inky water. A narwhal's back humped up, the point of its twisted tusk tearing the water. The men paddled hard, grabbing their harpoons. Mikele deferred to Jens, but before he could throw, the narwhal disappeared. The fjord was ice-stubbled; the sea it flowed into was still.

Autumn, 1999

October. No falling leaves, no sap rising, no elk bugling, no sandhill cranes rising from ponds, no firestorms in aspen trees. Only ice and the hanging bullion of the sun, its auric twilight. I returned to Qaanaaq to see the sun go down for the last time this year. After five days of traveling to get here, I felt fog-dulled, dream-sweetened. By coincidence Torben was on the same plane with me from Kangerlussuaq—we were linked by planes and met only in midair.

We looked out the plane window at the weather. In his golden hair there was gray. I touched the back of his hand and he shivered. Sila, he said, is the power behind the natural world. It is the life spirit that directs us, an awareness of who we are. As we headed toward darker skies, he started grinning. "In darkness, new ice shines."

Faithful as always, Hans Jensen met me at the heliport, quiet and smiling. "Let's walk to town," I said. We strolled arm in arm, straining against a stinging breeze, leaving my dufflebags behind to be picked up later. The view from the front windows at the hotel was of consummate twilight. Morning was twilight and midday was twilight and night was twilight. The sun hung. We were living in a crawlspace below and above gravity's dictum.

Jens and Niels came by in the morning. They were going north to hunt walrus near Neqe. Did I want to come? Yes, of course. In the morning I found myself pulled by the trance of the dogtrot, the fibrillations of trace lines vibrating above ice. Looking down from a moving sled I read

the passing coastline. The cold was white-knuckled at 15 below zero Celsius, near zero Fahrenheit—much colder than the previous May. Jens, Niels, and I squeezed together for warmth. The dogtrot and pant-breath lulled and kept me awake.

"*A da, da, da, da,*" Jens cried to his dogs. The ginger-colored leader was still in front. He had survived the bout of distemper, but "Shaggy," who used to rumble along on the sidelines, was gone. The young dogs who were puppies in May were full-grown and tied in with the others. The dogs dug into the new ice with their claws, carving their calligraphic signs of passage. If I could have read their script, what would it say? "North. Hungry. Meat. Happy to be going anywhere."

The day the sun goes down, the schoolchildren—about 150 of them—go up onto the hill behind the village and have a little ceremony. They sing "Good-bye, sun, please come back," Jens told me. "They are a little sad, I think. But for us, it is the beginning of the hunting year, the best time to harpoon walrus. Sometimes we go to Herbert Island and sometimes to Neqe, and we stay out for a month or two. The ice is still thin and the walrus break through it with their heads, so it is easy for us to see where they are."

Walrus eat clams from the sea bottom, which they feel out with their whiskers. They only give birth every two years. When the babies get tired, they ride on the mothers' backs. They migrate but not far. Their only enemies are humans and polar bears.

"We hunt walrus with harpoons," Jens told me. "The skin isn't too good for much now. We eat some of the meat and the rest makes good dog food. The ivory we sell to the Kommune and the people in town use it to make carvings which they sell. It's a way to make money in the dark time."

New ice flattened the fjord. At times it was translucent—a window to another world; in other places it was a mirror that had gone blind. New ice buckled and rolled as we glided—a following sea, a wave of water that had changed molecules and become solid.

On October 24, the ice was glass, mocking the idea of solidity. Solid space stands for emotional grasping; an ephemeral cataract, making opaque what it is we long to see. As the countdown to sunset ticked on, we traveled in perpetual twilight. Daybreak and dusk were one. Night never came; day never came. There was no destination except north. The coastal rock that pressed out from Greenland's margins appeared to be only a moat between eternal ice floes: the one that floated atop the ocean, and the one that rode heavy on the land—the inland ice. The colors in the sky were green, apple, purple, tangerine, and white. Regardless, we mourned the imminent passing of the sun.

Earlier I read more news from the *Soho* spacecraft: the sun was burning brighter and hotter as it extinguished itself; it was a fresh fire each instant. Under its surface, rivers of charged gas sluiced down, fiery bands moved at varying speeds, between which sunspots formed. A new star appeared in the frame of the Hubbell telescope. Although it is similar to our sun, its diameter is many times bigger—big enough to fill the entire orbit made by the earth.

We trotted north. The air was clear and crisp. A pane of new ice had been laid down on the sea, a looking glass through which I tried to glimpse the nature of things: what did a mirror image really show, and in plumbing the depth of translucence, what do we find?

The panting and trotting of the dogs was all I heard. Was I seeing through a glass darkly or into an emptiness that was bright? It is said that emptiness inspires compassion, but first you have to wade across the waters of uncertainty.

Icebergs were pink, ice was blue, open water was red. Polar bears roamed around under these colored lights, sticking their paws down a breathing hole to bash an inquisitive seal on the head. Foxes followed bears, who sometimes killed promiscuously, leaving plenty behind for their fox friends; yet foxes are so high-strung, an unexpected loud noise can cause them to die of fright.

Schools of walrus pursued schools of ringed seals and the seals were in turn lured by the tasty delights of sea scorpions and schools of cod. Traveling blindly, hunters glided above their prey, hoping for clues to the animals' whereabouts.

My Greenlandic friends said that a lemming's house was arranged just like a traditional Inuit house, with sleeping platform, a low entryway, and the refuse heaped outside in neat piles. They admired the lemming's character. They are strong-willed and resourceful, just like an Eskimo, they said. Lemmings are meat and insect eaters. One summer Peter Freuchen saw a pair of butterfly wings lying outside a lemming hole.

I rested my head against Niels's shoulder. Was it jet lag or the constant forward movement of the sled that made me sleepy? The cold wind on my face was a flame. Had we gone back to a time when there was only darkness, when humans and animals were intermixed, when water burned? I'd had a dream about fox fur—the lining of Niels's and Jens's anoraks puffing out around their faces, wrists, and waists as if they were humans trapped inside animals' bodies.

In the legend "The Man Who Took a Fox to Wife," a man who wanted a wife different from all the others married a she-fox. When they met up with a man who had married a hare, the men decided to exchange wives for a while. The husband of the hare didn't like the way the fox wife smelled; rebuffed, she ran away and lived with a worm. When the fox's original husband went to find her, the worm challenged him. It turned out that many lifetimes before, the fox had burned that very worm to death. After fighting with the worm, the man was never the same, so he went off to live with the strand dwellers, who were dwarfs. They ate what they called the shoulder of a walrus, but it was only the wing of an eider duck, and their houses were very small. People like this aren't seen now, but in the old days people knew them. The man lived with the dwarfs for a long time. Then he went back to his own house and lived alone.

When I woke, the top of the sky had gone purple. Sun burned low at the hard edge of the world. What was holding it there that long? The sun cut through the horizon's silver thread, demarcating heaven and earth like a welding torch, burning, burning. It hurt to look, yet I couldn't take my eyes away. A haze of salmon-colored glitter fell through air: the sun was a golden eye pulsing.

All the rest-above, below, and all around—was see-through solidity, which is emptiness. Why didn't the sled crash through? I gasped and laughed. This can't be! Jens's quick eyes darted from the dogs to me and back to the dogs. He saw that I was happy but couldn't imagine why, nor could I. Which made it even funnier.

We rushed over an unseeable world of animals in their water homes under the ice. The narwhal were gone—they'd already migrated south with their calves to a fishery, where they'd poke their grooved tusks through bottom sand searching for halibut. But there were plenty of walrus and seals. When I looked up Peter Freuchen's 1921 Fifth Thule Expedition notes to read about marine mammals, his entry on walrus was almost blank. He wrote: "Walrus are subject to certain laws of which we know nothing."

Ahead was Siorapaluk, Neqe, and Etah. I suggested to Jens that if things got bad for hunters here, they could move north and reinhabit these historic sites. He told me that fifteen years ago a group from Qaanaaq did just that, but failed. They couldn't make enough money selling skins to buy what they now needed—coffee and sugar, toilet paper, and pencils for the kids.

"In that case, the government should make you their national treasures," I said, but he didn't understand what I meant. He blinked, looked away, and talked to the dogs.

We traveled. If I tipped my head way back, the sky was navy blue with red lace. The sled heaved up and down as if we were passing over a small ocean of rubber. I gulped twilight, drank fire, levitated on the artesian spring of air. The sun was behind us, hanging over Cape Parry, Savissivik, Dundas Village, over Thule Air Force Base, over polluted Bylot Bay. I asked Jens why the sun's passage across the sky seemed to stop on this day. He smiled and shrugged. Maybe the harpoon's vibrating arc pierced the sun and dragged it down to the horizon where we wait for seals and walrus to come. The disk of the sun and the rounded top of the walrus resembled each other. Months before, I saw a walrus burst through ice, his bulbed head like a fist pushed through glass—all this only to breathe—but the harpoon struck and his breath was taken from him.

For seven years I'd watched shore ice grind winter into summer; now autumn laid its *mille-feuilles* of new ice down, and snow that didn't melt last year slowly bulked up and deformed itself until it was a glacier.

"Balance and justice," Torben said. "Those are European ideas. Here, the weather directs us. Up here, joy and sorrow, death and birth, are not measured out in teaspoons. Cannibalism, infanticide, jealousy, revenge, evil spirits, and a great joie de vivre—this is the cup from which all northern Greenlanders drink."

As the sky darkened we could see the moon. It lay lazily on its back, the top half buzz-cut sharp. "It's almost time," Niels said, fumbling for a cigarette. I thought of the twenty-one moons just discovered around Uranus, none more than twelve miles in diameter. Too bad we didn't have a handful of them. It would mean more light in dark days. Niels puffed and coughed. Movement was life. When Jens stopped the sled, the dogs lay down quietly. They were waiting.

Slowly, we turned to look: over the Politiken Glacier the sun hovered, its heat mirages buckling up the horizon in fire. "Ice is a clear mirror and beneath it, the broken sea. Which is which?" Muso Soseki asked in the thirteenth century. I thought of the small asteroid just discovered that makes a complete rotation every 10.7 minutes and twirls ten times as fast as any other known body in the solar system. From it, the sun climbs above the horizon every ten minutes in continual sunrises. But the opposite was happening here. One sunset and that was it until the next calendar year.

Gitte, with whom I'd watched the sun rise years before in Uummannaq, was not here to make a pronouncement on its retreat. I thought of her tearful farewell at Thule Air Base under the thumping blade of the helicopter. Instead of *"Sono io,"* she might now say, "I am not I."

All month the shadows of our dogs have leaned at odd angles on the ice in cubist disrepair, looking like a second team pulling. Now those familiar shadows stretched to their limit, snapped, then disappeared. Jens stopped the sled. Are we dead? I asked. Jens and Niels stood motionless. A faint light glazed the sky. Time is asymmetrical. Then the icebergs went blank, shedding their red glow like memory, and the burning gilt of the sun slipped from sight.

After, I remembered falling asleep again to the soft tempo of dogs trotting. We had gone hunting and now we were headed home. The ice was a wide elastic stretched over the ocean's torment. Smooth, smooth, wild, smooth. Fog wavered and flounced, ice floors melted and refroze, glaciers inching forward carrying gifts of garnet-studded rock, rivers of pitch flowed around a sun that had gone southward.

"*Huughuaq, huughuaq,*" Jens shouted in darkness, waking me. The dogs raced ahead. We had never gone this fast. Then they stopped suddenly. Ahead, there were patches of open water. I craned my neck to see, rising to my knees: the polynyas were dark hands lying palms up, waiting to hand us down to a watery underworld.

"It is not easy living on a mirror," Jens said. "This is a dangerous time of year. You can't go along on your dogsled just dreaming. You have to be awake. You have to be *ilihamahuq*—wise about things—because the ice wants to trick you."

We stretched our legs by the sled. The dogs rolled on the ice to cool themselves. There was still light in the sky, yet it felt like night, even though it was only noon. We yawned. The purple air above our heads looked burnt, as if there had been a fire.

Soon it would be November, the month of unbroken night. The ice floor would be only weakly lighted when there was a moon. The Greenlandic word to denote this time of year is *Tutsarfiq,* meaning "one is listening," as if light were a divine presence whom we ask for mercy and tell our stories.

Knud Rasmussen wrote of an East Greenland shaman who had put a curse of death on some of his villagers. His cruelty was avenged: the survivors murdered him. To avoid being haunted by his spirit, the villagers "severed the head from the body, put it in a harpoon bladder, and threw it into a lake. The eyes were taken out and placed in a soapstone lamp where they were to remain for the rest of the winter; this was in order to blind the dead man's soul."

I recall how snowblindness felt—as if my eyes were being scratched by glass. But how did it feel to have a soul that had been blinded?

Silanigtalersarput. "Working to obtain wisdom." From the root word *sila,* meaning weather and consciousness, natural power. When a shaman had acquired all the powers he needed—to sit atop a great boulder and move it all the way into the water, to fly under water to Nerrivik's world and persuade her to make the hunting better, to sneak over the inland ice and recapture a lost soul—then, after all that, he worked to obtain wisdom. This meant that at night, when the seal oil lamps had been extinguished, he could see as well as when they were lit;

he could see everyone and everything around him; he could see through their clothes and skin into their souls. The shamans said, "The life of a man is frail; to those who can see, it is as if their souls were about to glide from their body all the time."

Jens bent straight-legged at the waist to untangle the dogs' traces. Once, when they took off before they were supposed to, the lines wound around his legs and he fast-danced out of the entanglement, jumping straight up, clearing the lines as they snapped taut. Now I watched: his hands were so used to the feel of these lines, he didn't have to look. Torben had said, "When the hunters are out on the ice they don't stop to think. They act directly."

The walrus tooth Jens had given me two springs ago was hanging from a thong around my neck. When he saw it, he smiled. "*Aaveq*," he said. "Walrus. Let's see if we can find some."

I sat as the sled veered off, going around black patches of open water. "Now as far as you can imagine there is new ice," Jens said. "You must look very carefully. It is hard to see where the ice stops and where the water begins. On a calm day, they look just alike. It is easy to make a mistake and go under. Many hunters have disappeared that way. And maybe it will happen to us too. Yes. At this time of year, the ice comes to teach us how to see."

Epilogue, January 2001

It begins with ice and ends with ice. I once watched a baby seal rub its own eyes at birth to see the new world—that's how it is with me each time I go to Greenland. A glacier's calving torment sounds like thunder. Whoosh . . . another continent is born, severed from its mother ice. Slowly, it floats out, pitching topsy-turvy all alone on indigo, ice-encrusted waves.

In the twilight months of October, when the sky goes tangerine and gray, I think of winter as being purely shadow. In February, light returns. Blink, blind. An eye opens and darkness, like a phantom, bends away.

My north-pointing compass oscillates: spinning south, it keeps jouncing back around to N again and I return to see old friends. In Nuuk, the capital city of Greenland, the peripatetic Aleqa Hammond now works for the ICC, the International Circumpolar Conference, an organization that seeks to bring together all the peoples of the polar north. At the other extreme, in the far north, Ikuo Oshima does a dance on clear and dangerous new ice, then dashes off beyond the last human habitation to hunt walrus. At home again in Qaanaaq after a month visiting children and grandchildren in Denmark, Torben Diklev, curator and archeologist, has returned refreshed, together again with his Danish girlfriend, Tine.

Jens and Ilaitsuk are at home, caring for yet another grandchild.

Contemplating global warming, Jens says, "Maybe soon there will be no ice at all and we will have to find some other way to live. Maybe learn to water-ski!" he says laughing. "We'll let the ice tell us what it wants us to do. That's how it has always been."

Qaanaaq residents have gone online and when I'm elsewhere, we communicate by e-mail and check each other's weather: −22 degrees^F at Thule Air Base; 79 degrees above zero where I live. "Computers are fine, but on the dogsled," Jens says, "a human being is free to be who he is." So saying, he goes down to the ice, harnesses his dogs, and glides away.

Even as the hunters of the far north lose their traditional life—blame it on weather changes plus economics—Jens, Ilaitsuk, Mikele, and Ikuo, among others, continue to keep up their traditional hunting practices when not jumping on helicopters to testify before Parliament or going in front of the television camera. Sophie, once a shaman's apprentice, has begun forgetting things. "Her mind has reversed," Hans Jensen said sadly. She has lost almost all her dances and songs.

An airport is being built in Qaanaaq and it will no longer be necessary to transit through Thule Air Base. Hans and Birthe Jensen will be busier than ever with guests at their tiny hotel. They contemplate a vacation. Europe in winter sounds fine to them. Any other time of year would be too hot.

Far to the south in Illulissat, in what north Greenlanders call "West Greenland," where the sleds are small and the path from one town to the next is over land, not ice, I find that Elisabeth Jul, once chief of staff at the regional hospital, has gone to live with a carpenter in Denmark and is practicing medicine there. Her neighbor, Ono Fleischer, who once traveled by dogsled to Alaska with Jens Danielsen following Rasmussen's route, completed a journey around Hudson Bay, some of the most isolated and weather-battered terrain in the Arctic.

In Uummannaq, Ann is still queen bee of the Children's House, dispensing her generosity everywhere, and Olejorgen makes his annual trips to Melville Bay and beyond. He gets leaner and darker and still dreams of spending a year in Siorapaluk just hunting.

On Ubekendt Ejland, Hans Holm and his two children, Marie Louisa and Hendrik, have vacated their house in Illorsuit. "We left suddenly with only what we could carry," Hans told me. They settled in Jutland near Hans's brother-in-law and sister. Hans bicycles nine kilometers to and from his work on a dairy farm and the children are enrolled in school. "They went from a class of three to one of twenty-three, and here it is all Danish and English. At home I speak to them in Greenlandic so they won't forget who they are.

"Everything is so new for them . . . the smell is new, the language, but they are very popular and I think they will end up with a wider angle to make decisions later in life. As for Illorsuit, well, the settlement is changing. It is easier to be a loser now because they have exchanged some of the old ways for the Internet, the snow scooter, and, of course, the booze. So if you aren't technically trained or have only enough money for beer, then you have an excuse to fail. That was not possible before. Failure meant certain death. Now, too many people are not living in the old ways, making it with just a knife and a string and only eating seal."

Hans continued: "It is strange to find myself not far from the place I left more than thirty years ago when I was in my early twenties and escaping from architecture school. The children and I landed back here with almost no money. I'm not used to asking for anything, but I had to at first, just to get a place to live. Now that we are settled, we can exist on almost nothing. Greenland taught us that. But oh, I miss home . . . I miss it. . . . If I'd been alone, I would have stayed.

"Marie Louisa is taking care of a horse, has joined the gymnastics team, and is swimming. Hendrik is still acting in the plays he makes up for himself. It was harder for him because he is younger. Some days it feels as if we are still in motion, still landing, with one leg in each camp—one in Illorsuit, one in Denmark. You can imagine how many things are completely new for the children—rain, trees, flowers, grass, animals, cars, and so many people.

"But now I can look out the windows and sometimes feel joy. I think I have a little bit of power that will help me here. When traveling by train I listen to other people's problems. It's always rather small things, you know, just peanuts. Then I know how lucky the children and I are. Those things don't bother us because we have lived with something bigger—we have lived, you could say, inside the weather, and out on the ice, being hungry and seeing people and animals die, and every day, just being in the midst of beauty.

"But here the children are safe from people and forces that would have destroyed them. Even in Denmark, we think and speak in Greenlandic, we can still live with what we know from home and at the same time go forward toward some new thing."

In late October darkness spread like cream over Greenland's humped-up back of ice. But nothing could diminish the population of spirits who still live on the glaciers, mountains, and beaches: sprites with no noses, giants traveling open water in half-kayaks, inland ice dwellers, naked spirits who steal hunters' seals, mountain dwarfs, and stones that are alive.

As black days came unnumbered, merging with night, the *pulaar*— visits between villagers—started up again. They told new stories about animal and human doings, about the demise of their traditional lifeways and melting ice caps, and waited, in their cold heaven, for the coming of light.

A Note on Sources

My study of the Arctic would not have been possible without the writings of Knud Rasmussen and the ten volumes of notes from the Fifth Thule Expedition, five volumes of which are by Rasmussen and the others, on the material culture of the Inuit and the flora, fauna, and geology of the far north, by his team members. At one time or another, I carried these compendiums with me on dogsleds up and down the west coast of Greenland. Published in Danish and later translated into English in the early part of the twentieth century, they provide an ethnographic record of the entire polar north: how the Inuit people lived before modernization in Greenland, Arctic Canada, and northern Alaska.

In addition, the books of Peter Freuchen, Rasmussen's partner in the Arctic Station at Thule, provide an entertaining and enthusiastic view of their years together in the Arctic from a slightly different perspective.

In Uummannaq I used the personal library of Ann Andreasen and Olejorgen Hammekin for works published in Denmark about Greenland, unavailable in America.

During my stay in the village of Illorsuit on Ubekendt Ejland, I brought with me and read three books by the American painter Rockwell Kent about his stay there.

Also indispensable to my understanding of northwestern Greenland was *The Last Kings of Thule* by the French ethnographer Jean Malaurie, who lived for a year in the village of Siorapaluk.

Ikuo Oshima's brief autobiography, published only in Japanese, was generously translated for me in one all-night session by a Japanese journalist, Ken Yanagawa, who happened to be visiting Qaanaaq while I was there.

There are many fine works about the Arctic, new and old, and I have listed only a few of them—those that seemed indispensable to my study of Greenland at the time.

Bibliography

Brody, Hugh. *Living Arctic: Hunters of the Canadian North.* Seattle: University of Washington Press, 1987.

Christensen, N. O., and Ebbesen, Hans. *Thule: In Days of Old.* Charlottenlund: Arktisk Institut, 1985.

Fienup-Riordan, Ann. *Boundaries and Passages: Rule and Ritual in Yup'ik Eskimo Oral Tradition.* Oklahoma City: University of Oklahoma Press, 1994.

Finn, Gidd. *The History of Greenland.* Vols. 1 and 2.

Fortescue, Michael D. *Inuktun: An Introduction to the Language of Qaanaaq, Thule.* Copenhagen: Institut fir Eskimologi, 1991.

Freuchen, Peter. *Adventures in the Arctic.* Edited by Dagmar Freuchen. New York: Julian Messner, 1960.

———. *Peter Freuchen's Book of the Eskimos.* Edited by Dagmar Freuchen. Cleveland: World Publishing, 1961.

———. *I Sailed with Rasmussen.* New York: Julian Messner, 1958.

Grownnow, Bjarne. *The Paleo-Eskimo Cultures of Greenland.* Copenhagen: Danish Polar Center, 1996.

Hambry, Michael, and Alean, Jurg. *Glaciers.* Cambridge, England: Cambridge University Press, 1994.

Harper, Kenn. *Give Me My Father's Body: The Life of Minik, the New York Eskimo.* Iqaluit, NWT: Blacklead Books, 1986.

Kane, Elisha Kent. *Arctic Explorations: The Second and Last United States*

Grinnell Expeditions in Search of Sir John Franklin. Hartford, Conn.: R. W. Bliss, 1869.

Kent, Rockwell. *Greenland Journal.* New York: Ivan Obolensky, 1962.

———. *N by E.* Middletown, Conn.: Wesleyan University Press, 1978.

———. *Salamina.* New York: Harcourt, Brace, 1935.

Lindberg, David C. *Theories of Vision from Al-Kindi to Kepler.* Chicago: University of Chicago Press, 1976.

Malaurie, Jean. *The Last Kings of Thule: With the Polar Eskimos as They Face Their Destiny.* Chicago: University of Chicago Press, 1985.

Norman, Howard. *Northern Tales: Traditional Stories of Eskimo and Indian Peoples.* New York: Pantheon Books, 1990.

Oshima, Ikuo. *A Hunter's Memoir from Siorapaluk.* Japan, 1989.

Peary, Robert E. *The North Pole, its discovery in 1909 under the auspices of the Peary Arctic Club.* New York: Frederick A. Stokes, 1910.

Peary, Josephine Diebitsch. *My Arctic Journal: A Year Among Ice-Fields and Eskimos.* New York: Contemporary Publishing, 1893.

Pielou, E. C. *A Naturalist's Guide to the Arctic.* Chicago: University of Chicago Press, 1994.

Rasmussen, Knud. *Across Arctic America: Narrative of the Fifth Thule Expedition.* Westport, Conn.: Greenwood Press, 1969.

———. *Greenland by the Polar Sea: The Story of the Thule Expeditions from Melville Bay to Cape Morris Jesup.* London: Heinemann, 1921.

———. *Notes on the Life and Doings of the East Greenlanders.* New York: AMS Press, 1976.

———. *The People of the Polar North: A Record.* New York: AMS Press, 1976.

———. *Report of the Fifth Thule Expedition, 1922–24.* Vols. 1–10. New York: AMS Press, 1976.

Vol. 7, no. 1: *Intellectual Culture of the Iglulik Eskimos.*

Vol. 7, nos. 2 and 3: *Observations of the Intellectual Culture of the Caribou Eskimos.*

Vol. 8: *The Netsilik Eskimos.*

Vol. 9: *Intellectual Culture of the Copper Eskimos.*

Vol. 10, no. 2: *The Mackenzie Eskimos.*

Vol. 10, no. 3: *The Alaska Eskimos; as Described in the Posthumous Notes of Knud Rasmussen.*

Ross, John. *A Voyage of Discovery: . . . for the purpose of exploring Baffin Bay and enquiring into the probability of a North-west passage.* London: Longman, Hurst, Rees, Orme, & Brown, 1819.

Bibliography

Soseki, Muso. *Sun at Midnight:* 23 Poems. Translated by W. S. Merwin with Soiku Shigematsu. New York: Nadja, 1985.

Stefansson, Vilhjalmur. *Greenland.* Garden City, N.Y.: Doubleday, Doran, 1942.

Vaughn, Richard. *The History of Northern Greenland.*

Weems, John Edward. *Peary, the Explorer and the Man.* Boston: Houghton Mifflin, 1967.

Young, Steven B. *To the Arctic: An Introduction to the Far Northern World.* New York: John Wiley, 1994.

Acknowledgments

Heartfelt thanks to the many people who befriended and helped me during my visits to Greenland. Their wide-armed hospitality and many kindnesses will always be cherished, especially: Ann Andreasen and Ole-jorgen Hammekin, who took me under their wing on my initial flight from Baffin Island to Greenland and invited me to come north with them to Uummannaq and without whose generosity I couldn't have written this book; Aleqa Hammond, who taught me so much about traditional and contemporary Inuit thought; the intrepid doctor Elisabeth Jul, who showed me where to find the keys to her house and opened her heart to me many times; Hans Holm, for taking me in when I had no warm clothes and no place to stay, and his splendid children, Marie Louisa and Hendrik, whom I love; Aliberti, for taking me on his sled; Hans and Birthe Jensen, gracious hosts, helpmates, and translators in Qaanaaq; Jens and Ilaitsuk Danielsen, formidable hunters and gentle souls; Hans Niels Kristiansen, who translated for me; Torben Diklev, whose brilliance and friendship has helped me in many ways; and Ikuo Oshima, for a glimpse of his enlightened being. *Qajanaq*.

Thanks also to Poul Karup and Esther Hammekin, and Maritha and Motzflot Hammekin in Nuuk; to Ono Fleischer and Silver in Ilulissat; to Arne Fleischer, Hans Peter Kristensen, Gitte Mortensen, Ludwig, and Pipaluk in Uummannaq; to Kristian Moller and Nikolai Moller in Illorsuit; to Birthe in Ukkusissat; to Imina Heilman, Sophie Kristiansen, and Mikele Kristiansen in Qaanaaq; to Thyge, Steen, Jack, and Guy at Thule Air Base; to Jens Fog Jensen, John Pind, Erik Christoffersen, and the Andreasen family in Denmark; and to photographer Robert Van der Hilst and Chris Anderson.

Because of these people and many others who shared their food, houses, dogsleds, and stories, I now think of Greenland as a home away from home.

Gratitude to my loyal and brilliant editor, Dan Frank, and to my steadfast agent, Liz Darhansoff, for two decades of guidance and moral support. Their patience in awaiting the delivery of this long overdue book has been exemplary. I hope it was, in some way, worth the wait.

And finally, thanks to those who stayed behind, caring for animals and domestic details, thus allowing me to be way for long periods of time: Bill Hawksworth, Linda and John Kiewit, Aaron Young, and Randy Gilchrist; to my sister, Galen, to my dear departed friends John and Linda Kiewit; and, for his insights, love, and visual inspirations, to Tony Bright.

Permissions Acknowledgments

Grateful acknowledgment is made to the following for permission to reprint previously published material:

THE HEIRS OF KNUD RASMUSSEN: Excerpts from *Iglulik Eskimo* vol. 7, no. 1, *Netsilik Eskimo* vol. 8, *Copper Eskimo* vol. 9 from *The Fifth Thule Expedition* by Knud Rasmussen. Reprinted by permission of W. Bentzen on behalf of the Heirs of Knud Rasmussen.

THE RANDOM HOUSE GROUP LTD.: Extracts from *Greenland by the Polar Sea* by Knud Rasmussen, published by Heinemann. Reprinted by permission of The Random House Group Ltd.

THE WYLIE AGENCY, INC.: Excerpts from *Sun At Midnight: Poems and Sermons* by Muso Soseki, translated by W.S. Merwin and Soiku Shigematsu. Copyright © 1985 by W.S. Merwin. Reprinted by permission of The Wylie Agency, Inc.

Index

About the Author

Gretel Ehrlich is the author of A Match to the Heart; The Solace of Open Spaces; Heart Mountain; Islands, the Universe, Home; Questions of Heaven; A Blizzard Year; John Muir, Nature's Visionary; *and three books of poetry. She is a recipient of an NEA Fellowship, a Guggenheim Fellowship, a Bellagio Fellowship, the Whiting Award, and the Harold V. Purcell Award from the American Academy of Arts and Letters. She lives in California and Wyoming.*

ELLESMERE ISLAND

Cape
Bryant

Black Horn Cliffs

Sherard Osborn Fjord

Hall
Basin

Kennedy Channel

St. George's
Fjord

Cape
Constitution

WASHINGTON LAND

KNUD RASMUSSEN LAND

GREENLAND